ALSO BY
ANDREW NAGORSKI

The Nazi Hunters

Hitlerland:
American Eyewitnesses to the Nazi Rise to Power

The Greatest Battle:
Stalin, Hitler, and the Desperate Struggle for Moscow That Changed the Course of World War II

Last Stop Vienna *(A Novel)*

The Birth of Freedom:
Shaping Lives and Societies in the New Eastern Europe

Reluctant Farewell:
An American Reporter's Candid Look Inside the Soviet Union

1941

SIMON & SCHUSTER
New York London Toronto Sydney New Delhi

THE YEAR GERMANY LOST THE WAR

ANDREW NAGORSKI

Simon & Schuster
1230 Avenue of the Americas
New York, NY 10020

First Simon & Schuster hardcover edition June 2019

Interior design by Lewelin Polanco

Manufactured in the United States of America

1 3 5 7 9 10 8 6 4 2

Library of Congress Card Number: 2018030143

ISBN 978-1-5011-8111-5
ISBN 978-1-5011-8112-2 (ebook)

As always, for Krysia

CONTENTS

CAST OF CHARACTERS

Germany

Adolf Hitler (1889–1945): Nazi Party leader who became chancellor in 1933 and took the additional grandiose title of Führer in 1934 following the death of President Paul von Hindenburg.

Joachim von Ribbentrop (1893–1946): foreign minister who signed the German-Soviet Nonaggression Pact in 1939, which set the stage for Germany's invasion of Poland that marked the start of World War II. He was the first of the major Nazi war criminals to be hanged in Nuremberg.

Albert Speer (1905–1981): Hitler's chief architect and, later, from 1942 to 1945, his minister of armaments and war production. Tried and convicted in Nuremberg for war crimes and crimes against humanity, he served a twenty-year sentence in West Berlin's Spandau Prison.

Franz Halder (1884–1972): chief of the German army's general staff from 1938 to 1942. Although he worked closely with Hitler during that critical period, he was later implicated in the July 20,

1944, plot to assassinate Hitler and sent to the Dachau concentration camp. After the war, he testified in Nuremberg against the Nazi leaders on trial there. His war diaries have proved invaluable to historians of the Third Reich.

Heinz Guderian (1888–1954): the commander of panzer units and proponent of the blitzkrieg (lightning war) tactics that were employed so effectively in the initial German conquests of World War II. An early favorite of Hitler's, Guderian repeatedly clashed with the German leader over his handling of the invasion of the Soviet Union. In December 1941 Hitler dismissed him, but Guderian was recalled to wartime duty in 1943.

Georg Thomas (1890–1946): the German army general who was the chief economist of the Wehrmacht (the armed forces) and a longtime specialist in procurement. Thomas tried to warn Hitler of the dangers of launching a wider war but later helped design the Nazis' Hunger Plan for the Soviet Union. Implicated in the July 20, 1944, plot to assassinate Hitler, he was arrested and held prisoner until the end of the war. He died in American captivity in 1946.

Soviet Union

Joseph Stalin (1878–1953): general secretary of the Communist Party and, as of May 1941, premier of the Soviet Union.

Vyacheslav Molotov (1890–1986): close associate of Stalin who held a variety of top Communist Party and state posts. As foreign minister, he was most famous for signing the German-Soviet Nonaggression Pact, also known as the Molotov-Ribbentrop Pact. Expelled from the Communist Party in 1962 as a result of de-Stalinization, he was reinstated in the Party in 1984, two years before his death.

Georgy Zhukov (1896–1974): chief of the general staff and Stalin's top general who led the defense of Moscow and other major campaigns all the way up to the drive on Berlin in 1945.

Anastas Mikoyan (1895–1978): Politburo member and member of the State Defense Committee, among other assignments. Despite his long association with Stalin, the Armenian "old Bolshevik" outlasted him biologically and politically, participating in Nikita Khrushchev's de-Stalinization campaign.

Ivan Maisky (1884–1975): Soviet ambassador to the United Kingdom from 1932 to 1943. In his extensive diaries, he chronicled his frequent interactions with British officials from Winston Churchill on down. He later participated in the Yalta and Potsdam Conferences. In 1952, shortly before Stalin's death, he was arrested and accused of espionage and participation in a Zionist conspiracy. He was released in 1955.

Britain

Winston Churchill (1874–1965): prime minister from 1940 to 1945, and from 1951 to 1955.

Anthony Eden (1897–1977): foreign secretary from 1935 to 1938, 1940 to 1945, and 1951 to 1955. Succeeded Churchill as prime minister from 1955 to 1957.

Lord Beaverbrook, William Maxwell Aitken (1879–1964): Canadian-British newspaper publisher who was an early supporter of appeasement but then held a variety of positions in Churchill's War Cabinet: minister of aircraft production, minister of supply, and minister of war production. Along with Averell Harriman, he led the Anglo-American delegation to meetings with Stalin in Moscow in 1941.

Lord Ismay, General Hastings Ismay (1887–1965): Churchill's chief military adviser, who supported providing aid to the Soviet Union but was wary of Stalin's political and territorial ambitions. In 1952 he became the first secretary general of the North Atlantic Treaty Organization (NATO).

Harold Nicolson (1886–1968): Conservative member of Parliament (MP) and staunch supporter of Churchill, who also worked in the Information Ministry. His diaries and letters provide revealing testimony about the atmosphere in wartime London.

John Colville (1915–1987): Foreign Office staffer who was assigned to 10 Downing Street at age twenty-four in 1939. When Churchill took office in 1940, "Jock" Colville worked closely with him on a daily basis, serving as his principal private secretary. He, too, kept detailed diaries.

United States

Franklin Delano Roosevelt (1882–1945): president from 1933 to his death early in his fourth term in 1945.

Harry Hopkins (1890–1946): Roosevelt's close adviser who embarked on special missions to London and Moscow. As the president's "personal representative" to Britain, he cultivated strong personal ties with Churchill. He oversaw the Lend-Lease program and advocated unconditional aid to Stalin's Soviet Union.

W. Averell Harriman (1891–1986): dispatched by Roosevelt to Britain to handle all Lend-Lease matters there, since Hopkins was only an occasional visitor. Along with Lord Beaverbrook, he led the Anglo-American delegation to Moscow, where the two men held extensive talks with Stalin.

John Gilbert Winant (1889–1947): former Republican governor of New Hampshire and Roosevelt's pick as ambassador to Britain, succeeding the defeatist Joseph Kennedy. He also developed an excellent rapport with Churchill.

Raymond E. Lee (1886–1958): the popular, well-connected military attaché in the US embassy in London. A staunch supporter of US aid for Britain, the army general played an important behind-the-scenes role in preparing for America's entry into the war.

Charles Lindbergh (1902–1974): famed aviator who became the most prominent spokesman of the America First isolationist movement.

INTRODUCTION

On *June 28, 1940, shortly* after the German invasion of France and that country's capitulation, Adolf Hitler visited Paris for the first and only time in his life. During the mere three hours he spent in the French capital, there was no victory parade. The ostensible reason was the fear of British air raids. But the German leader later offered another explanation: "We aren't at the end yet."

At that point, Hitler's Germany had reached its apogee. It had already dismembered Czechoslovakia, annexed Austria, and conquered Poland, Denmark, Norway, the Netherlands, Belgium, and Luxembourg, culminating in its especially satisfying humiliation of France. The German military machine looked to be unstoppable.

Nonetheless, Hitler understood that his messianic dream of a new Germanic empire was only partially fulfilled. Three leaders stood in his way. Britain's Winston Churchill, who replaced Neville Chamberlain as prime minister at the moment that France fell, was proclaiming Britain's defiance and determination to fight back. The Soviet Union's Joseph Stalin remained a de facto but uncertain ally since the signing of the Nazi-Soviet pact less than a year earlier, with neither tyrant completely trusting the other not to strike. And across the Atlantic, President Franklin D. Roosevelt was promising to keep the United States out of the conflict, but there was no doubt about his sympathy for an increasingly isolated Britain.

So instead of participating in military festivities in Paris, Hitler used the short visit as an opportunity to get a quick look at the city's cultural landmarks.

Accompanied by his favorite architect Albert Speer and other aides, he drove directly to the Paris Opera, where an attendant took him on a tour of the empty, lavishly ornamented building. According to Speer, Hitler "went into ecstasies about its beauty." Then the German delegation took in the Madeleine church, the Champs-Élysées, and the Trocadero before making another brief stop, this time at the Eiffel Tower.

The highlight of the tour, though, was Les Invalides, where Hitler lingered at Napoléon's tomb. Pierre Huss of the International News Service was one of a small group of correspondents from Berlin who were allowed to witness the scene. The Nazi leader looked lost in his thoughts. "He folded his arms and murmured something we could not hear," Huss recalled. "His lips moved, as if he were talking to himself, and once or twice he shook his head."

Hitler came "out of his trance" and leaned forward on the balustrade to stare down at Napoléon's tomb. "Napoléon, *mein lieber,* they have made a bad mistake," he said. Huss admitted: "It startled me, standing there across from a live warlord and a dead emperor." The correspondent also did not understand what Hitler meant.

The German leader promptly explained to everyone around him: "They have put him down into a hole. People must look down at a coffin far below them. . . . They should look up at Napoléon, feeling small by the very size of the monument or sarcophagus above their heads. You do not impress people if you walk in a street and they are on top of a building. They must look at something above them; you must be the stage and center of attraction above the level of all eyes."

Hitler was applying the same principles of staging that had proven devastatingly effective at his rallies as he rose to power. In talking about Napoléon, he was also talking about himself. "I shall never make such a mistake," he continued. "I know how to keep my hold on people after I have passed on. I shall be the Führer they look up at and go home to talk of and remember. My life shall not end in the mere form of death. It will, on the contrary, begin then." H. R. Knickerbocker, another Berlin-based American correspondent, wrote that it would be wrong to dismiss the analogies between Napoléon and Hitler. "Hitler is the nearest thing to Napoléon since Napoléon," he argued in his book *Is Tomorrow Hitler's?*, which was published in 1941, after he had left Germany. He quoted a French colonel who had marveled at Hitler's "miraculous sense of timing," and explained to American readers that the German leader's military successes were a result of the fact that he was "always right." As if catching himself, Knickerbocker tacked on a caveat: "Well, nearly always."

As far as Hitler was concerned, no qualifiers were necessary. On the evening when he returned from Paris to his temporary field quarters in a northern French village, he invited Speer to join him for dinner. "Wasn't Paris beautiful?" he declared. "But Berlin must be made more beautiful." Then he added casually: "In the past, I often considered whether we would not have to destroy Paris. But when we are finished in Berlin, Paris will only be a shadow. So why should we destroy it?"

While Hitler knew that he had not yet achieved total victory, his message was that it was coming soon—and Speer needed to start making preparations for a capital worthy of the new empire and its brilliant modern-day emperor. As Field Marshal Wilhelm Keitel put it in the aftermath of the French campaign, Hitler had proven himself to be "the greatest military commander of all time." By then, according to the Swiss psychiatrist Carl Jung, the German people had convinced themselves that Hitler was their messiah or at least the equivalent of an Old Testament prophet who would "lead them to the Promised Land."

To the growing ranks of the true believers, victory was no longer a question of "if" but "when."

A competing narrative was beginning to take shape even before Hitler's visit to Paris and his subsequent return to Berlin, where he was welcomed with cheers, strewn flowers, and the ringing of bells across the city. It was carefully crafted by Churchill, first in his speeches and then in his memoirs. Following the collapse of France and the spectacular evacuation of 338,000 British and Allied troops from Dunkirk by the Royal Navy and a flotilla of small boats, the prime minister rallied his countrymen with his famous speech on June 4, 1940. Facing a possible German invasion, he pledged to "defend our island, whatever the cost may be, we shall fight on the beaches, we shall fight on the landing grounds, we shall fight in the fields and in the streets; we shall never surrender . . ."

But for all that imagery of resistance on land, the next battles were in the skies over England. There, in what became known as the Battle of Britain, Germany suffered its first defeat. The Luftwaffe could not cripple the Royal Air Force, which was bolstered by an influx of Polish, Czech, and Commonwealth pilots. Hitler thereby failed to gain the air superiority his forces needed to launch an invasion of that island nation. "Upon this battle depends the survival of Christian civilization," Churchill told the House of Commons on June 18, rallying his countrymen and all those who were seeking to liberate their occupied lands to make this "their finest hour."

In many accounts of the war, this is presented as the critical period marking the end of Hitler's string of victories and the beginning of the reversal of fortunes that would lead to Germany's defeat. "The Second World War seemed to have been decided early—not in May 1945, but after less than a year, in June 1940," wrote German historian Christian Hartmann. To a limited extent, this is accurate. The Battle of Britain was the first turning point—but it fell far short of a decisive one.

And despite Churchill's insistence that he had always believed in victory, he was not immune to moments of doubt. In the largely overlooked recollections of Scotland Yard detective W. H. Thompson, his longtime bodyguard revealed one such occasion. Returning from his meeting with King George VI at Buckingham Palace on May 10, 1940, after Chamberlain had tendered his resignation and German troops launched their invasion of France, Churchill was uncharacteristically subdued.

"You know why I have been to Buckingham Palace, Thompson?" he asked.

Thompson replied that he understood that the king had "at last" asked him to form a new government. "I only wish that the position had come your way in better times, for you have taken on an enormous task," he added.

Churchill had tears in his eyes as he replied: "God alone knows how great it is. I hope that it is not too late. I am very much afraid that it is. We can only do our best."

There was nothing inevitable about the subsequent sequence of events. As John Winant, who frequently traveled to London and would become US ambassador to Britain in 1941, pointed out: "You could not live in London in those early years and not realize how narrow was the margin of survival. It would have taken so few mistakes to bring about defeat. . . . There were many times in the early years of the war when you felt that the sands would run out and all would be over."

In fact, Joseph Kennedy, Winant's predecessor as ambassador, had not only advocated a policy of appeasement but also widely predicted that Britain would not be able to withstand the Nazi onslaught. After Poland fell in September 1939, Kennedy reported that military experts were not giving Britain, backed by its French ally, more than a "Chinaman's chance" against Germany. Both in Washington and London, he was seen as "a defeatist," and he kept predicting Britain's demise even after his return to the United States.

Another foreign ambassador in London, the Soviet envoy Ivan Maisky, wrote in his diary on May 20, 1940, as France was collapsing: "The Anglo-French bourgeois elite is getting what it deserves. . . . We are witnessing the fall of the great capitalist civilization, a fall similar in importance to that of the Roman Empire." Despite his close social ties with many top British officials, Maisky was relishing what he saw as Britain's—and, by extension, the whole capitalist world's—comeuppance.

As for the defeated French, most of their leaders saw no choice but to accept Hitler's armistice, which meant nothing less than surrender. They not only predicted that Britain would follow their example but sounded eager for it to do so. The French military commander General Maxime Weygand offered a bleak prediction: "In three weeks, England will have her neck wrung like a chicken."

Even some of Churchill's staunchest supporters could not help but feel despair as the German blitzkrieg rolled across France. Conservative MP Harold Nicolson made a suicide pact with his wife, the poet and novelist Vita Sackville-West, securing poison pills they pledged to use if they were about to be captured by German invaders. In a letter to Sackville-West, Nicolson wrote that he did not fear that kind of "honourable death." What he did fear, however, was "being tortured and humiliated."

Churchill soon managed to lift the spirits of Nicolson and most of his countrymen, aided by the heroism and skill of the pilots who prevailed in the Battle of Britain. Their successes forced the indefinite postponement of Operation Sea Lion, the German plan for an invasion of Britain, in September.

Nonetheless, for the rest of 1940, the war could be described as an uneven stalemate. England had not collapsed, but waves of German bombers took part in the Blitz, dropping their deadly cargo on London, Coventry, and other cities. In the Battle of the Atlantic, U-boats and other German vessels targeted British ships, seeking to further isolate the lone holdout against the Nazi tide. On most of the Continent, the new German masters reigned supreme, unleashing a previously unimaginable reign of terror to subjugate the local populations. The decisive turning points had not been reached yet.

But they would be in 1941.

What transpired in that critical year set the trajectory that would lead to Nazi Germany's ultimate destruction. It was the year of Germany's "attack on the whole world," as German writer Joachim Käppner put it. By the end of 1941, Hitler had taken almost every wrong decision possible. His early successes in Operation Barbarossa, the invasion of the Soviet Union that he launched in late June, had turned into the first defeat of the German army on the outskirts of Moscow. His decision to make mass murder and terror his weapons of choice, not just in the first stages of the Holocaust but also in his treatment of Soviet POWs and others in the newly conquered territories, were already beginning to work against him.

The leader who seemed to be so "gloriously right," as the American correspondent H. R. Knickerbocker had put it earlier, was by then disastrously wrong.

What accounted for this stunning turnaround in the short span of one year? What possessed Hitler to gamble again and again, raising the stakes each time? Once it was clear that Britain was not going to be added to his list of quick conquests, he gambled on delivering a swift knockout blow to the Soviet Union. When that failed, he not only welcomed Japan's attack on Pearl Harbor on December 7, 1941, but rushed to declare war on the United States, thereby putting an end to the efforts of isolationists such as Charles Lindbergh and the America First movement to keep their country out of the conflict. As a result, Churchill's Britain could boast two new powerful allies: the Soviet Union and the United States.

And what possessed Hitler to pursue a policy of terror and enslavement as his armies scored their initial successes in the western Soviet Union, where many Soviet POWs and local inhabitants would have otherwise welcomed any invader who promised liberation from Stalin's tyranny? One key part of that rule-by-terror approach was "the Shoah by bullets" carried out by Einsatzgruppen, special squads assigned the task of shooting Jews, Gypsies, and other "enemies" of Nazi rule. It was no accident that 1941 was the year when the Holocaust was set in motion, although the further coordination of the logistics was then left to the Wannsee Conference that took place on January 20, 1942.

To outsiders and even to some of his inner circle, Hitler's actions in 1941 often looked like lunacy. With the benefit of hindsight, it is clear that he had chosen a path that could only lead to the destruction of his country, his movement, and himself. But a "deranged monster" theory hardly provides adequate explanation for the fateful course he charted, or the mayhem perpetrated in his name. Nor does it explain the roles of the Allied leaders who benefitted from his key miscalculations and parlayed them into a strategy that led to victory in 1945.

World War II was much more than a clash of two opposing political and military alliances. It was at heart a worldwide struggle instigated by a man and a movement whose race-based ideology and inner conviction of infallibility defied common sense. Yet at the same time, it was propelled by a perverse internal logic based on a worldview that made perfect sense to its creator and his devoted followers.

Nineteen forty-one would prove to be the year when the war escalated into a truly global conflict, with Hitler scoring impressive short-term tactical victories while condemning his Third Reich to defeat. His actions also guaranteed that the Third Reich's murderous policies would continue to take their toll right up until the end of the fighting, dooming millions. Finally, they allowed fellow mass murderer Joseph Stalin, his onetime ally-turned-foe, to dictate the shape of the postwar world, leaving Europe split into two antagonistic camps. This Cold

War division remained frozen in place for nearly a half century afterward. That, too, was a legacy of 1941.

A personal note is in order here. During the many years that I worked as a *Newsweek* foreign correspondent based in cities such as Bonn, Berlin, Moscow, and Warsaw, World War II never felt like a distant abstraction. Its legacy remains a source of constant debate, its horrors a source of constant fascination. The latter raises fundamental questions not just about how someone like Hitler could have come to power but also about basic human nature. As a result, the books I have written since then all deal with various aspects of Hitler's rise, the war, the Holocaust, and the search for justice afterward.

Each of those projects, along with my reporting for a broad array of articles earlier, helped provide me with research and interviews that I could draw upon for this book. In particular, the numerous interviews I conducted while working on *The Greatest Battle*, my book about the battle for Moscow, helped me emphasize the key difference between Hitler and Stalin in 1941: how Hitler's megalomania led him to multiply his mistakes as the year progressed, while Stalin's megalomania did not prevent him from charting a more calculated course to salvage his country and regime.

Given the passage of time, many of those who participated directly in these events are no longer with us, making my previous interviews all the more valuable. But even at this late date, I was able to find and interview some survivors from that era who I had not tracked down before. At the same time, the literature about World War II has kept growing, which meant that I could benefit from a variety of new studies with new perspectives.

My experiences as a foreign correspondent during the final years of the Cold War and the seismic upheavals that led to the collapse of the Soviet empire have prompted me to keep returning to a central theme: the role of the individual in history. History looks inevitable only in retrospect: in reality, it is shaped by the choices of both political leaders and their subjects, by the powerful and the dissidents—and, at times, by the element of pure chance.

In writing about contemporary events and recent history, I always look for the pivotal moments, actions, and decisions that produced the outcomes we now take for granted. An examination of those moments, especially if it includes a close look at the motivations of the key players, can shed new light on events that are often only partly understood.

In the broader histories of World War II, a single year's significance can be hard to discern. This book is an attempt to bring the importance of 1941 sharply into focus.

ONE

"MAD LOGIC"

On *January 1, 1941, Ivan Maisky,* the long-serving Soviet ambassador in London who frequently both vexed and intrigued his British hosts, made a bold prediction. "This will be the decisive year of the war," he wrote in his diary. "Hitler must make a supreme effort (most probably in spring or summer) in order to bring the war to an end this year—in his own favor, of course." It would be "catastrophic" for Germany if the war extended into 1942, he added, because by then, both British and US military production would be in full swing, and the Anglo-American allies would be "capable of simply raining bombs and shells on Germany." Thus, Hitler needed to deliver "a final, decisive knockout blow" in 1941. While Maisky wrote his diary in Russian, he sprinkled in English words for emphasis—which was the case for "supreme effort" and "knockout blow."

"But where? In which direction?" he mused. "I think it will be directed against England, for a blow in any other direction cannot produce a decisive effect."

Maisky was right in the first part of his prediction: 1941 would prove to be the decisive year of the war. But the Soviet envoy was wrong about the direction of Hitler's next blow. Like his boss Joseph Stalin, he refused to believe the mounting evidence that German plans for the invasion of the Soviet Union were already under way.

This was a huge strategic misjudgment—and far from the only one. As events unfolded in 1941, it became glaringly apparent that the two totalitarian tyrants were miserable judges of each other's character and mind-set. Stalin was made to look the fool first, but Hitler would soon follow.

The irony is that these two leaders should have understood each other better than anyone else. After all, despite their ideological differences, they had a tremendous amount in common: cynicism, cunning, and staggering brutality. When they concluded their infamous nonaggression pact, signed by their foreign ministers, Joachim von Ribbentrop and Vyacheslav Molotov, on August 23, 1939, they both knew they were green-lighting the start of a new war, allowing the Germans to invade Poland from the west on September 1 and the Red Army to attack from the east on September 17. They were both eager to destroy the Polish state and divvy up the spoils—and, in the process, they appeared to realign themselves against new common enemies: Britain and France.

While proclaiming a new era of cooperation between Moscow and Berlin, Molotov declared in a speech to the Supreme Soviet on October 31: "A short blow at Poland from the German army, followed by one from the Red Army, was enough to reduce to nothing this monster child of the Treaty of Versailles. Now Germany stands for peace, while Britain and France are in favor of continuing the war. As you see, the roles have been reversed." He added that it was "not only nonsensical but also criminal to pursue a war 'for the destruction of Hitlerism' under the bogus banner of a struggle for 'democracy.'" Later, of course, when the two countries were at war with each other, Soviet propagandists would pretend that the Kremlin leaders never expressed such sentiments.

Even in terms of their personal biographies, Hitler and Stalin had much in common. Both men were born far from the political center of the countries they would come to rule: Hitler in Upper Austria, and Stalin in Georgia. Both men had fathers who believed in harsh discipline. Stalin's father was a cobbler who was probably illiterate. "Undeserved and severe beatings made the boy as hard and heartless as the father was," recalled a friend of the young Stalin. Hitler's father, who died when Adolf was only thirteen, was a short-tempered customs official who also did not hesitate to beat his son.

In that era, such parenting was commonplace, and plenty of boys with similar experiences grew up to lead normal lives. In Hitler's case, his years of drift after his father's death, including his failure to gain admission to the Vienna Academy of Fine Arts, probably played a bigger role in sustaining his sense of grievance than whatever mistreatment he experienced in his early years. But it is fair to say that both men's characters were shaped initially by their authoritarian fathers. The result, as General Dmitri Volkogonov, the former propaganda chief of the Red Army, wrote in his epic biography of Stalin, was someone who displayed "contempt for normal human values" and "despised pity, sympathy, mercy." That description could have fit either tyrant.

Both men also rose to lead their movements by appealing to a collective sense of grievance. Hitler denounced Jews, Communists, the Weimar government and everyone else he blamed for Germany's defeat in World War I, the humiliating terms of the Versailles Treaty, and the economic and political chaos that followed. Stalin claimed to represent the little people of tsarist Russia, even "the oppressed nationalities and the religions"—the same groups that he immediately labeled as enemies of the Bolshevik Revolution and persecuted when he took charge. Just like Hitler, he never hesitated to promise the exact opposite of what he delivered.

Once in power, both men quickly found pretexts to eliminate any potential rivals. On his deathbed, Vladimir Lenin famously warned against allowing Stalin to succeed him. "Stalin is too crude, and this defect, although quite tolerable in our own midst and in dealings with us Communists, becomes intolerable in a general secretary," he dictated on January 4, 1923. "That is why I suggest that the comrades think about removing Stalin from that post." The Party should find someone who is "more tolerant, more loyal, more polite, and more considerate to the comrades, less capricious, etc."

But that warning, delivered by Lenin's widow after her husband's death a year later, came too late. Potential rivals such as Nikolai Bukharin and Leon Trotsky not only lost out in the power struggle but also lost their lives. Bukharin was swept up in the purges of the 1930s, put on display in the leading show trial, and promptly executed; Trotsky fled to Mexico, where a Stalinist agent murdered him with an ice pick in 1940. Hitler made sure that Gregor Strasser, his sole potential rival, lost out in a party power struggle right before the Nazi takeover in 1933. On June 30, 1934, Strasser was among the scores of victims of Hitler's Night of the Long Knives, which gave a foretaste of the new German leader's reign of terror.

Stalin, who had taken power a decade earlier than Hitler, boasted a far more extensive record of terror, with millions of victims, than his German counterpart in this period. His Great Terror targeted not just Ukrainian peasants who resisted forced collectivization, along with autocrats and intellectuals, but also the entire power apparatus: the Communist Party, the People's Commissariat for Internal Affairs, or NKVD (as the forerunner to the KGB was known), and the armed forces. In many cases, the executioners soon found themselves among those who were executed; just like the French Revolution, the Bolshevik Revolution devoured its own children.

During 1937 and 1938 alone, the NKVD rounded up about 1.5 million people, of whom only about 200,000 were released later. Many were dispatched to the Gulag, but about 750,000 of that number were shot outright—their bodies dumped in execution pits near cities all across the country. Among the victims were top military officers, often accused of hatching plots with Nazi Germany at a time when the two militaries had cooperated with the official blessing of their governments. Most of the accused were also tortured mercilessly to elicit full confessions of their imaginary crimes at the show trials.

Stalin reviewed personally many of the execution lists, and dismissed appeals for mercy with his usual fury. "Swine and prostitute," he wrote on the appeal of General Jonah Yakir. His henchmen followed his lead. Politburo member Lazar Kaganovich added: "For a bastard, scum, and whore, there is only one punishment: the death penalty." For the families of the victims, the guilty verdicts and executions of their husbands and fathers were often only the starting point of their ordeal. Some of the "wives of enemies of the people" were then tried, sentenced—and, in some cases, shot just like their husbands.

Little wonder that Stalin greeted the news from Germany about the Night of the Long Knives with admiration. "Hitler, what a great man!" he declared. "This is the way you deal with your political opponents." Hitler was just as impressed by Stalin's reign of terror and, during the war, once declared: "After the victory over Russia, it would be a good idea to get Stalin to run the country, with German oversight, of course. He knows better than anyone else how to handle the Russians." This was more an ironical aside that a real recommendation, but it reflected Hitler's genuinely ambivalent feelings about his rival. Once Germany began to suffer setbacks on the Eastern Front, Hitler also mused that he should have followed Stalin's example by carrying out a purge of his top military officers.

In many other ways, too, the two dictators resembled each other. They were supposed to be ideological opposites, but it was hardly a coincidence that each built up their image as the all-knowing, all-powerful leader who deserved nothing less than public worship. Valentin

Berezhkov, who served as Stalin's interpreter for his meetings with German and later Allied leaders during the war, visited Berlin with a Soviet trade mission just after the German victory in France in June 1940. He observed Hitler as he arrived at the opera, where he was greeted by a frenzied crowd shouting *"Sieg Heil!" "Heil Hitler!"* and *"Heil Führer!"* This produced a startling reflection: "As I am watching all that, I am thinking—and the thought scares me—how much more there is in common between this and our congresses and conferences when Stalin makes his entry into the hall. The same thunderous, never-ending standing ovation. Almost the same hysterical shouts of 'Glory to Stalin!' 'Glory to our leader!' "

To those who harbored secret doubts about their own leader, the resemblances were uncanny—but they also noticed differences. Valeria Prokhorova was a student in Moscow during the time of the uneasy Nazi-Soviet alliance and the subsequent German invasion of her country. By then, many of her family members and friends had disappeared during the successive waves of Stalin's terror. In her eyes, the two dictators were "spiritual brothers," with the main difference one of style. "Stalin reminds me of a murderer who comes with flowers and candy, while Hitler stands there with a knife and pistol," she said.

As Hans von Herwarth, a German diplomat who served in Moscow in the 1930s, saw it, Stalin's "flowers and candy" approach could be highly effective. "Stalin struck me then as exuberant, not without charm, and with a pronounced capacity for enjoying himself," he wrote. "What a contrast he seemed to make with Hitler, who had so little zest for pleasure!" Herwarth may have heightened the contrast because of his dislike of Hitler. But he also pointed out "the feline manner in which he [Stalin] moved," likening him to "a kind of lynx or tiger." The image was that of an attractive yet dangerous animal.

And while tigers may look and even act alike, they can turn on one another very quickly. For Hitler, this was no mere theoretical possibility: he had been contemplating the conquest of his giant neighbor to the east from his earliest days, when he mapped out his Weltanschauung—his worldview—in his autobiographical screed *Mein Kampf.*

The Nazi Party was still in its infancy when Hitler launched his abortive Beer Hall Putsch in Munich. On November 9, 1923, along with World War I hero General Erich Ludendorff, he led the Brownshirts in their bid to topple the Bavarian government—with the further grandiose ambition of marching on Berlin and putting an end to the Weimar Republic. All this proved to be a short-lived fantasy when the state police met the Nazis with a burst of machine-gun fire. Found guilty of treason in early 1924, Hitler was dispatched to Landsberg Prison, where he received pampered treatment as a local celebrity—and then was released after serving less than nine months of his five-year sentence. During that short spell behind bars, he worked on the autobiography that would prove to be an invaluable tool as he sought to rebuild his movement.

To this day, many people who claim familiarity with Hitler's thinking have read only excerpts from *Mein Kampf.* That is hardly surprising. After all, much of the prose is so turgid that even his supporters had difficulty wading through it.

Otto Strasser was an early follower of Hitler but had the good sense to break with him and escape from Germany before he met the same fate as his brother Gregor did on the Night of the Long Knives. During the 1927 party congress in Nuremberg, he recalled, he was at a dinner with several top Nazi officials. When it became apparent that no one had read all of *Mein Kampf*, they agreed they would ask anyone who joined them if he had done so—and stick that person with the bill. "Nobody had read *Mein Kampf*, so everyone had to pay his own bill," Strasser reported.

The parts of the volume that are most familiar to the general public illustrate Hitler's obsessive anti-Semitism and determination to "wipe out the vermin," "a maggot in a rotting body," as he characterized Jews. "All who are not of good race in this world are chaff," he wrote. The Jew is "the eternal blood-sucker," and "the hissing of the Jewish world hydra" represents the greatest danger to the Aryan race. Conversely, he argued: "A state which in this age of racial poisoning dedicates itself to the care of the best racial elements must someday become lord of the earth."

But the sections that are worth examining more carefully, which signal the kind of thinking that spurred Hitler's major actions in 1941, focus on Germany's place in the world and, in particular, his determination to conquer and colonize Russia. Despite Hitler's marriage of convenience with Stalin at the beginning of the war and the German leader's occasional admission that he was impressed by the ruthlessness of his Soviet counterpart, they explain why he was never going to abandon that goal. Tactics dictated the Nazi-Soviet pact; his worldview dictated that it be short lived.

As Hitler explained, "*Germany today is no world power*" [his italics] and "*Germany will either be a world power or there will be no Germany.*" He envied Britain's far-flung empire but understood that Germany could look for new lands to conquer only within Europe. The alleged reason for his push for Germany's expansion: its need for Lebensraum—living space—to spread out its "excess population" and gain access to more natural resources. In Malthusian terms, he added: "If this earth really has room for all of us to live in, let us be given the soil we need for our livelihood." Anticipating the fact that other nations would hardly agree to this, he argued that "then the law of self-preservation goes into effect; and what is refused to amicable methods, it is up to the fist to take."

For Germany, the only logical direction to look was eastward—"by and large only at the expense of Russia." Political boundaries should not be taken seriously; what was important, he maintained, were "the boundaries of eternal justice." This vision dovetailed with his conviction that Russia was a land controlled by Jews, and Marxism "systematically plans to hand the world over to the Jews." In his mind, the Jewish race and the Bolshevik creed were inextricably linked. Therefore, "the end of Jewish rule in Russia will also be the end of Russia as a state." It would constitute the critical step in "a war of annihilation on Marxism" everywhere.

But Hitler was aware of historical precedent, which demonstrated that Russia could be a formidable foe. In World War I, he wrote, German forces had fought "without the slightest success" on the Russian front for three years. "The Allies almost laughed over this aimless undertaking," he wrote. "For in the end, the Russian giant with his overwhelming number of men was sure to remain the victor while Germany would inevitably collapse from loss of blood."

To achieve his goal, Hitler seemingly recognized that Germany had to find support elsewhere on the Continent. In *Mein Kampf*, he came to one conclusion: "For such a policy, there was but one ally in Europe: England." While he also mentioned Italy as a potential ally and praised Benito Mussolini as "the great man south of the Alps," he assumed that Germany would need at least the tacit backing of one of the bigger powers—and France, which he viewed as "the inexorable mortal enemy of the German people," was never an option. "England desires no Germany as a world power, but France wishes no power at all called Germany," he wrote.

In other words, France was still seeking the total destruction of Germany. England, on the other hand, could tolerate Germany as a continental power, leaving Britain as the uncontested global one. In essence, he was proposing his version of a grand bargain with Britain's rulers, an idea that he would return to again and again.

From his earliest days, though, Hitler was fully committed to implementing his vision, regardless of whether he could convince England to protect his back as he mobilized Germany to strike eastward—or to remain on the sidelines whenever he would choose to strike in the opposite direction against France. In February 1936, at his mountain retreat in Obersalzberg, Hitler told Albert Speer: "There are two possibilities for me: To win through with all my plans, or to fail. If I win, I shall be one of the greatest men in history. If I fail, I shall be condemned, despised, and damned."

At least in the latter part of his prophecy, he proved to be absolutely right.

Aside from his skills as an orator and stage master, Hitler displayed a mixture of talents and idiosyncrasies that kept those around him both in awe and frequently off guard. According to Percy Ernst Schramm, who served as Hitler's war diarist from 1943 to the end of the conflict, the dictator realized that most people had a hard time dealing with his piercing eyes. "Knowing this, Hitler looked people straight in the eye without blinking," he recalled. At the same time, Hitler was quite capable of telling jokes, drawing on his "phenomenal memory." Yet he could switch in a second from appearing gracious, particularly with women and children, to "ferocity—morally, uninhibited, ruthless, 'ice-cold.' "

Hans Karl von Hasselbach, one of Hitler's physicians, noted after the war that he had "an extraordinarily high estimation of his own capabilities," and that he considered himself to be an expert on almost any subject or country. But before the war, he demonstrated no interest in traveling outside of Germany and Austria to broaden his knowledge of foreign peoples and cultures. He was convinced he could teach himself everything he needed to know without stepping out of his familiar surroundings.

Hitler was indeed capable of learning enough to impress many of those around him. General Alfred Jodl, who worked closely with him on a daily basis, marveled at his "astounding technical and tactical vision" that allowed him to guide the development of new weaponry. He would routinely demonstrate his familiarity with details that no one expected him to know. For Schramm, though, this was a key element in his ultimate failure. "Even in technological questions, Hitler was his own worst enemy as he became more and more firmly convinced that he knew more than anyone else," he explained.

Hitler also considered himself an expert judge of others. In fact, as Hasselbach pointed out, Hitler "underestimated many of his opponents in an ominous fashion." This would prove to be true in his military, political, and economic calculations from the time he was preparing for war right up until his final days in his bunker in Berlin. It was particularly true in his dealings with the leaders of the other major powers who would soon be allied against him.

In *Mein Kampf*, Hitler unwittingly identified another one of his failings that manifested itself in his preparations for war: his disregard for the economic underpinnings needed for a successful military strategy. "Economics is only of second- or third-rate importance, and the primary role falls to factors of politics, ethics, morality, and blood," he wrote.

Hermann Göring, the head of the Luftwaffe, who was already considered the second most powerful man in the country, echoed those sentiments in a meeting with army officers in the summer of 1938. "The armed forces should not concern themselves with the fate of the economy," he told them, since he had "sole responsibility" for such matters. "The collapse of parts of the economy was irrelevant. Ways will be found."

Both before the outbreak of the war and in its early days, other members of Hitler's entourage, including within the military, attempted to warn the German leader that he was charting a dangerous course. They feared that his dismissing economic considerations, along with underestimating the strength and political will of Germany's likely opponents, could prove to be a fatal combination. Even Göring expressed similar concerns on occasion. But all of them would be overruled again and again.

In the buildup to the crisis over Czechoslovakia's Sudetenland in 1938, General Ludwig von Beck, chief of the general staff of the army, had been in the forefront of those issuing such warnings. He was particularly alarmed that Hitler would risk a war with the Western powers at a time when he was convinced Germany would not have the arms or the resources to prevail. Beck sought assurances from him that his pressure on Czechoslovakia would not lead to war, and he tried to rally his fellow senior officers to stand up to Hitler with him. He failed on both counts and resigned in August.

A small group of anti-Hitler conspirators had then hoped to enlist Beck's successor, Franz Halder, in their cause, possibly mounting a coup. According to Jacob Beam, a young staffer at the US embassy in Berlin who met one of the plotters, "The plan was to assassinate Hitler if he moved to the point of making war." Beam's senior colleagues were dismissive of his report, although it was consistent with what Halder and several other senior officers claimed at the end of World War II. But once Britain and France acceded to Hitler's annexation of the Sudetenland and signed the Munich Pact in September, any plans for overthrowing the dictator were abandoned. It was hard to argue with such spectacular success.

Field Marshal Erich von Manstein wrote after the war: "We had watched Germany's precarious course along the razor's edge to date with close attention and were increasingly amazed at Hitler's incredible luck in attaining—hitherto without recourse to arms—all his overt and covert political aims. The man seemed to have an infallible instinct."

When the appeasement deal was struck in Munich, and Chamberlain made his infamous "peace in our time" pronouncement, even Hitler appeared astounded by his victory. Earlier, William Shirer, the CBS correspondent in Berlin, had noticed Hitler's nervous tic as he made his demands for the Sudetenland. Observing Hitler upon his return to the German capital, he noted: "How different Hitler at two this morning. . . . I noticed his swagger. The tic was gone!"

But if Hitler had proven to his doubting generals that their fears of British and French intervention were misplaced at that point, the larger question of whether Germany literally could afford a new conflict remained open.

Two officials took on this issue directly. The first was Reich Finance Minister Schwerin von Krosigk. During that fateful summer of 1938, he was acutely aware of the soaring costs of Germany's rapid military buildup and the strain this was putting on the country's finances. He had raised taxes and increased borrowing, but worried how much longer he could maintain a steady course—and if a new war broke out, how long Germany could hold out against its foes.

In a memorandum that summer, he pointed out that "every war in the future will be fought not only with military means but also will be an economic war of greatest scope." Krosigk, who had firsthand experience in England as a Rhodes scholar, warned that Britain would be a formidable adversary in any conflict, even if it appeared weak at the moment, with its army far from ready. It had "two great trump cards," he wrote. "One is the soon-expected active participation of the United States of America in the war." The other was Germany's "financial and economic weakness."

If a war started, he warned, England would try to outlast any initial German victories, waiting for the Reich to become "weaker and weaker" because of its economic vulnerabilities. By then, the United States would supply England with arms and airplanes, altering the military balance. Krosigk's recommendation, which, not coincidentally, echoed the advice of Beck before his resignation, was for Germany to step back from confrontation, at least for the immediate future.

The other key figure in the battle to convince Hitler to slow down in his rush to war was Major General Georg Thomas, the Wehrmacht's chief economist and a longtime specialist in procurement. In 1939, as the German leader was signaling his intention to move against Poland next, Thomas offered another set of warnings about German-versus-Western capabilities. Like Krosigk and others, he already viewed

Washington as London's ally. Consequently, he explained to Foreign Ministry officials that, along with its empire, Britain could rely on "the United States as an armory and reservoir of raw materials."

Thomas offered specific calculations to make his case about the significance of this development. Comparing the combined planned defense expenditures of Britain, France, and the United States with the combined expenditures of Germany and Italy for 1939–1940, he calculated that the Western powers would be in a position to outspend Germany and Italy by the equivalent of at least 2 billion reichsmarks in 1940. And this was at a time when Germany was devoting a staggering 23 percent of its national income to military needs. Although Britain was increasing its military spending, it was at 12 percent, in Thomas's calculations, while the United States was at a mere 2 percent. According to his analysis, the balance of forces was certainly not in Germany's favor, and it was likely only to deteriorate further.

The United States, in particular, had plenty of room to beef up its military expenditures. Germany, on the other hand, was already stretching some of its resources to the limit. General Walter von Brauchitsch, the army's commander in chief, pointed out that shortages of rod iron, steel, and copper were hobbling the country's rearmament effort. Adam Tooze, the author of *The Wages of Destruction: The Making and Breaking of the Nazi Economy*, a detailed examination of the economy of the Third Reich and the debate about its implications for the war effort, explained what this meant: "Germany's 'wartime economy at peace' had reached a critical threshold."

Thomas kept insisting that his calculations about the industrial resources of the Western countries demonstrated that Germany should not risk a war with England and France by attacking Poland. Hitler was aware of his country's precarious position. But he also knew, as Tooze put it, "that the Third Reich had assembled both the largest and most combat-ready army in Europe, as well as the best air force" by the summer of 1939.

On August 26 Thomas pressed his case by providing new charts and tables to General Wilhelm Keitel. In his diary, Thomas recorded the reaction: "Was not well received, but K. [Keitel] agreed to speak to the Führer again." The next day, Thomas had the chance to raise the issue with Hitler directly. "Again sharp rebuke," he noted, adding that he was kicked out of the meeting. Hitler's final words to him: "Stop bothering me with the bloody Western situation."

What accounted for Hitler's anger? The German leader understood many of the negative trends that Thomas was projecting but did not accept his recommendation to hold off on the invasion of Poland. In effect, as Tooze explains in his authoritative study, Hitler drew the exact opposite conclusion, based on his own "mad logic" that made perfect sense to him: if Germany's position was likely to get worse over time, then this was the moment to strike.

On September 1, 1939, German forces launched their attack. It would be the first in a series of Hitler's decisions to ignore large, blinking yellow lights when contemplating military action. In Hitler's mind, all such warnings proved that his troops should race through them as fast as possible.

In his preparations for war, Hitler had recognized the danger of provoking his more powerful enemies to the east and west simultaneously. In that sense, the warnings of his subordinates had not gone completely unnoticed. As a result, the German leader pursued a two-pronged strategy. The first part was to ensnare Russia as a partner in the dismemberment of Poland, thereby guaranteeing that it would not become an immediate enemy on the battlefield. The second was a long-shot hope: as German troops were crushing Poland with an impressive display of overwhelming might, Britain and France would back down from their pledges to fight for that country; they would accept the seemingly inevitable, just as they had in the case of Czechoslovakia.

Despite Hitler's and Stalin's similarities and admiration of each other's ruthlessness, the two totalitarian leaders went into their provisional partnership with their eyes wide open. Hitler had spelled out his views about Russia's leaders in *Mein Kampf*: "Never forget that the rulers of present-day Russia are common blood-stained criminals; that they are the scum of humanity. . . . Furthermore, do not forget that these rulers belong to a race which combines, in a rare mixture, bestial cruelty and an inconceivable gift for lying, and which today more than ever is conscious of a mission to impose its bloody oppression on the whole world."

Stalin was well aware of Hitler's rants on the subject of his country—and his ambitions to make it the new frontier of a German empire. He had read those parts of *Mein Kampf* that left no doubt about Hitler's goal of conquering and enslaving Russia. Stalin had also read Konrad Heiden's *History of National Socialism*, which offered a clear warning about Hitler's tactics. "His promises cannot be regarded as that of a reliable partner," Heiden wrote. "He breaks them when it is in his interest to do so."

As the two sides wrapped up their negotiations for the nonaggression pact, they went through the motions of proclaiming their good intentions. When Ribbentrop arrived in Moscow to sign the agreement, he assured his Soviet hosts that Germany was focused on threats from the West, not from the Kremlin. Lifting a glass of champagne, Stalin proposed a toast to Hitler's health. But the Soviet leader let loose with his true feelings when Ribbentrop suggested a flowery preamble to the pact.

"The Soviet Union could not possibly present to the Soviet people in good faith assurances of friendship with Germany, when, for six years, the Nazi government has showered the Soviet government with buckets of shit," he declared. And during the signing of the pact, Stalin added, "Of course, we are not forgetting that your ultimate aim is to attack us."

Nonetheless, both leaders were delighted by the result. Hitler had the guarantee he needed that the Soviet Union would not choose this moment to attack him. Stalin, for his part, believed he had outsmarted both Hitler and the West, allowing him to seize eastern Poland and the Baltic states as well. "Hitler wants to trick us, but I think we've got the better of him," he told Ukraine's Communist Party leader Nikita Khrushchev.

Hitler's hopes for keeping Britain and France out of the conflict were quickly dashed. As late as August 29, just before Germany invaded Poland on September 1, General Halder noted in his diary: "The general impression is that Britain is 'soft' on the issue of a major war." At nine o'clock on the morning of September 3, however, Sir Nevile Henderson, the British ambassador in Berlin, delivered an ultimatum to the German government to cease all aggressive actions against Poland. If it failed to do so by eleven that morning, Britain would declare war on Germany.

Henderson had wanted to deliver the ultimatum personally to Ribbentrop, but the foreign minister sent his interpreter, Paul Schmidt, to meet him instead. Schmidt promptly took the British demand to the chancellery. Stepping into the office, he saw Hitler seated at his desk and Ribbentrop standing by the window. Schmidt translated the note for them. He later described the scene:

"When I finished, there was dead silence. . . . Hitler sat immobile, staring into space. He was not stunned, as was later asserted, nor did he rant, as others claimed. He sat absolutely silent and unmoving. After an interval, which seemed an eternity to me, he turned to Ribbentrop, who had remained frozen by the window. 'What now?' Hitler asked his foreign minister with a furious glare, as if to say that Ribbentrop had misinformed him about the probable reaction of the British. Ribbentrop replied in a muted voice: 'I assume that within the hour, the French will hand us a similar ultimatum.' "

Both Britain and France did declare war on Germany that day as promised. Interestingly, while the invasion of Poland on September 1 was the beginning of World War II, Nazi Germany treated that date as merely marking the "counterattack" against Poland. As long as the

Third Reich existed, Germans were taught that World War II started on September 3, launched by Britain and France against them.

As the Poles soon learned, their allies were not ready to assist them in any significant way. Despite the valiant resistance of Polish forces, the German invaders overwhelmed them quickly with their superior firepower, as Hitler had anticipated. The initial British action of dropping leaflets over Germany looked almost comically ineffective—more a display of impotence than power. But even when the first bombing raids began, with British planes attacking German ships and other military targets, the conflict was promptly dubbed "the phony war." It signaled the Western powers' inability to seriously slow, much less reverse, Hitler's momentum.

This allowed the German leader to continue to minimize the significance of his miscalculation about Britain and France. "He stuck unswervingly to his opinion that the West was too feeble and too decadent to begin the war seriously," Speer recalled. But once again, it would be Hitler who would push to escalate the conflict to the point where his enemies had no choice but to take it seriously and act accordingly.

Despite the success of the Polish campaign, those military skeptics who had tried to slow down Hitler's rush to war tried to push their case again—this time while Hitler was preparing to target France. On November 5, 1939, General Brauchitsch presented Hitler with statistics about the problems with Wehrmacht equipment, maintaining that more time was needed to prepare for any new offensive. Hitler's response was to berate him at length and to angrily denounce the "sabotage" of the Wehrmacht commanders.

A month later, Thomas, the Wehrmacht's economic expert, argued that more steel should be diverted to export production rather than allocated almost entirely to the military. In a long war, he warned, as he had before the invasion of Poland, Germany would falter if it did not bolster its economic base.

Relaying Hitler's response, General Keitel told him: "The Führer himself has recognized that we cannot last out a war of long duration. The war must be finished rapidly." In other words, Hitler was once again taking the appeals of his subordinates about the need for more time to prepare for the next stage of the war as a reason to arrive at a diametrically opposite conclusion: all their supporting arguments, he insisted, buttressed his case for immediate action.

In March 1940 Hitler wrote to Mussolini that Britain was fully committed to an all-out war. Its introduction of the draft and rearmament program meant that "a significant shift in the balance of forces in our favor was barely conceivable." The upshot: Germany needed to take advantage of its current strength before the balance of power shifted to its enemies.

Given the subsequent string of victories of his armies in Western Europe, particularly in France, Hitler's mad logic appeared to be vindicated yet again.

For Stalin, the speed and breadth of Hitler's successes was deeply unsettling—and not something he had anticipated. Khrushchev was with him when he heard about France's surrender. "He was racing around cursing like a cab driver," Khrushchev recalled. "He cursed the French. He cursed the English. How could they allow Hitler to defeat them, to crush them?" Stalin also revealed his underlying fear: all of this would allow Hitler "to beat our brains in."

Stalin had plenty of reasons to feel vulnerable. In stark contrast to the German record of swift conquest, the Soviet Union's attack on tiny Finland on November 30, 1939, turned into a protracted winter war, which Politburo member Anastas Mikoyan described later as a "shamefully conducted" campaign. Stalin had predicted victory in two weeks, allowing him to install an already prepared puppet government and turn Finland into the Karelo-Finnish Soviet Republic. Instead, the Finns fought back ferociously, stunning the ill-prepared Soviet forces.

As Khrushchev noted in his memoirs, "Most of our troops were ground up by the Finns." The casualty figures confirm this bleak assessment: more than 125,000 Soviet troops perished in the conflict, while Finnish losses totaled about 48,000. When the Finns were finally forced to accept the Moscow Peace Treaty in March 1940, they lost a good chunk of their territory—but they had succeeded in humiliating the Kremlin. None of that was lost on Hitler and his generals. "The Germans could see that the USSR was a giant with feet of clay," Khrushchev added. "Hitler must have concluded that if the Finns could put up such resistance, then the mighty Germans would need only one powerful blow to topple the giant."

As for Stalin, Khrushchev concluded, he had "lost his nerve" after his pyrrhic victory. "He probably lost whatever confidence he had that our army could cope with Hitler." In fact, Stalin would later complain to Churchill and Roosevelt that "the Red Army was good for nothing" in the Finnish campaign.

As Hitler saw it, there was another reason to feel increasingly confident that the Red Army would not be able to survive an all-out attack by his forces. The German leader may have admired the brutality of Stalin's purges of his top brass, but he also recognized that the wave of show trials and executions had taken its toll on the armed forces. In 1938 Kliment Voroshilov, the defense commissar, reported the "impressive" tally for the Red Army, which had been cleansed of more than forty thousand men. "The purge was drastic and thorough," he said. "We purged everyone that it was necessary to purge, starting with high positions and finishing with the low ones."

The results were devastating. Konstantin Rokossovsky, who was imprisoned for two years but was lucky enough to survive and even emerge as a top general during the war, declared: "This is worse than when artillery fires on its own troops." The top ranks were hit the hardest. Three of the five marshals, thirteen of the fifteen army commanders, and eight of the nine fleet admirals were among the victims, and so on down the chain of command. "So many were executed that the high command as well as middle and lower echelons were devastated," Khrushchev wrote. "As a result, our army was deprived of the cadres who had gained experience in the civil war, and we faced a new enemy unprepared."

Khrushchev was not alone in that assessment. According to Stepan Mikoyan, his father, Anastas Mikoyan, did not hide his feelings in their discussions at home. The loss of so many experienced military officers, he told him, "produced the most damaging effect on both the preparation for repelling Hitler's attack and the course of the war itself." Stalin's biographer General Volkogonov insisted that the purges "forged the defeats of 1941 which were to bring millions of new victims."

But those were judgments made later. The key question in the period of the nonaggression pact was how Stalin and Hitler viewed their respective strengths and weaknesses, and what decisions they should make based on that analysis. Not surprisingly, they reached diametrically opposite conclusions.

Recognizing his country's vulnerabilities, many of his own making, Stalin acted as if he could rely on the de facto alliance he had forged with Hitler to keep the peace between them—at least for a good while. He may have realized that this was only a temporary state of affairs, but he wanted to stretch it out as long as possible to allow him to bolster his country's forces. Besides, so long as the war was taking place elsewhere in Europe, the Western world was in the kind of crisis that might work to the advantage of Soviet long-term interests.

To keep Hitler at bay, Stalin made sure his subordinates honored the trade and other agreements with Germany, while the Germans regularly fell behind in their deliveries. During the run-up to the German invasion of his country, the Soviet Union provided huge amounts of oil, wood, copper, manganese, rubber, grain, and other supplies. In April 1941, for example, it sent 208,000 tons of grain, 90,000 tons of oil, and 6,340 tons of nonferrous metals to Germany. As the warnings mounted from Stalin's spies and elsewhere that he was only strengthening a formidable military opponent who was about to turn against him, Stalin was even more insistent on keeping those commitments. He wanted to prove to Hitler that he was not suspicious of him, figuring that the German leader was more likely to strike if he came to the opposite conclusion.

Khrushchev summed up the practical implications. "So while those sparrows kept chirping, 'Look out for Hitler!' Stalin was punctually sending the Germans trainload after trainload of grain and petroleum. He wanted to butter up Hitler by living up to the terms of the Molotov-Ribbentrop Pact!"

The "sparrows" included Soviet spies abroad. In June 1940, while German forces were still fighting in France, Colonel Ivan Dergachev, the Soviet military attaché in Bulgaria, sent a report from a source who predicted the armistice with France and "within a month's time" an attack on the Soviet Union. "The purpose would be to destroy Communism in the Soviet Union and create a fascist regime there," he wrote. Other reports were more accurate about the timing of the invasion, which was still a year away. A source code-named Ariets reported from Berlin on September 29, 1940, that Hitler planned to "resolve problems in the east in the spring of next year."

The warnings would multiply in early 1941, but Stalin was not listening.

Hitler had also played the game of seeking to reassure Stalin. As soon as the Molotov-Ribbentrop Pact was concluded, he instructed Admiral Wilhelm Canaris, the head of German military intelligence known as the Abwehr, to refrain from any operations that could be seen as targeting the Soviet Union. The spy agency immediately abandoned its efforts to cultivate sources there. In a directive on March 26, 1940, Canaris relayed those orders. "Nothing must be done to offend the Russians," it declared. As Canaris's biographer

Hans Höhne pointed out, "The result of this self-inflicted paralysis was the Abwehr had almost no idea of what was going on inside Russia."

The difference between Hitler and Stalin was that the German leader had never abandoned the goal that he had first spelled out in *Mein Kampf*: the conquest of Russia. After the failure of the Luftwaffe to dominate the skies over Britain and thereby prepare the way for an invasion of that country, Hitler refocused on that original objective. His reasoning why this was the next obvious move was, as always, convoluted. Nonetheless, he characteristically insisted that it made perfect sense, rejecting the advice of anyone who dared to voice any objections or doubts.

In a discussion with his military leaders on July 31, 1940, Hitler argued that the fulfillment of his dream of conquering Russia would solve his other problems as well—in fact, it would be the key to victory in the global struggle. According to General Halder's account, he made the following points:

"*Britain's hope lies in Russia and the United States.* [Halder's italics] If Russia drops out of the picture, America, too, is lost for Britain, because elimination of Russia would tremendously increase *Japan's power* in the Far East."

"*Russia is the Far Eastern sword of Britain and the United States* pointed at Japan." Once Russia was defeated, he reasoned, the Japanese would tie down the Americans in the Far East. Those developments would also seal the fate of Britain. "*With Russia smashed, Britain's last hope would be shattered.* Germany then will be master of Europe and the Balkans."

Hitler's conclusion: "*Decision: Russia's destruction must therefore be made a part of this struggle. Spring 1941. The sooner Russia is crushed the better.*"

As was the case before Hitler unleashed his forces against Poland and then Western Europe, some of his officials were skeptical about the wisdom of taking on their huge Eastern neighbor. Serving in the German embassy in Moscow in the 1930s, Herwarth—whose anti-Nazi views had prompted him to forge close ties with Western diplomats—soon learned that any attempt to warn Berlin against underestimating Russia's capabilities could backfire. "We decided that our responsibility was to point out the continuing strength of the Soviet Union," he recalled. But when he and his colleagues did so, "Hitler interpreted our reports in exactly the opposite way to what we had expected. Learning that the Russians were still strong and were likely to grow yet stronger, Hitler resolved that he had better strike immediately, lest the Russians grow to the point where they could dictate their terms to all Europe."

More senior officials who put forward other arguments against invading Russia met with a similar response. Ernst von Weizsäcker, the Foreign Ministry's secretary of state, observed that such an action "would only give a fresh boost to British morale," since it would be seen as a sign of "German uncertainty about the success of our war against Britain." Admiral Canaris, another skeptic, pleaded with General Keitel to warn Hitler against underestimating Russia's ability to fight back. "My dear Canaris, you may know something about military intelligence," Keitel replied. "Being a sailor, you surely don't propose to give us any lessons in strategic planning."

In making his case for an attack on Russia, Hitler invoked not just political and military calculations but also economic ones—despite his impatience with Thomas and other subordinates who had attempted to use economic arguments against embarking on a hasty war. On January 9, 1941, he told his generals that victory in Russia would make Germany invulnerable. "The gigantic spaces of Russia conceal immeasurable riches," he declared. "Germany must dominate them economically and politically."

The irony was that Germany had come to rely on the steady flow of Russian supplies since the signing of the Molotov-Ribbentrop Pact. Without the Soviet Union's massive shipments of animal feed, oil, metals, and minerals, both Germany's military and civilian economy would have been severely weakened. Colonel Eduard Wagner, the quartermaster general of the army, declared that "the conclusion of the treaty has saved us."

A few examples of the significance of Soviet supplies prove his point. In 1940 Germany received 65 percent of its chrome ore, 74 percent of its phosphates, and 55 percent of its manganese from Russia. But instead of considering how a German invasion of Russia could jeopardize that flow, Hitler fixated on the notion that a speedy and successful military campaign would provide his country with the "immeasurable riches" he mentioned to his generals. All the arguments about Germany's economic vulnerabilities would then become irrelevant.

During the discussions in the summer and fall of 1940 about an invasion of the Soviet Union, Field Marshal Fedor von Bock was largely out of the loop while on extended sick leave. But on December 3, Bock's sixtieth birthday, Hitler came to see him, bringing a small gift and delivering a blunt message. "After some preliminary inquiries about my health, he told me that it will be necessary to eradicate the Soviet Union from the face of the earth," Bock recalled. "I was somewhat surprised by the Führer's statement and remarked that Russia's enormous terrain and untested military strength would make this a difficult task, even for our powerful forces."

His visitor abruptly turned "cold and stiff," Bock noted. Hitler insisted that it was "Germany's destiny to launch this great crusade against Bolshevism." Switching back to a friendlier tone, he told Bock that he expected him to play "a decisive role" in that crusade. In fact, Bock would command Army Group Center, the forces whose mission it was to conquer central Russia and Moscow itself.

Two weeks later, on December 18, Hitler issued his Directive Number 21, "Case Barbarossa." Its opening paragraph:

"The German Armed Forces must be prepared, even before the conclusion of the war against England, *to crush Soviet Russia in a rapid campaign* ('Case Barbarossa')."

Like so much about this rush to expand the war to the Eastern Front, even the selection of the name of the operation suggested dubious preparation. Barbarossa was the nickname of Frederick I, the German emperor who drowned while trying to lead his troops to the Holy Land in 1190.

Hitler had convinced himself that his troops would pull off another stunningly swift victory. By the spring of 1941, he declared, they would be "visibly at their zenith," while Soviet forces would be at "an unmistakable nadir." As he put it in early January, "Since Russia has to be beaten in any case, it is better to do it now, when the Russian armed forces have no leaders and are poorly equipped."

His commanders still harbored doubts. Gerhard Engel, Hitler's army adjutant, noted in his diary on December 18 that General Halder had asked him to find out if the dictator "really intends war or is only bluffing." Engel, who acted as a go-between between the military brass and Hitler, may have been projecting those doubts onto Hitler when he wrote: "I am convinced that F. [Der Führer] still does not know what will happen. Distrustful of his own military leaders, uncertainty about Russ(ian) strength, disappointment over British stubbornness continue to preoccupy him."

On January 28, 1941, Halder wrote in his diary: "BARBAROSSA: Purpose is not clear. We do not hit the British that way. Our economic potential will not be significantly improved. Risk in the West must not be underestimated."

On February 1 Bock was summoned for another meeting with Hitler. "He regards Russia's collapse as a foregone conclusion," the field marshal noted. When Bock warned Hitler that his armies could suffer setbacks, the German leader was unfazed: "I am convinced that they will think a hurricane has hit them!"

A traditional Prussian militarist, Bock immediately began preparing diligently to lead his troops into the Russian heartland, whatever his misgivings. But only two weeks later, he was startled by the discovery that many of his units were short on rations due to cutbacks in supplies. "If the rations are being reduced now, what will happen when we have moved into Russia's interior, far from our bases of supply?" he wrote in his diary.

Hitler was not asking himself those kinds of questions. He had repeatedly proven the doubters wrong before, and he fully intended to do so again. During his meeting with his generals three weeks earlier, he had already envisaged Germany, flush with the anticipated victory in Russia, ready for a "war against continents." In other words, if the United States joined the conflict, Germany would have the resources of its newly conquered eastern territories to draw upon as it would inevitably crush that enemy as well.

TWO

"TWO PRIMA DONNAS"

By *most accounts, Winston Churchill's* defining—and most challenging—moment came during the Battle of Britain in the summer and fall of 1940, when the Luftwaffe tried and failed to achieve mastery of the skies over his country in preparation for a possible German invasion. But by Churchill's own account, he found himself in an even more unsettling situation a few months later, at the start of 1941. "Looking back upon the unceasing tumult of the war, I cannot recall any period when its stresses and the onset of so many problems all at once in rapid succession bore more directly on me and my colleagues than the first half of 1941," the prime minister wrote in his memoirs.

The Battle of Britain had turned into the Blitz, the German bombing campaign against mostly civilian targets, which would result in forty-three thousand deaths before it had largely run its course in May 1941. There were the battles with German U-boats, the widening war in North Africa, and looming German threats in the Balkans. "No part of our problem in 1941 could be solved without relation to all the rest," Churchill added. Noting how stretched his country's military and economic resources were, he declared: "And we had to do all this for a long time alone." Then, referring to the previous year with a colorful metaphor, he concluded: "After shooting Niagara, we had now to struggle in the rapids."

By contrast, Hitler was still projecting to the outside world an image of confidence in victory. "The Führer is serene about the future prospects of the war," Count Galeazzo Ciano, Mussolini's foreign minister and son-in-law, noted in his diary on January 1. Unlike his American counterparts in London who were reporting on a capital struggling with devastation and shortages on a daily basis, Henry Flannery, William Shirer's successor as the CBS correspondent in Berlin, recorded his almost surreal sense of detachment from the conflict. "We in Berlin hardly knew a war was on during the early part of 1941," he recalled. "There were no air raids to disturb our rest, and the conflict seemed far away."

Not so in London, where the windows in the office of Harold Nicolson, who was then working for the Ministry of Information, were blown out by a dropped bomb; Nicolson escaped because he was touring outside the British capital at the time. Such near misses appeared to only steel British resolve. "There is no doubt that the feeling is growing that similar treatment of the Germans is the only thing they will understand," he wrote on January 2. "We are fighting devils, and I don't see why we shouldn't fight like devils in order to let them see what it is like."

Britain was in no position to make good on such sentiments then. With the United States still officially on the sidelines and Russia still honoring its pact with Hitler, it had no powerful ally fully committed to the fight. But the mere fact that it was holding out while struggling in the rapids was a remarkable accomplishment.

From the moment he took office in May 1940, Churchill had rallied his people by putting them at the center of the "We are alone" narrative, portraying them as the brave holdouts against the Nazi tide sweeping across the rest of Europe. Aside from the prime minister, other top officials reinforced that message. "Personally, I feel happier now that we have no Allies to be polite to and to pamper," King George VI declared.

General Hastings Ismay, Churchill's chief military assistant during the war, added: "We were now alone. So, far from being alarmed, we were relieved, nay, exhilarated. Henceforward everything would be simpler. We were masters of our own fate." Conservative MP Victor Cazalet, who, like Churchill, had sounded the alarm about Hitler's intentions early and often, noted dourly: "France vanquished, out of War, defeatist, and anti-Britain." Yet he, too, insisted that "some people have even gained confidence that it is better to be on our own."

But, in reality, Britain was not completely alone, not even in those perilous early days. The spectacular evacuation of British, French, Polish, and other forces from Dunkirk and other French ports meant that the nucleus of a new coalition was already forming; it became the base of operations for all those who wanted to carry on the struggle.

Among them was my grandfather, Zygmunt Nagorski, who was a member of the Polish government-in-exile that had been evacuated from its previous headquarters in Angers, France. "For us, this island became the only country where it was possible to continue the fight," he recalled. His fellow Polish exiles called their new temporary home "Last Hope Island." Belgium's Foreign Minister Paul-Henri Spaak was one of the very few members of his government who decided to escape to London while most of his countrymen resigned themselves to German rule. "One hope was left—Britain," he recalled. "We realized it was on Britain that we had to gamble."

General Charles de Gaulle made a similar decision when Marshal Philippe Pétain, the country's famed military leader in World War I, capitulated to Hitler. Upon his arrival in London, de Gaulle vowed in a BBC broadcast that "the flame of French resistance must not and shall not die." In theory, he had the credentials to aspire to lead his countrymen in that effort. In his 1934 book *Vers l'armée de métier* (the English edition was called *The Army of the Future*), he had already issued a stark warning: "United Germany, favored by our illusions, cemented by our disasters, consolidated by our haste to limit the results of our recent victory of 1918, has put the colossus in a position to hurl itself upon the West in a single instantaneous bound."

To prevent that from happening, de Gaulle had argued that France needed to modernize its army, combining tanks and infantry into highly mobile units capable of striking fast while working closely with the air force, rather than relying on entrenched defenses and traditional infantry formations. His book sold a mere 750 copies in France, and Marshal Pétain and most of the top brass barely deigned to acknowledge such theories. The Maginot Line and infantry units, they insisted, would offer the country protection.

Given his failure to win support for his recommendations, de Gaulle's claim to leadership when he arrived in London was tenuous at best. "I was starting from scratch," he admitted later. "Not the shadow of a force or of an organization at my side. In France, no following and no reputation. Abroad, neither credit nor standing." Except, that is, from Churchill, who immediately offered him the microphone of the BBC to broadcast his messages to his countrymen, which allowed de Gaulle to become the voice of the Free French.

After spending six weeks in England, American author John Gunther observed the impact of the influx of foreigners. "London is not the capital of one country," he wrote. "It is the capital of six or eight." He was referring to all the governments-in-exile and representative offices set up by those who had fled from their occupied lands. "Polish soldiers guard British shores," he added. "Polish and Czech and other foreign flyers fight with the RAF."

But while all this meant that Churchill knew that his people were not completely alone in their fight, he also understood that he needed far more than the exiles who had made it across the English Channel to have a shot at victory. His primary focus was on the powerful country across the Atlantic, and, in particular, President Roosevelt. For all the prime minister's efforts to nurture this relationship and win more support for Britain, Churchill was encouraged by the signals from Washington but far from fully confident.

On New Year's Eve 1940, he wrote to Roosevelt: "Remember, Mr. President, we do not know what you have in mind, or exactly what the United States is going to do, and we are fighting for our lives." He concluded his message by sending his best wishes "in the New Year of storm that is opening upon us."

In one of his famous "*This* is London" broadcasts that same evening, CBS's Edward R. Murrow offered a sober assessment of the war: "Britain has been hit hard and cruelly—will be again—but she still stands where she did." Then he added a pointed message to his countrymen across the Atlantic. "You have not been promised blood and toil and tears, and, yet, it is the opinion of nearly every informed observer over here that the decisions you take will overshadow all else during this year that opened an hour ago in London."

Aside from its power as a rallying cry, Churchill's "We are alone" message came naturally to a politician who had experienced more than his share of political isolation. Today it is easy to forget how, on the eve of the war, as the American diplomat Robert Murphy put it, Churchill was written off as a "has-been, which was the general opinion at that time in England as well as in Europe."

As first lord of the Admiralty during World War I, he was grievously wounded by the failure of his ambitious Gallipoli campaign that was meant to knock the Ottoman Empire out of the war and open the sea route to Britain's ally Russia. Instead, both sides sustained massive casualties, and eventually the Allies were forced to withdraw. While there was plenty of blame to spread around, Churchill took the fall, resigning from the government and returning to military duty to serve on the Western Front.

After the war, he resumed his political career, but most of the 1930s constituted his "wilderness years," when, as a Conservative backbencher in Parliament, he held no government posts. He alienated many of his colleagues by fiercely opposing any concessions to Mahatma Gandhi's movement for Indian independence and by initially siding with King Edward VIII during the abdication crisis. While his early and frequent warnings about the dangers of appeasement would later prove decisive in the struggle for power, he was still seen as a lonely figure often prone to reckless words and deeds.

Even when Germany's invasion of Poland demonstrated how accurate Churchill had been about Hitler's intentions, his political prospects continued to look doubtful. John "Jock" Colville, a twenty-four-year-old Foreign Office staffer who was assigned to work at 10 Downing Street at the outbreak of the war, noted in his diary that Neville Chamberlain's failed appeasement policies had been completely discredited. "But there is really nobody to take his place," he wrote on November 8, 1939. "[Foreign Secretary Viscount] Halifax has not the forcefulness and Winston is too unstable."

Nonetheless, Chamberlain appointed Churchill to his old post of First Lord of the Admiralty at the start of the war, recognizing his prescience about the German threat. In that capacity, Churchill began pushing in early 1940 for Britain to take the offensive in neutral Norway by cutting off Swedish iron ore supplies to Germany and mining Norwegian territorial waters. But the ill-prepared mining operation started just as Hitler was dispatching his ships and troops to occupy that country. Despite some victories by the British, French, and Polish forces sent to secure Narvik and other Norwegian strategic objectives, the Allies were soon forced to evacuate.

The confusion and failure of the Norwegian campaign could have been a final fatal blow to Churchill's reputation and shakily revived political career. After all, as he acknowledged, given the prominent part he played in pushing for and orchestrating those events, "it was a marvel that I survived and maintained my position in public esteem and parliamentary confidence."

The reason he not only survived but also rose to the top was that a growing number of his parliamentary colleagues concluded that Chamberlain could no longer be trusted to lead a wartime nation and that Churchill was the only credible alternative. Whatever his past and more recent failings and miscalculations, he had been proven absolutely right about his warnings about Hitler and the need to prepare for a momentous military struggle. "At last, we had Churchill," Harold Macmillan, a staunch supporter and future prime minister, wrote with evident relief.

Churchill immediately began not only mobilizing his countrymen but also laying the groundwork for a full alliance with the United States.

After Germany's invasion of Poland, Roosevelt reached out to Churchill, reminding him in a letter dated September 11, 1939, that they had held "similar positions" in World War I, since they were responsible for their respective navies. "I want you to know how glad I am that you are back again in the Admiralty," he wrote, urging him to "keep me in touch personally with anything you want me to know about." Leaving no doubt that this would be a direct line of communication, he added: "You can always send sealed letters through your pouch or my pouch." In other words, any correspondence would go by diplomatic pouch, but the diplomats—especially Ambassador Kennedy, who made no secret of his defeatist views—would not be involved.

Churchill eagerly took him up on his offer, signing his letters "Naval Person." As General Raymond E. Lee, who served under Kennedy as the US military attaché but vehemently disagreed with him about Britain's chances for survival, noted in his diary the following month: "He [Kennedy] has been wrong on many points about the war and I don't believe Churchill has had much use for him, preferring to deal directly with Roosevelt."

Kennedy was hardly pleased. On a visit to the White House at the end of the year, he asked Roosevelt to explain the reason for this high-level private correspondence. Much to his surprise, the president responded by harking back to the first time he saw Churchill. "I have always disliked him since the time I went to England in 1918," he told Kennedy. He had been on an official visit to London as assistant secretary of the navy, attending a dinner of the British Cabinet, which included Churchill. "He acted like a stinker at the dinner I attended, lording it all over us," he recalled.

Knowing Kennedy's antipathy to Churchill and seeing his irritation with their private correspondence, Roosevelt may have deliberately sharpened his language. But he did not apologize in any way for bypassing his envoy in his dealings with Churchill. "I'm giving him attention now because there is a strong possibility he will become prime minister, and I want to get my hand in now," he said.

Although Churchill did not even recall Roosevelt's presence at the dinner in 1918, both men were wary of each other. To the American, Churchill's staunch defense of the British Empire—particularly his opposition to Gandhi's independence movement in India—marked him as an old-school imperialist. To Churchill, Roosevelt's seeming equivocation on the seminal issue of whether his country should be involved directly in the new global conflict proved a source of frequent exasperation. He complained that the American was inclined to "follow public opinion rather than to form it and lead it."

There was certainly truth in that. Roosevelt's close friend Robert H. Jackson, who served as solicitor general and then attorney general before his appointment to the US Supreme Court in July 1941, aptly summed up the "peculiar difficulty" Roosevelt faced. From the beginning of the war through his 1940 reelection campaign and until Pearl Harbor, "if he made any move that looked like getting the country ready for war, he was charged with being a warmonger," Jackson wrote. "But he felt obliged to take some steps that would prevent us from being caught unawares. He had a dual policy. One was a policy of peace. The other one was a policy for preparing for war. Each step that he took in favor of one of those policies was construed as an abandonment, or perhaps insincerity, concerning the other. So it was difficult for him to move."

Given their memories of the previous war, most Americans recoiled from the idea that "our boys" could be dispatched to the new one. Famed aviator Charles Lindbergh, who had visited Germany in the 1930s and reported on the growing strength of its air force, was the most prominent proponent of the isolationist movement that gave birth to the America First Committee in September 1940. As he had explained earlier, he was convinced the United States needed to stay clear of the conflict on a continent dominated by Hitler and Stalin—and, in any case, the Soviet Union represented the real threat to European civilization.

If the war turned into a contest between those two powers, Lindbergh wrote, "a victory by Germany's European people would be preferable to one by Russia's semi-Asiatic Soviet Union." Since Hitler would not live forever, he added, "the Germans would eventually moderate the excesses of his Nazi regime." Apart from other factors, his argument made no sense because Hitler was a decade younger than Stalin; in theory, he should have outlived his Soviet counterpart.

During Churchill's first months in office, the British leader also had to combat the perception that his country was fighting a losing battle. "Democracy in Britain is finished," Kennedy reported to Roosevelt on May 20 as France was collapsing. Across the Atlantic, many officials were thinking the same thing. "In July of 1940 very few of us in Washington believed that Britain, even under Winston Churchill's inspired leadership, could long hold out against Nazi Germany," Undersecretary of State Sumner Welles recalled. If that was the case, the isolationists argued, any American effort to change the outcome would not only be wrong but also futile.

On May 7, three days before he took over as prime minister, Churchill had offered a more upbeat—but still cautious—assessment of America's position. "The mighty Republic of the United States proclaims itself on our side, or at our side, or, at any rate, near our side," he told the House of Commons.

Once he moved to 10 Downing Street, Churchill immediately did everything he could to propel Roosevelt in the direction of preparing more openly for war. His son, Randolph, later recalled his encounter with his father when he returned to London on May 18 while on leave from military training. He found him shaving in front of a mirror, dressed only in a silk undershirt. Telling his son to sit down, he declared: "I think I see my way through"—leaving no doubt that he meant he could lead his country to victory. When Randolph responded that he didn't see "how you can do it," Churchill turned around and vowed: "I shall drag the United States in."

Churchill was not about to drag Roosevelt anywhere, but he unleashed his full powers of persuasion on him right from the start. On May 15 he sent his first message to the American leader as prime minister—and altogether he would send 950 messages to him during the war, receiving about 800 messages in return. The messages were delivered to the US embassy in London, which sent them as encrypted telegrams to Washington. Invoking their common background, as Roosevelt had in his first message at the start of the war, Churchill signed his cables "Former Naval Person" instead of just "Naval Person," as he had when he was at the Admiralty. "Although I have changed my office, I am sure you would not wish me to discontinue our intimate private correspondence," he explained.

Judging purely by his rhetoric, Roosevelt was already convinced in 1940 that his country needed to provide all the assistance it could to Britain. In his State of the Union address on January 3, he had warned his countrymen against the illusion that they could "live within a high wall of isolation while, outside, the rest of civilization and the commerce and culture of mankind are shattered." But he also expressed his understanding of "the feelings of those who warn the nation that they will never again consent to the sending of American youth to fight on the soil of Europe." He added hastily that "nobody has asked them to consent—for nobody expects such an undertaking."

Following Germany's victories in Western Europe, he warned even more strongly against the isolationist notion that the United States could become "a lone island in a world dominated by the philosophy of force." In his speech at the University of Virginia on June 10, he declared: "Such an island represents to me and to the overwhelming majority of Americans today a helpless nightmare of a people without freedom—the nightmare of a people lodged in a prison."

But Churchill knew all too well that none of this lofty language guaranteed the level of American material support he was hoping for, much less the kind of direct military involvement that he believed would be his country's ultimate salvation. In his May 15 telegram to Roosevelt, the new prime minister offered a blunt assessment of the "darkened" situation, noting that he expected Germany to attack Britain next, "both from the air and by parachute and airborne troops." While vowing to continue the war alone if necessary, he warned that "the voice and force of the United States may count for nothing if withheld too long." The result could be "a completely subjugated Nazified Europe established with astounding swiftness, and the weight may be more than we can bear."

Specifically, he asked for "the loan of forty or fifty of your older destroyers" to bridge the gap until Britain's new ones were completed; antiaircraft equipment and ammunition; and steel and other materials. Churchill promised to "go on paying dollars for as long as we can, but I should like to feel reasonably sure that when we can pay no more you will give us the stuff all the same."

Roosevelt's response was not encouraging. He pointed out that Congress would have to authorize the loan or gift of the older destroyers, and the timing was not right for him to make such a request. The clear implication was that domestic opposition to deepening the country's involvement in the war was still very strong. The opponents included General George C. Marshall and other top military leaders, who argued that it was too risky to provide supplies that could fall into enemy hands if the Germans conquered Britain.

When Churchill learned about such sentiments from Lord Lothian, his ambassador in Washington, he did not conceal his irritation. Handing another message for Roosevelt to Colville, he snapped: "Here's a telegram for those bloody Yankees." To Lothian, he complained: "Up till April, they were so sure the Allies would win that they did not think help necessary. Now they are so sure we shall lose that they do not think it possible."

But Churchill's efforts began to pay off as Roosevelt sought ways to provide immediate assistance. On June 1 he authorized sending "surplus" military supplies to Britain, including eighty thousand machine guns, ammunition, and a half million rifles produced during the previous war. Significantly, General Marshall had recommended this action, reversing his stance on such aid. Tank parts soon followed, and the two sides concluded a destroyers-for-bases agreement on September 2. In return for allowing the United States to establish naval and air bases with ninety-nine-year leases on British possessions, the Americans started sending over their old destroyers.

It was far from a perfect arrangement, and the Royal Navy quickly complained that the first destroyers they received were in terrible condition. But Churchill recognized it was a bargain that allowed Roosevelt to sell the deal to a skeptical Congress and public; more importantly, it meant that better ships and a vast array of other military equipment would follow. After Roosevelt won reelection in November, the British leader wrote to him that he had "prayed for your success and that I am truly thankful for it."

Churchill still expressed his annoyance with the slow response to his subsequent requests for more aid—and particularly with what he viewed as unduly harsh demands by the Americans for prompt payment for all deliveries. Given his country's rapidly dwindling gold and US dollar reserves, he pleaded with Roosevelt for a more generous arrangement. The president's response came in one of his radio broadcasts known as fireside chats. On December 29, he declared: "In a military sense, Great Britain and the British Empire are today the spearhead of resistance to world conquest. They are putting up a fight which will live forever in the story of human gallantry."

While still insisting that his country was not heading toward war, he vowed to make it "the great arsenal of democracy," adding that Britain's dwindling financial resources would not be a hindrance to making it the chief beneficiary. At a press conference a few days earlier, he explained that he would treat Britain the way he would a neighbor who wanted to use his garden hose to put out a fire. He would not respond to his neighbor's request by saying, "Neighbor, my garden hose cost me fifteen dollars; you have to pay me fifteen dollars for it." Instead of asking for payment, he would expect to get the garden hose back "after the fire is over."

This kind of folksy reasoning proved critical to winning support for the Lend-Lease Act that was drafted by the beginning of January 1941, sparking the decisive debate in Congress during the next two months about just how far the country could go in supporting Britain. Roosevelt's speechwriter Robert Sherwood credited the neighbor analogy with convincing most Americans "that there couldn't be anything very radical or very dangerous in the President's proposal to lend our garden hose to the British who were fighting so heroically against such fearful odds."

The wording of the act itself offered Roosevelt the kind of broad latitude Churchill wanted. Under its terms, he would be able to send military and other supplies to "the government of any country whose defense the President deems vital to the defense of the United States." The Americans would "lend" those supplies, without any requirement for immediate repayment or specification of what form such repayment might take.

It was precisely this broad latitude that alarmed the isolationist camp. Republican Senator Robert A. Taft pointed out that the bill would "give the president power to carry on a kind of undeclared war all over the world, in which America would do everything except actually put soldiers in the frontline trenches where the fighting is."

As 1941 began, there was no certainty that Congress and the American people would accept those provisions. Both Roosevelt's supporters and the isolationists were gearing up for an intense battle.

In *Mein Kampf*, Hitler pointed to what he felt was a major mistake of Germany before World War I: its belief that it could compete with Britain's far-flung empire by pursuing its own colonial policy. "I would have thought it sounder if Germany, renouncing her senseless colonial policy and renouncing her merchant marine and war fleet, had concluded an alliance with England against Russia, thus passing from a feeble global policy to a determined European policy of territorial acquisition on the Continent," he wrote.

Hitler's notion that Britain could have been Germany's ally rather than its foe in the early part of the century stuck with him during his ascension to power—and into World War II. "His regret at not having made an ally out of England ran like a red thread through all the years of his rule," Speer wrote in his memoirs. Hitler fixated on certain ideas early and never let go of them completely, no matter how compelling the evidence was to the contrary. This was particularly true in his assessment of Britain and the United States during the critical period when his policies were driving those countries closer together—and certainly true of his subsequent massive miscalculations about the ability of the Soviet Union to resist German might.

"Hitler actually knew nothing about his enemies and even refused to use the information that was available to him," Speer added. "Instead, he trusted his inspirations, no matter how inherently contradictory they might be." The most dramatic example of this, according to Speer, was how Hitler would call England "'our enemy number one' while at the same time hoping to come to an arrangement with that enemy." Engel, Hitler's army adjutant, noted in his diary on December 18, 1940: "Hopes Eng(lish) will relent; does not believe USA will enter war."

From the moment that Britain and France declared war on Germany after its invasion of Poland, Hitler sought to convince himself and his entourage that, according to Speer, they had done so "merely as a sham, in order not to lose face before the whole world." A typical headline of the *Völkischer Beobachter,* the Nazi Party daily, read: "Germany's Will for Peace—No War Aims Against France and England."

Hitler continued to make such "peace" overtures in private as well as public. On March 4, 1940, he met with James D. Mooney, the president of the General Motors Overseas Corporation, who was engaged in a quixotic effort to avert a wider war at the suggestion of German officials. Hitler told Mooney that Germany was willing to respect England's world power status so long as Germany was respected in a similar way. He claimed that this could be the basis for a peace agreement with Roosevelt, which could then lead to arms reductions and new international trade. Mooney sent five messages to Roosevelt about that encounter and other meetings with German officials, only to receive a brush-off from the White House.

In the aftermath of the Battle of Britain and during the continuing onslaught of the Blitz, Hitler grew increasingly frustrated with the refusal of the island nation to submit to his will. "The Führer is greatly puzzled by Britain's persisting unwillingness to make peace," General Halder noted on July 13, 1940. On November 24 Propaganda Minister Joseph Goebbels asked in his diary, "When will Churchill surrender?" He added, "But Churchill is not yet considering surrender." Two days later, Goebbels vented his anger further in another diary entry about the English. "Their best weapons are their phlegm and their stupidity," he wrote. "In their position, any other nation would have collapsed long since."

That same month, Molotov visited Berlin, meeting with his German counterpart, Ribbentrop. While the Soviet foreign minister was attending a banquet in his honor, the RAF attacked the city, forcing his hosts to retreat with him to Ribbentrop's bunker. When Ribbentrop insisted that Britain was finished, the normally dour Molotov delivered his best riposte ever. "If that's so, then why are we in this shelter, and whose bombs are those falling?" he asked.

Much of the exasperation of Hitler and his entourage with Britain was aimed personally at Churchill. When Chamberlain appointed him first lord of the Admiralty right after the invasion of Poland, Hermann Göring emerged from Hitler's office, dropped into the nearest chair, and declared: "Churchill in the Cabinet. That means that the war is really on. Now we shall have war with England." Yet Hitler never completely abandoned the idea of convincing the British to see the wisdom of his putative peace offers.

To the limited extent that Hitler considered the role of the United States in his geopolitical calculations, he exhibited the same propensity to see only what he wanted to see as he did with Britain. In the early 1920s, when Hitler was the leader of the fledgling Nazi Party in Munich, Ernst "Putzi" Hanfstaengl, a Harvard graduate of mixed German-American parentage, served as his chief propagandist and occasional adviser. In a postwar interview with Hitler biographer John Toland, Hanfstaengl claimed that he had tried to educate him about the growing importance of the United States, offering him "his big chance. . . . to reduce the chasm between Washington and Munich."

Pointing out that it was America's entry into World War I that determined the final outcome, he told Hitler: "If there is another war, it must inevitably be won by the side which America joins." While Hitler conceded his point, he didn't seem to register it. His ideas about America were "wildly superficial," Hanfstaengl concluded, and his main preoccupation was the Jews, who were allegedly pulling all the strings there. In *Mein Kampf*, Hitler illustrated his point. "It is Jews who govern the stock exchange forces of the American union," he wrote, describing them as "the controlling masters of the producers" of that country. The only American Hitler admired, according to

Hanfstaengl, was Henry Ford, whom the Nazi leader described as a "great man" because of his fierce anti-Semitism.

Hitler conceded in *Mein Kampf* that England's position was unique in Europe "because of her cultural and linguistic bond with the American union," and at times he appeared to recognize the economic potential of the United States. But he consistently underestimated its military potential. In remarks to his generals on September 14, 1940, he predicted: "America's rearmament will not reach its peak before 1945." Later that year and in early 1941, he began to shorten his estimates for when the United States could significantly contribute to Britain's defense, but he was still a captive of his prejudices and wishful thinking.

Speer offered a telling summary of Hitler's views: "The Americans had not played a very prominent part in the war of 1914–1918, he thought, and moreover had not made any great sacrifices of blood. They would certainly not withstand a great trial by fire, for their fighting qualities were low. In general, no such thing as an American people existed as a unit; they were nothing but a mass of immigrants from many nations and races." According to an account of one of Hitler's conversations in April 1940, he had characterized American arms production as "the biggest swindle on earth. . . . simply a joke."

As early as April 26, 1939, Louis Lochner, the Associated Press bureau chief in Berlin, had written to his children back home: "I fear the Germans make one big mistake: they completely underestimate the potential forces arrayed against them. . . . Queer that the top leaders in Germany should repeat their mistake of 1914–1918! Remember how they used to scoff at the possibility that America could ship troops across the ocean? Now they drill into the German people that England is decrepit and won't fight; that France is torn with domestic strife; that the USA is a big bag of wind, etc., etc. A great pity!" Hitler was right about France, but woefully wrong about Britain and the United States.

Those miscalculations would have disastrous consequences in the long run—but only if Churchill's efforts to enlist US help on a large scale met with success. That meant winning the battle for the hearts and minds of the American people during the Lend-Lease debate that dominated the headlines in the first months of 1941.

Aside from providing limited aid for Britain in 1940, Roosevelt began to lay the groundwork for his country's future direct involvement in the conflict if it came to that. On September 16 he signed into law the first peacetime draft in US history, requiring all males between the ages of twenty-one and thirty-five to register for it. "We cannot remain indifferent to the philosophy of force now rampant in the world," he declared. "We must and will marshal our great potential strength to fend off war from our shores. We must and will prevent our land from becoming a victim of aggression."

At the start of 1941, with Lend-Lease hanging in the balance, Roosevelt was even more explicit about the threats that his countrymen needed to be concerned about. In his "Four Freedoms" State of the Union speech on January 6, he asserted that "at no previous time has American security been as seriously threatened from without as it is today." Once again declaring his opposition to "enforced isolation for ourselves," he denounced "the new order of tyranny that seeks to spread over every continent today." He added that "the assailants are still on the march, threatening other nations, great and small." Rejecting appeasement, he concluded: "The American people have unalterably set their faces against that tyranny."

In reality, many of his countrymen were far from that decided about their stance, but Roosevelt's speech was designed to convince them otherwise. All the nation's efforts, he argued, should be focused on "meeting this foreign peril." That meant speeding up the production of planes, ships, ammunition, and other goods essential to the war effort—not just for the US arsenal but also for "those nations which are now in actual war with aggressor nations." He did not name Britain, but everyone knew who he was talking about. Reinforcing the message that repayment would come in the future in various forms that were left deliberately vague, he spelled out his plan to the embattled democracies: "We shall send you, in ever-increasing numbers, ships, planes, tanks, guns. This is our purpose and our pledge."

Asking citizens to put "patriotism ahead of pocketbooks," Roosevelt promised to build up the country's defense program by raising taxes. The purpose, he continued, was to defend the four freedoms: of speech and worship, and from want and fear. America should defend "human rights everywhere," not just at home.

It was a grandiose vision, and it was no accident that the Lend-Lease bill was given the number HR 1776, tying it to the ideals of the American Revolution. The isolationists were quick to launch their counterattack, arguing that Roosevelt was asking for unlimited authority to do whatever he wanted with the country's resources. "Never before has the US given to one man the power to strip the nation of its defenses," charged Burton Wheeler, the Democratic Party's fiery isolationist senator from Montana. Alluding to the government's farm program, he added: "The Lend-Lease program is the New Deal's triple-A foreign policy; it will plow under every fourth American boy." Roosevelt shot back that this was "the most untruthful, the most dastardly, unpatriotic thing that has ever been said."

Republican Congressman Hamilton Fish III, another fervent critic of Roosevelt, appealed to Lindbergh to testify before the House Committee on Foreign Affairs against the pending Lend-Lease legislation. As he saw it, this was the heaviest piece of artillery that the isolationists could deploy in their battle. The aviator was more than happy to oblige.

On January 23 Lindbergh testified in a committee room that was packed with about a thousand people, including photographers, motion picture camera operators, reporters, and onlookers attracted to the scene both by his celebrity and the seriousness of the issue at hand. While his supporters applauded him often, his four and a half hours of testimony included numerous awkward exchanges, usually triggered by questions from Lend-Lease backers such as Congressman Luther A. Johnson.

The Texas Democrat pressed Lindbergh whether he was sympathetic to England's cause. "I am in sympathy with the people on both sides, but I think it would be disadvantageous for England herself, if a conclusive victory is sought," he replied. "I am in sympathy with the people and not with their aims."

Somewhat incredulous, Johnson asked Lindbergh whether he didn't believe that it was in America's best interests for England to win. "No sir, I think that a complete victory, as I say, would mean prostration in Europe; would be one of the worst things that could happen," he declared.

Lindbergh argued that it would be best to achieve "a negotiated peace," seemingly oblivious to what any negotiation with Hitler inevitably entailed. That could happen only if "neither" side won, he added, which would be his preferred outcome.

Responding to other questioners, Lindbergh insisted that American involvement in the war "would be the greatest disaster," and he refused to blame Germany for starting the war, suggesting that Britain was equally guilty. As for his silence about the brutality of the Nazis, he maintained coolly "that nothing is gained by publicly commenting." Although the worst atrocities in German-occupied lands were still underreported at that point, many Americans had already heard enough to be shocked by his display of callous indifference. According to a commentary in the *Richmond News Leader,* "Millions would vote today to hang Lindbergh or to exile him."

The isolationist camp hailed Lindbergh as a truth teller, but his version of the truth appeared to have made no new converts. In fact, it probably backfired, weakening rather than strengthening the isolationist cause. On February 9 the House approved the Lend-Lease Act by a vote of 260 to 185; on March 8 the Senate followed suit by a margin of 60 to 31.

Amid all the maneuvering to win over the Americans, Churchill and his government had plenty of other distractions. Colville, the prime minister's aide, recorded a sensational bit of news in his diary on January 1, 1941. Acting on a tip that Admiral Emile Muselier, the commander of the Free French navy, was involved in a spy ring for the collaborationist Vichy government with another Frenchman and two French women, MI5 agents carried out the arrests. "One of the ladies was found in bed with a doctor attached to the Free French forces," Colville noted with evident relish. "In the house of the other was found the second secretary of the Brazilian embassy, stark naked. It was through the Brazilian embassy that information was passed to Vichy. The admiral himself was found to be in possession of dangerous drugs."

There was only onc problem with the operation: the tip was based on forged documents. Although General de Gaulle and Muselier had an uneasy relationship that would later result in a complete break, the French leader delivered an ultimatum to the British to free him. Britain did so, and Churchill offered de Gaulle a personal apology. Farcical notes aside, such episodes provided a graphic illustration of the tensions that played out in London at the time, especially in the exile community. Raymond Aron, another member of the French contingent in the British capital, who was the editor of *La France Libre* (Free France), observed pointedly: "Exile accentuates the most disagreeable aspects of politics; there is a proliferation of intrigues, gossip, hidden antagonism, superficial agreements."

But the most pressing business remained the transatlantic relationship, and Roosevelt did not wait for formal passage of the Lend-Lease bill to seek to strengthen the bond between him and Churchill. The president dispatched Harry Hopkins, his closest adviser, to London as "my personal representative," according to his official letter of authorization. Hopkins was in frail health and dreaded air travel, but he was eager to carry out his mission, which was both to assess Churchill up close and convey a message of reassurance that Roosevelt was determined to win the political battle on the home front over aid for Britain.

Churchill had not known who Hopkins was when he was first informed of the planned visit, but once he was apprised of his close ties with Roosevelt, he spared no effort on his welcome. He dispatched Brendan Bracken, his parliamentary private secretary, to meet the British Overseas Airways Clipper that took him on the final leg of his five-day journey from Lisbon to Poole, a coastal town in southern England. When Hopkins failed to emerge from the plane after the other passengers had disembarked, Bracken found him still in his seat, "looking sick and shrunken and too tired even to unfasten the safety belt."

Bracken then took a special train to London, arriving there with Hopkins on January 9. Sir Eustace Missenden, the general manager of the Southern Railway, recalled later how carefully it had been prepared: "Mr. Churchill had given instructions that the best was to be done, and arrangements were made for the most modern Pullman cars to be formed in the train. The conductors wore white gloves; a good meal, with liquid refreshment, was available, together with papers, periodicals, etc. Mr. Harry Hopkins was obviously impressed."

In his first meetings with fellow Americans, Hopkins revealed his frame of mind. Herschel Johnson, the chargé d'affaires at the US embassy, was delighted to see that he was intent on learning about what Britain needed to survive. "Harry wanted to find out if they were asking for *enough* to see them through," he recalled.

Hopkins was especially eager to meet CBS's Murrow, whose broadcasts he had listened to, inviting him immediately to Claridge's hotel, where he was staying. He told the newsman: "I suppose you could say that I've come here to find a way to be a catalytic agent between two prima donnas," referring to his boss and Churchill. He expected these two powerful men with huge egos to clash on occasion, he explained, so he needed to get a measure of the prime minister. Before leaving Washington, Hopkins had asked numerous diplomats about Churchill and had grown weary of the effusive praise he heard. "I suppose Churchill is convinced that he's the greatest man in the world!" he remarked.

Hopkins met the prime minister for the first time the next day, lunching with him at 10 Downing Street. Writing to Roosevelt afterward, he noted that the residence was "a bit down at the heels because the Treasury next door has been bombed more than a bit." Over soup, cold beef, and a salad followed by cheese and coffee, accompanied by a light wine and port, Hopkins assessed the "rotund—smiling—red-faced gentleman" who had welcomed him to England. But before Churchill launched into an overview of the war, Hopkins brought up "a feeling in some quarters" that his British host did not like America or Roosevelt. "That set him off on a bitter tho fairly constrained attack on Ambassador Kennedy, who he believes is responsible for this impression," Hopkins reported. "He denied it vigorously."

The mood improved as Hopkins explained that the purpose of his visit was to evaluate the extent of Britain's needs to win the war. Churchill launched into an overview of the fighting and the prospects for his country. "He thinks the invasion will not come, but if they gain a foothold in England with a hundred thousand men, 'we shall drive them out,'" Hopkins related. Churchill pointed confidently to the impending defeat of Italian forces in Africa, but conceded that Greece was almost certainly lost. Hopkins marveled later at his host's drive and determination. "God, what a force that man has," he said. His earlier skepticism had completely vanished.

It was, in turn, the American visitor who impressed Churchill and his entourage the next day at Ditchley, the country house in Oxfordshire that served as the prime minister's frequent weekend haven during the war. Lord Chandos, the president of the Board of Trade who was often at Ditchley, recalled that Churchill went all out to further impress Roosevelt's envoy, employing "his sonorous elegance, his sense of history, of man's destiny and Great Britain's part in it" in a "majestic monologue" that was nothing short of "enthralling." He talked about why his country was fighting against tyranny and for "the right of man to be free," seeking "no treasure. . . . no territorial gains."

After a pause, the prime minister asked Hopkins: "What will the president say to all this?"

While everyone looked on in anticipation, the visitor took his time before replying. "Well, Mr. Prime Minister, I don't think the president will give a dam' for all that," he said. A thought flashed through Chandos's mind: "Heavens alive, it's gone wrong."

But after another pause, Hopkins added: "You see, we're only interested in seeing that that goddamn sonofabitch, Hitler, gets licked." The ensuing laughter signaled that, as Chandos related, "at that moment a friendship was cemented which no convulsion ever undermined." After the meal, Colville recalled, Churchill turned "very mellow" and "smoked the biggest cigar in history."

Shortly before he had flown off to England, Hopkins had alerted Averell Harriman that the president was planning to tap him for a major war-related job. Harriman, who had known both Franklin and Eleanor Roosevelt since his school days at Groton, an exclusive boarding school in Massachusetts that Roosevelt had attended earlier, came from an immensely wealthy railroad family. The Harrimans had always backed Republican candidates—until Averell and his sister, Mary, voted first for Alfred E. Smith in 1928 and then for Roosevelt in the ensuing elections, signaling their switch in allegiance to the Democrats. In the battle over aid for Britain, Harriman spoke up forcefully on the side of the president, dismissing the critics who claimed that he was appropriating dictatorial powers in his push for the Lend-Lease bill.

"If we are to aid Britain, let's be practical and grant the president power to make our aid effective," Harriman declared in a speech to the Yale Club on February 4. Speaking at the Traffic Club of Washington on February 13, he added: "I see no place in this debate for the cry of dictatorship at home." The entire debate came down to the question of whether the United States would aid Britain. "I have made my decision," he concluded. "I am not willing to face a world dominated by Hitler."

Five days later, Roosevelt invited Harriman to the White House and made the job offer that Hopkins had signaled was coming. "I want you to go over to London and recommend everything that we can do, short of war, to keep the British Isles afloat," the president instructed him. To the reporters who clamored for his job title, Roosevelt responded, only half jokingly, that he'd call Harriman "expediter" or "defense expediter." In practical terms, this meant overseeing all aspects of the Lend-Lease program, dealing with everyone from Churchill on down to make sure it functioned effectively.

Harriman immediately accepted the assignment. On March 15, four days after Roosevelt signed the Lend-Lease Act, he arrived in England. He was promptly whisked off to Chequers, the official country home of British prime ministers, where Churchill welcomed him "most warmly," as Harriman recalled.

By then, Churchill had been on the receiving end of numerous assurances that the United States would live up to its pledges to aid his country. And it wasn't only New Deal Democrats who were providing them. Wendell Willkie, Roosevelt's Republican opponent in the 1940 election, had visited England in January. A liberal Republican, he had strongly supported the introduction of a peacetime draft and expressed little sympathy for the large isolationist contingent within his party. Nonetheless, in the heat of the campaign, he had appeared to flirt with them by repeatedly vowing to keep US troops out of Europe. "If you elect me president, they will not be sent," he declared. "If you reelect the third-term candidate, I believe they will be sent."

Willkie's sister Charlotte, the wife of Commander Paul Pihl, the naval attaché for air at the US embassy in Berlin, went even further. She assured German officials and Luftwaffe officers attending her popular Sunday afternoon salons that, if her brother won the election, he would keep that promise.

Although Roosevelt had offered similar assurances to American voters, Willkie later came to regret his rhetoric. After the election, he once again embraced a more internationalist position, backing the president in the Lend-Lease battle.

When Willkie met Roosevelt for the first time in the White House on January 19, a day before taking off for England, the president wrote a note for him to take to Churchill. He introduced his former rival by saying: "He is truly helping to keep politics out over here," alluding to Willkie's efforts to make sure that the push for Lend-Lease did not dissolve into a purely partisan dispute with the Republicans, whose ranks included the majority of leading isolationists. The president also quoted Henry Wadsworth Longfellow's poem "The Building of the Ship":

Sail on, O Ship of State!
Sail on, O Union, strong and great!
Humanity with all its fears,
With all the hopes of future years,
Is hanging breathless on thy fate!

The message could not have been clearer: Roosevelt was intent on helping Britain prevail, no matter how fierce the opposition might be in the United States to his policies. Churchill wrote to the president the next day that he was "deeply moved" by the poem.

Willkie was also moved by what he saw on his visit. "He is astonished by our attitude," Nicolson noted in his diary. The visitor was particularly startled by the way traffic continued to flow as usual through London's Trafalgar Square when the sirens sounded to warn of a raid by twenty-five German planes, and pedestrians continued to feed the pigeons under Nelson's Column. "I must say, the indifference of the London public to daylight raids has to be seen to be believed," the Tory MP added.

For all the displays of stiff-upper-lip resolve and despite the welcome news of support coming from Roosevelt's envoys, Nicolson and many Brits were still far from convinced that the worst was over. On March 9 Murrow reported for CBS: "There was no dancing in the streets when the Lend-Lease bill was passed, for the British know from their own experience that the gap between legislation and realization can be very wide." Nonetheless, Murrow added, "There is great courage and a blind belief that Britain will survive."

Part of that courage, Murrow believed, stemmed from the fact that the British maintained the "old feeling of superiority over all other peoples." Undoubtedly, Churchill embodied that feeling better than anyone else. It was hard to imagine a more tenacious and convincing wartime leader.

Yet even his most fervent supporters continued to have their moments of doubt. "It will require all our strength to resist the appalling attack by air and submarine which is shortly coming on us," Nicolson wrote on March 2. "We shall be shattered and starved. . . . The only hope is that America and Russia will come in on our side." Otherwise, he worried that a domestic movement could arise that would seek to unseat Churchill and replace him with an appeaser. "That will be the end of England," he concluded darkly.

These were only Nicolson's private thoughts, recorded in his diary, and they alternated with more upbeat declarations of faith in victory. But they indicated just how long a journey still lay ahead—and how uncertain its outcome.

THREE

"WHOLLY MISGUIDED"

On *April 18, 1941, Stalin* showed up at a Moscow railway station to see off Japan's Foreign Minister Yosuke Matsuoko. It was highly unusual for the Soviet leader to make such a personal gesture, but not surprising given the fact that Matsuoko had signed the Japanese-Soviet Neutrality Pact a few days earlier. Japan had also signed the Tripartite Pact with Germany and Italy on September 27, 1940, pledging to "recognize and respect the leadership of Germany and Italy in the establishment of a new order in Europe" while the European partners pledged similar respect for "the leadership of Japan in the establishment of a new order in Greater East Asia." But Stalin was convinced he had secured a guarantee against a Japanese attack on his country, and he clumsily tried to flatter Matsuoko. "We both are Asiatics," Stalin told him.

What was even clumsier and more startling was how Stalin used the occasion to plead with the German diplomats who were on the railway platform also bidding farewell to Matsuoko. Spotting German ambassador Count Friedrich von der Schulenburg, he threw his arm around his shoulders and proclaimed, "We must remain friends, and you must now do everything to that end!" A little later, when he saw Colonel Hans Krebs, the military attaché, he first checked that he was indeed German and repeated his message: "We will remain friends with you in any event."

Stalin achieved his goal of impressing Schulenburg, an aristocrat who was singularly unperceptive in his observations of the Soviet Union—as well as in his assessments of Hitler's intentions. When the count assured the wife of the American ambassador at a party in early 1941 that Russia and Germany would not go to war with each other, he wanted to believe it. Later, Schulenburg began to recognize that he had been misreading the signals, but he kept trying to convince his superiors in Berlin that they should take Stalin's appeals to "remain friends" seriously—long after the decision to invade was finalized. "I honestly believe that in realizing how serious the international situation is, Stalin has made himself personally responsible for preserving the USSR from a conflict with Germany," he argued.

Schulenburg had been played for a fool by his government. As Goebbels noted in his diary, the envoy had been kept in the dark about the key deliberations leading up to the invasion. He didn't have "the faintest idea" about them, the propaganda chief wrote. "There is no doubt that one does best if one keeps the diplomats uninformed about the background of politics. They must sometimes play a role for which they don't necessarily have the theatrical abilities, and even if they did possess them, they would undoubtedly act an appeasement role more convincingly and play the finer nuances more genuinely, if they themselves were believers in appeasement."

Although Hitler and his generals had been discussing the invasion plans for months, they had also kept them a secret from their Japanese partners. Shortly before Matsuoko received a lavish welcome in Berlin on an earlier leg of his European journey in March, the German high command issued a directive stating: "No hint of Operation Barbarossa must be given to the Japanese." But Japanese officials knew, at least in general terms, what Hitler had in mind. At a breakfast for Matsuoko in Hitler's chancellery, Bock sat next to General Hiroshi Oshima, Japan's ambassador in Berlin. The envoy, who struck CBS correspondent William Shirer "as more Nazi than the Nazis," assured the field marshal that he was in agreement with Germany's plan to destroy Stalin's Communist state.

While Hitler was intent on not sharing details of his plans with Matsuoko, he volunteered a commitment that would prove significant after Pearl Harbor. He would not permit the United States to fight its enemies one at a time, he told his Japanese guest. "Therefore, Germany would intervene immediately in case of a conflict Japan-America, for the strength of the three pact powers was their common action. Their weakness would be in letting themselves be defeated singly."

Aside from Schulenburg, the other person who proved to be deluding himself about Hitler's immediate intentions was Stalin. In this respect, he demonstrated how similar he was to the German leader in his stubborn refusal to believe anything that contradicted his wishes and worldview. Hitler had convinced himself that all the arguments against launching an invasion only reinforced the need for quick action; similarly, Stalin had convinced himself that the proliferation of new warnings about a looming German invasion could only be a trick aimed at luring his country into a new conflict—particularly when those warnings were emanating from the West.

On March 20 US Undersecretary of State Sumner Welles told Konstantin Umansky, the Soviet ambassador in Washington, that "it is the intention of Germany to attack the Soviet Union." Laurence Steinhardt, the US ambassador in Moscow, repeated that warning on April 15 in discussions with a top Soviet official. Churchill sent a similar warning to Stalin a few days later. But again the Soviet leader was not listening. As Hans von Herwarth, the German diplomat who had served in Moscow, pointed out, "There was near unanimity among the Western embassies in Moscow that Stalin had a higher regard for the Germans than for the other Western powers, and that he certainly trusted them more."

Stalin's distrust extended to his own spies as well. The Soviet military intelligence operatives in Berlin, who had sent warnings in the second half of 1940 from their source code-named Ariets, dispatched a new report quoting him as saying on February 28, 1941, "that war with Russia has definitely been decided on for this year." Other Soviet military missions delivered similar bad news. On March 13, 1941, Bucharest, Romania, quoted a German major as saying, "We have completely changed our plan. We will move to the east, against the USSR. We will obtain grain, coal, and oil from the USSR, and that will enable us to continue the war against England and America." According to one Bucharest source, "The German military are drunk with their successes and claim that the war with the USSR will begin in May."

On March 26 Bucharest added that "the Romanian general staff has precise information that in two or three months Germany will attack the Ukraine." The report predicted that the attack also would be aimed at the Baltic states, "hoping for an uprising there against the USSR," and that Romania would participate in the war and be rewarded with Bessarabia, the border territory that Stalin had seized from it. The mission went on to report Germany's growing confidence that it would defeat the Soviet Union in a matter of weeks.

Stalin's reaction was not only to dismiss those reports but also to rid himself of Ivan Proskurov, the head of Soviet military intelligence, who had consistently refused to buckle under the pressure to deliver better news. He replaced him with Filipp Golikov, who began relaying the reports from those of his officers who were picking up German disinformation. In March, for instance, the Soviet military attaché in Budapest, Hungary, who had no credible sources, dismissed all talk of a German invasion as English propaganda. He reported that "at the present time, a German offensive against the USSR is unthinkable before the defeat of England."

This is exactly what Stalin wanted to hear, and Golikov endorsed such conclusions enthusiastically to please his boss. All the reports of an imminent German attack "must be assessed as disinformation emanating from English, and even perhaps from German intelligence," he insisted, adding the odd twist that Berlin might be participating in some convoluted conspiracy. Golikov continued to send on reports like the one from his Prague station on April 17 predicting, "Hitler will attack the USSR in the second half of June"—although distancing himself from it. Within three days, it landed back on Golikov's desk with Stalin's note in red ink: "English provocation! Investigate!"

Those kinds of "provocations" continued to arrive from Moscow's spies. Reporting on the transfer of an increasing number of German troops from Western Europe to the border with the Soviet Union, Major General Vasily Tupikov, the Soviet military attaché in Berlin, concluded at the end of April: "The USSR figures as the next enemy." On May 9 he added details of the German war plan. According to his summary, "Defeat of the Red Army will be complete in one or one and a half months with arrival of the German army on the meridian of Moscow."

Richard Sorge, the Soviet master spy in Tokyo, delivered report after report to his superiors in military intelligence that were right on target—and especially infuriated Stalin. Born in Baku, Azerbaijan, of a Russian mother and a German father who was an oil engineer, Sorge was raised in Germany, fought in World War I, and joined the Communist Party. After working in Moscow for the Communist International (Comintern), which maintained contacts with Communist movements around the world, he ostensibly broke off his Communist ties and moved to Tokyo as the German correspondent of the *Frankfurter Zeitung.*

Portraying himself as a dedicated Nazi, Sorge ingratiated himself with German ambassador Eugen Ott and his staff and with senior Japanese officials, while also drinking heavily and carrying on affairs with several of their wives and lovers. His exploits fascinated even the postwar occupiers of Japan, whom he didn't live to see. According to a US military intelligence report, Sorge was "intimate with some 30 women in Tokyo during his years of service, including the wife of his good friend, the German ambassador, the wife of his foreign assistant, and the mistress of this same assistant."

Making full use of his access to inside information, Sorge provided some of the first reporting in late 1940 that a German attack was likely. On December 18 he warned that "the Germans could occupy territory on a line Kharkov, Moscow, Leningrad." Subsequent reports provided more evidence for his claims; Golikov responded by cutting back his expenses, which Sorge characterized correctly "as a kind of punishment." But the spy refused to be silenced. On May 15, he reported that the German invasion would begin on June 21 or 22; on June 13 he declared: "I repeat: Nine armies with the strength of 150 divisions will begin an offensive at dawn on June 22." Stalin's response was to dismiss him as "a little shit who has set himself up with some small factories and brothels in Japan."

Stalin reacted in the same way to the NKVD's foreign intelligence operatives when they produced reports that paralleled those of their military counterparts. Harro Schulze-Boysen, who worked in the Germany Air Ministry and was code-named Starshina, was an invaluable asset who kept warning of the impending invasion, reporting on June 17 that "the blow can be expected at any time." When Stalin saw his report, he declared that Starshina should be sent back to "his fucking mother."

Stepan Mikoyan, the son of Politburo member Anastas and a fighter pilot during the war, pointed out that such behavior was a product of Stalin's "extreme distrust" of everyone, including his agents. "In his opinion, everyone was capable of deceit or treason." In his memoirs, the younger Mikoyan added that Stalin ordered a recall of his resident agents so that, in Stalin's words, he could "grind them into dust in the camps."

After the defeat of France, Speer overheard Hitler speaking with two of his top generals, Jodl and Keitel. "Now we have shown what we are capable of," he told them. "Believe me, Keitel, a campaign against Russia would be like a child's game by comparison." On another occasion, Hitler told Jodl, "We have only to kick in the door, and the whole rotten structure will come crashing down." Again and again, he insisted that Operation Barbarossa, the invasion of the Soviet Union, would produce another quick victory—and most of his subordinates echoed those sentiments dutifully, varying the clichéd metaphors only slightly. "Russia will collapse like a house of cards," Goebbels wrote in his diary.

Any remaining doubters understood the risks involved in trying to contradict those wildly optimistic predictions. General Thomas, the Wehrmacht's economic expert who had tried to warn against expanding the war to Western Europe, was capable of pointing out how risky it was to envisage only the best-case scenarios for an attack on the Soviet Union. In January 1941 his staff was preparing reports that warned about the dangers of disrupting the peaceful flow of supplies from Russia, and the prospects for shortages of fuel and rubber. In short, they were predicting that the invasion was likely to have far more negative than positive economic consequences.

But as Hitler kept promising an economic windfall from the invasion, Thomas changed his tune abruptly. In his report to the Führer on February 20, he declared that German forces would quickly gain control of 70 percent of Soviet industrial potential along with four million tons of grain from the Ukraine—in effect, fulfilling Hitler's prophecies. In light of Germany's swift victories in Western Europe, Thomas may have been worried about appearing unduly negative again. More likely, though, he could not resist the pressure from the top to produce the kind of optimistic estimates that Hitler was expecting to see.

Not everyone surrendered completely to such pressure. There was no disguising the fact that there was a huge demographic imbalance between the two totalitarian states, which meant that Stalin had a far larger pool of manpower to draw on. The Soviet Union's population stood at about 170 million on the eve of the war, while Germany's numbered about 84 million. The German invaders would have to achieve a swift victory or else face new call-ups of Soviet troops that they could not match. To do so, Hitler was counting on the fact that he could field a better-equipped, better-trained, and better-organized army.

But while German per capita income was estimated to be two and a half times higher than Russia's in 1940, and it had poured vast resources into its rapid military buildup, the modernization of the Wehrmacht was far from complete—in particular, when it came to mechanization. In 1941 only 33 of its 130 divisions were motorized for blitzkrieg purposes, with the others continuing to rely heavily on horses to transport artillery and supplies while most of their soldiers marched on foot.

In his April 28 memorandum, where he voiced his doubts that the defeat of Russia would prompt Britain to surrender, Ernst von Weizsäcker, the Foreign Ministry's secretary of state, also warned that a quick victory might prove to be impossible. Even if the Germans overran the western Soviet Union and reached Moscow, he noted, at least some of the Red Army was likely to survive farther east, leading to a prolonged conflict. "The well-known passive resistance of the Slavs" would come into play, he wrote. "We would be victors over Russia only in a military sense and would, on the other hand, lose in an economic sense."

But Hitler and many of his generals remained convinced that a swift victory over Russia was all but inevitable, allowing them to dismiss anyone who still had the temerity to voice contrary views. General Günther Blumentritt told his colleagues in April that "fourteen days of fighting" might prove enough to achieve victory, especially since, as he added later, they would be fighting against "ill-educated, half-Asiatic" troops. Other military estimates ranged from six to ten weeks.

By comparison, Hitler almost looked cautious when he predicted a campaign that would last no more than four months, possibly three.

The German leader was well aware that Napoléon had waited till late June 1812 to lead his Grande Armée into Russia, which proved to be a fatal mistake. The French emperor's battered forces eventually retreated during the fierce Russian winter, suffering catastrophic losses. To avoid a similar fate, Hitler initially planned on sending in his troops on May 15, 1941. Even if the Soviet forces held out for the full four months, he figured that this earlier date would afford him more than enough time to achieve victory before the first snows.

With Hitler's confidence soaring about the ultimate outcome of the invasion, he also felt free to address other problems in the broader war. And thanks to Mussolini, his putative ally, he felt compelled to do so just when his focus should have remained on the final preparations for Operation Barbarossa. Jealous of Hitler's string of early victories that had left him looking like a marginal figure, Il Duce had decided in the fall of 1940 to spring his own surprise and prove that he, too, could conquer swiftly. When Hitler came to see him in Florence on October 28, Mussolini announced proudly, "Führer, we are on the march! Victorious Italian troops crossed the Greco-Albanian frontier at dawn today!"

As Hitler put it to his generals, Mussolini's action proved to be a "regrettable blunder," and Italian troops were in retreat a few days later. In the midst of his preparations for Operation Barbarossa, Hitler drew up plans for Operation Marita, a German offensive in Albania and Greece to salvage the situation. According to his directive of December 13, 1940, German troops would seize control of much of that area in another blitzkrieg action. That way, most of them would become available quickly "for new deployment"—meaning for the Russian campaign.

Those plans were soon upended by another setback. In March 1941 the Yugoslav government that had just signed on to the Tripartite Pact, ostensibly ensuring that it would be a reliable German ally in the struggle for control of the Balkans, was overthrown in a coup. The new government, led by Air Force General Dusan Simovic, withdrew immediately from the pact, jeopardizing Germany's plans to attack Greece from the north. An enraged Hitler pledged "to smash Yugoslavia militarily and as a state," making sure that Belgrade was destroyed in the process. In early April German forces attacked both Yugoslavia and Greece, with the Luftwaffe delivering on Hitler's promise to devastate Yugoslavia's capital.

In military terms, the German offensive succeeded in both countries, despite the efforts by British troops and the Royal Navy to shore up the Greek resistance. But those victories came at a price. While ordering Operation Marita, Hitler had told his generals, "The beginning of the Barbarossa operation will have to be postponed by four weeks." As his adjutant Major Engel noted in his diary on March 24: "Our imminent intervention [in the Balkans] has made him throw his entire conception out of the window: the great objectives have all to be put back, and it is now impossible to launch the attack on the Soviet Union in the second half of May." As if trying to reassure himself, he added: "By themselves, a couple of weeks earlier or later are not necessarily so bad, but we do not want to be surprised by the Russian winter." The earliest alternative date would be at the end of June, he concluded. "For this entire crap, we have unfortunately to thank the Italians."

In *The Rise and Fall of the Third Reich*, Shirer acknowledged Mussolini's role but laid the blame for the delay of Operation Barbarossa where it belonged: on Hitler. "This postponement of the attack on Russia in order that the Nazi warlord might vent his personal spite against a small Balkan country which had dared to defy him was probably the most catastrophic single decision in Hitler's career," he wrote.

In fact, Hitler's far bigger and more fundamental mistake was to underestimate the risks of attacking the Soviet Union at all. He would also make subsequent tactical misjudgments that competed with his handling of the Balkan campaign for "the most catastrophic single decision" title. But there was no doubt that the delay in launching Operation Barbarossa increased the chances for failure.

When Foreign Minister Ribbentrop arrived in Rome in May, he told Mussolini: "Russia will be dispatched in the space of three months." Count Ciano, his Italian counterpart, was not convinced. Calling the planned invasion "a dangerous game. . . . without a definite purpose," he wrote in his diary: "The story of Napoléon repeats itself."

Even some of Hitler's top generals had entertained similar doubts. Back in January 1941, Bock had worried that, without the swift destruction of the Red Army and the capture of Moscow, the result would be "a long, drawn-out war, beyond the capacity of the German armed forces to wage." On April 4 Halder wrote in his diary: "Foreign Armies East now admits that strength of Russian army in European Russia must be higher than estimated originally."

There were other troubling signals as well. As part of his ongoing effort to demonstrate to Stalin that he was observing the terms of their nonaggression pact, Hitler permitted a Soviet military delegation to visit German tank factories and training areas that spring. He ordered that the visitors should be shown everything, so as not to arouse suspicion. When the Germans showed them the Panzer IV, the Russians protested that this could not be their newest and heaviest tank, as their hosts claimed. In fact, it was the best tank the Germans had at the time. As General Heinz Guderian, the army's most famous tank commander, recalled after the war, this led him and some of his colleagues to conclude that the Russians must have had something better in their own production line. Soon enough Guderian would be able to confirm that for himself.

Shortly before the invasion, Hitler also sent military staffers to give briefings on the Soviet economy. They claimed that the country wouldn't be capable of producing good armaments quickly to replace its anticipated early heavy losses. After one such lecture, Admiral Wilhelm Canaris, the head of military intelligence, turned to his colleagues. "Gentlemen, do you really believe all the nonsense you heard today?" he asked. "To the best knowledge of the experts in my department, the entire situation is quite different. So far, no one has succeeded in defeating and conquering Russia!"

But, keeping in mind Hitler's unrelenting push for an invasion whose outcome he viewed as certain, most of his top generals tried to suppress their occasional doubts. As Guderian put it, the speed of Hitler's earlier victories "had so befuddled the minds of our supreme commanders that they had eliminated the word *impossible* from their vocabulary." They were too intimidated by Hitler, and too acutely aware that he had proven the doubters wrong before, to speak up. Before he was hanged at Nuremberg in 1946, Keitel attributed his willingness to accept Hitler's optimistic predictions to both ignorance and blind faith. "I believed in Hitler and knew little of the facts myself," he said. "I'm not a tactician, nor did I know Russian military and economic strength. How could I?"

At the same time, the military brass grasped at anything it felt justified the Führer's optimism. On May 5, for example, Halder wrote: "Russian higher officers' corps decidedly bad (depressing impression). Compared with 1933, picture is strikingly negative. It will take Russia twenty years to reach her old level." Aside from making such misleading predictions, the general also seized on highly inaccurate information about Soviet infrastructure, however dubious the sources. Back on March 11, he had reported: "Intelligence on new roads in Russia, which would indicate existence of better road net than heretofore assumed." Nothing could be further from the truth, as the invasion force would learn soon.

In an address to top military leaders who were summoned to the Reich Chancellery on March 30, Hitler left no doubt that he expected them to employ far more ruthless tactics in the coming war against Russia than they did during the conquest of Western Europe. "The war will be such that it cannot be conducted in a knightly fashion," he declared. "It must be waged with unprecedented, merciless, and unrelenting harshness. All officers must rid themselves of old-fashioned and obsolete theories." This kind of a war was "beyond the comprehension of you generals," he continued, and he expected nothing less than "unquestioning and unconditional obedience" in carrying out all his orders.

Bock, the traditional Prussian militarist, turned to Generals Brauchitsch and Halder during this presentation. "What does the Führer mean?" he asked. "Will we have to shoot civilians and noncombants?" He received only evasive replies, he noted. But Bock should certainly have known the answers to his questions by then; his apparent reluctance to face the truth was a form of evasiveness in and of itself.

It wasn't just a matter of dispelling any remaining illusions that German generals were still expected to observe rules of war about not shooting civilians. Hitler was preparing for a war against Europe's largest Slavic nation based on his theory of racial conquest that he expounded upon in *Mein Kampf* and never reconsidered. As he stressed repeatedly, the Slavs were *Untermenschen*, a species of subhumans who ranked only slightly above the "vermin" Jews—and this accounted for the need to treat them far more brutally than other conquered peoples. "This war will be very different than the war in the west," he told the generals. "In the east, harshness today means lenience in the future."

The other decisive factor, as Hitler put it, was the war against Communism. As conveyed in summary form by Halder, the German leader delivered a blunt message:

> *Clash of two ideologies.* Crushing denunciation of Bolshevism, identified with a social criminality. Communism is an enormous danger for our future. We must forget the concept of comradeship between soldiers. A Communist is no comrade before or after the battle. This is a war of extermination. If we do not grasp

> this, we shall still beat the enemy, but thirty years later, we shall again have to fight the Communist foe. We do not wage war to preserve the enemy. . . . Extermination of the Bolshevik commissars and of the Communist intelligentsia.

Along with Hitler's decision to invade the Soviet Union in the first place, the implementation of this combination of racial and ideological reasoning would prove to be one of his most fundamental mistakes of 1941. It would rule out any serious attempt to convince the Soviet people, who had already experienced more than a decade of Stalin's policies of mass murder and terror, that they should view the German invaders as liberators rather than as new oppressors.

The Nazi planners who were preparing for the occupation of Soviet territory were not at all reticent about spelling out the impact their policies would have on their new subjects. To ensure the fulfillment of Hitler's dream that the Ukraine would provide a seemingly endless supply of grain to feed his people and armies, they prepared their Hunger Plan for the Soviet Union, which envisaged the starvation of the "surplus" local population. According to the estimates, this could mean deliberately starving between 20 million and 30 million people. As Erich Koch, who would become Hitler's governor of the Ukraine, put it, the object of the occupation was not "to bring blessings on the Ukraine but to secure for Germany the necessary living space and a source of food."

Summarizing Hitler's remarks at a dinner with him and other generals shortly before the invasion, Bock wrote in his diary: "If following the victory over Russia we are able to at least feed the elements of the armed forces that will remain there—all told about 65 to 75 divisions—off the land, Germany's food and raw material needs will be guaranteed indefinitely."

General Thomas, the Wehrmacht's chief economic expert, who had by then thrown himself fully into planning the most brutal aspects of the occupation policies, met with representatives from other government agencies on May 2. As Thomas's office summarized, the meeting offered these stark conclusions:

1. The war can only be continued if the entire Wehrmacht is fed from Russia in the third year of the war.
2. If we take what we need out of the country, there can be no doubt that many millions of people will die of starvation.
3. The most important issues are the recovery and removal of oil seeds, oil cake, and the only then the removal of grain.

Aside from their sheer callousness, these policies vastly overestimated the Ukraine's agricultural potential after a decade of Stalinist forced collectivization and mass starvation. On the eve of the war, the region produced only a small amount of grain for export outside of the Soviet Union. The German planners were convinced they could deal with this problem by starving the Soviet population further, allowing millions more to die or, in some cases, to emigrate to Siberia. Major cities, not just in the Ukraine but also in other parts of the Soviet Union, would be deliberately cut off from their traditional sources of food, which would be diverted to German needs.

As far away as Tokyo, Sorge, the Soviet master spy, picked up on Germany's occupation goals. The first, as a German military courier who visited the Japanese capital told him, was "to occupy the European grain area of the Ukraine," while the second was "to obtain at least a million or two million captives to supplement the German scarcity of labor and use them for agriculture and industry."

The notion of Slavic slave labor serving the German master race was also one of Hitler's fundamental tenets. As he put it in *Mein Kampf* and his speeches, the conquest of Slavic lands would provide a vast pool of workers to work in Germany, making up for manpower shortages in agriculture and industry caused by the growing number of young men joining the military and other security forces. In mid-1939, right before the invasion of Poland, the German workforce totaled 39.4 million, according to official statistics. Even with the addition of 350,000 prisoners of war and 800,000 other foreigners working in the country, the total dropped to just over 36 million a year later. The trend was clear from early on, and the pressure on the Nazi overlords of occupied territories to make up for the chronic shortfalls in the labor force would only intensify as the war progressed.

Underlying all those draconian policies was an unshakable belief in terror as the most effective tool in crushing all resistance. Even before Hitler spelled out his detailed orders, many of his generals were preparing their troops for the kind of warfare that his rhetoric had already signaled. On May 2 General Erich Hoepner, the commander of the Fourth Panzer Group, instructed his troops that they were about to participate in "the old struggle against Slavdom, the defense of European culture against Moscovite-Asiatic inundation, the repulse of Jewish-Bolshevism." This struggle, he added, had to be fought with "unprecedented" measures. "Every military action must in conception and execution be led by the iron will mercilessly and totally to annihilate the enemy," he declared. "In particular, there is to be no sparing the upholders of the current Russian-Bolshevik regime."

Shortly afterward, Hitler's Barbarossa Decree and other directives explained that the German invaders had carte blanche to shoot anyone suspected of guerrilla activity, whatever their military or civilian status, and to organize collective reprisals against entire villages. In theory, "the breaking of a civil law, such as murder, rape, or robbery," was still not permitted; but when such acts were deemed to be part of the campaign of conquest, no soldier was be considered guilty of any crimes.

The most explicit instructions came in the form of the infamous Commissar Order that was first drawn up more than a month before the invasion. It mandated the execution of all political officers in the Red Army units, even if they attempted to surrender. According to the version of the order dated June 6, those ideological enforcers "are the real leaders of resistance. . . . [who] have initiated barbaric, Asiatic methods of warfare." There could be only one way to handle such enemies, it added: "As a matter of principle, they will be shot at once, whether captured *during operations or otherwise showing resistance.*"

In an earlier note, General Jodl did not bother to disguise the cynical nature of subsequent protestations that such policies were prompted by Soviet behavior. "We must reckon with retaliation against German fliers; therefore it will be best to picture the whole action as retaliation," he wrote.

By then, most German officers were not about to question Hitler directly about anything, but some did find ways to express their unease about the specific targeting of the political commissars. When Major Engel, Hitler's adjutant, visited Poland in May, he noted in his diary that two generals, Hans von Salmuth and Henning von Tresckow, "consider it to be a very bad thing and fear it will be counterproductive amongst the troops." Tresckow told him: "If international law is to be broken, rather the Russians do it than ourselves!"

According to Engel's diary entry on May 23, Field Marshal von Kluge "pleaded with me to get F. [the Führer] to change the dangerous Commissar Order." He also asked that the Einsatzgruppen, the security services' special killing squads, be placed under tighter military control. "There had been some very bad goings-on in Poland, and he had to intervene personally on several occasions," Engel noted. "Considered political tactics in Poland as very unfortunate."

If such tactics were already producing "unfortunate" results for the occupiers in Poland, they would soon trigger disastrous results in the Soviet Union. The problem was that Hitler was willfully blind to the lessons of Poland—and their far more serious implications for his newest military offensive. If anything, he treated Poland as the successful test run for the doctrines and methods that he would employ on a much larger scale farther east.

In its February 15, 1941, issue, the *Polish Fortnightly Review*, published by Poland's government-in-exile in London, ran a chilling piece under the headline "The German Mass Murders of the Polish People." It reported: "The German extermination of the Polish people has not stopped; on the contrary, recent information indicates that they have acquired still greater and more frightful dimensions." Because of the rapid organization of an extensive underground resistance movement within Poland, Polish officials in London were able to keep abreast of developments in their occupied homeland. While some of the generalizations of their reports were questionable, they offered largely accurate information on the specific acts of violence on a daily basis.

What was happening was more than a tragedy for the Poles: it was a harbinger of the way Nazi rhetoric about its Slavic neighbors along with their large Jewish minorities would translate into terror and mass murder not just in Poland but also in the Soviet Union. On the eve of the attack on Poland, Hitler had explained to his subordinates that the goal was the "annihilation of Poland," just as he would later announce the same goal for Russia. "We must all steel ourselves against humanitarian reasoning!" he told them. Heinrich Himmler, the head of the SS and the Gestapo, echoed those sentiments: "It is essential that the great German people should consider it as its major task to destroy all Poles." During the conquest of Poland in September 1939, Reinhard Heydrich, Himmler's chief lieutenant, conveyed terse but unambiguous instructions: "Housecleaning: Jews, intelligentsia, clergy, nobility."

A year later, Himmler told a gathering of SS officers that "we had to harden our hearts at the shooting of leading Poles. We had to be so ruthless, or otherwise we would have had to pay for it later." Almost as an aside, he added: "This is something that you ought to hear, but it is also something you should forget right away." The SS officers were meant to learn the lesson well for future conflicts—the looming attack on Russia was certainly on Himmler's mind—but he also wanted them to be ready to deny the crimes as needed.

Such messages from the top led to a terrifying level of violence from the earliest days of the occupation. Whenever a German was wounded or killed, the *Polish Fortnightly Review* reported, "in revenge, the Germans murder a hundred or more quite innocent Polish inhabitants of the given locality." One of the orders issued by Field Marshal von Bock to his invading troops left no ambiguity on that score: "If there is shooting from a village behind the front and if it proves impossible to identify the house from which the shots came, then the whole village is to be burned to the ground." This also signaled the tactics that would be employed in the Soviet Union.

The Polish publication provided graphic examples of such actions: "In the peasants' fields of the village of Szczuczka, in Lublin province, ammunition was found buried. The Germans at once drove two hundred peasants into a barn, locking them in, after which they raked it with [gun]fire and finally set light to it. . . . At Zeran, near Warsaw, and at neighboring localities such as Targowek, some three hundred persons were arrested and bestially tortured on the spot, after which eighty-six of the men and six women were shot."

Even within this litany of murder, there was a special fury reserved for Jews. "At Ostrow Mazowiecki, in Warsaw province, a Jewish shop was burnt down, after the entire stock of goods had been confiscated. Some six hundred male Jews were driven outside the town and shot down with machine guns. The wounded were finished off, and some were buried while still alive."

The other victims who were singled out immediately: patients in mental hospitals. One of many such incidents: "At Chełm Lubelski, a Gestapo detachment surrounded the local asylum and ordered the doctors and personnel to leave the place. Then they killed all the patients, 428 persons in all, with revolver shots, and in addition 40 healthy children who were looked after as war refugees in one of the wings of the building were also executed."

The February 1941 report concluded with a tally of those executed up to that point: "The total number of people murdered by the Gestapo throughout the German-occupied area exceeds 70,000." In fact, regular troops as well as militias composed of ethnic Germans who had lived in Poland were responsible for many of the executions as well.

The extent of the executions far exceeded the killings in other German-occupied territories. On February 6, 1940, Hans Frank, the governor general of the General Government, as the part of Poland that had not been directly annexed by Germany was called, explained to a correspondent for the Nazi newspaper *Völkischer Beobachter* why his administration employed different tactics than elsewhere. In Prague, he observed, the Germans maintained the practice of putting up posters for every seven Czechs who were shot. If he tried to do the same thing in Poland, he said, he would run out of trees to pulp for the posters needed to list each group of seven Poles who were shot. As he put it on another occasion, "We nevertheless bear the enormous responsibility of ensuring that this area remains firmly in German hands; that the backbone of the Poles is broken for all time."

To achieve that goal, German forces in Poland initially included five Einsatzgruppen, the special execution squads with a total of about three thousand men, who targeted a long list of "enemies of the state"—anyone suspected of resistance activity, along with members of the Polish elites and Jews. Drawn from the SS, the police, and other security services, these killers would become known for their singular ruthlessness even in an invading force that routinely resorted to extreme violence; they were often responsible for the burning of villages, mass shootings, and other acts of terror. These were the units that Field Marshal von Kluge warned Major Engel about.

General Johannes Blaskowitz, the military commander in chief in occupied Poland, was disturbed enough by the reports of mass executions streaming in that he refused to keep silent. He shared his misgivings—and some of the graphic details—with Colonel Helmuth Stief, a visiting member of the general staff. Stief subsequently wrote to his wife: "This extermination of entire families with women and children is only possible through subhumans who do not deserve to be German. I am ashamed to be a German."

Blaskowitz followed up with an exceptionally blunt report on November 27, 1939. He called the Einsatzgruppen "execution commandos" and chastised the police for doing almost nothing to maintain order while they "only spread terror among the population." The mass murders of Poles and Jews, he wrote, were "wholly misguided. . . . for this will neither destroy the idea of a Polish state in the eyes of the mass of the population, nor do away with the Jews." He also warned of "the tremendous brutalization and moral depravity which is spreading rapidly among precious German manpower like an epidemic."

Hitler's reaction was predictable. "One cannot wage war with Salvation Army methods," he declared, scorning his general's "childish attitude." In February 1940 Blaskowitz offered the additional practical argument that such continued terror would only lead to the further growth of the Polish resistance, tying down an occupation force of five hundred thousand men in Poland for the indefinite future. As a result of such accurate predictions, Hitler soon sidelined Blaskowitz, although he was returned to more senior command posts in the final period of the war.

Mass arrests were the other tool of terror and repression. According to the dark humor of the times, there were three categories of Poles: "those who have been in prison, those who are in prison, and those who will be in prison." In fact, that saying may have originated in the Soviet Union, where it was all too accurate a description during Stalin's reign of terror. In the parts of Poland annexed by Moscow in 1939, mass arrests, deportations of Poles to the east, and executions were also commonplace.

But there was a significant difference between the two occupation zones: Polish Jews realized quickly that their chances for survival were better if they crossed into Soviet-occupied territory, and about three hundred thousand did so. Many of them were arrested and dispatched to the Gulag along with Polish Catholics, but they were not targeted because they were Jews; as far as the Soviet authorities were concerned, they were simply part of the larger group of highly suspect Poles. In that sense, the Soviet zone was the lesser of two evils for them.

No area of Polish life was sacrosanct under either occupier. On November 6, 1939, the Germans summoned professors and other personnel of the Jagiellonian University in Krakow, one of Europe's oldest centers of learning, ostensibly for a lecture titled "The Attitude of the National Socialist Movement Toward Science and Learning." The city's Gestapo chief announced to the assembled Poles that the university had manifested anti-German attitudes; at the same time, SS troops surrounded the building and began beating and arresting the professors. Of the 183 Poles who had shown up, 168 were sent to the Sachsenhausen concentration camp, where several of them died.

The targeting of top educators, along with other cultural and political leaders, was no accident. While planning their conquest of eastern lands, starting with Poland, the Nazis envisaged a system that would keep the Slavs deliberately uneducated, with the majority of their schools shuttered. In May 1940 Himmler declared that the subjugated Slavs should receive no education beyond the fourth grade of elementary school. "The sole goal of this schooling," he explained, "is to teach them simple arithmetic, nothing above the number five hundred, writing one's own name, and the doctrine that it is divine law to obey the Germans. . . . I do not think that reading is desirable."

Such policies reflected Hitler's instructions to his military leaders on October 18, 1939: "Polish intelligentsia must be prevented from establishing itself as a new governing class. Low standard of living must be preserved. Cheap slaves." The term "low standard of living" was a euphemism; the reality was a policy that was a prescription for widespread hunger and starvation, mitigated only by the ingenuity of Polish farmers and a black market that blossomed quickly. This wasn't yet the full-blown Hunger Plan that was drawn up later for the Soviet Union, but it was certainly a preview.

The deliberate impoverishment and terrorizing of the Poles was supposed to make it easy to round up slave labor for Germany. Ironically, a year before the war, the Poles and Germans had worked out an agreement that allowed sixty thousand Polish workers to help with the German harvest; both sides benefitted, since the prewar unemployment rate in Poland was very high. But when the occupation started, and Frank's superiors demanded that he dispatch up to a million Polish workers to Germany, his attempts to seek volunteers produced meager results. Word of the harsh treatment of the twenty thousand Poles who did volunteer soon spread.

In March 1940 Himmler issued a decree ordering Polish laborers in Germany to wear a violet letter *P* on their clothing, and they were banned from using public transport, going to church or movies, or having sexual relations with Germans. This meant that any pretense of choice was quickly abandoned. Forced labor—"cheap slaves," as Hitler had put it—was now the order of the day. In towns and villages, Poles did everything possible to elude capture.

In theory, the occupiers could have experimented with a more rational policy of economic exploitation, offering modest incentives to encourage greater cooperation and productivity within the broader context of their coercive policies. But Hitler was not about to entertain any such notions, either in Poland or later in the Soviet Union. Instead, he concluded that more terror, not less, would ensure both military and economic success everywhere on the Eastern Front.

It wasn't just Stalin's spies and Western governments who were warning the Soviet leader of the imminent invasion threat. As far back as August 14, 1940, Hitler dropped a clear hint of his thinking about timing when he requested a schedule of Soviet deliveries for the period "until the spring of 1941." And in the run-up to the invasion, the Germans steadily recalled diplomats and families from the embassy in Moscow. On the eve of the attack, the German presence had been reduced to just over a hundred people. Valentin Berezhkov, the Kremlin interpreter who also served in the Soviet embassy in Berlin during this period, pointed out that the equivalent number for the Soviet side was about a thousand people. "Stalin, concerned about making Hitler suspicious, had forbade us from reducing the number of our employees in Germany," he wrote.

Yet, just as no one could convince Hitler that it was folly to attack the Soviet Union, no one could convince Stalin that it was folly to believe that Hitler was not about to launch the war against his eastern neighbor that he had first promised in *Mein Kampf*. Some German military preparations had been obvious for more than a year. German planes flew frequently into Soviet air space, clearly on reconnaissance missions. Initially, Red Army border troops opened fire on some of the planes, and Soviet planes scrambled to intercept them. On one occasion, five German planes landed in Soviet territory, ostensibly because they had lost their way before running out of fuel.

Stalin's response was to restrict the actions of his own troops. NKVD Directive 102 on March 29, 1940, read: "In case of violations of the German-Soviet border by German aircraft or balloons, do not open fire. Limit yourselves to preparing a report on the violation of the state frontier." On April 5 NKVD chief Lavrenty Beria issued another order to his border troops: in case of any confrontations, they should "strictly see to it that bullets do not fall on German territory."

The Germans offered the lame explanation that the frequent overflights were a result of the fact that several flight schools were located near the border. At the same time, the number of incidents kept growing: between April 19 and June 19, 1941, there were 180 of them. Stalin continued to look for excuses to write them off as insignificant. "I'm not sure Hitler knows about those flights," he declared.

In an unmistakably groveling tone, an official Soviet note informed the German government that border troops had been instructed not to fire on its planes "so long as such flights did not occur frequently."

All of which sparked speculation whether Stalin was committed to a policy of complete appeasement. The Turkish ambassador in Moscow sent a dispatch to his home office, which was intercepted by the Germans on May 15, portraying Stalin as willing to do almost anything to convince Hitler he genuinely wanted peace. "Stalin is about to become a blind tool of Germany," he wrote.

Some historians have argued that, on the contrary, Stalin was contemplating a preemptive attack on Germany—but there is little supporting evidence for this theory. A far more compelling case can be made that he deluded himself to the very end that he could stall the Germans. After all, as Stalin's biographer Isaac Deutscher pointed out, Tsar Alexander I made peace with Napoléon, which provided him with four years to prepare for war. Stalin was probably hoping for at least a year's reprieve to better prepare his underequipped forces. In March 1941 he received the news that only 30 percent of his tank and armored units could be adequately supplied with the parts they needed to operate. A month before the German attack, his generals reported: "Fulfillment of the plan for the supply of military technology the Red Army needs so acutely is extremely unsatisfactory."

Speaking to the graduates of the military academy on May 5, Stalin seemed to acknowledge the looming threat more than he had before, while at the same time attempting to project confidence about the ultimate outcome of any military confrontation. "Is the German army invincible?" he asked. "No, it is not invincible." He warned that the Nazi leaders "are beginning to suffer from dizziness" from their military successes. "It seems to them that there is nothing that they could not do." He added pointedly that Napoléon enjoyed a similar string of successes at first—before "his army began suffering defeats."

But if Stalin was playing for time during the period of his de facto alliance with Hitler, he had squandered much of the time he already had. One example was the handling of the Soviet defensive lines. In the 1930s, heavily fortified lines were built along the Soviet Union's western borders. When those borders moved farther west as a result of the Nazi-Soviet pact, Stalin decided to largely abandon the old fortifications and build new ones along the new dividing line between the two totalitarian powers. This would prove to be a costly mistake.

Petro Grigorenko, who as a young soldier had helped build the original fortifications, recalled that in the spring of 1941, Stalin ordered the blowing up of "tens of thousands" of them before the new fortifications were completed and outfitted with adequate artillery. As a result, when the Germans invaded, most of the new concrete emplacements were easily overrun. "I do not know how future historians will explain this crime against our people," the future general and dissident wrote later. "No better gift could have been given to Hitler's Barbarossa plan. How could this have taken place? Stalin's justification must have been that he was insane."

Or that he was still clinging to the belief, notwithstanding all the evidence to the contrary, that his country could watch indefinitely from the sidelines as Germany kept fighting its battles elsewhere. Speaking to his aides shortly after the German invasion of Poland in September 1939, Stalin had characterized the war as one "between two groups of capitalist countries." He added: "We see nothing wrong in their having a good fight and weakening each other." In that scenario, he could imagine the Soviet Union as the long-term winner, not only consolidating its hold on the Baltic states and eastern Poland but also expanding its power and influence further. Even as Hitler made his final preparations for Operation Barbarossa, Stalin appeared to be trying to will this vision into reality.

The Soviet leader's message was echoed by many of his foreign envoys. In an interview with the International News Service in London on June 3, Ambassador Maisky predicted that Germany would not be strong enough to defeat both Britain and the United States, which he believed would sooner or later feel compelled to enter the war. Asked if the Soviet Union would help in the struggle against Germany, Maisky replied that his country was "the only neutral power in the world" and intended to maintain that status, while seeking the best possible relations with all the countries involved in the war. According to a Polish government report based on a source inside the news service, the editors concluded there was nothing new in Maisky's statements and spiked the interview.

When British Foreign Secretary Anthony Eden warned Maisky on June 13 of the growing concentration of German troops on the Soviet border, the envoy once again insisted that he did not believe they would attack. Even in his diary entries, Maisky refused to acknowledge the mounting evidence that he was wrong; like his boss in the Kremlin, he was still in denial. "Hitler is not yet ready for suicide," Maisky wrote on June 18. "A campaign against the Soviet Union is, after all, tantamount to suicide."

Back in Moscow, those who served Stalin knew that they had to be extremely careful about how they presented the reports that contradicted what he wanted to hear. Just a day before the German invasion, Beria relayed a note from Vladimir Dekanozov, the Soviet ambassador in Berlin, warning that the attack was imminent. The secret police chief prefaced it with a declaration that addressed Stalin by his first name and patronymic: "My people and I, Joseph Vissarionovich, firmly remember your wise prediction: Hitler will not attack us in 1941!"

In the short-term, Stalin was demonstrating that he was even more delusionary than Hitler.

FOUR

"OUR PLYMOUTH BRETHREN"

In *February 1941, on the* eve of his departure for London to take up the post of US ambassador to the Court of St. James's held earlier by Joseph Kennedy, John Gilbert Winant met with Roosevelt for final instructions. The president asked him "to keep Winston Churchill and the British government patient while the American people assessed the situation," Winant recalled. He also wanted him "to make plain to the people of Great Britain that we believed in their cause, that Nazism and Fascism were incompatible with the American way of life." Roosevelt pointed to the introduction of the first peacetime draft, along with the pending Lend-Lease Act and the transfer of destroyers to Britain as evidence of how those beliefs were being translated into action. "We had made our decision to do everything short of war," Winant concluded.

As the popular Republican governor of New Hampshire who regularly defied his party's bosses and dogmas, Winant had backed the New Deal early, organizing public works projects and signing up for relief programs for his state's citizens. Even before Winant stepped down as governor in 1935, Roosevelt nominated the man he dubbed

"Utopian John" as the first US representative to the International Labour Organization. Winant eagerly accepted the job and moved to Geneva, Switzerland, only to return to Washington in August 1935 to serve as chairman of the newly created Social Security Board. Roosevelt was delighted to enlist a liberal Republican in the battle for public opinion for his most important new social program. Once that battle was won, Winant returned to the ILO in Geneva, taking over as the organization's director in 1939.

Winant witnessed Hitler's early conquests and made no secret of his opposition to them. He traveled to Prague as the Germans dismembered Czechoslovakia, and later observed the collapse of France. "I had seen sectors of the front from a plane while the battle of France was raging," he wrote. "I left Paris the day before the Germans marched in." He also witnessed the arrival in Britain of the soldiers evacuated from Dunkirk and "the effects of aerial warfare over England." All of which did not go unnoticed elsewhere. In Geneva, the German and Italian secret police monitored his activities; in Germany, the press portrayed him as an enemy.

By the time he was ready to take up his appointment in London, Winant was a confirmed internationalist who harbored no doubts about the necessity of supporting Britain. Before his departure, Winant accepted an invitation to address the New Hampshire legislature. While many of his countrymen were still uncertain how to respond to the war in Europe, Winant delivered an unambiguous message echoing Roosevelt's rhetoric. "We are today 'the arsenal of democracy,' the service of supply against the aggressor nations," he declared. "Great Britain has asked that we give them the tools that they may 'finish the job.' We can stand with them as free men. . . . In a just cause, and with God's will, we can do no less."

When he landed in Britain in March, a special train deposited him at Windsor Station, where King George was waiting to accompany him on his first visit to Windsor Castle. "It was the first time in the history of Great Britain that a king had gone to meet an ambassador,"

Winant pointed out with evident pride. He understood fully the reason for this unprecedented gesture: Britain was still in peril and desperately needed his country's help. As Winant's train pulled into London's Paddington Station after his visit to Windsor, a German air raid was taking place.

The new ambassador's British hosts were predisposed to greet his arrival enthusiastically, especially given his predecessor's record of gloomy predictions about their chances of survival and barely concealed opposition to Roosevelt's Lend-Lease program and anything else that tied the fate of their two countries more closely together. Upon his return from Britain, former presidential candidate Wendell Willkie told the columnist Joseph Alsop that "the British people hate Joe Kennedy."

On a flight from Palm Beach, Florida, to Washington in early 1941, Kennedy made clear that those feelings were mutual. Franklin Roosevelt Jr., the president's second youngest son, who was on leave from the navy, boarded the same flight, and the two of them got into an intense discussion about the situation in Europe. As the younger Roosevelt recalled later, "He was convinced that Hitler would ride over Europe and that we should pressure England into negotiating the best peace it could." When another passenger tapped Kennedy on the shoulder, asking him in what sounded like an English accent to keep his voice down, the former envoy confessed to the young Roosevelt, "I hate all of those goddamned Englishmen, from Churchill on down."

From the moment Winant arrived in London and received a note from Churchill expressing his eagerness to meet him, the new ambassador's relationship with the prime minister could not have been more different. In his memoirs, Churchill pointed out gratefully that this was a period when "the President was moving step-by-step ever more closely with us."

But Churchill was still seeking every possible assurance that the support from across the Atlantic would continue to grow, and he chafed at the delays in gearing up US arms production and expediting deliveries. In Washington, Lord Halifax, who had taken over as Britain's ambassador following the death of Lord Lothian, also complained regularly about the disarray of the Roosevelt administration as it tried to transform the president's promises into reality. Dealing with Washington's tangled bureaucracies, he said, was "like hitting wads of cotton wool."

Winant found that all doors were open to him, starting with the prime minister, who included him in his inner circle from the very beginning—so much so that the new ambassador quickly found himself romantically involved with actress Sarah Churchill, the prime minister's daughter. Winant's wife, a wealthy socialite, continued to live in New Hampshire, visiting London only from time to time; Sarah, who, at twenty-seven, was a quarter century younger than Winant, had drifted apart from her husband, an Austrian-born Jewish musician and comedian, although she still appeared in public with him.

Winant did not allow his secret personal life to interfere with the main focus of his new assignment: developing a close working relationship with his lover's father. He quickly helped resolve an impasse between Washington and London about the final terms of the destroyers-for-bases deal that had been announced six months earlier, signing the agreement on March 27. Along with Averell Harriman, who had also arrived in Britain by that time to coordinate the US aid effort, Winant accompanied the prime minister not only to Chequers but also on his visits to cities hit by German air raids.

Impressed by what he saw of the British leader both in public and private, Winant described Churchill as "this stocky figure, with a slight stoop, striding up and down, suddenly completely unconscious of any presence beyond his own thoughts—a power of concentration I was to see repeated many times in many circumstances." Churchill and his aides, in turn, were rapidly won over by Winant. Colville, his young staffer, praised "his unassertive shrewdness and wisdom." One evening when the two men were conferring, German bombers struck again. "He did not even raise his head," Colville noted approvingly.

Despite his success in politics and the immediate praise he won in London, Winant, while strikingly handsome, did not cut a dashing figure. He was at best a mediocre public speaker, and he could be almost painfully reticent. When Winant paid his first visit to Maisky, the Soviet ambassador noted the "somewhat strange impression" he made. "Tall, dark-haired, with slow, demure manners, a listless, barely audible voice, and a pensive, introspective look, he is the polar opposite of his predecessor, the vociferous, jaunty, loquacious, and flighty Joe Kennedy," he wrote in his diary. "I had to strain my ears to catch Winant's words."

Maisky mocked Winant for his decision "to play the democrat" by not moving to the ambassador's residence and living in a modest apartment in the embassy instead. But to his British hosts, the new envoy's low-key style and frequent walkabouts after German bombing raids were further evidence that the new American in town was both serious about his job and on their side.

At a lunch for Winant at the Savoy Hotel two weeks after his arrival, Churchill welcomed him as "a friend and faithful comrade," pointing out that "you come to us at a grand turning point in the world's history." While the BBC broadcast his remarks, the prime minister concluded with his usual eloquence: "You, Mr. Ambassador, share our purpose. You'll share our dangers. You'll share our interests." He added that their two countries would also one day "share the crown of victory."

Unlike Churchill, Winant read his speech in his quiet, sometimes halting voice. But he delivered exactly the message that his hosts wanted to hear about how the United States would provide "the tools—the ships, the planes, the guns, the ammunition, and the food—for all those here and everywhere who defend with their lives freedom's frontiers." He added: "A new spirit is abroad. Free people are again cooperating to win a free world, and no tyranny can frustrate their hopes."

The press reaction was ecstatic. According to the London *Sunday*

Times, Winant had scored "an extraordinary triumph." The *Daily Herald* declared that "his words were more than oratory. They were a declaration of faith."

On March 21 Minister of Information Duff Cooper and Harold Nicolson, the MP who worked for him, hosted a lunch for British editors. Despite the sometimes difficult negotiations with Washington about the destroyer-for-bases deal that was just about to be signed, he warned them "not to antagonize the United States." He praised the Lend-Lease bill as "probably the most decisive fact of the war," and claimed, as Nicolson noted in his diary, that he was "sure that America will be in the war before long."

Cooper's message was that the British press, along with its political leaders, needed to keep convincing not just their own countrymen but also the Americans that the war could and would be won. Otherwise, he suggested, the United States could very well stay out of the conflict—and Britain's hopes of victory could be dashed. In other words, public perceptions would shape reality as much as warships and guns.

Hans Dieckhoff, who had served as the last German ambassador to Washington before the war and then returned to the Foreign Ministry in Berlin, concurred that American public opinion was an essential factor. In a memo on March 10, he emphasized that its evolution "will depend on the progress of the war." His prediction: "If Germany succeeds in defeating the English decisively in the near future, then in all probability, American public opinion will be in favor of staying out of the war; if the war continues undecided for a considerable time, then there is considerable danger that public opinion will develop in the direction of a growing willingness to enter the war."

For all their displays of public optimism, British leaders were all too aware how precarious their country's position still was. The German U-boat campaign was taking a heavy toll on British and

Commonwealth ships seeking to maintain the flow of supplies to the island nation. In the three months ending with May, Churchill noted, U-boats sank 142 ships, 99 of them British. The German victories in Greece and Yugoslavia, although they would delay Hitler's plans to invade the Soviet Union, provided another demonstration of Nazi might. In Libya, General Erwin Rommel, the "Desert Fox," was scoring victories with his Afrika Korps that had been dispatched to help the beleaguered Italian forces in their battles with British troops.

And while the Luftwaffe had failed to win the Battle of Britain, its bombers had resumed their attacks on London and other cities. On April 16, after a late-evening meeting with Winant at the US embassy, Colville was caught in another bombing raid as he walked back to 10 Downing Street. "Bombs came down like hailstones," he noted, adding laconically, "I had quite a disagreeable walk." Three days later, he was more explicit about his fears in another diary entry: "Certainly as I walk through the streets, I look at London's landmarks more carefully now, with a feeling that it may be the last time I see them."

It wasn't just the young Churchill aide who experienced such premonitions: his boss was not immune to them either. On May 2 Colville reported that the prime minister was "gravely depressed" by the news that Washington had rejected his government's request that it help prevent Germany from seizing the Azores and the Cape Verde Islands (although, in the end, Hitler did not do so) and by more bad tidings from the high seas and the Middle East. Churchill, "in worse gloom than I have ever seen him," as Colville put it, dictated a telegram reflecting his somber mood to Roosevelt. Then, speaking to Harriman, his chief military assistant General "Pug" Ismay and him, the prime minister described "a world in which Hitler dominated all Europe, Asia, and Africa and left the US and ourselves no option but an unwilling peace."

Churchill called the moment a decisive one, warning that if Hitler gained control of Iraqi oil and Ukrainian wheat, not even "our Plymouth brethren"—referring to the Americans—would be able to guarantee a turnabout in fortunes. On the train that morning, Colville reported that Clementine, Churchill's wife, asked him: "Jock, do you think we are going to win?"

From his perch in the ministry of information, Nicolson had been picking up on the signs that the general public was also increasingly worried and weary, and he pondered what could be done about it. "From the propaganda point of view, all that the country really wants is some assurance of how victory is to be achieved," he noted in his diary on April 13 as German forces were gaining the initiative in Libya. "They are bored by talks about the righteousness of our cause and our eventual triumph. What they want are facts indicating how we are to beat the Germans." Then he added: "I have no idea at all how we are to give them those facts."

When General Raymond E. Lee, the dapper US military attaché in London, died in 1958 at the age of seventy-two, his obituary in the *New York Times* pointed out that no one "was ever more popular in that post both with the American residents in the British capital and with British government officials." The reason: throughout the German bombing raids in 1940 and 1941, the newspaper explained, "he retained absolute faith that the Royal Air Force would be successful in the defense of the British Isles."

Lee not only sounded convinced of his belief in victory but also sought to imbue the same faith in others, especially those who were responsible for shaping public opinion back home. During the Blitz, he became disturbed by the frequency with which the American press described London as "devastated" by the bombings. He summoned several American correspondents to his office, where there was a pile of dictionaries on his desk—and then read them the definition of *devastated*. Inviting them to look out the window, he made the point that the scene outside did not match the definition he had just read. "London is not devastated, and if you want one soldier's opinion, it will not be devastated," he said.

But even Lee, who had battled so hard to counter the pessimism of his first boss, Ambassador Kennedy, and others, felt some of the same anxieties that afflicted his British counterparts that spring. From late January to the end of March, he participated in the ABC-1 Conference, as the first American-British-Canadian military staff planning meeting was called, acting as an adviser to the American delegation. Held in Washington, the conference laid the groundwork for extensive military cooperation between Britain and the United States, based on the implicit assumption that the Americans were likely to enter the war. But given Washington's official position as a nonbelligerent, the proceedings were strictly secret, limited to a small group of participants. Calling themselves "technical advisers to the British Purchasing Commission," the British delegates took the precaution of wearing civilian clothes.

According to presidential aide Robert Sherwood, the staff talks "provided the highest degree of *strategic preparedness* that the United States or probably any other nonaggressor nation has ever had before entry into war." The extreme secrecy, he wrote, was necessitated not so much because of fears that Germany or Japan might learn of these consultations; the real reason was that they could provide ammunition to the isolationists at home who were already charging that the Roosevelt administration was plotting to bring the country into the war. If those plans had fallen in the hands of Congress or the press, Sherwood noted, "American preparation for war might have been well-nigh wrecked and ruined."

After such a successful conference, Lee should have felt relieved and fairly relaxed on his return journey to London in early April. But during his stopover in Lisbon, the military attaché appeared to suffer a near panic attack about the secret documents he was carrying back with him. They contained the results of the military deliberations in Washington, including the operational and deployment plans for US and British troops in case his country entered the war. He was also carrying a secret letter from Roosevelt to Churchill. The loss of these documents, he noted, would be "completely irreparable."

Since he was staying at a hotel before his flight to England, he entrusted those documents to members of the US legation in Lisbon for safekeeping. After a late dinner, he went to sleep—only to wake up at two thirty in the morning "in the midst of a most tremendous nightmare." Only half awake, he remembered that Lisbon was a center for international spying, full of Nazi agents, and that he had entrusted the documents to "these American representatives who were not Americans at all." In his nightmare, one of them had driven straight for the border to hand them over to the Germans. He rushed to the legation in the morning to check that he was only imagining all of this—but then, just to be sure, he took back the documents, locking himself into his hotel room until his departure.

Lee's plane landed in Poole late in the evening on April 10, and he went to spend the night in the neighboring town of Bournemouth before catching the morning train to London. As he was pouring his coffee in his new lodgings, he heard "four loud thuds which sounded like bombs some distance off," he wrote. When he and other guests came out to look, they saw the glow from the flames rising from a large hotel in Poole that had been hit. After he and the others had turned in, they were awakened by the landlady knocking on their doors, telling them to get downstairs, where it was safer. This time, only a half block away, the local Woolworth store had been set ablaze, and more German bombers were circling overhead. Finally arriving in London, Lee felt a tremendous sense of relief once he had handed over Roosevelt's letter for transmission to Churchill and locked up the other documents.

The other source of relief for Lee was his first meeting with Winant, who had arrived in London during his absence. "What a contrast to the interview I had first with Kennedy, who was crude, blatant, and ignorant in everything he did or said," Lee wrote in his diary. "It is evident that Winant and Churchill are already on the best of terms, and I am sure they will remain so."

Nonetheless, Lee's first week back in London left him in a dour mood. "I think I notice a considerable deterioration in many directions, which I might not have noticed had I not been away," he wrote. The food situation had worsened, he pointed out, and people looked "more solemn." At the movies, audiences were subjected to the kind of blatant propaganda that the authorities had shied away from before. He watched a film with British troops in training shouting "Kill! Kill! Kill!" and observed that this was something he had not seen earlier.

While Lee hoped that American aid would allow the RAF to extend its bombing raids deeper into Germany, he worried about "the race against time." The vital question was "whether our support will arrive soon enough to bolster up what is a gradually failing cause." Judging by his diary, he was far less optimistic than his public pronouncements indicated.

"Mr. Black," probably an alias for one of his intelligence sources who met him during this period, did nothing to improve Lee's spirits. The gist of his message to Lee was that the Germans "are convinced that assistance from the United States can never reach England soon enough to affect the final issue." Even a few British officials appeared intent on conveying a sense of desperation in their dealings with the numerous emissaries from the United States, instead of the unwavering confidence that Churchill projected on almost every occasion. Lord Beaverbrook, the minister for aircraft production, asked General Henry "Hap" Arnold, who had been busy expanding the US Army Air Corps: "What would you do if Churchill were hung, and the rest of us [were] hiding in Scotland or being run over by the Germans?" According to Lee, Arnold concluded that his British hosts "were putting on a show to impress him" about the urgency of the situation.

Some of the Americans were suitably impressed. On April 10 Harriman wrote to Roosevelt: "England's strength is bleeding. In our own interest, I trust that our Navy can be directly employed before our partner is too weak." In a letter to Harriman dated April 29, William Bullitt, who had served as US ambassador first to Russia and then to France until its collapse, wrote: "The President is waiting for public opinion to lead, and public opinion is waiting for a lead from the President. . . . Nothing drastic will happen unless either the President leads or Hitler supplies an incident which public opinion will consider an affront to the national honor."

In the interim, American journalists in Europe played an increasingly direct role in that battle for public opinion.

Dorothy Thompson was one of the first female foreign correspondents to achieve celebrity status, building her reputation on her usually incisive reporting from Europe for a variety of American publications starting in the 1920s. As far back as 1923, in the aftermath of the failed Beer Hall Putsch, she had tried to meet Hitler. When his Nazi Party began gathering momentum following the 1929 stock market crash and the subsequent economic depression, Thompson finally succeeded in lining up an interview with him, in November 1931. She did the interview for *Cosmopolitan* but made full use of the opportunity, quickly turning out a book titled *I Saw Hitler!* The slim volume made a huge splash when it was published in 1932, just as its subject was figuring prominently in all the stories flowing from Germany.

Unfortunately for Thompson, the book trumpeted her biggest misjudgment during her otherwise impressive career. She explained accurately how Hitler was counting on subverting the democratic system instead of trying to overthrow it by force, as he had tried to do earlier: "The people were to 'awaken,' and Hitler's movement was going to vote dictatorship in!" But she completely misread his political prospects—despite all the signs that his new strategy was working.

"When finally I walked into Adolph Hitler's salon in the Kaiserhof Hotel, I was convinced that I was meeting the future dictator of Germany," she wrote. "In something less than fifty seconds, I was quite sure I was not. It took just that long to measure the startling insignificance of this man who has set the world agog." She described Hitler as "inconsequent and voluble, ill-poised, insecure . . . the very prototype of the Little Man," referring to the title of a bestselling novel of that era by German writer Hans Fallada. His eyes, she added, "have the peculiar shine which often distinguishes geniuses, alcoholics, and hysterics." As a result, she concluded that Hitler was unlikely to rise to the top, and, even if he did, "he will smite only the weakest of his enemies."

To her credit, Thompson returned to Germany after Hitler took power to write hard-hitting articles about the Nazis that led to her expulsion from the country in 1934 for her "anti-German" attitude, demonstrating that she was not about to underestimate him again. Nor was she reticent about trying to rally her countrymen to support Britain once the war started. In the heat of the domestic fight over the Lend-Lease bill, she abandoned any pretense of journalistic detachment and joined the fray on the side of the Roosevelt administration.

In her introduction to the pamphlet *The Battle of 1776*, which contained the text of the Lend-Lease bill along with statements by Roosevelt and Secretary of State Cordell Hull, Secretary of the Navy Frank Knox, and Secretary of War Henry Stimson, Thompson insisted that "there was nothing more urgent" than the passage of the pending legislation.

Offering an exposition on how Hitler's Germany was systematically engaged in "the pulverization of nations," she explained that this process had also destroyed the essential ingredients—"law, culture, institutions"—that had once constituted the German nation. In its place, there now was "a race of people held together not by a state. . . . but a tribe held together by a secular church, a pagan religious order, the Nazi Party."

Then, in a passage that sounds eerily contemporary but would surely be denounced as politically incorrect if it were penned today, she wrote: "It is this order, this secular religion, which, like Mohammed's movement to which it bears more historical resemblance than anything else, is subjecting the civilized world. And wherever it arises, nations end. The nation is destroyed, not only by its military occupation, but by the systematic destruction of its basic institutions." If Germany managed to prevail over Britain, she added, it would be folly to believe that the United States would not be its next target. A defeated England "would become the base for the domination of the Atlantic Ocean and the encirclement of the Americas. . . . we will have lost a war without ever having moved a weapon."

Thompson aligned herself with the Roosevelt administration more openly than some of her former Berlin-based colleagues did, but she was far from alone in doing so. *Chicago Daily News* correspondent Edgar Ansel Mowrer, who won the Pulitzer Prize for his incisive reporting on Hitler's rise to power, was forced to leave Germany in 1933 under pressure from the new Nazi regime. In the summer of 1940, his publisher, Frank Knox, who by then was secretary of the navy, instructed him to accompany William "Wild Bill" Donovan on a visit to Britain. Roosevelt was sending Donovan, who would soon head the spy operation known as the Office of Strategic Services (OSS), on a mission to assess the British mood and chances for survival, since he did not trust Ambassador Kennedy's judgment.

After their meetings with Churchill and other top officials, the two emissaries agreed on what they would report back to the president. As Mowrer put it [his italics], *"Britain under Churchill would not surrender either to ruthless air raids or to an invasion."*

It was hardly surprising that those correspondents who had witnessed Nazi behavior up close were eager to help fight the battle to influence public opinion back home. On December 1, 1940, as he was wrapping up his tour in Berlin for CBS, William Shirer noted in his diary that if Hitler continued to score victories in Europe and Africa, he would then launch an attack on the United States "unless we are prepared to give up our way of life and adapt ourselves to a subservient place in his totalitarian scheme of things." Hitler would not be able to dominate the world as long at the United States stood in its way, Shirer concluded. "The clash is as inevitable as that of two planets hurtling inexorably through the heavens toward each other." In mid-1941 the publication of his *Berlin Diary: The Journal of a Foreign Correspondent* allowed him to share those uncensored thoughts with a large audience of readers, as the book quickly rose to the top of the bestseller lists.

At the same time, Joseph Harsch, the *Christian Science Monitor* correspondent who had also recently returned from Berlin, published *Pattern of Conquest*, a compilation of his twelve-part series in the newspaper that echoed many of Shirer's and Thompson's themes. "The question before the American people is a clear one," he wrote. In the titanic struggle for global dominance, "America can either belong to that dominant force or submit to it." To prevent a German victory, the United States needed to "take its stand with Britain." He added: "The two together can unquestionably defeat Germany."

Not all American correspondents had started out as such ardent opponents of Hitler. Henry Flannery, Shirer's CBS successor in Berlin, who arrived in November 1940 to overlap with him briefly, did not immediately share Shirer's vehemently anti-Nazi outlook. "I was one of those people who were known as 'open minded'—who did not believe that Nazi Germany was necessarily a threat to the United States, who believed it was at least possible we might do business with Hitler," he recalled. But as Flannery began to learn more about the country he was covering, including its secret program of "mercy killings" of the physically and mentally disabled, he changed his views quickly.

So long as Germany still hoped to keep the United States out of the war, its officials made a show of treating American correspondents with some restraint. But as Washington ramped up its support for Britain in early 1941, the reporters felt increasingly vulnerable. On March 15 the Gestapo arrested Richard Hottelet of United Press "on suspicion of espionage," and he was locked up until July 8, when he was just as abruptly freed and allowed to return to the United

States. Hottelet's real crime, according to his colleague Howard K. Smith, the future ABC anchorman, was that he could "no longer hide his nausea" when he listened to Nazi propagandists. Since the Nazis were looking for someone to arrest so that they could intimidate the other American reporters in Berlin, Smith concluded, Hottelet was the obvious target.

Like so many Nazi actions, this kind of harsh treatment only reinforced the revulsion that most of the remaining correspondents felt about the regime they were covering. And as they shed any lingering inhibitions about displaying such feelings in their reports to their readers, they contributed further to the evolving shift in mood back home.

If those who had served in Berlin found it easy to cast the Nazis as the embodiment of evil, the American correspondents in London offered the other side of the narrative, largely accepting Churchill's portrayal of his country as a heroic holdout against the German war machine. "The United States had an exceptionally fine team of correspondents in London at that time," wrote Minister of Information Cooper. "They were, almost without an exception, anti-German, and they rendered great service to the common cause."

Throughout the Battle of Britain and the Blitz, Murrow's "*This* is London" broadcasts riveted his American listeners with their descriptions of the toll that German bombs took on a daily basis—and, most importantly, conveyed to them the quiet courage of London's citizens and the inspiring leadership of Churchill. When the new prime minister addressed the House of Commons following the fall of France and the evacuation at Dunkirk, Murrow reported, "He spoke the language of Shakespeare with a direct urgency such as I have never before heard in that House."

Murrow was hardly alone among the American correspondents who told the story of British defiance. Quentin Reynolds, a roving correspondent for *Collier's Weekly*, summed up his impressions from London at the end of 1940, pointing out that the terror tactics Hitler had employed successfully in subduing most of continental Europe proved a failure during the Blitz. Instead of quivering, "London yawned," he wrote. "Terror as a weapon against the English is about as effective as a cream puff would be in a fight against Joe Louis." But it was Murrow's broadcasts that had the greatest impact.

Eric Sevareid, who worked in the CBS London bureau with Murrow, maintained that his colleague did not see his role in directly political terms. "Murrow was not trying to 'sell' the British cause to America," he wrote. "He was trying to explain the universal human cause of men who were showing a noble face to the world. In so doing, he made the British and their behavior human and thus compelling to his countrymen at home." His influence, the correspondent added, made him far more important than his country's official envoy, who was still Kennedy during most of his broadcasts. "*He* [Murrow] was the ambassador, in a double role, representing Britain in America as well as America in Britain," Sevareid concluded.

Murrow's accounts undoubtedly predisposed visiting American reporters to pick up on the themes of his reporting. Ernie Pyle, the Scripps-Howard correspondent whose folksy style and courage won him a Pulitzer and huge fame before he was killed by a Japanese sniper in 1945, arrived in Britain in December 1940 and stayed until March 1941. *Ernie Pyle in England*, his speedily published book, was an unabashed ode to the English spirit, completely overlooking any doubts among the populace. "In three months, I have not met an Englishman to whom it has ever occurred that Britain might lose the war," he wrote.

The Americans who had lived longer in Britain knew that the reality was not that simple: the English harbored the same doubts and fears that anyone would as the skies filled with German bombers. But, according to Sevareid, "The British were still afraid of one another" when it came to showing their emotions; it was simply bad form to do so. "One could panic in the heart, but two together could not show it, nor a hundred in a group." Significantly, Sevareid's ruminations on this subject appeared in his memoir that was published after the war. During England's moment of greatest peril, he and his colleagues were not inclined to share such nuanced analysis.

To a visitor like Pyle, the public displays of everyday courage were both endlessly impressive—and infectious. Describing his feelings toward the end of his stay, he wrote: "I had been in London so long I had acquired the London outlook, the London casualness, the London assurance that no matter what happens, we can stand it. The Londoner's psychology is like that of the aviator—somebody will get killed tonight, but it'll always be somebody else, never me."

In January 1941 the Goebbels propaganda ministry lauded the America First Committee as "truly American and truly patriotic." This suggested that the German regime still hoped the isolationists could block or at least slow Roosevelt's push to shore up Britain. With the passage of the Lend-Lease Act, those hopes took a direct hit. On March 11, after the House and Senate votes, Goebbels complained in his diary that the opposition in the United States had "given up the struggle," pointing to the "ever-wider reverberations" of the Lend-Lease legislation. "London, of course, is seizing it eagerly, like a drowning man clutching at a straw."

Although Hitler continued to maintain that the United States would not be able to gear up fast enough to have a decisive impact on the war, the Lend-Lease news prompted him to launch "frequent tirades against the Americans, particularly Roosevelt," as Engel put it. The new legislation gave him "additionally major problems." According to his army adjutant's summary of his remarks to a small group of top party officials and generals on March 24, Hitler also claimed it "gave him a cause for war." He added that he had no intention of availing himself of that cause yet, but that time would come.

"Eventually there would be war with the USA," Hitler declared. "Roosevelt, and behind him Jewish finance, wanted war and had to want war, for a German victory in Europe would bring with it enormous losses of capital for American Jews in Europe." He bemoaned the fact that Germany did not have bombers capable of reaching American cities as a way of teaching a lesson "to American Jews." But he explained that "a merciless war on sea traffic" would limit the effectiveness of the US supply effort. Besides, he added, "The Americans could not do everything, and the capacity of their armaments industry was still limited."

Halder dutifully echoed those sentiments in his diary entry a month later, noting on April 26 that Washington was ill prepared for an outright confrontation in other ways as well. "If USA entered the war now, we would have to reckon only with the peacetime army," he wrote. But not all of Hitler's generals were so dismissive. Unsettled by the Lend-Lease news, Bock wrote in his diary that the Americans "have done everything now except actually send troops to Europe." His troubled tone indicated that he saw nothing positive in this development.

Given the closer US-British ties, Hitler was more determined than ever to project unwavering confidence in an ultimate German victory. His plans to attack Russia would not only fulfill the promises of expansion to the east that he had first spelled out in *Mein Kampf*, he believed, but also demonstrate to a stubbornly unbending Britain and its supporters in Washington the futility of trying to thwart his ambitions. "We no longer have much respect for the USA," Goebbels wrote in his diary on March 10. "The only thing that impresses the Jews there is a show of power."

Although Goebbels assumed his boss's dismissive attitude toward Roosevelt and his countrymen, he betrayed unease about Churchill's strong leadership. "If he had come to power in 1933, we would not have been where we are today," he wrote on May 8 after studying a volume of Churchill's speeches and essays from the late 1930s. "And I believe that he will give us a few more problems yet." Then, as if trying to reassure himself, he added: "But we can and will solve them. Nevertheless, he is not to be taken as lightly as we usually take him."

In the midst of Hitler's preparations for Operation Barbarossa and Churchill's efforts to keep strengthening his country's links with Washington, a totally unexpected visitor literally dropped out of the sky over Scotland, catching both leaders by surprise. On May 10 Rudolf Hess, Hitler's deputy—who had been at his side from the earliest days of the birth of the Nazi movement in Munich—flew a Messerschmitt 110 from Augsburg and disappeared from German territory, heading over the North Sea. Although Hess was an experienced pilot, he had never practiced parachuting from a plane; near Glasgow, he did exactly that, injuring his leg as he extricated himself from the cockpit.

After his plane crashed and exploded, he found himself in a field facing a Scottish farmer, telling him and later the Home Guard members who quickly showed up that he was German and needed to get a message to the Duke of Hamilton. A RAF wing commander who had been part of the British delegation to the 1936 Berlin Olympics, Douglas Douglas-Hamilton claimed he had no memory of meeting Hess during a reception for top Nazi officials there. But Hess had decided this was the person he needed to reach to carry out his mission.

As Hess told Hitler in a letter he had left behind and then his captors, his goal was to convince the British to make a separate peace with Nazi Germany. In fact, as Hitler admitted later, Hess had come to see him a few days before his flight and asked whether he still believed, as he had written in *Mein Kampf*, that the two powers could make a deal. Hitler declared that he hadn't changed his views, although at that point he must have felt he was responding to a rather academic question.

Fittingly, Churchill was watching a Marx Brothers movie at Ditchley Park when he was interrupted by the news of Hess's arrival—relayed in a phone call from Hamilton, who had just met him.

"I thought this was fantastic," Churchill recalled. "The report, however, was true." An analogous situation for him, he added, would have involved Foreign Secretary Eden, "my trusted colleague," parachuting from a stolen Spitfire into Germany. In other words, it was impossible to imagine.

If the British prime minister was perplexed, Hitler was furious when he learned what his deputy had done. The German leader was in the Berghof, his Alpine retreat, about to meet Speer to go over his sketches envisaging a victory parade in 1950 in the German capital, redone in grandiose style. On the eve of his most dramatic act of aggression—this one, against the Soviet Union—Hitler was already contemplating the splendor of future celebrations. Waiting downstairs, Speer encountered two of Hess's aides, who asked his permission to deliver Hess's letter to Hitler first. Speer had no idea what had happened, and he started flipping through his sketches once more as they went into Hitler's salon. "I suddenly heard an inarticulate, almost animal outcry," Speer recalled.

Hitler was badly shaken and embarrassed by what he viewed as a personal betrayal. "Hess always had crazy ideas," he told his lieutenants once it was confirmed that he had landed safely. The next day Hitler, added that "all his ideas were on the borderline between reality and madness." As Goebbels noted, "The Führer is absolutely shattered. . . . People are asking, rightly, how a fool like this could have been next in line to the Führer."

Whatever concerns Nazi officials had about the domestic reaction, Hitler's immediate priority was to reassure Mussolini that this was a rogue act by a mentally unstable individual and not indicative of any deeper crisis of his regime. He dispatched Foreign Minister von Ribbentrop to Rome, who arrived there "discouraged and nervous," according to his Italian counterpart Count Ciano. During Ribbentrop's meeting with Mussolini, the Italian leader ended up comforting his German visitor. But afterward, Mussolini told Ciano that he considered the Hess affair "a tremendous blow to the Nazi regime," as the foreign minister put it. Mussolini was jealous and resentful of German victories, while his own troops had suffered repeated setbacks; as a result, he welcomed the news about Hess, convinced "this will have the effect of bringing down German stock, even with the Italians."

Hitler and Goebbels worried about how Churchill and his team would handle their unexpected visitor—and especially what propaganda mileage they'd get out of him. Goebbels believed at first that the affair was causing "appalling damage," given the huge play it received everywhere in the press. He also had a different worry. "The main danger is that they will use him to give authenticity to faked atrocity reports," he wrote. But by the next day, Goebbels was perplexed by the fact that Britain was not issuing any phony statements in Hess's name, which is clearly what he would have done if the situation were reversed. "We are dealing with dumb amateurs over there," he concluded.

In reality, Churchill had no intention of playing games with his prisoner, who, as he wrote to Eden, "like other Nazi leaders, is potentially a war criminal." Hess was to be treated as a prisoner of war, kept isolated but comfortable while his interrogators both studied him and learned whatever they could from him. "He should be treated with dignity, as if he were an important general who had fallen into our hands," the prime minister instructed.

Churchill wrote to Roosevelt on May 17, explaining what the interrogators had learned already and his strategy for handling the case. "Here we think it best to let the press have a good run for a bit and keep the Germans guessing." Hess's message, as summarized by Churchill, was that Germany was certain to emerge victorious and, therefore, Britain should make peace with Hitler, allowing the British Empire overseas to survive "in exchange for a free hand for him in Europe." As Churchill put it to Roosevelt, "This is the old invitation to us to desert all our friends in order to save temporarily the greater part of our skin."

But Hess insisted that Hitler would not negotiate with the present British government—in short, with Churchill. Instead, he seemed to believe there were pro-German elements in Britain, perhaps associated with the monarchy, who could take charge. This may have explained his determination to reach the Duke of Hamilton, on the mistaken assumption that he would be receptive to that kind of appeal. He may have also thought that the duke could get him access to King George.

Churchill's other concern, which also explained his cautious handling of the Hess affair, was how Stalin would react to it. As the prime minister wrote in his memoirs, Soviet officials were "deeply intrigued. . . . and they wove many distorted theories around it." At a time when Stalin was convinced that both London and Washington were supplying disinformation about a pending German attack on his country, this was hardly surprising. Over dinner three years later, Stalin asked Churchill about the story behind the Hess affair. When Churchill explained that Hess was truly a deluded man on a personal mission, Stalin was no less suspicious. "I had the feeling that he believed there had been some deep negotiation or plot for Germany and Britain to act together in the invasion of Russia, which had miscarried," the prime minister recalled.

Hess, whose prestige and importance had visibly diminished in Hitler's inner circle before his solo flight, may have hoped to restore his standing by this spectacular act. Along with Speer and other top Nazis, he was put on trial in Nuremberg after the war. Given a life sentence, he ended up in Spandau Prison with Speer and five other convicted Nazis who had avoided the death penalty. Talking to Speer shortly before the architect's release, Hess confirmed that he had wanted to make the deal he had proposed with Britain. "Hess assured me in all seriousness that the idea had been inspired in him in a dream by supernatural forces," Speer wrote. "He said he had not at all intended to oppose or embarrass Hitler."

By 1966, all the other Nazi prisoners in Spandau had been released, and Hess remained as its sole occupant. In 1987 Hess was ninety-three, frail and nearly blind, yet he managed to strangle himself by wrapping an electrical cord around his neck. The four Allied powers—the United States, Britain, France, and the Soviet Union—were in charge of Spandau Prison. But like Hitler, they had found it impossible to control his actions.

For all the headlines it garnered, the Hess affair proved to have no lasting significance. "I never attached any serious importance to this escapade," Churchill wrote. "I knew it had no relation to the march of events." Nonetheless, Hess unwittingly exposed the dynamic among the four major players at that critical moment before German forces marched on Russia: the undercurrent of tensions between Hitler and Mussolini; Stalin's all-too-visible paranoia about Churchill—and, by extension, Roosevelt; and, as demonstrated by the calm tone of Churchill's letter to Roosevelt explaining what had happened, the growing rapport between the two Western leaders.

While the Lend-Lease program represented a giant step forward in Washington's push to aid Britain, Roosevelt had offered other encouraging news as well. On April 11 he cabled Churchill that the United States was extending its security zone and patrol areas much farther into the North Atlantic, as far as the twenty-sixth meridian (west)—effectively taking responsibility for monitoring all shipping in the Western hemisphere. American ships would not yet escort British convoys, but they would inform them of any enemy activity they detected, including the location of "aggressor ships or planes." In his response to Roosevelt on April 16, Churchill wrote: "Admiralty received the news with the greatest relief and satisfaction."

Nonetheless, the prime minister was increasingly worried about the scale of British losses at sea. On May 24 Harriman was a guest of Churchill at Chequers when British ships confronted the *Bismarck*, the Nazis' imposing new battleship, and the cruiser *Prinz Eugen* in the North Sea. At seven in the morning, Harriman woke to find the prime minister dressed only in a yellow sweater that covered his short nightshirt, leaving his pink legs exposed, as his visitor recalled. "Hell of a battle going on," Churchill told him. The news was not good: the British battleship HMS *Hood* had taken a direct hit that set off a massive explosion, sinking the ship and killing all but 3 of its 1,421 men. The *Bismarck* was also hit, but initially managed to elude its British pursuers as it set course for the French port city of Brest.

This gave Harriman the chance to watch his host in action. "For three days, Churchill concentrated his full attention on the chase, ordering out every available ship and aircraft in spite of the generally foul weather," he recalled. The *Bismarck* was finally cornered and sunk on May 27; about 2,300 sailors went down with it. The ship that was supposed to be the pride of the Third Reich's navy failed to survive its first mission.

That same evening, Roosevelt delivered an address from the East Room of the White House on the radio. "From the point of view of strict naval and military necessity, we shall give every possible assistance to Britain and to all who, with Britain, are resisting Hitlerism or its equivalent with force of arms," he vowed. If that sounded like the president was edging even closer to direct involvement in the war, the very next day he appeared to backpedal, insisting that he was not about to ask the navy to protect convoys directly, or to ask Congress for changes in the Neutrality Acts.

Roosevelt was acutely aware that Lindbergh and the America First movement still had considerable appeal. Speaking to a rally of fifteen thousand supporters in Saint Louis on May 3, Lindbergh kept pounding away at his message that Britain was doomed and it was futile for the United States to try to rescue it. "No matter how many planes we build in America and send to England, we cannot make the British Isles stronger than Germany in military aviation," he declared.

Robert Sherwood, Roosevelt's speechwriter, wrote that the isolationists' cumulative attacks on the president—including their incendiary rhetoric claiming that he would "plow under every fourth

American boy"—had taken its toll on his boss. "Whatever the peril, he was not going to lead the country into war—he was going to wait to be pushed in."

As for his countrymen, many of them were torn between their conflicting desires to stay out of the war and to help Britain. In a Gallup poll published at the end of April, 81 percent of the respondents opposed entering the war at that time; but as the polling organization put it, "if it appeared that the only way to beat Germany and Italy was for the US to go to war, 68 percent would now say 'Go.'"

The epicenter of the war was about to shift, however. Despite the continued fierce battles at sea and Germany's successful invasion of Crete in late May, London and other British cities suddenly felt a respite from bombing raids. "We are puzzled why, in this lovely weather, the Germans have not seriously attacked us by air," Nicholson wrote in his diary on June 17. Speculating on the reason for the abrupt change, he added: "It may be that they are massing on the Eastern Front as part of the intimidation of Russia." In his Information Ministry job, he was not privy to the intelligence reports indicating that Hitler had much more than intimidation in mind; he was about to launch Operation Barbarossa.

Once again, Hitler was acting according to his own brand of logic, which was reflected in General Halder's diary entry on June 4. The imminent attack was "based on the need to remove Britain's last hope for continental support and to build a Europe finally without Britain," he wrote. "Once this mission is completed, we will have a free hand, especially with air and naval arms, to bring Britain down finally."

In Hitler's mind, the swift conquest of Russia would be only a short interval before the final reckoning with Britain.

FIVE

"WHAT SHALL WE DO?"

Right *up until the last* moment when Hitler's armies struck in the early-morning hours of June 22, Stalin persisted in his state of denial about German intentions. Two days before the invasion, the supervisor of the Baltic port of Riga, Latvia, had called Politburo member Anastas Mikoyan with news that should have set off the final alarm bells: the twenty-five German cargo ships in the port at that moment had received instructions to leave the next day, whether or not they had completed their unloading and loading of cargo. Mikoyan went straight to Stalin, urging him to order that the German ships not be allowed to depart. "It's going to be a provocation," the Soviet leader responded angrily. "We cannot do it. Instruct them not to impede the ships and to let them go."

On the night of June 21, three German deserters from the front lines separately crossed to the Soviet side to warn that the attack was coming at dawn. In each case, the news was relayed up the chain of command. Once again, Stalin insisted that these were provocations—although he did belatedly agree to place his border troops on alert. He also issued an order to shoot Alfred Liskov, a young

Communist worker from Berlin who was the third German deserter, "for his disinformation."

Liskov's "disinformation" proved to be all too accurate only a few hours later. Shortly after three in the morning, the gargantuan German military machine swung into action. The German army that launched the attack numbered 3.05 million men and included 3,550 tanks, 2,770 aircraft, and about 600,000 horses, whose job it was to transport weaponry and other supplies. Another half million troops were provided by Finland and Romania, which were allied with Germany. This was the biggest military force ever assembled, and marked the beginning of an epic conflict between the two totalitarian powers that, on average, involved about nine million troops from both sides at any one time.

The German invasion force was divided into three parts. Army Group North was to direct its assault through the Baltic states, with Leningrad as its ultimate target. Army Group South was to mount the drive on the Ukrainian capital of Kiev. But it was Army Group Center that was the most heavily equipped, boasting half of the German armored divisions and its most famous panzer units. Its assignment was to encircle and take Minsk and then continue the push due east toward Moscow. As the fighting moved in that direction, the single largest concentration of troops would be involved in the battle for Moscow.

When the first artillery shells began to fly on June 22, Corporal Ernst Busch, a member of the German Signal Corps who spoke Russian, picked up an uncoded Red Army message: "We are being fired on. What shall we do?" The response from Russian headquarters was in code, but another member of Busch's unit deciphered it quickly. "You must be mad!" it read. "And why is your signal not in code?" Given the orders that had been flowing from the Kremlin, such initial expressions of disbelief were as understandable as they were absurd.

At four o'clock, General Georgy Zhukov, chief of the general staff, called Stalin's dacha to wake him and let him know about the reports coming in from all over the western Soviet Union about heavy German shelling and bombing. Arriving at the Kremlin a short time later, Stalin was still reluctant to accept the full import of the news he was receiving. He speculated that the German military could be acting on its own initiative. "Hitler surely doesn't know about it," he declared. Then he ordered Molotov to meet with German Ambassador Schulenburg to find out the real story behind the reports from the border, clearly hoping there was still a chance that they were wrong.

As instructed by his government, the German envoy had already requested a meeting with Molotov to deliver an unambiguous message. He arrived at five thirty in the morning, just as Goebbels was reading on German radio an announcement dictated by Hitler. It blamed the Russians for "continual infringements" on the border, and claimed that German troops had engaged in "a prolonged firefight" to drive back Red Army patrols that had "once more crossed into the Reich." This was accompanied by Hitler's purported ideological-geopolitical justification for the invasion:

"[T]he hour has come in which it is necessary to go into action against this conspiracy of the Jewish-Anglo-Saxon warmongers and Jewish power holders of the Bolshevik Center in Moscow."

At his meeting with Molotov, Schulenburg delivered his government's message, although not hiding his disappointment with its contents that undid all his efforts to keep the peace between their two countries. Like the statement that Goebbels was reading out at the same time, it claimed that the Nazi regime had been forced "to take immediate military countermeasures" against the growing Russian threat on its borders. Incredibly, Molotov asked the German envoy what this statement could mean. As the Soviet note taker at the meeting reported drily, "Schulenburg replied that, in his opinion, it meant the beginning of the war."

Still acting as if Hitler could be convinced to change his decision, Molotov protested that Soviet troops were only involved in routine maneuvers, and there was no military buildup at the border. Schulenburg replied that there was nothing he could add on the subject. Molotov went back to Stalin to relay the news that "the German government has declared war on us." The Soviet leader muttered, "Ribbentrop deceived us, the scoundrel!"

But it was Stalin who had excelled at deceiving himself.

The invaders were astonished that—despite all their preparations, which had been impossible to hide—the Red Army defenders were so clearly unprepared for their onslaught. "Tactical *surprise* of the enemy has apparently been achieved along the entire line," Halder wrote in his diary on day one. Two days later, Goebbels's diary entry read: "Military developments in the East are excellent beyond all our expectations."

Goebbels pointed with particular pride to the success of the Luftwaffe in targeting the Soviet air force, whose planes stood in neat formations on airfields in the western districts, offering ideal targets. As for the small number of Soviet planes that managed to take off, the propaganda chief noted, "They are falling like flies." On day one of the invasion, the Germans destroyed about twelve hundred Soviet planes in all, while Luftwaffe pilots freely roamed the skies, attacking ground troops and civilians at will. Major General I. I. Kopets, the commander of the Soviet air force for the Western Front, had vowed to shoot himself if his planes were wiped out in a surprise attack. Seeing the results of the first day, he did exactly that.

On the ground, the news was equally grim for the defenders—and equally astonishing for the attackers. Hans von Herwarth, the former diplomat in the German embassy in Moscow, crossed back into Soviet territory with the Wehrmacht. When his regiment's artillery let loose against the Red Army positions before dawn on June 22, this made "an awesome impression," he recalled, lighting up the terrain under the still-dark sky. For several hours, the defenders' guns were silent.

"We had caught them unprepared—and, as many Russians told us later, not even dressed for the day." This was hardly a unique experience. When German troops shelled the western Ukrainian city of Lvov, the Soviet troops there also failed to respond. After their commander was taken prisoner, he explained that at first he believed the Germans had hit them by mistake during a training exercise—and he had obeyed the orders not to respond to "provocations."

As Herwarth put it, "The fighting spirit of the Soviet infantry could not have been lower." Once his unit broke through enemy lines, "the soldiers of the Red Army abandoned all resistance, throwing away their weapons and waiting to be taken prisoner." Guarded often by a single German soldier, long lines of newly minted POWs marched wherever they were told. Herwarth described the captives as "uniformly cooperative and, equally important, the information they gave us was precise and reliable."

Nothing could have been more alarming to the bewildered Soviet leadership, which later would try to whitewash this litany of setbacks by claiming that its soldiers and civilians offered fierce resistance right from the start. In the ensuing mythology of the "Great Patriotic War," no one was willing to surrender voluntarily, and no one ever had any doubt that the Red Army under Stalin's brilliant leadership would emerge victorious in the long run. Those who were on both sides of the rapidly moving front lines knew differently. But soon the invaders' relentlessly brutal treatment of both Soviet POWs and the civilian population produced a new resolve to fight back.

During the first month, German troops took advantage of the Soviet forces' disarray to drive eastward at a staggering pace, advancing about 450 miles. The letters that Wehrmacht soldiers wrote home in those early days reflected their soaring morale. "I feel born anew," Lance Corporal Henry Nahler wrote on June 26. He described with evident pride the thunder produced by German weaponry during the initial assault; as German bombers appeared in the skies, he added, "people ran like mad along the roads with their belongings." He also reported that he was able to celebrate those early victories by drinking a bucket of fresh milk and eating two fresh eggs that he found in a barn. "Generally speaking, everything was very cozy and festive. The Russians didn't direct any artillery against us."

Others expressed their complete faith in Hitler's leadership. "If the Führer has decided to do something like this, he will certainly succeed," wrote a noncommissioned officer with the last name of Bering. A Lance Corporal von Dirdelsen boasted that his company had advanced twenty-five miles in the first three days, destroying three Soviet bunkers in the process. Although he admitted that many officers were killed during this initial push, he claimed their bravery served as inspiration for the others to fight harder. "We will defeat the country with the mad government and beat the Red Army," he proclaimed, echoing Nazi propaganda.

On the other side of the rapidly shifting front lines, the demoralization of the Red Army troops was easily understandable. Vyacheslav Dolgov, who had just graduated from military school the day before the invasion, was immediately sent to serve as a political officer in the Novgorod region on the northwestern front. More than sixty years later, as a retired general living in Moscow, he described himself as a true believer "in the iron fist and the genius of Stalin" in those days. But he also recalled vividly the fear all his fellow soldiers felt as they were sent into battle without even the most basic equipment. "We asked our commander to give us weapons, since we were sent to fight without guns. We were told to seize weapons from the enemy and defeat them with their guns," he recalled. "We would sometimes manage to get some guns from the Germans, but that was why there were so many casualties. I saw fields covered with dead bodies."

One reason why Dolgov's unit—and many others—were sent into battle with very few guns was that the Germans had quickly captured or destroyed large stockpiles of Soviet weapons and other supplies near the western border. They had been placed there with no consideration of the fact that this would make the job of the invaders all that much easier.

The results were macabre, contributing to the massive casualties of the defenders, which would soon total in the millions. Ilya Druzhnikov, a book illustrator in his midforties who was immediately called up and sent to the front with other recruits in cattle cars, recalled the scene of "total chaos" that greeted them. In his unit, there was only one rifle available for every ten men, which meant that unarmed men trailed every armed man. Whenever an armed man fell, the next man was supposed to pick up his weapon. The officers were ready to shoot anyone who dared move in the wrong direction—away from the fighting instead of right into it. Periodically, the recruits were ordered to go to the fields and strip the corpses of everything they could carry: weapons, ammunition, and clothing.

Not surprisingly, many Red Army troops looked for any way to surrender in those early days. It was the job of political officers such as Dolgov to prevent that, and he recalled seeing "cowards" surrendering in large numbers. "These were desperate Russian soldiers who had taken off their white underwear and were waving it to surrender," he said. Other soldiers fled into the woods, surviving there as long as they could by eating berries and boiling water from the bogs in their helmets after taking out the lining. Dolgov was wounded for the first of several times during the war. Of the two thousand to three thousand men in his regiment, only seventy-five survived.

In the early morning hours of June 22, as German troops were scoring their quick first victories, Soviet radio aired innocuous programming, ignoring the news from the front and the German radio broadcasts justifying the invasion. This official silence was another indicator of Stalin's unwillingness to acknowledge the rapidly escalating catastrophe on his country's western border. First, he was in denial about the reality of the invasion itself—and then in denial about the capabilities of his troops, who were singularly ill-prepared to fight back.

In the initial denial stage, defense commissioner Semyon Timoshenko called General Ivan Boldin, the deputy commander of the western military district, at his headquarters in Minsk. "Comrade Boldin, remember no action is to be taken against the Germans without our knowledge," Timoshenko told him. "Will you please tell [General Dmitry] Pavlov that Comrade Stalin has forbidden to open artillery fire against the Germans."

"But how is that possible?" Boldin yelled. "Our troops are in full retreat! Whole towns are in flames; people are being killed all over the place."

Once Stalin had to accept the overwhelming evidence that a full-scale invasion was under way, he started issuing new orders that reflected an equal level of ignorance about the balance of opposing forces. The Stavka, as the Soviet Supreme High Command was called, ordered frontier troops "to attack enemy forces with all the strength at their disposal, and to annihilate them wherever they had violated the Soviet border." As for the air force, it was ordered to strike "mighty blows" and "smash the main enemy troop concentrations and their aircraft on its airfields." Soviet bombers were supposed to hit the East Prussian cities of Königsberg and Memel; Soviet forces in the southwestern region were supposed to capture the Polish city of Lublin, thirty miles across the border.

Stalin's orders must have come across as the ravings of a madman. By the time those instructions were issued, much of the Soviet air force in the west was already destroyed, and most of the frontier Red Army frontier units had disintegrated.

On some level, the Soviet dictator understood that all of his actions could reflect badly on him. It was no accident that the orders flowing to the front were signed by Timoshenko, Zhukov, and Georgy Malenkov, a member of the Kremlin inner circle—but not by Stalin.

Once the assembled political and military leaders realized that they had to announce the fact that the war had started, they urged Stalin to do so. He ducked that responsibility. "Let Molotov speak," he said. His aides still tried to convince him that it wasn't the foreign minister but the supreme leader who people would expect to address them "at such a significant historical moment." But Stalin wouldn't budge. "That was certainly a mistake," Mikoyan wrote later. "However, Stalin was so depressed that he didn't know what to tell the nation."

Stalin helped Molotov draft his address, which he delivered on the radio at noon. Every Soviet citizen who was alive then still remembers this broadcast. Molotov called the German invasion "an unparalleled act of perfidy in the history of civilized nations." He pointed out that it occurred "despite the fact that there was a nonaggression pact, the terms of which were scrupulously observed by the Soviet Union." Completely overlooking his country's acquiescence and partnership in Nazi aggression up to that point, he denounced Germany's enslavement of "the French, the Czechs, the Poles, the Serbs, and the peoples of Norway, Denmark, Holland, Belgium, Greece, and other countries." The "arrogant Hitler" would meet the same fate as Napoléon in Russia, he vowed. And in a final line that particularly resonated with his audience, he declared: "Our cause is just. The enemy will be crushed. Victory will be ours."

Soviet citizens far from the front may have taken this show of confidence at face value, and they may have believed the first Soviet radio bulletins about the fighting later that evening. Those broadcasts reported that the Germans had scored "minor successes" along the border, but, in most cases, "attacks were repelled with heavy enemy casualties." For his part, though, Stalin was increasingly aware of the desperation of the situation. German forces of Army Group Center, the troops that were driving straight east through Belorussia, were making rapid progress. On June 28, they captured the Belorussian capital of Minsk, trapping four hundred thousand Red Army troops.

The city may not have been a major strategic target, but Stalin had expressed his determination to defend it. The loss hit him hard. The next day, he told his entourage: "Lenin left us a great inheritance and we, his heirs, have fucked it all up!"

After that dire pronouncement, Stalin retreated to his dacha, where he would lie down without undressing but mostly pace restlessly from room to room, eying Lenin's illuminated portrait and the three phones there, expecting more bad news. The following day, he did not follow his normal routine of returning to the Kremlin. Callers were told "Comrade Stalin is not here and is unlikely to be here." For two days, Politburo members and other top officials were left to wonder whether he was still in charge or had suffered some sort of breakdown. According to Mikoyan's account, "Molotov said that Stalin was in such a state of prostration that he wasn't interested in anything, he'd lost all initiative and was in a bad way."

A delegation of Politburo members, including Molotov and Mikoyan, finally made their way nervously to the dacha. They feared Stalin, but they feared a leadership vacuum even more, especially at such a critical time. When they arrived, they found Stalin seated in an armchair in the small dining room. He looked at the visitors and asked, "What have you come for?" As Mikoyan recalled, "He had the strangest look on his face, and the question itself was pretty strange, too. After all, he should have called us in." Mikoyan realized that Stalin assumed that they were about to arrest him.

Molotov told Stalin about the proposal to set up a State Defense Committee to preside over the war effort. "With whom as its head?" Stalin asked suspiciously. Both Molotov and secret police chief Beria told him he would be in charge. Stalin looked both surprised and relieved. "Fine," he said. For a leader who was always convinced he was surrounded by potential enemies and assassins, this was the moment when he could begin to shed his worst fears.

But the results of Stalin's stubborn refusal to heed the multiple warnings about the looming German invasion—along with his colossal mistake of seeking to reassure Hitler by avoiding anything that looked like overt preparation for war—were all too visible. He seemed to have undergone a startling transformation: he no longer projected the image of the all-powerful tyrant. Khrushchev observed that in those early days, he was "a different Stalin, a bag of bones in a gray tunic."

When Khrushchev told Stalin that the fighting was going badly because so many Red Army troops lacked weapons, Stalin did not try to pretend this was not the case. "Well, they talk about how smart Russians are," he replied in a low voice. "Look how smart we are now."

Stalin's sardonic remark was little consolation to Khrushchev when he called later from Kiev to ask for weapons. According to Khrushchev's account, that led to the following testy exchange when he got Malenkov on the line:

"Tell me, where can we get rifles?" Khrushchev asked. "We've got factory workers here who want to join the ranks of the Red Army to fight the Germans, and we don't have anything to arm them with."

"You'd better give up any thought of getting rifles from us," Malenkov replied. "The rifles in the civil defense organization here have all been sent to Leningrad."

"Then what are we supposed to fight with?"

"I don't know—pikes, swords, homemade weapons, anything you can make in your own factories."

"You mean we should fight tanks with spears?"

"You'll have to do the best you can. You can make firebombs out of bottles of gasoline or kerosene and throw them at the tanks."

Khrushchev felt "dismay and indignation" at what he saw as the consequence of Stalin's string of misjudgments and lack of preparation. "Here we were, trying to hold back an invasion without rifles and machine guns, not to mention artillery or mechanized weapons!" he lamented.

Given the realities of Stalin's Soviet Union, only one man could aspire to rebuild his countrymen's confidence that they could not only withstand the German onslaught but also emerge victorious in the long run. And it had to be someone who no longer looked or sounded like "a bag of bones in a gray tunic."

Stalin finally addressed his countrymen over the radio on July 3, seeking to boost their morale at a time when his troops were still suffering defeat after defeat. The most important part of the speech turned out to be its opening lines, even before he began his account of the military situation. "Comrades! Brothers and sisters! Men of our army and navy! I am addressing you, my friends!" Stalin declared.

In another country, such a greeting might have sounded perfectly normal—but not in the Soviet Union. Stalin had never before addressed his people as "brothers and sisters" and "my friends." All of his actions and words had made clear that they were merely his subjects. Now the despot was appealing to them as partners in the common struggle. This was unprecedented—and his listeners felt it. They also understood that his speech carried much more weight than Molotov's and signaled that Stalin was fully in charge again.

The body of his speech was a mixture of half-truths and outright lies, along with a heavy dose of self-justification and predictable threats, aimed not just at the Germans but also at his countrymen. Although he was appealing to them in more human terms than before, the Stalin who was reassuming his leadership role was still the Stalin of old. For those who were used to submitting to his will, whatever the price, this, too, offered a form of reassurance.

Stalin praised "the heroic resistance of the Red Army," claiming that they had already destroyed the "finest divisions and finest air force units" of the German invaders. While admitting that "the enemy continues to push forward, hurling fresh forces into the attack," he insisted that those gains were only temporary. "History shows that there are no invincible armies and never have been," he declared, echoing his speech to the graduates of the military academy in May. "Napoléon's army was considered invincible but was successfully beaten by Russian, English, and German armies." Like Napoléon's forces, he vowed, the German invaders "will be smashed" on Soviet soil.

Trying to explain the speed of the German drive eastward from the border, he pinned the blame on "conditions favorable for the German forces and unfavorable for the Soviet forces." The German forces were fully mobilized, he added, "whereas Soviet troops had still to effect mobilization and move up to the frontier." Predictably, he failed to accept his responsibility for this state of affairs. Instead, the culprits were the Germans who had "treacherously" violated the nonaggression pact.

To justify his deal with Hitler, Stalin claimed that it "secured our country peace for a year and a half and the opportunity of preparing its forces to repulse Fascist Germany should she risk an attack on our country despite the pact." The problem with this reasoning was that it was contradicted by his admission that his forces were not prepared when the attack came. But he was counting on his countrymen to accept his reasoning, no matter how contorted and contradictory it was. In Stalin's universe, his pronouncements were correct simply because they came from him, the *vozhd*—the leader—and woe to anyone who suggested otherwise.

To drive home that message, he also promised to wage "a ruthless fight against all disorganizers of the rear, deserters, panic-mongers" and to "exterminate spies, saboteurs, and enemy parachutists." Military tribunals would mete out justice to anyone guilty of "panic-mongering and cowardice." Whenever retreat would prove to be absolutely necessary, he added, all equipment and supplies had to be evacuated or destroyed. "The enemy must not be left a single engine, a single railway car, not a single kilogram of grain or a liter of fuel," he said. The fact that this would leave nothing for civilians caught in the struggle either was of no concern to him.

Stalin had taken a few sensible steps during the tumultuous period between the start of the German invasion and his speech. On June 24, for example, he set up a Council of Evacuation, acknowledging implicitly that German forces were likely to gain control of large swathes of Soviet territory for the indefinite future. Its assignment was to transport entire factories, their workers, and supplies to eastern regions of the country beyond the reach of the Germans. Under its auspices, 2,593 major enterprises were among the approximately 50,000 smaller factories and workshops that were soon shipped eastward. Their equipment was broken down on the original premises, loaded up, and then reassembled at their new locations by evacuated workers, often in brutally harsh conditions.

On July 3, even before Stalin delivered his radio address that evening, a top secret part of the emergency plans was put in motion: the evacuation of Lenin's mummified body from the mausoleum in Moscow's Red Square to Tyumen, a small city more than a thousand miles due east of the capital. This was no minor detail of the much more elaborate preparations to evacuate factories and machinery: Stalin saw the preservation of his predecessor's body as absolutely critical to continuing his rule.

The deification of Lenin was both a means of solidifying the mythology of the Bolshevik Revolution that he had led, and of legitimizing his successor's stranglehold on power. If the German invaders managed to reach Moscow—which, given their rapid progress to date, seemed increasingly probable—and if they then seized Lenin's body, this would be both a major military victory and a crushing political and psychological blow. It would represent the triumph of Fascism over Communism, the cult of Hitler over the cult of Lenin—and, by extension, of Stalin. As long as the capital was in danger, the Soviet leader and his Politburo were determined to keep Lenin's body safe.

But keeping Lenin intact was no easy matter, even in the mausoleum. When I interviewed him in 2004, Ilya Zbarsky was the sole survivor of the handful of caretakers who accompanied Lenin's body on the journey to Tyumen. (He died in 2007.) His father, Boris Zbarsky, was one of the two men who had carried out the original daring embalming work on Lenin, which involved removing his internal organs and soaking the body in chemical baths; he was also put in charge of moving the body to safety. In 1934 Ilya, who was studying biochemistry at Moscow State University, had joined his father as part of the mausoleum's team of scientists who constantly worked on preserving Lenin's body for viewing.

On the evening of July 3, NKVD cars picked up Boris, Ilya, Sergei Mardashev, who was another member of the preservation team, and their families, depositing them at a siding of Moscow's Yaroslavsky Station. They then boarded a special train that carried them and forty Kremlin guards on their four-day journey with their precious cargo. The train wasn't refrigerated, which meant that the scientists had to work hard to protect the body, lying in a wooden coffin, from deterioration in the stifling summer heat. Ilya put curtains on the windows to block out the sun, switching shifts with his father and Mardashev. They took turns dabbing the body with special fluids as the train moved steadily through an unending string of green signals.

In Tyumen, Lenin was treated as a "secret object," hidden away in a two-story, guarded tsarist villa. There, too, the scientists had to deal with the lack of refrigeration, soaking Lenin in chemical baths about 70 percent of the time, according to Ilya's estimate. Although the threat to Moscow receded in 1942, Stalin did not allow the body to return until March 1945, as the war was ending. Ilya Zbarsky later viewed Lenin as "more a symbol of terror than a hero," but he still exuded a quiet pride that he had been part of the team that preserved him during the war—out of Hitler's reach.

As more reports of his troops' rapid progress came in, Hitler felt almost giddy at times. He had been determined to attack the Soviet Union for a long time, but he knew he was taking a huge risk.

"Since I struggled through to this decision, I again feel spiritually free," he wrote to Mussolini. "I am now relieved of these mental agonies." On the same day that Stalin delivered his radio address, General Halder wrote in his diary: "It is thus probably no overstatement to say that the Russian campaign has been won in the space of two weeks." But he added a note of caution: "The sheer geographical vastness of the country and the stubbornness of the resistance, which is carried on by all means, will claim our efforts for many weeks to come."

The clear implication was that the backbone of the Red Army had been broken already—and that German forces would be engaged in a mopping-up operation over many more weeks, not months. This left Hitler free to contemplate the fall of the major Soviet targets in the very near future.

On July 8 Halder wrote in his diary: "It is the Führer's firm decision to level Moscow and Leningrad and make them uninhabitable, so as to relieve us of the necessity of having to feed the populations through the winter. The cities will be razed by the air force. Tanks must not be used for that purpose." Then in a sentence that appeared to quote Hitler directly, he wrote: "A national catastrophe which will deprive not only Bolshevism, but also Muscovite nationalism, of their centers."

On July 14, Halder marveled at the "astonishing progress" of General Guderian's panzer forces. "Some of the enemy are running away in wild flight, some are making a stand," he reported. Two days later, "Schneller [speedy] Heinz," as the tank commander was called, reached Smolensk, the next big city to fall after Minsk. Once again, the Germans encircled hundreds of thousands of Red Army troops, killing or capturing most of them. The invasion was only three weeks old, but Moscow was a mere 230 miles farther east. On July 21 German bombers attacked the Soviet capital for the first time. Stalin's assurances notwithstanding, the Red Army looked like it wasn't capable of stopping the German forces from continuing their drive all the way to Moscow—if Hitler ordered them to do so.

Over dinner with his entourage on July 27, Hitler was in an expansive mood, outlining his vision not just for Moscow and Leningrad but also for the entire territory he expected to conquer. The new German empire, he explained, would extend 200 to 300 kilometers (124 to 186 miles) east of the Urals. While the invading force numbered in the millions, he was convinced that the new German masters would be able to control that expanse "with 250,000 men plus a cadre of good administrators." He pointed to the British Empire as the source of his confidence that such a modest occupation force could rule effectively. "Let's learn from the English, who, with 250,000 men in all, including 50,000 soldiers, govern 400 million Indians. This space must always be governed by Germans."

But he quickly made clear that he was not contemplating anything resembling a semi-enlightened form of colonialism, which might also include a modicum of decent treatment of the conquered peoples. They would be subjugated mercilessly and denied basic education, he declared. The goal would be "to Germanize this country by the immigration of Germans and look upon the natives as redskins. . . . In this business, I shall go ahead cold-bloodedly."

Yet at this critical juncture, with Operation Barbarossa only five weeks old, Hitler was far more conflicted than he appeared at such gatherings. On July 28, just a day after his discourse about the future of the German empire, he confided his doubts while strolling with his adjutants Gerhard Engel and Rudolf Schmundt in Wolf's Lair, his military headquarters in East Prussia. Engel noted in his diary that Hitler "was not sleeping at night, since he was uncertain about many things." The focus of that uncertainty had to do with his sense that he had to make a choice about how best to capitalize on the early victories of his troops—in other words, where they should concentrate their efforts next. As Engel put it, "Within his breast, two souls wrestled: the political-strategic, and the economic."

If Hitler chose to make political-strategic goals his priority, "he would say that the two principal suppurating boils had to be got rid of: Leningrad and Moscow," Engel continued. "That would be the heaviest blow for the Russian people and the Communist Party."

But if Hitler chose to focus on economic targets, his priorities would be quite different, according to Engel. "Whereas Moscow was a big industrial center, the south was more important, where oil, wheat, more or less everything was located necessary to keep the country going. A land where milk and honey flowed." That land, as Hitler had explained as far back as when he wrote *Mein Kampf*, was the Ukraine.

Hitler believed that the choice between politics and economics came down to a decision whether his forces should attack Moscow or Kiev first. This was a decision that could prove as significant as Stalin's stubborn refusal to believe that Germany would strike when it did. In the war in the east, the two tyrants were alike in insisting that only they could make those calls—for better or worse.

As Halder had already recorded in his diary, German forces were encountering stiff resistance in some places where they least expected it, even as they overran many of the Red Army units in the early days of the invasion. At the Brest fortress right across the border, for example, Soviet troops, along with their wives and children, held out under a steady barrage of German artillery and machine-gun fire longer than seemed humanly possible. Some of them kept fighting from the fort's tunnels and ramparts for up to a month. The Germans had expected to sweep by the fortress quickly; instead, they found themselves almost pleading as they appealed to the holdouts over loudspeakers. "Russians surrender. German command guarantees your lives," they declared. "Moscow has already capitulated." German pilots dropped leaflets all along the Red Army front lines repeating this outlandish claim. "Moscow has surrendered," they asserted. "Any further resistance is useless. Surrender to victorious Germany now."

There was a special irony to the lengthy delay at Brest. The city was a part of Poland before the war, and when the Germans invaded in 1939, Polish troops had also made a stand in and around the same fortress. (My father was one of the Polish defenders who survived.) After Soviet forces had invaded Poland from the east, and Hitler and Stalin agreed on a division of the spoils, the Germans had handed Brest over to the Red Army.

Fedor von Bock, the commander of Army Group Center, was struck by the determination of the Red Army in Brest. "The Russians are defending themselves stubbornly," he wrote in his diary on June 23. "Women have often been seen in combat. According to statements made by prisoners, political commissars are spurring maximum resistance by reporting that we kill all prisoners! Here and there Russian officers have shot themselves to avoid being captured."

On June 27, five days after the start of the invasion, Goebbels conceded in his diary that the battles weren't as one-sided as his propaganda was making them out to be. "The Russians are suffering huge losses in tanks and aircraft," he wrote. "But they are fighting well and have learned a great deal since Sunday [the day of the invasion]." Two days later, Halder mentioned reports "that the Russians are fighting to the last man."

The other obstacle the Germans faced was the abysmal state of Russia's road network—contrary to Halder's preinvasion "intelligence" that it was better than assumed. "We were not prepared for what we found because all of our maps in no way corresponded to reality," General Gotthard Heinrici recalled after the war. In the same June 23 diary entry where Bock noted the fierce resistance of the Red Army at Brest, he complained: "Lack of culture and the state of the roads are indescribable."

German officers discovered quickly that most of the roads marked on their maps were unpaved and often woefully neglected. In the dry days of summer, they usually served their purpose, but as soon as the rains started, they turned into mud swamps. On July 7 Bock bemoaned the fact that his Fourth Panzer Army had been caught in the rain for two days—enough to offer a preview of the much bigger problems they would face in the late summer and fall. "This has made the conditions of the roads frightful and placed an unusually heavy strain on men and materiel," he wrote.

All of which signaled that, despite their initial progress, German forces were in for a long slog, in the literal and broader sense, if they did not score close to a knockout blow during that first summer. When Napoléon had invaded Russia 129 years earlier, also in late June, his Grande Armée made it all the way to Moscow—which was abandoned by the Russians and partly set ablaze. Forced to retreat after failing to score a decisive victory over the scattered Russian forces, his troops froze and starved in the harsh winter conditions, while Cossacks torched villages and fields that might have provided them sustenance. Of the 550,000 to 600,000 French and allied troops who took part in Napoléon's Russian campaign, about 400,000 perished, with less than a quarter of that number dying in battle.

Hitler had always insisted that his far bigger, modern army was capable of achieving victory before it would have to face similar winter conditions. But there were signs early on that he was more worried about Napoléon's example than he let on—and that this was influencing his thinking about where to concentrate his forces next. "The Führer has an instinctive aversion to treading the same path as Napoléon," General Jodl explained. "Moscow gives him a sinister feeling. He fears that there might be a life-and-death struggle with Bolshevism."

To be sure, Hitler was in exactly that kind of life-and-death struggle with Bolshevism already, triggered by the launch of Operation Barbarossa. But from the beginning, he emitted conflicting signals about duplicating Napoléon's march on Moscow, despite his predictions of easy conquests. Goebbels, always attuned to Hitler's thinking, noted in his diary on July 4 the "excellent" situation on the central front but added: "I ban any special emphasis on Moscow from German propaganda. We must beware of fixing the gaze on this one, fascinating goal."

Hermann Göring had tried to convince Hitler that the destruction of Moscow "could be done by the Luftwaffe alone," as Engel noted in his diary. But the Führer's adjutant also pointed out that Hitler had become "a little skeptical" of Göring's claims after his failure to deliver on his promise to bomb the Allied troops gathered at Dunkirk a year earlier. He had assured Hitler that there was no need to send troops into the French port, since his planes could do the job more effectively. Guderian had expected to attack Dunkirk with his tanks, only to be stopped by Hitler's order, which allowed the successful evacuation of British and French troops there. The panzer commander was angered by Hitler's decision then, convinced that he had missed an opportunity to cripple Britain's military forces—and he was equally incensed when the German leader began reconsidering the plans to take Moscow.

So was Bock, his commander of Army Group Center. On July 13 he wrote in his diary: "The enemy is only really beaten at one place on the Eastern Front—opposite Army Group Center. . . . What matters now is to completely smash this foe and make it impossible for him to establish another new front before Moscow."

But Hitler was suddenly unwilling to act decisively, demonstrating a lack of the audacity that had propelled his forces to earlier victories. On July 28 his aide Schmundt visited Bock to brief him on Hitler's priorities. A clearly angry Bock summarized Hitler's message in his diary: "The main thing is to eliminate the area of Leningrad, then the raw materials region of the Donets Basin [in the Ukraine]. The Führer cares nothing about Moscow itself." Two days later, Hitler's Directive Number 34 stated: "Army Group Center will go over to the defensive, taking advantage of the suitable terrain." In other words, he was instructing his troops to put off any plans to reach Moscow.

Both Bock and Guderian, whose troops were already putting up signs reading "To Moscow," were infuriated by the new orders. When Guderian flew to his army group's headquarters, he was instructed to send his tanks and troops to join the fighting around Gomel, a city southwest of their current location in Smolensk—"that is to say, toward Germany," as Guderian noted. When he, too, met Schmundt, Guderian urged him to convince Hitler to reconsider his decision in favor of "a direct push to capture Moscow, the heart of Russia."

A new directive from Hitler's headquarters on August 12 appeared to contradict Schmundt's assertion that the German leader no longer cared about the Soviet capital. It declared that the goal was still "to deprive the enemy, before the coming winter, of his government, armament, and traffic around Moscow, and thus prevent the rebuilding of his defeated forces and the orderly working of government control." But—and here was the catch—it called for delaying the efforts to achieve that goal. "Before the beginning of the attack on Moscow, operations around Leningrad must be concluded," it stated.

When Walter von Brauchitsch, the commander of the army, tried to argue for a resumption of the drive on Moscow on August 18, Hitler responded that the army's plan "is not in accordance with my intentions." He spelled out his new priorities: "The most important aim to be achieved before the onset of winter is not to capture Moscow but to seize the Crimea and the industrial and coal region on the Donets, and to cut off the Russian oil supply from the Caucasus area. In the North, the aim is to cut off Leningrad and to join with the Finns."

Toward the end of August, Guderian flew to Wolf's Lair to make a final attempt to dissuade Hitler from sending his troops south to Kiev instead of east to Moscow. But by then, Brauchitsch was no longer willing to back him—and, in fact, he tried to block him from making his case. "I forbid you to mention the question of Moscow to the Führer," he told him. "The operation to the south has been ordered. The problem now is simply how it is to be carried out. Discussion is pointless."

Guderian was not easily put off. Joining a meeting between Hitler and his top generals, he seized the opportunity to make his case. When Hitler asked him whether his troops were capable of "making another great effort," he replied: "If the troops are given a major objective, the importance of which is apparent to every soldier, yes."

"You mean, of course, Moscow?" Hitler said.

Guderian replied "Yes" and asked for the chance to spell out his reasons. He pointed out Moscow's role as the country's major communication and transportation hub, a major industrial center, and "the political solar plexus" of the country. He argued that its capture would have "an enormous psychological effort" on Russia and the world. This, in turn, would make it easier to score victories elsewhere, including in the Ukraine. But he warned that if his and other troops were diverted to other targets, "it would then be too late to strike the final blow for Moscow this year." Like most officers, he was acutely conscious of the dangers of waiting until the onset of fall and winter weather, when conditions for any major new military push would become increasingly difficult.

Hitler did not interrupt him, but he wasn't swayed, either. He returned to his theory that the most important task was to seize the agricultural and raw material resources of the Ukraine first. "My generals know nothing about the economic aspects of the war," he declared, leaving no doubt that he was sticking with his orders to make Kiev the next target. Guderian was dismayed to see all the others in the room nodding in agreement. He felt completely alone, abandoned by even those who had earlier agreed with the argument that Moscow was far more important.

As a result, Guderian found himself fighting in the battle for Kiev during the first half of September. The German forces carried out the kind of pincer movements they had used at Minsk and Bialystok, inflicting massive casualties on the Russian defenders and rounding up hundreds of thousands more prisoners. But it was a grueling battle, fought in part in pouring rain, suggesting that the hardships would only multiply in quick order. "Only a man who has personally experienced what life on those canals of mud we called roads was like can form any picture of what the troops and their equipment had to put up with and can truly judge the situation at the front and the consequent effects on our operations," Guderian wrote.

Hitler was not such a man. Despite the cost of the victory of Kiev, he signaled a return to the plan to seize Moscow. On September 6 he ordered other units of Army Group Center to focus on "destroying the enemy forces located in the area east of Smolensk by a pincer movement in the general direction of Vyazma"—the next key town and railroad junction on the road to Moscow. And on September 16 Hitler issued the directive that would be the basis for launching Operation Typhoon, the drive against Moscow, on September 30.

It looked increasingly like Hitler believed his forces could do it all: not just achieve his goals in the Ukraine but also mount a successful assault on the Soviet capital in quick succession.

In his postwar memoirs, Erich von Manstein, the skilled military strategist who served as the commander of the Fifty-Sixth Panzer Corps during Operation Barbarossa, described the tensions between Hitler and his generals in this pivotal moment. The German dictator, he noted, was "utterly unscrupulous, highly intelligent, and possessed of an indomitable will." He did not hesitate to contradict Halder and other generals, telling them that as a frontline infantryman in World War I, he had better military instincts than they did as professional officers. Manstein admired Hitler's grasp of military technology and other subjects, but he was far from convinced. "What he lacked, broadly speaking, was simply *military ability based on experience*—something for which his 'intuition' was no substitute," he wrote.

While the commanders wanted to focus their military might in the center of the front where they were strongest, Hitler believed he could send his main force in multiple directions. Given "the vastness of theater of operations, Germany did not possess adequate forces" to succeed with such a diffuse strategy, Manstein concluded.

What prompted Hitler to be so sure he could succeed, disregarding the pleas of his commanders to keep the focus on Moscow? Part of the answer could be found in his conviction that his earlier military victories, which led to the conquest of most of the rest of Europe, were a product of what he believed to be his audacious genius, despite many similar warnings that he would fail. More often than not, he truly believed that he could do no wrong. But those closest to him, like Engel, also realized that at other times, despite his efforts to project an image of utter certainty, he could be indecisive and jittery.

In the case of his decision to overrule his generals, another factor may have been involved. Norman Ohler, the author of *Blitzed: Drugs in the Third Reich,* first published in Germany in 2015 and then in English in 2017, reported that Hitler's quack doctor Theodor Morell began administering heavy doses of steroids and other doping agents to him after he fell ill with fever and diarrhea in his bunker at Wolf's Lair in August 1941. As Hitler became more and more dependent on Morell's improvised mixtures of drugs, his natural tendency to believe in his own infallibility was strengthened, even as "the injections began to throw his body into chaos," Ohler maintained.

Ohler's carefully researched study also revealed the extent that German troops were pumped up with the methamphetamine Pervitin, especially during the blitzkrieg attacks on Poland, France, and then the Soviet Union. The German military soon cut back on the distribution of those "boosting pills" once it became apparent that they were both addictive and, for some soldiers, highly dangerous. But Morell ignored all such evidence as he continued to treat his patient with more and more injections, which may help explain some of Hitler's increasingly bizarre behavior as the war progressed.

Like Stalin, Hitler was already convinced that no one was more capable than he was. Given their predispositions, it was hardly surprising that both leaders were quite capable of making major mistakes.

The difference was that Stalin's major mistakes came early on, when he ignored the signals that the Germans were about to attack and left his troops woefully exposed, unprepared, and underequipped as they faced the invaders, leading to staggering loses. Hitler's mistakes were about to become much more apparent as the fighting continued into late summer and early fall.

At times, it appeared that the two men were competing for the title of "the world's most willfully blind dictator." It was their calculations—and, more significantly, gross miscalculations—that were determining the trajectory of the war.

SIX

"STEP ON IT!"

R*eturning to London on Friday,* June 20, after a trip to the United States, Ambassador Winant looked "very tired and disheveled," as his military attaché General Lee recalled. This was hardly surprising. His short trip back was packed with briefings on Lend-Lease and other forms of US-British cooperation, along with broader discussions about the state of the war that generated conflicting headlines. "Winant Reports Britain Thinks Victory Certain," one read, while another proclaimed: "British Position Extremely Grave but Not Disastrous, Winant Says."

Although formally not yet a belligerent, the United States was increasingly a party to the conflict. On May 21 a German U-boat had sunk the SS *Robin Moor*, an American cargo ship, in the South Atlantic. Roosevelt told Congress later that this was "a warning that the United States may use the high seas of the world only with Nazi consent"—and that his administration would never yield to such pressure. Winant believed he had been targeted personally by the Nazis when he had taken off for Lisbon on the first leg of his trip back to the United States in late May. In a clear security breach, his embassy had released the date of his trip and its planned route. "The Germans picked up the information and sent out a plane to intercept us," he wrote, "but the British had provided fighter escort planes, and the German was shot down."

Winant kept his visit short because of the pending German invasion of the Soviet Union, which was anticipated by Churchill and Roosevelt, if not by Stalin. Winant was convinced that his urgent need to return to London "contributed to an accident I can never forget." When his flight's captain landed in Montreal because of engine trouble, Winant insisted that they fix the problem immediately and keep flying rather than spend the night there. As a result, the captain kept the propellers running after they landed while an engineer came out to check on the plane. In the nighttime darkness, a young soldier on guard duty walked into one of the spinning propellers and was immediately cut to pieces.

All of which undoubtedly added to Winant's physical and emotional exhaustion upon his return. But he had barely stepped out of his plane when he received an invitation to spend the weekend with Churchill and Eden at Chequers. As Lee noted, the ambassador probably would have preferred to spend the weekend recovering from his journey, but the British leaders "want to find out exactly what is going on in Washington as soon as possible." Lee added that "things are at such a critical pass in view of the Russian crisis that there is no time to be lost by anybody."

Churchill had cabled Roosevelt a week earlier to let him know that the German attack was imminent, checking to make sure the two of them were in agreement on their reaction to this anticipated development. "Should this new war break out, we shall, of course, give all encouragement and any help we can spare to the Russians, following the principle that Hitler is the foe we have to beat," he wrote. Upon his arrival at Chequers, Winant relayed Roosevelt's response that, if the Germans launched their invasion as expected, he would support publicly "any announcement that the prime minister might make welcoming Russia as an ally."

At dinner on Saturday, Churchill hosted Winant along with Eden, Cabinet Secretary Edward Bridges, and their wives. The British leader repeated that a German attack on Russia was now certain, and that Hitler was hoping to garner support from right-wingers in both Britain and the United States for that action. But the German dictator would be proven wrong, Churchill insisted, and everything should be done to help Russia. Winant assured him that his country would take the same attitude.

After dinner, Churchill took a walk on the croquet lawn with Colville, picking up on the same theme. The private secretary asked him whether, as a staunch anti-Communist, he wasn't troubled by the notion of helping the Kremlin. "Not at all," Churchill replied. "I have only one purpose, the destruction of Hitler, and my life is much simplified thereby. If Hitler invaded hell, I would make at least a favorable reference to the devil in the House of Commons."

Woken at four the next morning by a call with the news about the German attack, Colville made the rounds of the bedrooms of Churchill, Eden, and Winant to relay the information, producing "a smile of satisfaction" from each of them, as he recalled. Churchill's butler appeared in Eden's bedroom and presented him a large cigar on a silver platter. "The prime minister's compliments, and the German armies have invaded Russia," he declared. As Eden noted later, "We savored the relief, but not for me at that hour the cigar." Instead, he and Churchill immediately began discussing how to react.

Churchill started working on a radio address to be broadcast by the BBC that evening. Despite the gravity of the situation, he acknowledged the irony of the task ahead of him: pledging support for the other totalitarian state based on terror. Sir Stafford Cripps, the British ambassador to Moscow, was also visiting Chequers that weekend. During lunch, as Colville recorded in his diary, Churchill teased Cripps that "Russians were barbarians," and that "not even the slenderest thread connected Communism to the very basest type of humanity"—in other words, it was a completely inhumane system.

According to Colville's account, "Cripps took it all in good part and was amused."

Eden was less amused when he realized that he would not have time to vet Churchill's address, since the prime minister did not finish writing it until twenty minutes before he went on the air. He need not have worried, since it proved to be another masterful Churchill performance.

"We have reached one of the climacterics of the war," the prime minister declared. "Hitler is a monster of wickedness, insatiable in his lust for blood and plunder." He added that the German attack was no surprise to him, and that he had warned Stalin that it was coming. He did not specifically point out that Stalin had ignored his and other warnings, but it was not hard to read between the lines when he declared: "I can only hope that these warnings did not fall unheeded."

The critical sections of his speech spelled out the rationale for supporting the Soviet Union now that it was under attack. "The Nazi regime is indistinguishable from the worst features of Communism," he said. "No one has been a more consistent opponent of Communism than I have for the last twenty-five years. I will unsay no words that I've spoken about it. But all this fades away before the spectacle which is now unfolding." Just as he had told Colville and the others, there could be only "one aim and one single irrevocable purpose": the destruction of Hitler's regime. "From this nothing will turn us. Nothing."

Then, in one of his most famous oratorical formulations, he added: "We will never parlay; we will never negotiate with Hitler or any of his gang. We shall fight him by land; we shall fight him by sea; we shall fight him in the air, until, with God's help, we have rid the earth of his shadow and liberated its people from his yoke."

Pledging British help "to Russia and the Russian people," he also spoke with new assurance about Washington's role. "It is not for me to speak of the action of the United States, but this I will say: if Hitler imagines that his attack on Soviet Russia will cause the slightest division of aims or slackening of effort in the great democracies, who are resolved upon his doom, he is woefully mistaken."

Winant's latest message from Roosevelt had helped convince Churchill that he could make such a sweeping statement, even if both his government and Washington were far from confident that their predictions that Hitler's armies could be stopped would prove accurate anytime soon.

While welcoming the news that the Germans would now have to focus on the Eastern Front, providing at least some relief for Britain, many top officials in London and Washington were, in fact, decidedly pessimistic about the Red Army's chances against the invasion forces. On June 16 Cripps had told the War Cabinet that the consensus among fellow diplomats in Moscow was that Russia would not be able to hold out for more than three or four weeks. John Dill, the chief of the Imperial General Staff, told Eden that the Soviet side might be able to resist a little longer, but his general assessment circulated quickly that the Germans "would go through them like a hot knife through butter."

In Washington, Secretary of War Stimson provided Roosevelt with his forecast. "Germany will be thoroughly occupied in beating Russia for a minimum of one month and a possible maximum of three months," he wrote. But he still viewed Operation Barbarossa as "an almost providential occurrence," since it effectively ruled out an invasion of Britain and would limit Germany's ability to mount new offensives in Africa and the Middle East. It also offered new possibilities for Roosevelt, he added. "By this final demonstration of Nazi ambition and perfidy, the door is opened wide for you to lead directly toward the winning of the battle of the North Atlantic and the protection of our hemisphere in the South Atlantic."

In London, Soviet Ambassador Ivan Maisky was well aware of the "great skepticism concerning the Red Army's efficacy." He also recognized that, to put it mildly, his country had a public relations problem. He pointed out the "bewilderment" of the British people about the sudden change in the Soviet Union's role in the war. "Psychologically, this is quite understandable," he noted in his diary. "Only recently, 'Russia' was considered a covert ally of Germany, all but an enemy. And suddenly, within 24 hours, it has become a friend! This transition was too abrupt, and the British *mentality* has yet to adjust to the new state of affairs."

If anything, Maisky understated the intense resentment of his country's policies in many British circles. "Apart from the revolting record of the regime," General Hastings Ismay wrote, "their treachery in signing up with Hitler in August 1939 could not easily be forgiven, and they had done their best to damage our war effort ever since. How could we be friends with people like that?" Ismay also contemplated the same question that had been on the minds of some of his American counterparts earlier during the discussions about aid to Britain. If the forecasts of a quick German victory in Russia proved correct, he noted, any Western aid could end up in the wrong hands. "The help given to Stalin, at great sacrifice to ourselves, would have been wasted, and we ourselves would be in greater danger than ever."

Churchill hadn't forgotten the Kremlin's earlier behavior either or talked himself into believing that Stalin suddenly would be an ideal partner. Writing about Hitler's invasion of Russia in his memoirs, he offered a biting commentary: "Thus the ravings of hatred against Britain and the United States which the Soviet propaganda machine cast upon the midnight air were overwhelmed by the German cannonade. The wicked are not always clever, nor are dictators always right." But even the canny prime minister probably didn't realize just how much time and frustration would go into nurturing the relationship with the dictator who was now his ally.

Maisky praised Churchill's radio address promising aid to Russia.

"A forceful speech! A fine performance!" he wrote—but only in his diary. "Precisely what is most needed today." No such message was forthcoming from Stalin. In fact, Churchill was stunned that his strong declaration of support for the Soviet Union met with no reaction from the Kremlin. "The silence on the top level was oppressive," Churchill noted. Trying "to break the ice" and elicit a response, he wrote directly to Stalin on July 7, reiterating his promise of aid. "We shall do everything to help you that time, geography, and our growing resources allow," he declared. "The longer the war lasts, the more help we can give."

Stalin did not write a reply until July 18, finally thanking him for his assurances of support and describing their two countries as "fighting allies in the struggle against Hitlerite Germany." But that first letter also contained a demand that the Kremlin would consistently push from then on: the establishment of a second front against Hitler in the West—in other words, sending British troops to the Continent to fight the Germans there. "A front in northern France could not only divert Hitler's forces from the East, but at the same time it would make it impossible for Hitler to invade Great Britain," he asserted.

Churchill was glad to be communicating directly with Stalin, but he rejected the Soviet leader's appeal for a second front with barely concealed irritation. "You must remember that we have been fighting alone for more than a year, and that, though our resources are growing and will grow fast from now on, we are at the utmost strain both at home and in the Middle East by land and air," he wrote, explaining that British naval forces were also stretched to their limit in the Battle of the Atlantic.

But this and similar messages failed to stem a steady stream of such complaints and demands from the Soviet side. As Churchill put it, "I received many rebuffs and only rarely a kind word. . . . The Soviet government had the impression that they were conferring a great favor on us by fighting in their own country for their own lives."

At a time when they were in no position to contemplate anything of the sort, Britain's military leaders were particularly galled by Stalin's repeated demands for a second front. "He might as well have demanded the moon," Ismay wrote, acidly pointing out that the Kremlin leader had exhibited "neither penitence nor shame" for cutting a deal with Hitler in 1939 and assisting Germany with deliveries of supplies while Britain fought alone. "How tired we were to become of that slogan 'Second Front.'"

A. P. Herbert, a popular writer and independent member of Parliament, composed a poem encapsulating those feelings:

Let's have less nonsense, from the friends of Joe . . .
In 1940, when we bore the brunt.
We could have done, boys, with a Second Front.
A continent went down a cataract,
But Russia did not think it right to act.
Not ready? No. And who shall call her wrong?
Far better not to strike until you are strong.
Better, perhaps (though this was not our fate),
To make new treaties with the man you hate.
Alas! These shy maneuvers had to end
When Hitler leaped upon his largest friend
(And if he'd not, I wonder, by the way,
If Russia would be in the war to-day?)

But for all the justified grumbling and outright resentment of Russia, Churchill faced little internal opposition to his policy of providing aid to his country's new ally. Both government officials and ordinary citizens instinctively understood that the prime minister's approach offered the best possibility of capitalizing on the rapidly shifting constellation of forces. Strengthened Russian resistance to the German invaders would benefit Britain directly—and, indirectly at first, the United States. Ironically, it was Hitler's decision to strike that provided the most compelling rationale for the rapid emergence of the broadened alliance arrayed against him.

In the United States, the isolationists tried to seize on the escalation of the conflict in Europe to revive their drive to keep America out of the war. Shortly after the German invasion of the Soviet Union, Lindbergh ridiculed the notion of Russia as an ally in a speech to an America First rally in San Francisco. "The murderers and plunderers of yesterday are accepted as the valiant defenders of civilization today," he declared. Then, echoing the arguments he had made during the debate over the Lend-Lease Act, he added: "I tell you that I would a hundred times rather see my country ally itself with England, or even with Germany with all of her faults, than with the cruelty, the godlessness, and barbarism that exists in Soviet Russia. An alliance between the United States and Russia should be opposed by every American, by every Christian, and by every humanitarian in this country."

On the other end of the political spectrum, Communist Party activists in the United States, who had been holding "peace" rallies to denounce supporters of Britain as warmongers and imperialists, abruptly switched sides. As Roosevelt's aide Robert Sherwood noted with obvious delight, "The next day, the *Daily Worker* [the Communist newspaper] was pro-British, pro–Lend Lease, pro-interventionist, and, for the first time in two years, pro-Roosevelt."

Lindbergh was certainly vulnerable to the charge that he was an apologist for Hitler. "No one has ever heard Lindbergh utter a word of horror at, or even aversion to, the bloody career that the Nazis are following, nor a word of pity for the innocent men, women, and children who have been deliberately murdered by the Nazis in practically every country in Europe," Harold Ickes, Roosevelt's secretary of the interior, declared. At the same time, American Communists and their sympathizers, like most of their counterparts in Europe, had remained unabashed apologists for Stalin even during the period of his pact with Hitler. But, aside from the battle of the apologists, there was a more serious debate about how Washington should respond to the new situation that involved fundamental questions about the handling of Russia policy.

While Roosevelt had immediately followed Churchill's lead by offering "all the aid we possibly can to Russia," others in Washington were wary of that approach. On June 22, after hearing of the German invasion, Senator Harry Truman expressed the sentiments that, while hardly practical, reflected the ambivalence many Americans felt. "If we see that Germany is winning, we ought to help Russia, and if Russia is winning, we ought to help Germany, and that way let them kill as many as possible, although I don't want to see Hitler victorious under any circumstances."

George Kennan, who honed his analytical skills as a young US diplomat in Moscow in the 1930s and then served in the US embassy in Berlin, did not go that far—but he, too, voiced strong reservations to the policy Roosevelt was signaling. On June 24, in a letter from Berlin to Loy Henderson, a former Moscow colleague now back in the State Department, he warned that "we should do nothing at home to make it appear that we are following the course Churchill seems to have entered upon in extending moral support to the Russian cause."

Russia had "no claim on Western sympathies," Kennan argued, since it clearly wasn't fighting for the same ideals as the West. "Such a view would not preclude the extension of material aid wherever called for by our own self-interest," he concluded. "It would, however, preclude anything which might identify us politically or ideologically with the Russian war effort."

The origins of such disagreements about Russia could be traced back to the earliest days of the Roosevelt era. When the new president took office in 1933, he made it a priority to reach out to the Kremlin leaders, ending the long period when the United States and much of the West still treated them as representatives of an illegitimate, dangerous regime. On November 16 of that year Washington and Moscow formally established diplomatic relations, and Roosevelt dispatched William Bullitt, a fervent advocate of the new policy of rapprochement, as the first American ambassador to the Soviet Union.

But Bullitt would soon become disillusioned by Stalin's regime, particularly its paranoia and xenophobia that translated into successive waves of mass terror. The envoy also warned his superiors in Washington that the Soviet Union posed a real danger to the West, despite Roosevelt's hopes that it would develop more democratic institutions and abandon its aggressive notions about spreading Communism elsewhere. In a message to Secretary of State Hull on April 20, 1936, Bullitt wrote that it was Soviet policy to make friends with democrats "in order the better eventually to lead those democrats to the firing squad." Kennan and other younger diplomats within the embassy mostly supported the ambassador's views.

Roosevelt showed no inclination to accept such recommendations for a tougher policy based on a realistic appreciation of the nature of the Soviet regime. He replaced Bullitt with Joseph Davies, his friend who was married to General Foods heiress and major campaign contributor Marjorie Merriweather Post. Davies had no Russia expertise and accepted most Soviet propaganda at face value. He fawned over Stalin, extolling his "sly humor" and "great mentality" in a letter to his daughter on June 9, 1938, as he was wrapping up his two-year stint in Moscow. "It is sharp, shrewd, and, above all things else, wise, at least so it would appear to me," he wrote. "If you can picture a personality that is exactly opposite to what the most rabid anti-Stalinist anywhere could conceive, then you might picture this man."

Davies even attended some of the infamous purge trials, and his reports on them to Washington echoed Soviet accounts of these events. He wrote to Hull: "It is my opinion so far as the political defendants are concerned sufficient crimes under Soviet law, among those charged in the indictment, were established by the proof and beyond a reasonable doubt to justify the verdict of guilty of treason and the adjudication of the punishment provided by the Soviet criminal statutes." In other words, Stalin's regime was perfectly justified in executing the victims of the purges. Davies argued that, by executing all those it deemed to be its political opponents, the Soviet rulers had strengthened their position.

From his next posting in Brussels and later back in the United States, Davies continued to urge Roosevelt to share his benevolent view of the Kremlin. Shortly after the German invasion of the Soviet Union, Davies published his book *Mission to Moscow*, which reads almost like a parody of Soviet propaganda. Soviet leaders "are moved, basically, by altruistic concepts," he wrote. "It is their purpose to promote the brotherhood of man and to improve the lot of the common people. . . .They are devoted to peace." This did not prevent him from not only justifying Stalin's purges of the army and other institutions but also applauding them. "There were no fifth columnists in Russia in 1941—they had shot them," he declared. "The purge had cleansed the country and rid it of treason."

As German troops scored their initial victories in Operation Barbarossa, Davies wrote to Harry Hopkins in a somewhat more sober vein. He claimed that the Red Army "has been more effective than was generally expected" in early combat, while still acknowledging that the German offensive could succeed in capturing most of the European part of the country, including Moscow. But he predicted that, in such a scenario, Stalin and his government would operate from east of the Urals, coordinating continued resistance to the occupation force. To encourage Soviet resistance and ensure that Stalin was not tempted to strike a new bargain with Hitler, he urged Roosevelt to follow Churchill's lead by promising full support for Russia. "Word ought to be gotten to Stalin direct that our attitude is 'all out' to beat Hitler and that our historic policy of friendliness to Russia still exists," he concluded.

Diplomats such as Kennan who were pleading for a more nuanced approach—coupling any aid to the Soviet Union with a hardheaded evaluation of the nature of its regime—were appalled by Davies's performance as ambassador in Moscow and his subsequent pleading on behalf of the Kremlin. "Had the President wished to slap us down and to mock us for our efforts in the development of Soviet-American relations, he could not have done better with this appointment," Kennan stated, reflecting the view of many of his colleagues.

But Hopkins shared many of Davies's assumptions about Russia—and he became the point man on Russia policy in the immediate aftermath of the German invasion. This meant that the emerging new relationship between Moscow and Washington was already rigged in favor of an outcome that offered Stalin a distinct edge.

In mid-July Roosevelt sent Hopkins back to England to continue his discussions with Churchill and other British leaders about a broad range of subjects: the agenda for the upcoming Atlantic Conference, the first wartime meeting between him and Churchill, which was to take place at sea in August; the progress so far in delivering on Lend-Lease aid; and a general review of the state-of-play of the broader conflict, with a focus on the German campaign in Russia. As Sherwood pointed out, "all deliberation on all phases of the war at that time, including American production and Lend Lease, depended on the question of how long Russia could hold out." The problem was that both sides in the US-British talks had little idea how to answer that question.

In Moscow, the authorities displayed "unbelievable reticence" in sharing any information with the British military mission, as Colville noted in his diary. "Now, in their hour of need, the Soviet government—or at any rate—Molotov—is as suspicious and uncooperative as when we were negotiating a treaty in the summer of 1939," he added, alluding to the failed British-Soviet talks right before Stalin and Hitler made their pact.

Major Ivan Yeaton, the US military attaché in Moscow since 1939, was highly critical of his British counterparts, who he felt relied solely on official communiqués. He was equally critical of his predecessor, Colonel Philip Faymonville, who other staffers believed suffered from the same kind of "definite pro-Russian bias" as Ambassador Davies did. Yeaton scorned Faymonville's "dependence on Soviet handouts" and sought out military attachés from other embassies who shared his critical views. He also collected more than a dozen militia citations for violating the wartime travel rules, driving at night, and seeking to slip out of the city to get closer to the fighting.

By comparing his impressions with those of other foreigners and the accounts of refugees fleeing the German offensive, Yeaton wrote highly pessimistic assessments of the Soviet Union's chances of holding off the Germans. "I could find no shred of evidence on which to base an optimistic report," he recalled later. He added that his reports sparked resentment both among British officials and members of the Roosevelt team such as Hopkins, who were eager to find justification for an infusion of aid to the Soviet Union.

During Hopkins's July visit to London, he and Winant met with Maisky at the American embassy. According to the Soviet envoy, this produced no major breakthrough on aid. "Hopkins assured me that Roosevelt was ready to provide the USSR with every kind of support in the struggle against Hitler, but warned me at the same time against cultivating any illusions regarding the speed and scope of American armaments aid." Nonetheless, Maisky was intrigued by a question Hopkins asked: "What could be done to bring Roosevelt and Stalin closer?"

Maisky wasn't immediately sure what Hopkins was driving at, but he was impressed by his "obvious sympathy for the Soviet Union," and would later conclude that he was "much more sympathetic" to Soviet needs than Churchill was. In his memoirs, Maisky wrote, "Harry Hopkins has remained as one of the most advanced people among the leading personalities in the bourgeois world during the Second World War."

As Maisky learned two days after his initial meeting with Hopkins, the presidential envoy had a very specific goal in mind when he had talked about bringing the leaders of their two countries closer together. After consulting with Churchill about the possibility of arranging an RAF flight for him from Scotland to Russia, Hopkins sent a cable on July 25 to Roosevelt proposing that he make the trip. It would allow him to hear from Stalin directly about his country's prospects—and to encourage him to keep resisting the German invaders. "I think the stakes are so great that it should be done," he wrote. "Stalin would then know in an unmistakable way that we mean business on a long-term supply job."

Roosevelt promptly granted his approval but urged Hopkins to make the trip right away so that he could be sure to return in time for the Atlantic Conference scheduled for early August. Winant urgently tracked down Maisky late in the evening of July 28, calling him back to the American embassy. When the Soviet envoy arrived, Winant pulled out the passports of Hopkins and two assistants, saying only that they were leaving on a train for Invergordon, Scotland, in a half hour en route to a flight to the Soviet Union. "I'll explain everything to you afterward," Winant told him. "For now, just give me the visas."

There was no time to return to the Soviet embassy for the proper forms, and Maisky decided to improvise: he wrote out by hand an authorization in Hopkins's passport, adding only an official seal as a precaution. "Such a visa, I imagine, has never been recorded in the annals of our diplomacy," he noted in his diary. Winant rushed off to catch Hopkins at Euston Station, where he had already boarded the special train that was about to depart—and handed him his passport through the window. "I still believe that his journey was a turning point in the war," Winant wrote later, taking pride in his supporting role.

Ironically, though, none of that paperwork was necessary. By the time the RAF's Catalina seaplane took off on its mission with Hopkins sitting during much of the twenty-one-hour flight on the machine gunner's stool near the tail, a Soviet military delegation was fully prepped to greet Roosevelt's personal representative when he disembarked in the Russian city of Archangel—and never asked for his passport. Instead, they offered their guest his first taste of Soviet hospitality: a "monumental" four-hour meal, with multiple courses featuring cold fish and caviar, and the inevitable vodka toasts. "Vodka has authority," he reported later. "It is nothing for the amateur to trifle with." Then, after only two hours' sleep, he boarded his flight to Moscow, where he was met by Laurence Steinhardt, who had succeeded Davies as ambassador to Moscow.

When Roosevelt had appointed Steinhardt, he probably believed the new envoy would be nearly as pro-Soviet as Davies. A wealthy New York lawyer who had already served as ambassador to Sweden, Steinhardt was a liberal Democrat with family credentials that indicated as much. His uncle Samuel Untermeyer was a major campaign contributor who was openly sympathetic to the Soviet Union. But like Bullitt, the earlier predecessor, Steinhardt soon grew sharply critical of Soviet policies at home and abroad—and irritated by the heavy-handed Soviet surveillance, restrictions, and bureaucratic regulations that made life maddeningly difficult for his embassy's staff.

As Yeaton noted approvingly, the ambassador was "ready to stand up to Soviet obstruction tactics when necessary." In December 1940 Steinhardt told Hull and Welles, his superiors in Washington: "I think we should match every Soviet annoyance by a similar annoyance here against them." The Kremlin was not amused by such recommendations, and Soviet officials derided him in typically virulent fashion. Konstantin Umansky, his Soviet counterpart in Washington, called Steinhardt "a wealthy bourgeoisie Jew who was permeated with the foul smell of Zionism."

In his first conversations with Steinhardt, Hopkins asked whether Yeaton's cables about the military situation were accurate. In other words, was the war going as badly for the Russians as the military attaché maintained? Steinhardt offered a nuanced answer. He pointed out that Russia's historical record demonstrated that, while its troops performed ineptly at times, they fought fiercely when defending their homeland—which indicated they should not be underestimated. But it was extremely difficult to know where things stood, he added, because the Kremlin's obsessive secrecy and fear of foreigners meant that diplomats assigned to Moscow could only piece together fragmentary information. Hopkins replied that he viewed his visit as an opportunity to break through the wall of suspicion to obtain a fuller picture.

His means of doing so was to go straight to the top. Stalin was only too happy to receive him, spending several hours with him in face-to-face talks during the next two evenings. After Hopkins conveyed the messages of support from Roosevelt and Churchill, the Soviet leader provided an overview of the military situation and discussed his specific requests for supplies. Most significantly, he left his visitor in awe of him, which was clearly his goal. As Hopkins had told Maisky, he wanted to bring Stalin and Roosevelt closer together on a personal level—even if by proxy. His visit represented a major step in that direction, since it only strengthened Roosevelt's predisposition to believe that he could nurture a mutually beneficial relationship between them.

Hopkins was impressed as much by Stalin's delivery and appearance as by his message. "Not once did he repeat himself," he recalled later. "He talked as he knew his troops were shooting—straight and hard." He described Stalin as "an austere, rugged, determined figure in boots that shone like mirrors, stout baggy trousers, and snug-fitting blouse. He wore no ornament, military or civilian." As Hopkins saw it, even Stalin's short stature was another indication of his strength. "He's built close to the ground, like a football coach's dream of a tackle," he declared. "He's about five foot six, about a hundred and ninety pounds. His hands are huge, as hard as his mind."

Reporting to Roosevelt on the substance of his meetings, Hopkins summarized Stalin's view of the war at that point. Despite the initial setbacks his forces had suffered, the Soviet leader insisted that the Germans had underestimated his forces. "Stalin said that his soldiers did not consider the battle lost merely because the Germans at one point and another broke through with their mechanized forces," Hopkins wrote. The invaders were already overextended, Stalin maintained, and "even the German tanks run out of petrol." The Soviet leader also insisted that the Red Army's large tanks were better than Germany's, and that, while the Luftwaffe had more planes available at the front than the Soviet air force, many of them were second-rate.

But it was Stalin's specific requests for supplies that provided the most compelling indication that he really envisaged a long-term struggle. He asked for a long list of items, including antiaircraft guns, machine guns, aluminum for the construction of planes, high-octane fuel, and more than one million rifles. "Give us antiaircraft guns and the aluminum, and we can fight for three or four years," he told Hopkins. He also reported that resistance fighters behind German lines were already making life difficult for the invaders.

As Hopkins summarized Stalin's remarks, "The might of Germany was so great that, even though Russia might defend itself, it would be very difficult for Britain and Russia combined to crush the German military machine." For that to happen, the United States needed to join the fight—and the Soviet leader was convinced this was an inevitability.

At that point, Stalin startled his visitor by urging him to convey the message to Roosevelt that he would welcome American troops under their own command on any part of the Russian front. As Hopkins noted in his report, "I told him that I doubted that our government, in event of war, would want an American army in Russia but that I would give his message to the President." The Soviet authorities' consistent refusal to allow Yeaton and other military attachés to visit the front, let alone participate in any action there, suggested that Stalin was simply throwing out this offer for dramatic effect.

But Hopkins appeared to take almost everything he heard from Stalin at face value, even when he made sweeping statements that could be equally applied to the Soviet system. Hitler's greatest weakness, according to Stalin, "was found in the vast numbers of oppressed people who hated Hitler and the immoral ways of his government," Hopkins reported. Stalin also spoke "of the necessity of there being a minimum moral standard between all nations," pointing out "that the present leaders of Germany knew no such minimum standard and that, therefore, they represented an antisocial force in the present world."

It was hardly surprising, therefore, that Hopkins had no patience for Yeaton, who had been sending a steady stream of reports highly critical of the Stalinist system and predicting a Soviet defeat, when they ran into each other at breakfast at the embassy. Hopkins promptly told the major that he was convinced that the Soviet Union would prevail in the conflict, and that the United States would provide it with "all possible military and economic assistance." This aid would never be used as a bargaining chip, he added.

Yeaton was dismayed. Alluding to Hopkins's poor health, he wrote later, "His enthusiasm to get us involved in this war and his readiness to negotiate with Stalin on an 'I trust you' basis gave me reasons to question whether or not his illness had affected his mind." Facing Hopkins, Yeaton still tried to explain the reasons for his more pessimistic view of the military situation and the nature of Stalin's regime. "When I impugned the integrity and methods of Stalin, he [Hopkins] could stand it no longer and shut me up with an intense 'I don't care to discuss the subject further,'" Yeaton reported.

The next morning, the two men met at breakfast again, and Yeaton tried to patch things up. He apologized to Hopkins for upsetting him and, as he put it, "begged for his help." If the United States and the Soviet Union were to be allies, he explained, it was vital for him to be able to move about freely to assess the military situation. In other words, the Kremlin should be told to stop restricting the movements of Western military attachés. Hopkins's response, Yeaton noted, was "a cold, emphatic 'no.'" Hopkins was sticking to his proclaimed policy of not using American assistance as leverage, even in such procedural matters.

Right before Hopkins had taken off for Moscow, he signaled that his mind had been already made up on such issues. Colonel Faymonville, Yeaton's predecessor who had been sidelined by the War Department because of his reputation as an apologist for Stalin, was effectively rehabilitated. On July 13 he was assigned to Washington's Division of Aid Reports, which oversaw Lend-Lease. His assignment was to help get the Russian aid program going.

When a Soviet military mission arrived on July 26, Faymonville served as its escort around Washington as the members pressed their hosts for quick action. He was so eager to accommodate them that he showed them classified documents. This led to charges that Faymonville had violated military regulations, and there was even talk of putting him on trial. But Hopkins and the Lend-Lease Administration offered him their full support, ensuring that no action was taken against him. On the contrary, he was soon given broader responsibility for the Russian aid program.

Roosevelt weighed in personally to reinforce the message that he wanted swift results on Russia. On August 2 he sent an emphatic note to Wayne Coy, who had been given oversight of the Soviet aid program while Hopkins was away. He pointed out that he had complained in the last cabinet meeting that six weeks after the German invasion, the United States had done "practically nothing" in terms of delivering the supplies Soviet officials had requested. "Frankly, if I were a Russian, I would feel that I had been given the runaround in the United States," he wrote. He ordered Coy to "with my full authority, use a heavy hand—act as a burr under the saddle and get things moving." He concluded with a blunt order: "Step on it!"

While both Roosevelt and Churchill were eager to convince Stalin of their support, the two Western leaders were also acutely conscious of the need to keep nurturing the ties between themselves. Churchill knew that his people were looking for any signs from the

United States that the country was moving closer to joining their fight for survival. For that to happen, he had to continue trying to sway American public opinion, not just Roosevelt and his team. To do so, he had to play a delicate game, avoiding the appearance of applying pressure tactics too bluntly or too directly. Instead, he had to skillfully wage a war for the hearts and minds of the American people.

As had happened during the Battle for Britain, the Blitz, and debate over the Lend-Lease Act, the American correspondents who were stationed in London or dropped in for reporting stints were often his best allies. And by then, it was apparent which of those correspondents could be counted on not just to provide favorable accounts but also to participate openly in that effort. Churchill and his government were more than eager to help them, providing them with extraordinary access and public platforms beyond their normal outlets.

One of the favorites was Quentin Reynolds, the roving correspondent for *Collier's Weekly*. In the spring of 1941, his book *The Wounded Don't Cry*, about the fall of France and the Battle of Britain, was selling well in England—somewhat to the author's surprise. "I wondered how the Blitz-weary Britons could enjoy reading about experiences that could be neither new nor pleasant for them," he recalled. A London literary critic explained to Reynolds that his timing was particularly good, since it was the first book published that provided the kind of first-person account of those events that British readers loved. "And, of course, you tell us how brave we are," he added. "Coming from an American, that pleases us to no end."

Duff Cooper, the minister of information, extended an unusual invitation to Reynolds. On Sunday nights, the BBC's fifteen-minute *Postscript to the Nine O'Clock News* normally featured Churchill or one of his Cabinet ministers or, on occasion, "a combat hero," as Reynolds put it. Cooper asked Reynolds to do the broadcast on June 29, offering his perspective as an American correspondent.

Reynolds decided to prepare a script in the form of an open letter to Joseph Goebbels. It skewered the Nazi propaganda minister's boss, calling Hitler "Mr. Schicklgruber," which was the original last name of the dictator's father. "I was impressed by the comic possibilities in that unfortunate last name," Reynolds recalled. Despite objections from a BBC program manager about his "rather rude" language on a Sunday evening, the American did not hold back: "I used every vocal trick I knew to create the effect of a prosecutor summing up the case against a murderer." As if to reinforce his message, German bombers appeared in the skies over London as he spoke.

During the next few days, the BBC was flooded with thousands of letters for Reynolds praising his performance. "God Bless you, Yank," one of them said. "You had the whole Elephant and Castle Underground Station roaring. It seemed easier to face the rest of the night after you finished off Mr. Schicklgruber." Churchill wrote as well, extolling his "admirable" broadcast. "Your words have given real pleasure and encouragement to a great many people in this island," he asserted.

Reynolds had been trying to interview the prime minister for a long time, and he immediately parlayed the new recognition to his advantage. Through Averell Harriman, who was in London overseeing the Lend-Lease program, he renewed his request. This produced an invitation to accompany Churchill and Harriman on their July 25 trip to observe some maneuvers with American-made tanks. At Paddington Station before boarding their train, Harriman introduced Reynolds to the British leader. "So you're the lad who did that *Postscript*," Churchill said, looking him over. "You have a style, Mr. Reynolds."

After they reached their destination in the countryside where the maneuvers were held, Reynolds had plenty of time to admire Churchill's style. It was stiflingly hot, but the prime minister looked animated as he discussed the performance of the tanks with Harriman and whenever he had the chance to greet the troops. "Somehow, he gave each man he spoke to the impression that he had come down from London especially to see him," Reynolds wrote. "He spread his charm upon officer and private, and the charm was contagious." When their train returned to London, Churchill invited Reynolds to join him for lunch at Chequers the next day. "I have an American visiting who I am sure can use your help," he said.

The American was Harry Hopkins, and Reynolds ended up spending the weekend at Chequers when the presidential envoy made his pitch to Roosevelt to send him to Moscow. Churchill asked Reynolds to help Hopkins prepare a radio address, which was meant to explain to the British public that the delays in getting more American supplies were due to the need to retool factories to produce more armaments—and not any indication of wavering support from Washington. Reynolds never hesitated, working with Hopkins to polish his message.

Reynolds also got the kind of inside look at Churchill and his entourage that he was hoping for—with glimpses of his wife Clementine's role as well. She was particularly concerned about Hopkins's health. "I am sure that Harry never got such a mothering in his life, except maybe from Mrs. Roosevelt," Reynolds observed. At the end of a family dinner, Clementine cautioned her husband to limit his liquor intake. "Always remember, Clemmie, that I have taken more out of alcohol than alcohol has of me," he replied—with Reynolds noting the affectionate tone in his voice.

Reynolds was suitably impressed by the man who was as eloquent and charming in private as in public. "Many great public figures, I have found, seem to dwindle in stature when one finally meets them informally," he wrote. "Churchill was not one of those. It was impossible to miss his aura of strength and confidence, even when he was chatting about trivialities."

Churchill knew, of course, that he was performing for his American visitors Hopkins, Harriman, and Reynolds. "Ah, that Hitler!" he told Reynolds. "When I think of the crimes he has committed! When this war has come to an end, something must be done about that man. If my allies agree, I would favor trying and exterminating him." If Hitler were to win, he continued, "I feel sure he would have me shot." He then added archly: "I would not like that, but I cannot say that my sense of righteousness would be outraged."

What impressed Reynolds even more was what Churchill failed to say. "It was noteworthy that, sitting there with three Americans, Churchill did not directly refer to the possibility of the United States' entry into the war," he pointed out. Instead, Churchill declared: "We have a long way to go, but with the help of our great friends across the sea, we shall get there." He left it to his American guests to ponder what form that help would ultimately take.

That same weekend, Dorothy Thompson also visited Churchill at Chequers. By then, the journalist's impassioned, pro-British syndicated columns were running in about two hundred newspapers in the United States. The "indefatigable fighter for freedom," as FDR's speechwriter Sherwood called her, had arrived for a monthlong whirlwind visit to Britain. She traveled all over the country, meeting everyone from Queen Elizabeth (the wife of King George VI and mother of Queen Elizabeth II) to ordinary soldiers and citizens, along with representatives of every government-in-exile in London; she also continued to churn out her columns and deliver hugely popular broadcasts on the BBC.

J. W. Drawbell, the editor of the *Sunday Chronicle* of London, which republished Thompson's columns regularly, played host and impresario, making sure she received near-royal treatment. He reserved three suites for her at the Savoy Hotel, where a team of Fleet Street assistants and secretaries juggled the crush of invitations for dinners, lunches, and speaking engagements, along with the complex logistics of her day-to-day schedule. Drawbell, who accompanied her almost everywhere during her stay, admitted later: "I was an exhilarated wreck when she left."

The reason for all the fanfare was not hard to explain. With her fervent advocacy of the Lend-Lease Act and denunciations of the isolationists, Thompson was viewed as the champion extraordinaire of the embattled British people. She was much more than a celebrity journalist; she embodied the hopes they had for America. In her BBC broadcasts during her visit, she only confirmed those feelings by telling her listeners exactly what they wanted to hear. Praising "the great British spirit" that was on display when they refused to succumb to German might after Dunkirk, Thompson declared:

"If you had given up in that awful moment, we would have given up too. Everyone would have given up. We would all have tried to buy our way out, or cringe our way in. This would have been a world populated by people who despised themselves. . . . You people in Britain have released more minds from fear than you can possibly imagine. That was the first act of liberation that you performed for the world."

In Plymouth, at the *Mayflower* steps and monument commemorating the Pilgrims who set out from there to seek religious freedom in the new world, she hailed Britain's role as the modern bastion of freedom, attracting those seeking to liberate their homelands from German rule. "The boats that come to England carry not only guns and food but Dutchmen and Poles, Norwegians and Czechs, who are the Pilgrim fathers of today, come to fight from here for states in which, through countless ages, men shall know liberty," she proclaimed.

She also directly addressed the German people on the BBC. Speaking in German, the language she had mastered when she lived in Berlin in the 1920s, Thompson said: "I know Germany, and I love Germany, and I believe in Germany. I hate and loathe this insane war. But I am not neutral in this war, I want Britain to win it. . . . I hated and fought the Nazi regime because I believed that it would destroy Europe and destroy Germany and destroy the whole of Western civilization if it were allowed to run its course unchecked." All her dire warnings about Hitler's intentions, she claimed, had proven to be correct. "In only one instance have I been wrong," she added. "I did not think that Hitler would at this moment attack Russia. I did not think he was so stupid." That latest action "will inevitably and certainly bring America into the war as an active instead of a passive partner."

All of which meant that "you cannot possibly win this war," Thompson concluded. "The great reserves of energy, resources, intelligence, and, above all, the sentiments of three-fourths of the people on this globe are against you."

When she met Churchill, he did not go so far as she did in predicting her country's direct involvement in the conflict—but he came closer than he had with Hopkins, Harriman, and Reynolds. "So much to do when all this is over," he mused. "A wonderful world—or a shambles and a prison. If you help make it. We can only do it with the Americans. You know that, don't you? We can't do it alone. That's clear, isn't it?"

After Thompson returned home, Drawbell wrote an adulatory book, *Dorothy Thompson's English Journey,* for British readers. He wanted to publish it in the United States as well, but Thompson told him not to do so. She feared that the book would be used by her opponents as evidence that she was a British agent. The charge was not true, of course. But, like CBS's Murrow earlier, she played a duel role as the de facto US envoy to Britain and the de facto British envoy to the United States.

Hopkins left Moscow on August 1, returning to Archangel where the RAF Catalina seaplane was waiting to ferry him back to Scotland. The plane's captain suggested delaying their journey because of rough weather, but Hopkins insisted on taking off right away. "Whatever it is, it will seem easy after what I've been doing the last couple of days," he said. The real reason for his urgency: he was due to meet up right away with the British battleship HMS *Prince of Wales* to join Churchill on his transatlantic crossing to his still-secret meeting with Roosevelt off the coast of Newfoundland.

The flight, which took twenty-four hours because of strong headwinds, was anything but easy. It didn't help that Hopkins had left his bag of medicines behind in Moscow. Or that when the seaplane came down in the sea lanes of the Scapa Flow, it was tossed about by the waves, and Hopkins had to jump into the launch sent to pick him up, with a sailor grabbing him to make sure he made it. Once aboard the *Prince of Wales*, he needed immediate medical care and sleep. Churchill cabled Roosevelt at the start of their journey: "Hopkins returned dead beat from Russia but is lively again now. We shall get him in fine trim on voyage."

Hopkins recovered well enough to brief Churchill on his meetings with Stalin and prepare his reports on them for Roosevelt. The two men also relaxed and played backgammon, with Hopkins reporting afterward: "He approaches the game with great zeal, doubling and redoubling frequently." The prime minister was clearly excited about the prospect of the summit with Roosevelt. "You'd have thought Winston was being carried up into the heavens to meet God!" Hopkins recalled later. Churchill was firmly convinced that it was Roosevelt's leadership that guaranteed America's support for Britain.

Roosevelt, too, was energized by his journey—especially enjoying the secrecy of it. The cover story was that he was taking a ten-day fishing trip on the USS *Potomac*, the presidential yacht, as a well-earned vacation. Instead, he boarded the USS cruiser *Augusta* in New London, Connecticut, confessing that "I feel a thrill in making a getaway—especially from the American press." Greeting Churchill on board the *Augusta* on August 9, the president told him with obvious delight: "At last we have gotten together."

During their three days of meetings at sea, the two leaders and their top aides reviewed the situation in Europe and the Far East, focusing particularly on the threat posed by Japan, and worked on the document that would be named the Atlantic Charter. They also discussed how to handle Russia. But it was a meeting that was as important for its symbolism as its substance. When Roosevelt visited

Churchill on the *Prince of Wales* for a Sunday-morning religious service, both men were moved by the sight of "the close-packed ranks of British and American sailors, completely intermingled, sharing the same books and joining fervently together in the prayers and hymns familiar to both," Churchill recalled. "It was a great hour to live. Nearly half those who sang were soon to die."

The Atlantic Charter the two leaders crafted left enough ambiguity about Roosevelt's intentions to allow him to break the news of the summit upon his return and insist that he had not committed the United States to entering the war. To the question of whether the country was "closer to entering the war," he replied "No!"—although he added that Americans hadn't woken up "to the fact that they had a war to win." He was still walking the narrow line between support for Britain and outright military involvement.

Churchill understood as much. The Atlantic Charter included the phrase "after the final destruction of the Nazi tyranny," which, the British leader noted, "in ordinary times would have implied warlike action." His assumption: these were not yet ordinary times, since Roosevelt could not win support for a declaration of war without some other dramatic development. In fact, on the day the summit ended, the US House of Representatives voted to extend the draft by a margin of only one vote, demonstrating the continued strength of isolationist sentiment. But the charter provided a set of common principles that Roosevelt believed would help him make the case for war as needed later, whenever that moment arrived.

Those principles echoed some of President Woodrow Wilson's "Fourteen Points" that he spelled out in a speech near the end of World War I, similarly based on lofty goals for a postwar world. Churchill and Roosevelt pledged that they would seek "no aggrandizement, territorial or other," for their countries, and that there would be "no territorial changes that do not accord with the freely expressed wishes of the peoples concerned." Once Nazi tyranny ends, everyone should also be free "to choose the form of government under which they will live."

Stalin had other ideas: he was already pushing for acceptance for his country's territorial and political gains that had been made possible by the now-defunct Nazi-Soviet pact—specifically, the annexation of eastern Poland and the Baltic states. But after listening to Hopkins's readout on his talks with the Soviet leader, Churchill and Roosevelt focused on what they viewed as the more pressing priority: responding to his appeals for aid.

Winding up their summit on August 12, they sent a joint statement to Stalin. "We are at the moment cooperating to provide you with the very maximum of supplies that you most urgently need," they assured him. "Already many shiploads have left our shores, and more will leave in the immediate future." But they sought to temper Stalin's expectations, pointing out that they had to allocate their resources to the many fronts of the war. They then proposed sending a high-level British-American delegation to Moscow to work out a joint plan of action for aid to Russia.

Churchill already knew something about the difficulties of dealing with his new Soviet ally, but, for now, he and Roosevelt believed they had finessed the problem. More significantly, the prime minister returned home with new confidence that he had forged a stronger bond with Roosevelt. As he put it in a BBC broadcast, he felt "uplifted in spirit, fortified in resolve."

Roosevelt's subsequent denials that the summit had pushed his country closer to war quickly dampened Churchill's mood, however. In a message to Hopkins on August 29, he wrote that Roosevelt's defensive pronouncements had sparked "a wave of depression" in Britain. He added: "If 1942 opens with Russia knocked out and Britain left alone again, all kinds of dangers may arise."

Neither possibility could be ruled out yet.

SEVEN

"SIMULTANEOUS WARS"

L*ike others in the German* invasion force that had crossed the border into Soviet-held territory on June 22, Hans von Herwarth, the former German diplomat in Moscow, was not quite prepared for the "astonishingly cordial" welcome his unit received from the inhabitants of the first villages and towns his unit entered. "The local population showed genuine kindness toward the German troops and pinned great hopes on our arrival," he reported. "Everywhere we went, we were greeted with bread and salt, the traditional Slav symbols of hospitality." Only the local Communist Party officials had fled, while most of the other inhabitants had ignored orders from Moscow to drive off their cattle and destroy their crops and grain reserves. According to Herwarth, they told the new arrivals repeatedly: "Now, thank goodness, we will be treated as human beings and will be given back our rights as men."

Such declarations demonstrated how little the villagers and townspeople knew about the invaders and the system they represented. "For many, Hitler was a savior who was expected to redeem the poor Ukrainians and Russians and secure them a brighter future,"

Herwarth wrote. They were not so much attracted to Nazi ideology, which they hardly understood, but to what they perceived as an opportunity to liberate themselves from Stalin's reign of terror, which they had felt most acutely in the form of forced collectivization, deliberate starvation, mass executions, and deportations. They eagerly handed over to the invaders lists of local Communist Party members, "against whom they wanted us to take action," Herwarth noted. And peasants asked impatiently about German plans for the hated collective farms. "Even the meanest peasant expected to get back his property and perhaps to end up with more than one cow," he added.

Coupled with the mass surrender of Red Army troops in the initial stages of Operation Barbarossa, this willingness of much of the civilian population to welcome—or, at least, not actively oppose—the invaders presented Hitler with a remarkable opportunity. If his forces had treated both the POWs and civilians with a minimal level of respect and decency, even if this were merely for show for a short period of time, they could have leveraged this remarkable situation to their advantage. Instead, as Herwarth recorded bitterly in his postwar memoir, the invaders resorted immediately to "oppressive and criminal methods." The result: "Hitler and his henchmen thus succeeded in driving large parts of the population back into the arms of Stalin."

In fact, it was Hitler who gave Stalin the chance to recover from the early German onslaught and rally his countrymen. By not only matching but often surpassing Stalin's reliance on terror and mass murder as a means of extending his rule, Hitler was setting the stage for Germany's defeat even as his armies racked up new victories. The Soviet leader could not have asked for a greater gift.

It was no easy task to outdo Stalin and convince many of his subjects that they had more to fear from the Germans than they did from him. After all, the Soviet record in the territories it controlled following the signing of the Nazi-Soviet pact was guaranteed to inspire both fear and hatred in the local populations. In what had been eastern Poland, the Soviet authorities deported an estimated two million of their new subjects between September 1939 and June 22, 1941. Hundreds of thousands died either in the horrific train convoys or after arriving at their remote destinations in the camps or places of exile in northern Russia, Siberia, and Kazakhstan. Many quickly froze or starved to death.

"At a time when the Germans were still refining their preparations for Auschwitz or Treblinka, the Soviets could accommodate a few million Poles and West Ukrainian additions to the population of their 'Gulag archipelago' with relative ease," wrote British historian Norman Davies.

Then there were the outright massacres of those Poles who Stalin feared might oppose Soviet domination, particularly Polish troops who were taken prisoner when the Red Army seized the eastern part of their country. In March 1940 the Kremlin decreed the "supreme punishment—execution by shooting" of 14,736 Polish army officers and officials, along with an additional 10,685 Poles held by the NKVD; the killings were carried out in early April. In 1943, German troops discovered the bodies of about four thousand of those Polish officers, each with a bullet hole in the head, in the Katyn Forest, near Smolensk.

Right up until the collapse of the Soviet Union, the Soviet authorities maintained that the Germans were trying to pin the blame for a Nazi atrocity on them. But it was clear that the timing of the killings—as indicated by the belongings of the victims that included letters, diaries, and other documents, all dated no later than April 1940—proved that the massacre took place when Soviet authorities were in control of the area. In a goodwill gesture to Poland in 1992, Russian President Boris Yeltsin finally released the order from the Politburo that officially confirmed this grim fact.

The Kremlin took longer to establish full control of the Baltic states, but there, too, it carried out mass arrests and deportations of anyone considered to be a potential "enemy of the people." On November 28, 1940, Lithuanian Interior Minister Aleksandras Guzevičius, a member of the Soviet puppet regime, issued a list of fourteen categories of people targeted for deportation: everyone from members of "leftist" and "nationalist" anti-Soviet parties, to officers of the Lithuanian and Polish armies and "all political émigrés and unstable elements."

Just one week before Operation Barbarossa, on the night of June 13–14, 1941, the Kremlin's overlords undertook their largest deportations. The numbers were smaller than for Poland, but for the tiny populations of those states, no less devastating. By most estimates, about sixty thousand Estonians, thirty-five thousand Latvians, and thirty-four thousand Lithuanians were deported to the east before the Germans struck. In Estonia's case, this constituted about 4 percent of its population, and for Lithuania and Latvia, about 1.5 percent to 2 percent.

Once the Germans launched their attack, the first instinct of the Soviet occupiers was to accelerate their deadly work. The NKVD had no intention of simply abandoning its political prisoners in the regions of Poland and the Baltic states that were about to change hands again; instead, it started executing them. In Lvov—or Lwòw, as it was known when it was part of Poland before 1939—they executed about four thousand prisoners before they had to flee, leaving behind their victims' machine-gun-riddled bodies. The NKVD and Red Army troops engaged in similar killing sprees across the region.

Behind the front lines, other prisoners were forcibly evacuated eastward, usually on foot. The resulting macabre scenes foreshadowed the death marches from the Nazi concentration camps at the end of the war, when the German front was collapsing. "Protest or not—all will walk," one Soviet guard told his prisoners. "Those who can't walk, we will shoot. We will leave no one for the Germans."

Little wonder that the German invaders were often welcomed at first. Heinz Hagermann, an NCO in the Sixth Infantry Division that moved into the border region that included Lvov, wrote that the troops were "warmly greeted, sometimes even with swastika banners, by happy faces and people relieved, finally, to have escaped the Bolshevik yoke, and terror! These people were almost completely cleaned out by the Bolsheviks, and they suffered atrocities—the political prisoners especially—that are almost beyond comprehension: mutilation, burning alive, the lot!"

But any jubilation was short lived. Captain Karl Haupt, whose troops were also greeted by villagers with bread, salt, and flowers in the western Ukraine, wrote that soon the locals turned passive and then "hostile through and through." On July 19 he lamented that "there is no place for trust, chumminess, or letting one's guard down." He followed up those observations by ordering his men to employ "the harshest, most ruthless measures" against the same villages that had looked so welcoming only a few weeks earlier.

Like most of his fellow German officers and men, Haupt failed to recognize how it was precisely those kinds of "ruthless measures" that were contributing to the growing resentment and resistance that they were meant to stamp out.

What passed for normal warfare was brutal enough. Yevgeniya Merlis, an eighteen-year-old nurse trainee at a hospital in Kharkov when the fighting started, recalled the frantic efforts to save wounded and dying Red Army soldiers—or at least to lessen their pain. "It's hard to describe how horrible it was there," she said in 2017, still haunted by those memories. "There were such screams from each cot." There were never enough painkillers; nor, during bombing raids, were there enough stretchers to carry all the patients to the bomb shelter. "You got to the floor, and they were calling 'Sister, me! Sister, me!' " she added. All too often, there was nothing she or anyone else could do to help them.

As gruesome as they were, the conditions in Merlis's hospital were hardly surprising given the lack of preparation for the German invasion and the chronic shortages that plagued the Soviet system. To be sure, nurses and doctors who worked on other fronts in World War II and in other wars could tell similarly chilling stories. But even in those early days of the German onslaught, the scale of the killing and suffering of both soldiers and civilians all too often surpassed anything that had happened up to that point.

This was no accident. It was a result of Hitler's calls for a war of annihilation against a people who were written off as subhuman and the preinvasion planning based on that assumption. For them, any normal rules of engagement did not apply. According to a directive issued by the Armed Forces High Command on July 23, "resistance in the occupied East should be broken not through 'the judicial punishment of the guilty,' but by inflicting such terror that the population would lose 'all inclination to resist.'" In response to the early signs of partisan activity, the military authorities instructed their troops to execute between fifty and a hundred Soviet citizens for every German killed.

But it was the Commissar Order—the directive to execute all political officers in the Red Army units, even those trying to surrender—that demonstrated most dramatically how Hitler was helping Stalin's cause. It convinced the Red Army commissars to rally their troops at any cost, since they soon realized that defeat meant an instant death sentence. After the war, Field Marshal von Manstein admitted as much. "The order simply incited the commissars to resort to the most brutal methods to make their units fight on to the end," he wrote.

In fact, even as they were preparing to launch Operation Barbarossa, some of Hitler's most fervent loyalists had recognized the danger of this policy. Army commander von Brauchitsch added a line to the instructions about such actions, suggesting that the commissars should be executed "inconspicuously." It wasn't shame that prompted that advice; it was calculation.

But when the Germans began encountering Soviet troops who fought back ferociously despite overwhelming odds, the top brass studiously avoided acknowledging the linkage to both the genuine patriotism of many of the defenders and to their own behavior. "The main reason why the Russian never surrenders is that, dim-witted half-Asiatic that he is, he fully believes the notion, drummed into him by the commissars, that he will be shot if captured," a directive to the Fourth Army declared.

In the buildup to the invasion, the Wehrmacht had prepared its men for the mission ahead by distributing pamphlets that combined denunciations of the commissars with anti-Semitic themes. "We would insult the animals if we described these mostly Jewish men as beasts," one such pamphlet declared. "They are the embodiment of satanic and insane hatred against the whole of noble humanity."

From the very beginning, most of the invaders viewed the Commissar Order, along with all the accompanying Nazi propaganda about inferior races, as proof that Hitler was perfectly serious when he urged his generals to abandon any notions of civilized warfare. The German troops killed and plundered at will, often boasting of their exploits in letters home. "One thing I can assure you: I'll see ten Russians croak before I do any starving," Erich Petschan wrote, demonstrating that the notion of a Hunger Plan for Russia was taken literally. Another soldier, Helmut Pabst, noted nonchalantly: "Willingly or unwillingly, the country feeds us."

While most commanders spurred their troops on, there were occasional objections—sometimes from unusual quarters. An SS report warned: "The positive attitude toward the Germans is being jeopardized by the indiscriminate requisitions by the troops. . . by individual instances of rape, and by the way the army treats the civilian population, which feel handled as an enemy people." That was exactly how they were handled, very deliberately.

A few German military leaders also voiced misgivings about the treatment of Red Army troops at first. On June 25 General Joachim Lemelsen, the commander of the Forty-Seventh Panzer Corps, decried the "senseless shootings of both prisoners of war and civilians."

Five days later, he complained that "still more shootings of prisoners of war and [Soviet] deserters have been observed, conducted in an irresponsible, senseless, and criminal manner. This is murder!" He added: "The German army is waging war against Bolshevism, not against the Russian peoples."

That was already a fictional distinction at that point, and Lemelsen left no doubt that any reservations he had were strictly limited. He supported the order that anyone identified as a political commissar or a partisan "should be taken aside and shot." Such measures, he added, were necessary to free the Russian people "from the oppression of a Jewish and criminal group."

Some commanders, such as General John Ansat, who led the 102nd Infantry Division, objected to using their troops to carry out the Commissar Order. His men were "no hangman's assistants," he declared. But he had no problem with delivering the captured commissars to "other units," knowing full well that this sealed their fate. In this way, Ansat could claim to have shielded his troops from direct involvement in the executions; they became hangmen's assistants once removed.

It wasn't only the Red Army commissars who had reason to fear capture by the Germans. The fate of the huge numbers of the troops who were quick to surrender when they were overrun by the invaders proved that ordinary soldiers could not hope for mercy either. When German newspapers began publishing photos of the POWs, it was to ridicule their "Asiatic, Mongol physiognomies" and their "degenerate qualities"—in other words, to confirm that they were indeed the *Untermenschen* depicted by Nazi propaganda.

Given those attitudes, Wehrmacht troops cared little for the POWs' survival and, in many cases, simply murdered them outright. "At this stage, we had hardly the time or the men to spare for rounding up prisoners," Field Marshal von Manstein wrote, referring to the early battles. He pointedly left unsaid what happened to those who weren't rounded up, but this was no mystery. In a letter home, a German soldier admitted that the first Russian he shot was a soldier who had just surrendered. "Since then, I have shot hundreds," he wrote. "I have such a rage. Since then, I took only one prisoner, a German."

Yet so many Red Army troops surrendered during the first months that the Germans had to set up a network of prison camps for them. In 1941 there were eighty-one such camps in the Soviet Union. As German historian Christian Hartmann wrote, the care of POWs should be "a routine task for a professional army," but everything about that task in Operation Barbarossa was "almost completely improvised." Many of the prison camps were little more than open fields with dugouts and huts, with the prisoners crowded together in horrific conditions. With Hitler and other Nazi leaders insisting that the Russians should be allowed to starve, it was hardly surprising that the POWs were among the first to do so. After all, as the popular German saying put it, "The Russian must perish that we may live."

A German report on conditions in one camp noted that the arrival of a water carrier triggered pandemonium among the thirsty, starving prisoners. "A ferocious brawl always breaks out, which can only be ended by shooting. Hunger revolts with incessant shooting are the order of the day." Hans Becker, a German soldier who went into a POW camp to find workers, described the terrifying spectacle he witnessed in a hut he entered: "A whirling mass of bodies staggered through the gloom, grunting, biting, and tearing at each other." Those men were attacking a fellow prisoner, "gouging his eyes out, twisting his arms off, and tearing his flesh with their nails," literally tearing him apart. Becker shouted for the men to stop but did nothing when they ignored him, "The murderers were now cramming the flesh down their throats," he reported.

All over the front, the appalling treatment of the POWs was glaringly evident. Herwarth, the former German diplomat, recalled seeing columns of prisoners "marching arm in arm but reeling like drunkards." The next morning, a fellow soldier pointed out the corpses of many of the POWs strewn nearby. Suddenly the truth dawned on him. "They had apparently not been fed for days, and their 'drunkenness' was the result of sheer fatigue," he wrote.

In his book *Operation Barbarossa,* Hartmann described the treatment of Soviet POWs as "the largest crime committed by the Wehrmacht." While the regular army also played a significant supporting role for the Einsatzgruppen, the SS, and others who carried out the mass murders of Jews, they were directly responsible for the handling of POWs. The toll of their victims fully justifies Hartman's assertion. During 1941, 3.3 million Soviet soldiers were captured; by February 1942, roughly 2 million of them were dead.

Aside from the obvious moral issues this raises, those statistics demonstrate the self-defeating nature of Hitler's policies. As word spread about German treatment of POWs, Red Army soldiers became increasingly determined to fight rather than surrender. And those who escaped captivity often eagerly enlisted in newly formed partisan units. Finally, the death of so many able-bodied Red Army POWs meant that they were not available to join the ranks of slave workers who were supposed to make up for the growing labor shortages in the Third Reich.

Starting in 1942, there were more attempts to exploit the POWs as laborers, and, in some cases, their treatment improved just enough to keep them alive. Nonetheless, by the end of the war, about 3 million out of 5.7 million Soviet POWs had perished. For many, captivity still amounted to a death sentence.

Some Soviet POWs spent their final days in Auschwitz, before the soon-to-be infamous concentration camp in German-occupied Poland played its central role in the Holocaust. A former army barracks located near the town of Oswięcim—or, in German, Auschwitz—it was initially used by the Germans to house Polish political prisoners.

The main camp received its first transport of 728 prisoners in June 1940, many of whom were affiliated with Polish resistance movements. In most cases, they were Catholics, since the deportation of Jews had not yet begun. Of the 150,000 Polish prisoners who ended up in Auschwitz, about 75,000 died there. But the death rate for the smaller contingent of Soviet POWs was much higher.

Once German forces began capturing huge numbers of Red Army troops, SS chief Heinrich Himmler offered to take responsibility for 100,000 POWs, with the idea of dispatching most of them to Auschwitz to serve as slave laborers. Starting in September 1941, about 15,000 Soviet POWs were sent there. They were promptly put to work on the construction of a second large complex of barracks at Birkenau, two miles away from the original Auschwitz facilities.

As hardened as they were by their own experiences, the Polish prisoners were horrified by the treatment of the Soviet POWs. "They were treated worse than any other prisoners," said Mieczyslaw Zawadzki, a Pole who worked as a nurse in a sick bay for the POWs. Fed only turnips and tiny rations of bread, they collapsed from hunger, exposure, and beatings. "The hunger was so bad that they cut off the buttocks from the corpses in the morgue and ate the flesh," Zawadzki added. "Later, we locked the morgue so they couldn't get in."

Nikolai Pisarev, a rare survivor from the first group of Soviet POWs sent to Auschwitz, recalled similar cases in the barracks when prisoners died in their bunks—and, in the morning, they were found with their buttocks cut off. One prisoner slipped into the kitchen and gorged himself with food, only to be caught by the Germans. "They put him in a cauldron and boiled him alive," Pisarev said, adding slowly: "The things I saw . . . They forced prisoners to eat their own excrement. The SS would rush into the barracks at night and force us to line up naked. If anybody had a big member, he was told to hold it up, and they would hit it with a riding crop."

Pisarev was one of the few participants in a mass escape attempt the following year who survived; with the help of sympathetic Poles, he then managed to pass himself off as a member of a Polish forced-labor brigade. But almost all the other Soviet POWs sent to Auschwitz perished within a few weeks or months. Pavel Stenkin, another survivor, estimated the average life span of the Soviet prisoners at two weeks. "It was death, death, death," he recalled. "Death at night, death in the morning, death in the afternoon. There was death all the time."

According to Rudolf Höss, the commandant of Auschwitz, some of the POWs were executed by firing squads. But about six hundred of the new arrivals were herded into an experimental gas chamber and killed with Zyklon B, the highly poisonous insecticide first developed to eliminate rats and insects. Höss donned a gas mask to observe the procedure. After the war, when he wrote his life story for the Polish authorities who hanged him in 1947, he recalled how quickly the victims died. "A short, smothered cry, and it was all over," he wrote, declaring how impressed he was by the new technique. "I had imagined that death by gassing would be worse than it was." Subsequent testimonies from both guards and prisoners dramatically contradicted his sanitized description of the process, which was not nearly as quick as he reported.

The barracks that the POWs built in the sprawling Birkenau complex were designed to cram in as many prisoners as possible. The original plan was to allocate 550 prisoners to each barracks, but SS planners upped that number to 744. The presumption was they would be filled with more Soviet POWs. But with those POWs dying rapidly in the newly conquered territories of the Soviet Union, the huge influx that Himmler had originally envisaged never materialized. As a result, Birkenau would soon play a different role.

It would be shaped, as Höss explained, by the growing determination of Hitler, along with his key subordinates like Himmler and Adolf Eichmann, to make good on the promises to eliminate the Jews. Referring to the use of Zyklon B on the Soviet POWs, Höss wrote: "I must even admit that this gassing set my mind at rest, for the mass extermination of the Jews was to start soon, and at the time, neither Eichmann nor I was certain how these mass killings were to be carried out."

This intersection between the fates of Soviet POWs and the Jews destined to perish at Auschwitz and other death camps illustrated how 1941 proved to be the pivotal year in the rush to genocide. As Rebecca Erbelding, a historian at the US Holocaust Memorial Museum, pointed out, "Nazi Germany fought two simultaneous wars: the military war against the Allies and the genocidal war against the Jews." While the first war started in 1939, when Germany invaded Poland, she added, "The second war began in 1941, when a decade of racial and religious persecution morphed into a plan to annihilate the Nazis' innocent enemies." In the words of Chaim Weizmann, the Zionist leader who would become the first president of Israel, "The Jewish calamity merged with, was engulfed by, the world calamity."

It was the invasion of the Soviet Union that triggered the rapid acceleration of that merger. Since Hitler had repeatedly defined Nazi Germany's foe as "Jewish Bolshevism," all killings of Jews could be explained as the elimination of this enemy. On September 12 Field Marshal Wilhelm Keitel called for "ruthless, energetic, and drastic measures above all against the Jews, the main carriers of Bolshevism." As partisan activity became more widespread behind enemy lines, the German invaders labeled all resisters Jews, whatever their origin. As they put it, "Where there's a Jew, there's a partisan, and where there's a partisan, there's a Jew."

Judging by their letters home, most German soldiers quickly internalized the propaganda messages from their superiors. "The battle against these subhumans, who have been whipped into a frenzy by the Jews, was not only necessary but came in the nick of time," Private Karl Fuchs wrote on August 4. "Our Führer has saved Europe from certain chaos."

As soon as German troops moved into Soviet territory, the massacres of Jews began. The SS mobile units known as Einsatzgruppen, composed of hardened veterans—many of whom had carried out killings of intellectuals, clergy, and Jews in occupied Poland—and special police units accompanied the invasion force. Order Police Battalion 309 entered the city of Bialystok in late June, immediately shooting and beating local Jews, while forcing many of them to gather at the marketplace and synagogue. When a desperate group of Jewish leaders went to the headquarters of the security division responsible for the area to plead for help, the general in charge turned away as one of the members of the police battalion urinated on them.

The Jews in the marketplace were then lined up and shot, while others in the synagogue were set alight. That fire in turn set off fires in nearby houses, where other Jews were hiding. The tally for the day's macabre events: about two thousand to twenty-two hundred Jews killed. And that wasn't the last of the killings in Bialystok. On July 12 two other police battalions filled the city's stadium with Jewish men. Their orders read: "All male Jews between the ages of 17 and 45 convicted as plunderers are to be shot according to martial law." The policemen collected the valuables of the "plunderers" and drove them to ditches on the outskirts of the city, formed firing squads, and kept shooting late into the evening—at that point, using the headlights of trucks to light up their targets. This time the tally was more than three thousand Jews.

Soon the roundups were producing more and more such massacres. They were increasingly composed of any Jews they could capture, including women and children, along with some Gypsies and other civilian "enemies." The terse reports of the killing squads would offer the name of the unit and the tally of its victims on any particular day. "August 25: Police Regiment South shot 1,324 Jews," for example, or "August 31: Battalion 320 shot 2,200 Jews in Minkovtsy."

The famed Soviet war correspondent and novelist Vasily Grossman later divided the war against the Jews into two parts: "the Shoah by bullets" and "the Shoah by gas," using the Hebrew term for the Holocaust. When the Germans invaded the Soviet Union, the Shoah by gas was not yet organized. Instead, the police battalions, and, even more so, the Einsatzgruppen, methodically carried out the Shoah by bullets. From the start of Operation Barbarossa to the end of 1941, the Germans and, in some cases, local collaborators murdered about six hundred thousand Jews.

Benjamin Ferencz, the US Army's twenty-seven-year-old chief prosecutor in the trial of twenty-two of the Einsatzgruppen commanders at Nuremberg, charged the defendants with "the deliberate slaughter of more than a million innocent and defenseless men, women, and children. . . . dictated, not by military necessity, but by the supreme perversion of thought, the Nazi theory of the master race." In his opening statement on September 29, 1947, he broke down the number of victims he cited to show how death on this scale was possible. The evidence indicated that four Einsatzgruppen, each composed of five hundred to eight hundred men, "averaged some 1,350 murders per day during a two-year period; 1,350 human beings slaughtered on the average day, seven days a week for more than one hundred weeks."

One of the defendants was Otto Ohlendorf, the commander of Einsatzgruppe D, probably the most notorious of the killing squads. A father of five who had studied both law and economics and boasted a doctorate in jurisprudence, Ohlendorf was one of the best-educated mass murderers in history. But he exhibited not a hint of remorse, either at the trial or when he was questioned earlier by the American psychiatrist Leon Goldensohn. He described matter-of-factly the way his men dispatched their victims during the early months of the Russian campaign.

"The Jews were shot in a military manner in a cordon," he told Goldensohn. "There were fifteen-men firing squads. One bullet per Jew. In other words, one firing squad of fifteen executed fifteen Jews at a time." The victims were men, women, and children. How many perished at the hands of his men during the year he spent in Russia? "Ninety thousand reported. I figure actually only sixty to seventy thousand were shot." Ohlendorf, like the other defendants, insisted he was only following orders. "All I had to do was to see to it that it was done as humanely as possible."

Shortly after he was sentenced to death by hanging, Ohlendorf exchanged a few words with Ferencz. "The Jews of America will suffer for this," he told him. As Ferencz recalled in an interview in 2013, "He died convinced that he was right and I was wrong."

Like their commanders, most of the rank-and-file executioners exhibited little or no remorse as they carried out their gruesome assignments. They were frequently given alcohol to deaden whatever feelings they might still have, and they were constantly urged to suppress any hint of compassion. This applied not just to those directly involved but also to regular troops who often played a supporting role. Field Marshal Walter von Reichenau declared in an order on October 10, 1941: "The soldier must have complete understanding for the necessity of the harsh but just atonement of Jewish subhumanity. This has the further goal of nipping in the bud rebellions in the rear of the Wehrmacht, which, as experience shows, are always plotted by the Jews."

The officers in charge were usually far more concerned with the practical difficulties of killing so many people than with any worries that their men would balk at carrying out their assignments. SS cavalry units were instructed to shoot Jews, but the order appeared to apply only to the men at first. The other part of the order read: "Drive the female Jews into the swamps." Taking those instructions literally, Franz Magill, the commander of one cavalry unit, reported: "Driving women and children into the swamps did not have the success it was supposed to have, as the swamps were not deep enough for sinking under to occur."

In his talks with Eichmann, Himmler, and other top Nazi officials,

Auschwitz commandant Höss was left with the impression that they were primarily bothered by the fact that the mass shootings were often conducted in chaotic conditions. "Many gruesome scenes are said to have taken place, people running away after being shot, the finishing off of the wounded and particularly of the women and children," he recalled. "Many members of the Einsatzkommandos, unable to endure wading through blood any longer, had committed suicide. Some had even gone mad. Most. . . . had to rely on alcohol when carrying out their horrible work." Far from everything that Höss wrote was reliable—for example, there was no need for any of the executioners to commit suicide. Those who did not want to keep killing could find a way to opt out, contrary to their assertions afterward that they had no choice. In those rare cases, they were simply reassigned to other duties.

But while the killings continued, including the slaughter of thirty-three thousand Jews at the ravine of Babi Yar after Kiev fell in late September 1941, the Nazi leaders were looking for new methods of mass murder. As they saw it, the special killing squads were doing their job well enough, but they weren't as fast and efficient as they wanted them to be given the remaining huge numbers of potential victims.

For a long time, the Nazis had equivocated on the ultimate fate of the Jews. After Germany attacked Poland on September 1, 1939, the Germans had quickly begun planning the creation of ghettos in major cities and towns. Less than three weeks later, on September 20, General Halder wrote in his diary: "Ghetto plan exists in broad outline; details are not yet settled; economic needs are prime considerations." The last part of his note indicated that in those early days of the war, there was at least some consideration of how to make the ghettos economically viable instead of using them as mere dumping grounds for Jews.

Some Nazi officials genuinely believed that they could make good use of the Jewish labor force. Hans Biebow, a Bremen businessman, served as the manager of the ghetto in Lodz, the Polish textile manufacturing city with the second-largest Jewish population after Warsaw. He pointed out to his superiors that almost all of the output of the ghetto's factories served the Third Reich's military needs. They were an "extremely sensitive component of the defense economy," he argued. But most Nazi officials had no interest in providing the ghetto's inhabitants with the food and other essentials required for them to remain productive. This even included Alexander Palfinger, Biebow's deputy. "The rapid dying out of the Jews is for us a matter of total indifference, if not to say desirable," he declared.

In his diary entry on December 19, 1939, Hans Frank, the governor general of occupied Poland, referred to the number of Jews estimated to be left in the territory that he presided over. "We cannot shoot 2,500,000 Jews, neither can we poison them," he wrote, sounding regretful that this was the case. "We shall have to take steps, however, designed to extirpate them in some way—and this will be done."

Most purported solutions still included the idea of further deportations rather than outright murder. When Germany invaded France in May 1940, the victors revived the so-called Madagascar Plan, which envisaged shipping four million Jews from German-controlled territory to the French island colony in the Indian Ocean, at a pace of one million per year. A totally impractical proposal, it was nonetheless seriously discussed by top Nazi officials, who believed the fall of France would be followed quickly by the defeat of Britain. When the Luftwaffe failed to win the Battle of Britain, Germany remained facing a formidable opponent in the skies and on the seas. As slim as the chances were for orchestrating such a massive transfer of Jews to Africa in peacetime, they evaporated altogether in the midst of the ongoing conflict.

Still, the notion of expelling Jews to some other distant destination lingered into 1941. SS Captain Theodor Dannecker, whom Eichmann had dispatched to Paris to deal with "the Jewish question" there, sent a memorandum on January 21 of that year to German offices in France about a "gigantic" task "whose success can be assured only through the most meticulous preparations." The task in question was "the carefully implemented complete deportation of the Jews prior to a colonization action in a yet to be determined territory."

Adam Rayski, a Polish-born member of the French Jewish resistance, wrote after the war that Dannecker's phrasing was open to differing interpretations. Was it, he asked, "an absence in Berlin at this time of a precise definition of the final objective, or rather a deliberate intention to keep this objective vague in order better to conceal it?" Rayski provided no answer.

Gerhard Engel, Hitler's army adjutant, offered a summary of the German leader's thoughts on the subject of what to do with the Jews in his diary entry on February 2, 1941: "In the first place, the war would accelerate the solution of the question; on the other hand, many additional difficulties would also present themselves." Reflecting on the occupied territories, Engel added, "If he [Hitler] only knew where the couple of million Jews could be sent: with so many, it was difficult to know."

The immediate initiation of the Shoah by bullets once Germany attacked the Soviet Union indicated that, at least for the Jews in the newly conquered territories, deportation was no longer considered an option. Jews from Western Europe could still be sent eastward, however. As Himmler wrote on October 10, it was "the will of the Führer that the Jews should be driven out step-by-step from west to east." But in the East, mass murder was already the norm.

Over a meal at his Wolf's Lair headquarters two weeks later, Hitler reminded Himmler and his chief lieutenant, Reinhard Heydrich, of his earlier prophecy that, in the event of a new war, "the Jew would disappear from Europe." He added: "It's not a bad idea, by the way, that public rumor attributes to us a plan to exterminate the Jews. Terror is a salutary thing."

In their search for new ways to speed up the killing, the Nazi leaders drew upon the experiences of their secret program targeting the physically and mentally disabled. In early 1939, before the invasion of Poland, as the US Holocaust Memorial Museum points out, they began this "first program of mass murder," which served as "a rehearsal for Nazi Germany's subsequent genocidal policies." The rehearsal included experiments with new methods of execution such as poison gas, which were then tried on Soviet POWs, Polish prisoners, and others.

In the early twentieth century, popular beliefs about the role of heredity and race in producing those viewed as inferior human beings fueled the eugenics movement in several countries. In Britain, its proponents focused on breeding people with "positive" traits; in the United States, the emphasis soon turned to forced sterilization to eliminate "negative" traits, which usually meant victimizing the poor and minorities. Before the movement was discredited by Nazi Germany's far more draconian practices, more than sixty-four thousand Americans underwent forced sterilization.

German proponents of eugenics, including prominent academics and doctors who had taken up the cause even before the Nazis assumed power, pushed more radical ideas. Along with Hitler, who spoke with revulsion about "those who perpetually soil themselves," they argued that the state should be free to kill anyone who was "unworthy of life." This had nothing to do with the usual definition of euthanasia: the voluntary ending of human life. It was a program of outright murder.

In May 1939 Hitler's physician Karl Brandt set up the Reich Committee for the Scientific Registering of Serious Hereditary and

Congenital Illnesses, whose euphemistic name barely concealed its purpose. Along with Philipp Bouhler of the Party Chancellery, Brandt led the effort to identify those slated for elimination. On August 18, 1939, the Interior Ministry ordered doctors and nurses to report all children under the age of three who were "deformed." In October parents were encouraged to send their disabled children to special pediatric clinics, where at least five thousand of them were killed by lethal injection or deliberate starvation.

The organizers of the Aktion T4, named for Tiergartenstrasse 4, the Berlin address where the coordinating staff was located, had no problem recruiting medical personnel for its program, which soon counted much larger numbers of adult victims. Hitler took the unusual step of signing the order for such killings. Bouhler and Brandt, it declared, were "commissioned with the responsibility of extending the authority of specified doctors so that, after critical assessment of their condition, those adjudged incurably ill can be granted mercy-death." One of Hitler's secretaries typed up the order for him to sign in October, but it was dated September 1, 1939—the first day of the war.

This backdating was no accident. The invasion of Poland offered an opportunity to extend that mission to the eastern part of the now expanded Reich and to suggest that somehow such killings were related to the war effort. The Einsatzgruppen and other security units murdered the patients of mental hospitals in the newly annexed territories. Most of the initial victims were Polish, but soon the distinction between Poles and Germans was largely ignored; if they were deemed to be unworthy of life, nationality offered no protection. Jewish patients were, by definition, placed in that category, regardless of their physical or mental condition.

At first, the victims were shot, often in forests near the hospitals that were emptied of their patients. Starting in October 1939, chemists of the Criminal Police (Kripo) and the SS began experimenting with executions using carbon monoxide in provisional gas chambers and sealed vans. Soon, six killing centers, with gas chambers disguised as showers, were in operation not only in the eastern parts of Germany but also elsewhere in the country.

Systematic murder on this scale within Germany was impossible to conceal entirely. Some of the American diplomats and correspondents stationed there recognized what was happening quite early. In October 1940 a German who had learned from a doctor about the Grafeneck killing center in the southern part of the country tipped off Charles Hulick, the US vice consul in Leipzig. Aside from relaying what he had learned about the killings there, he advised Hulick to look at the death notices placed by family members in the local newspapers. All of them had similar wording.

On October 26, for instance, the *Leipziger Neueste Nachrichten* ran a notice about a World War I veteran whose date of death was listed as September 23. "After weeks of uncertainty, I received the unbelievable news of his sudden death and cremation at Grafeneck in Württemberg." Other notices repeated those phrases about "the unbelievable news," varying only in terms of the location of death—in each case, mentioning a town with one of the killing centers.

Hulick's report from Leipzig, accompanied by twenty-two such death notices, was sent to the US embassy in Berlin. As a recent study suggests, CBS's William Shirer, who was one of the first American correspondents in Berlin to pick up on the story, probably saw that report. The US diplomats and journalists both mingled socially and frequently shared information. Since his broadcasts were subject to Nazi censorship, Shirer could not begin to tell his story publicly until he left Berlin in December and returned to the United States, where he published his famed *Berlin Diary* in June 1941.

In his diary entry dated November 25, 1940, Shirer wrote: "I have at last got to the bottom of these 'mercy killings.' It's an evil tale." He reported that the Gestapo "is systematically putting to death the mentally deficient population of the Reich." Henry Flannery, Shirer's CBS successor in Berlin, who arrived in November 1940 to overlap with him briefly, became suspicious of Nazi claims that British bombers were targeting German hospitals. He concluded that all of this was a cover-up for "their murder of the insane, crippled, hopelessly ill, even aged."

Within Germany, relatives of the victims received only their cremated remains, along with strict instructions not to ask questions or to "spread false rumors," Shirer noted. But Protestant and Catholic clerics expressed their objections to the practice. Most famously, Münster's Catholic Bishop Clemens August Graf von Galen denounced the euthanasia campaign in his sermon on August 3, 1941. He described openly how, "on instructions from Berlin," patients with incurable diseases were being forcibly removed from their homes and clinics—with their relatives learning of their deaths soon after. "There is little doubt that these numerous cases of unexpected death of the insane are not natural but often deliberately caused, and result from the belief that it is right to take away life that is unworthy of being lived," he declared. "Woe to us German people if we permit this heinous offense to be committed with impunity!"

From the beginning, Hitler had worried about the reaction of Germany's churches. While several priests who distributed copies of Galen's sermon were arrested, and some paid with their lives, the bishop remained free but under close surveillance. The Nazi leaders probably feared that his arrest or execution would have backfired. Partly as a result of Galen's courageous sermon, Hitler formally halted the T4 program three weeks later. By then, about seventy thousand people had perished in its killing centers.

But the killing of the psychologically and physically disabled, including children, soon resumed, continuing until the end of the war in a less centralized and even more secretive manner. Fearful relatives rarely spoke out, either because they genuinely did not realize what was happening or because they were "embarrassed by the stigma of carrying a 'degenerative illness' within their families," according to German historian Nicholas Stargardt. He added that the churches largely "fell silent" during this second phase of the killings. By most estimates, a combined total of at least two hundred thousand Germans were killed in the two different phases of the euthanasia campaign.

As historian Christopher Browning, the author of *The Origins of the Final Solution,* explains, there was an indisputable link between those actions and the pending fate of the Jews. "The killing of the handicapped and the Jews were two essential elements of the Nazis' wider vision of creating a racial utopia," he wrote. "The former was to cleanse the German race of its 'degenerate' or 'defective' elements. The latter was to destroy its ultimate enemy. They were two campaigns in the same crusade." And, most significantly, the T4 program proved to be the laboratory for the methods of mass murder that would be employed on a much larger scale in the war against the Jews.

For Stalin, Hitler's insistence on terror and mass murder as his weapons of choice in his simultaneous wars was no reason to rely less on his own standard draconian methods. On the contrary, the string of early German victories triggered a cascade of new threats and orders from the Kremlin. Stalin was particularly incensed to hear how many of his troops were surrendering to the invaders. "It was not the German attack that took Stalin by surprise but the collapse of our troops," Sergo Beria, the son of the NKVD chief Lavrenty Beria, wrote in his account of that period. The younger Beria was wrong in his contention that Stalin was not surprised by the attack itself, but he was right about the shock that the Soviet leader felt when he realized that discipline was breaking down in major units all across the front.

Stalin reacted by issuing orders that amounted to a death sentence not only for those who fled or wavered but also for many brave soldiers who stood their ground. On June 28 he spelled out his attitude toward his soldiers who were captured by the Germans. The "traitors who had fled abroad," as he called them, were to be punished immediately upon their return, and, in the meantime, their families were to be punished as well.

On August 16 Stalin issued his infamous Order 270 spelling out the specifics of his policy. "I order that (1) anyone who removes his insignia during battle and surrenders should be treated as a malicious deserter whose family is to be arrested as a family of a breaker of the oath and betrayer of the Motherland. Such deserters are to be shot on the spot. (2) Those falling into encirclement are to fight to the last and try to reach their own lines. And those who prefer to surrender are to be destroyed by any available means, while their families are to be deprived of all state allowances and assistance."

Ilya Vinitsky, a student at the Moscow Aviation Institute, volunteered for military service as soon as the Germans attacked—and quickly witnessed what such orders meant in practice. Assigned to the First Special Communist Battalion of Moscow, he was told, along with the other volunteers in this new unit, that they were entrusted with a special mission. Party officials explained that in the Baltic region, many soldiers had dropped their guns and either tried to escape or waited to surrender to the Germans. To put an end to such behavior, they declared, "The Central Committee authorizes you take whatever measures necessary—even executions."

Recalling those words as an octogenarian, Vinitsky fought back tears. Few memories are as painful to veterans of the Great Patriotic War, the official designation for World War II in Russia, as those of Soviet troops killing their own men. Like Hitler, Stalin was waging simultaneous wars right from the beginning. One was against the German invaders, and the other against those whom he deemed to be traitors or enemies within.

"We were proud we were assigned this special mission," Vinitsky declared. He claimed that he only rounded up deserters and didn't shoot any of them, marching them back to their main units. Most were relieved to have someone to tell them what to do, and they offered no resistance; in many cases, they had been left to fend for themselves when their officers were killed or fled. But some of Vinitsky's comrades admitted freely that they had executed soldiers to assert their authority. The special unit rounded up about fifteen hundred soldiers in all; Vinitsky did not know how many had been shot in the process.

According to a NKVD report, 667,364 soldiers who had "escaped from the front" were rounded up by October 10, 1941. Of those, 10,201 were shot, 25,878 were kept under arrest, and 632,486 were formed into new units—in many cases, penal battalions that were routinely sent on suicidal missions. During the course of the war, the ranks of the penal battalions were also filled with hundreds of thousands of prisoners from the Gulag.

Stalin wanted no exceptions in the application of his orders—even for members of his family. In July, Lieutenant Yakov Stalin, the dictator's elder son, found himself surrounded by German troops in Vitebsk. "I am Stalin's son, and I won't allow my battery to retreat," he announced, trying to follow his father's instructions. But he was captured, which meant he hadn't followed them to the end. When the Germans trumpeted the capture of their high-profile prisoner, Stalin was furious. "The fool—he couldn't even shoot himself!" he exclaimed.

The NKVD arrested Yakov's wife, Stalin's daughter-in-law Yulia, dispatching her to a camp for two years. The Germans would later offer to exchange Yakov for their famed Field Marshal Friedrich Paulus, who was captured in Stalingrad on January 31, 1943. Stalin refused, and, a few months later, his son carried out his father's wish. Stranded as a POW in Germany, Yakov committed suicide, reportedly by throwing himself on the camp's electrified fence.

Early in the war, the Germans suggested that a postal system should be set up for POWs of both sides. "There are no Russian prisoners of war," Stalin responded. "The Russian soldier fights on till death. If he chooses to become a prisoner, he is automatically excluded from the Russian community. We are not interested in a postal service only for Germans."

With no choice but to fight, Red Army troops began to perform better in the field. Hitler not only failed to exploit the resentment against Stalin's continuing reign of terror to win over the Soviet people, but also he gave them plenty of incentives to obey their orders to resist the invaders at all costs.

This was particularly true for Soviet Jews. The writer Ilya Ehrenburg, who had recently returned from living in Paris, summed up their sentiments in a speech he delivered in August 1941. "I grew up in a Russian city. I am a Russian writer. Now, like all Russians, I am defending my homeland," he declared. "But the Nazis have reminded me of something else: my mother's name was Hannah. I am a Jew. I say this with pride. Hitler hates us more than anyone else. And that does us credit."

Ehrenburg emerged as the most famous Soviet propagandist during the war, demonstrating that he could parry Nazi vitriol with his own. "Let us kill!" he urged his countrymen. "If you haven't killed a German in the course of the day, your day has been wasted."

Neither side was wasting many days.

EIGHT

"THE KINDLY ITALIAN GARDENER"

In *the August 4, 1941,* issue of *Life* magazine, Hanson W. Baldwin, America's most authoritative military writer, provided his analysis of the war up to that point. "The future depends in large measure upon the Russian campaign," he wrote. "A two to four months' victory in Russia (by 'victory,' I mean annihilation of the bulk of the Red Army) will put Germany in a far stronger position than ever before." His reasoning sounded much like Hitler's original rationale for launching Operation Barbarossa. By controlling the resources of the Ukraine and other parts of the Soviet Union, Baldwin argued, Germany would be "immune to blockade" and would have "completed the conquest of Europe." As a result, "Hitler's 'New Order' will be free to grow to its political and economic fruition."

Baldwin also examined another possibility, pointing out that "if the German drive into Russia bogs down into Napoleonic futility, Hitler himself may face eventual defeat." While his article was optimistically headlined "Blueprint for Victory," he sounded highly skeptical that this would prove to be the outcome. At best, he believed, Hitler would win in Russia only after a long campaign that would sap German strength and give Britain more time to rebuild its forces.

"But on the basis of all past experience—on our limited knowledge of the Red Army, on the operations of the first month—the world can anticipate another quick and decisive Germany victory," he wrote. For Britain, this would be catastrophic news. "If Russia and its resources fall easily within the Nazi orbit, victory is clearly beyond Britain's grasp," he concluded. "The best she can hope for is a negotiated peace."

In order to prevent this from happening, Baldwin urged his countrymen to join the war effort to stop Hitler, insisting that nothing short of such action could produce the blueprint for victory promised by the headline. He wanted to mobilize public opinion by offering his grim forecast of disaster if the Soviet Union did not receive a heavy infusion of aid from the United States.

As Stalin had effectively done when Harry Hopkins had visited him in Moscow, Soviet officials needed to both stress the urgency of their needs while convincing their Western counterparts that they would ultimately prevail. Despite the rapid advance by the German invaders and the massive losses they were inflicting on the Soviet defenders, some of those monitoring the fighting recognized that the balance of forces wasn't as one-sided as Baldwin and others were reporting. "In present instance, Russians are doing very well and should be encouraged to continue fighting, which they are showing they can do," General Lee, the US military attaché in London, noted in his diary on August 30. "They are bleeding, but the Germans are, too, and the latter can ill afford to lose all this blood, material, oil, and time." This was a view at odds with that of Major Yeaton, his counterpart in the US embassy in Moscow.

It wasn't just the Americans who were split on the question of whether the Soviet Union could hold out against the Germans. Two of the military attachés in the Japanese embassy in Moscow were delivering diametrically opposite readouts to their superiors in Tokyo in dispatches that were intercepted by the NKVD. Back in April, Colonel Michitake Yamaoka, the senior attaché, predicted a summer invasion, and he was convinced that the Germans would achieve victory by the end of the year. The rapidity of the initial German advance only strengthened his conviction that the Red Army would not be able to stop Hitler's forces. A Japanese newspaper correspondent who was in close contact with Yamaoka wrote in his diary on July 19, "The fate of Moscow will be resolved within a week." On August 11 he predicted: "Moscow should fall in early September."

But on the same day, Captain Takeda Yamaguchi, the naval attaché, reported that the German goal of achieving victory within two months was unrealistic. "If the war is conducted according to such plans, it will undoubtedly be lost, and we should probably expect an extremely dangerous situation in the future," he wrote to the Ministry of the Navy. By the following month, he was reporting that the Red Army was proving to be "pretty successful" in inflicting losses on the Germans, who by then were targeting Moscow.

For Tokyo, Berlin, and Moscow, the stakes in this debate were very high. Although Foreign Minister Yosuke Matsuoko had signed the Japanese-Soviet Neutrality Pact during his visit to Moscow in April, Stalin remained worried that Japan might attack from the east—especially if it looked like the Germans were about to score a quick victory against his country. From inside the German embassy in Tokyo, Richard Sorge, the Soviet spy, was reporting persistent German pressure on Japan to join the fighting. On July 1 Foreign Minister Ribbentrop predicted "the impending collapse of Russia's main military power and thereby presumably of the Bolshevik regime itself." This development, he added, "offers the Japanese the unique opportunity" to seize Vladivostok and keep going. "The goal of these operations should be to have the Japanese army in its march to the west meet the German troops advancing to the east halfway even before the cold season sets in."

This was a completely fanciful notion, since not even Germany's top generals could envisage such a meeting of the two armies, which would have required both to advance thousands of miles before the winter. But the idea was to entice Tokyo to strike, or at least to keep alive the notion of Japanese participation in the war against the Soviet Union. So long as Stalin could not rule out that possibility, he had to keep enough forces deployed in the Soviet Far East to fend off such an attack. Colonel Alfred Kretschmer, the German military attaché in Tokyo, did his part by suggesting how Japanese forces could seize control of Vladivostok and Siberia.

Sorge, who was working undercover in the German embassy's press section, took huge risks to try to convince Japanese officials that Operation Barbarossa was not succeeding as advertised. He reminded them of Napoléon's disastrous attack on Russia, arguing that Hitler's armies were likely to meet the same fate. He even told them that they should not believe the propaganda put out by his ostensible colleagues in the embassy, since he knew that the Soviet Union was not nearly as crippled militarily as they claimed.

But Sorge's primary task was to provide the Kremlin with the answer to its most pressing question: Were Japan's leaders seriously contemplating acceding to German pleas to enter the fight against the Soviet Union? During his trip to Moscow in late July, Harry Hopkins discussed the same question with Molotov. While the Soviet foreign minister did not expect an immediate attack from Japan, Hopkins reported to Roosevelt, "he felt that the Japanese would not hesitate to strike if a propitious time occurred."

Molotov conveyed his government's hope that Roosevelt would warn Japan that any such action would prompt the United States to join in the defense of Russia. In fact, US-Japanese tensions were already escalating. On July 26 Roosevelt had frozen Japan's assets in the United States after its forces moved into French Indochina, effectively imposing a trade embargo. Washington was wary of upping the ante further at that point. As a result, Hopkins responded that his government was monitoring the situation "with great care" but did not want to be "provocative" in its relations with Japan.

Nonetheless, both Roosevelt and Churchill were eager to demonstrate that they were ready to respond positively to Soviet appeals for help—even if Stalin and his lieutenants could drive them to total exasperation at times.

On August 29 Churchill responded by letter to Stalin's request for fighter aircraft. He informed the Soviet leader that 40 Hawker Hurricanes would reach Murmansk by September 6 and promised to expedite the shipment of 200 Tomahawks. Churchill also offered another 200 Hurricanes, for a total of 440 fighters, "if your pilots could use them effectively." But he added pointedly that "fighter aircraft are the foundation of our home defense" and were needed in North Africa as well. The implicit message: Britain could do only so much, given the precarious nature of its own military position.

Ambassador Ivan Maisky delivered Stalin's letter in reply on September 4. As Churchill noted with evident irritation, this was the Soviet leader's "first personal message since July." While thanking Churchill for the offer of more planes, he downplayed its significance, asserting that "these aeroplanes, which apparently cannot be put into use quickly and at once, but at different periods and in different groups, will be incapable of effecting serious changes on the Eastern Front."

Stalin underscored his point by admitting that the position of his forces had "considerably deteriorated" in the previous three weeks. "As a result, we have lost more than half of the Ukraine, and, in addition, the enemy is at the gates of Leningrad," he wrote. All of which presented "a mortal menace"—and not just to his country. "Germans consider it quite possible to smash their enemies singly: first Russia, then the English." Stalin, of course, failed to mention that Hitler had tried the reverse order earlier, hoping to defeat Britain first.

Then came Stalin's demands. To tip the balance, he declared, Britain needed "to establish in the present year a second front somewhere in the Balkans or France, capable of drawing away from the Eastern Front thirty to forty divisions," as well as supply the Soviet Union with thirty thousand tons of aluminum by early October, and provide "a *monthly* minimum of aid amounting to four hundred aircraft and five hundred tanks." Without such massive aid, he concluded, "the Soviet Union will either suffer defeat or be weakened to such an extent that it will lose for a long period any capacity to render assistance to its allies by its actual operations on the fronts of the struggle against Hitlerism." Stalin knew his letter would "cause dismay to Your Excellency," he concluded. "But what is one to do?"

The Soviet leader was right about Churchill's reaction, and his envoy did not help things by taking it upon himself to elaborate on Stalin's message. Maisky complained that Russia had been under attack for eleven weeks, struggling on its own to repel the huge concentration of German forces arrayed against it. Churchill was sympathetic to the country's plight, but his temper flared when Maisky asked "with an underlying air of menace," as the prime minister put it, how Britain could expect to win the war if it allowed Russia to be defeated.

"Remember that only four months ago, we in this island did not know whether you were not coming in against us on the German side," Churchill replied. "Indeed, we thought it quite likely that you would. Even then we felt sure we should win in the end. We never thought our survival was dependent on your action either way. Whatever happens, and whatever you do, you of all people have no right to make reproaches to us."

Maisky backed off. "More calm, please, my dear Mr. Churchill," he pleaded. As the ambassador recalled later, "I began to fear that in the height of his irritation, he might say a good deal that was unnecessary and thereby render our further relations more difficult."

Churchill promptly wrote back to Stalin in a more conciliatory vein, telling him that Britain would provide half of the total number of planes and tanks that he was asking for, while he hoped that the United States would supply the other half. But the prime minister was concerned enough about Stalin's letter and Maisky's tone during his visit that he also dispatched a note the next day to Roosevelt. "Although nothing in his language warranted the assumption, we could not exclude the impression that they might be thinking of separate terms," he wrote, alluding to lingering worries that Hitler and Stalin might once again strike a deal as they did in 1939.

Stalin did not help matters by sending Churchill a telegram on September 15 with another suggestion: "It seems to me that Great Britain could without risk land in Archangel twenty-five to thirty divisions, or transport them across Iran to the southern regions of the USSR. In this way, there could be established military collaboration between the Soviet and British troops on the territory of the USSR."

Churchill was stunned that Stalin could believe that Britain was in a position to do anything of the sort. "It is almost incredible that the head of the Russian government, with all the advice of their military experts, could have committed himself to such absurdities," he wrote in his memoirs. "It seemed hopeless to argue with a man thinking in terms of utter unreality."

But Churchill and Roosevelt knew that they had to deal with the tyrant, who could appear almost irrational at times. They understood that Stalin's underlying message, however offensive in its presentation, was largely correct: if the Soviet Union succumbed to the German onslaught, Hitler's position in the broader conflict would be strengthened dramatically.

In political terms, this gave Stalin a distinct advantage over the leaders of the other European states that Germany had conquered—and whose long-term goals were at odds with Stalin's geopolitical ambitions. Churchill and his team had sought to reassure the governments-in-exile and foreign troops in Britain that they were all allies in a joint enterprise, with the ultimate goal of not only liberating their homelands from Nazi occupation but also ensuring their complete independence in a postwar world. Polish and Czechoslovak pilots had already played a prominent role in the Battle of Britain, Polish troops were fighting alongside British units in North Africa, and Polish paratroopers in Britain were training for a future campaign to take back control of the Continent.

Recognizing the value of the new arrivals, Churchill's government assigned senior officials to act as liaison officers with the Poles, the Czechs, the French, and others. When Polish Prime Minister Władysław Sikorski, his government, and many of his troops escaped from France in June 1940, Conservative MP Victor Cazalet, a World War I veteran who had repeatedly warned about the danger that Hitler's Germany represented, took on the job of working with the Poles. He soon became a close friend of Sikorski's, traveling with him on visits to Polish units in Britain ("They make a very good show," he wrote on one such occasion) and also to the United States and Canada, where the Polish leader hoped to find new recruits.

As soon as Germany launched Operation Barbarossa, the Soviet Union and Poland were, in theory, on the same side. But the Poles had no intention of forgetting how Stalin had teamed up with Hitler to carve up their country or how two million of their countrymen, including the equivalent of several divisions of troops, had been deported to captivity in the east or simply disappeared. Noting that the Polish question was "at the root of our early relations with the Soviets," Churchill urged Ambassador Maisky and Sikorski's government to conduct negotiations in July 1941 aimed at getting the two sides to reestablish diplomatic relations and cooperate in the struggle against Germany.

The Poles wanted two clear commitments from Moscow: a declaration that the Nazi-Soviet partition of Poland was null and void, which would mean that the country would be restored to its pre-1939 borders at the end of the war, and the freeing of all Polish military personnel and civilians who were deported and imprisoned. This would allow the formation of Polish army units in the Soviet Union that would join the fight against the Germans.

At their talks, Maisky indicated immediately to the Poles that the Kremlin had other ideas about the borders of a reestablished Poland. "I explained that as we saw it, the future Polish state should only consist of Poles, and should cover those territories which were inhabited by Poles," he declared. The Polish negotiators understood that this formulation meant that the Soviet side intended to hold on to a large part of the territories it had annexed in 1939, since it viewed them as Ukrainian and Belorussian and had already conducted its version of ethnic cleansing there.

Sikorski was determined to reach an agreement, no matter how troubled he was by the Soviet stance and how much opposition he encountered within his own ranks. "Poles keep feeling they are giving away too much," Cazalet wrote in his diary as the two sides bickered over terms. "Ministers round Sikorski intriguing against him."

In a memorandum on July 1, Count Edward Raczynski, the Polish ambassador to Britain, argued that Sikorski should not be overly concerned about the specific provisions of any deal with Maisky. Given the rapid progress of the German invaders, the Soviet Union would "either be completely defeated and broken up into small political units, or at any rate pushed well beyond the Soviet-Polish frontier of 1939," he predicted. This meant that "the determination of our Eastern frontiers will not depend on the USSR." Instead, "our frontiers will eventually be determined by the victorious states, and presumably in the first instance by Britain and the USA."

But that was a minority view. Other Polish representatives realized that Stalin was already signaling his determination to dictate future peace terms, despite the fact that his country was fighting for its survival at that moment. When Sikorski signed the Polish-Soviet treaty on July 30, three of his ministers resigned in protest. Even some of his staunchest supporters felt that he had let them down. In an interview in 2016, when she was a still vivacious 103, his wartime secretary Walentyna Janta-Połczyńska recalled that she was convinced that the boss she adored lacked "the temperament that you needed to deal with the Russians."

Sikorski never felt he had any other option except to reach an agreement with Poland's historic foe. As Jan Ciechanowski, Poland's wartime ambassador in Washington, pointed out, "The British government was strongly pressing General Sikorski to speed up the conversations with the Soviets, instead of pressing the Soviets to accept the just conditions of Poland." Churchill conceded as much in his memoirs. Although Britain had gone to war over Poland, he was now intent on keeping his new Soviet ally in the fight against the Germans at all costs, especially if there was still any possibility of Stalin switching sides once again.

According to Churchill, he was not about to push Russia "to abandon, even on paper, regions on her frontiers which she had regarded for generations as vital to her security." As a result, the prime minister added, "We had the invidious responsibility of recommending General Sikorski to rely on Soviet good faith in the future settlement of Polish-Russian relations, and not to insist at this moment on any written guarantees for the future."

Aside from restoring diplomatic relations, the Polish-Soviet treaty did include provisions for the formation of Polish army units on Soviet soil and amnesty for Poles imprisoned there. The Nazi-Soviet pact of 1939 was declared invalid, but the territorial question remained unresolved. In Washington, Undersecretary of State Sumner Welles stated that he understood that the agreement "was in line with the United States policy of nonrecognition of territory taken by conquest." In the House of Commons, Anthony Eden claimed that his government did not recognize the territorial changes of 1939, but he added that this "does not involve any guarantee of frontiers by His Majesty's government." That was exactly what Maisky had hoped to achieve.

For Poles, as Ciechanowski put it, this was "the first swallow on the rising dawn of a new British policy of appeasement."

In the United States, public opinion was divided on the question of providing aid to the embattled Soviet Union. A Gallup poll taken in July 1941 indicated that 54 percent of Americans opposed such aid. By September, that number had decreased to 44 percent; however, the country remained deeply split even as German troops pushed deeper into the Russian heartland. "The American people don't take aid to Russia easily," Hopkins wrote to Britain's Minister of Information Brendan Bracken.

But, like Churchill, Roosevelt was fully committed to providing as much aid as possible to Russia. And he was willing to go to extraordinary lengths to try to convince his people that they should set aside their fears of the Soviet regime and focus on the goal of opposing Hitler. On September 11 Roosevelt met with Konstantin Umansky, the Soviet ambassador in Washington, to suggest that the Russians could help their cause by publicizing their putative commitment to freedom of religion, since this "might have a very fine educational effect before the next Lend-Lease bill comes up in Congress." Unlike Churchill, he was willing to encourage the whitewashing of Stalin's record to produce such an "educational effect."

One reason why Roosevelt tried to encourage Umansky to offer blatantly false assurances was that, just ten days earlier, he had focused his Labor Day speech on defending the freedoms of all Americans, including freedom of religion. Rhetorically at least, Roosevelt was sounding more and more like a participant in Britain's war effort rather than a supporter from the sidelines.

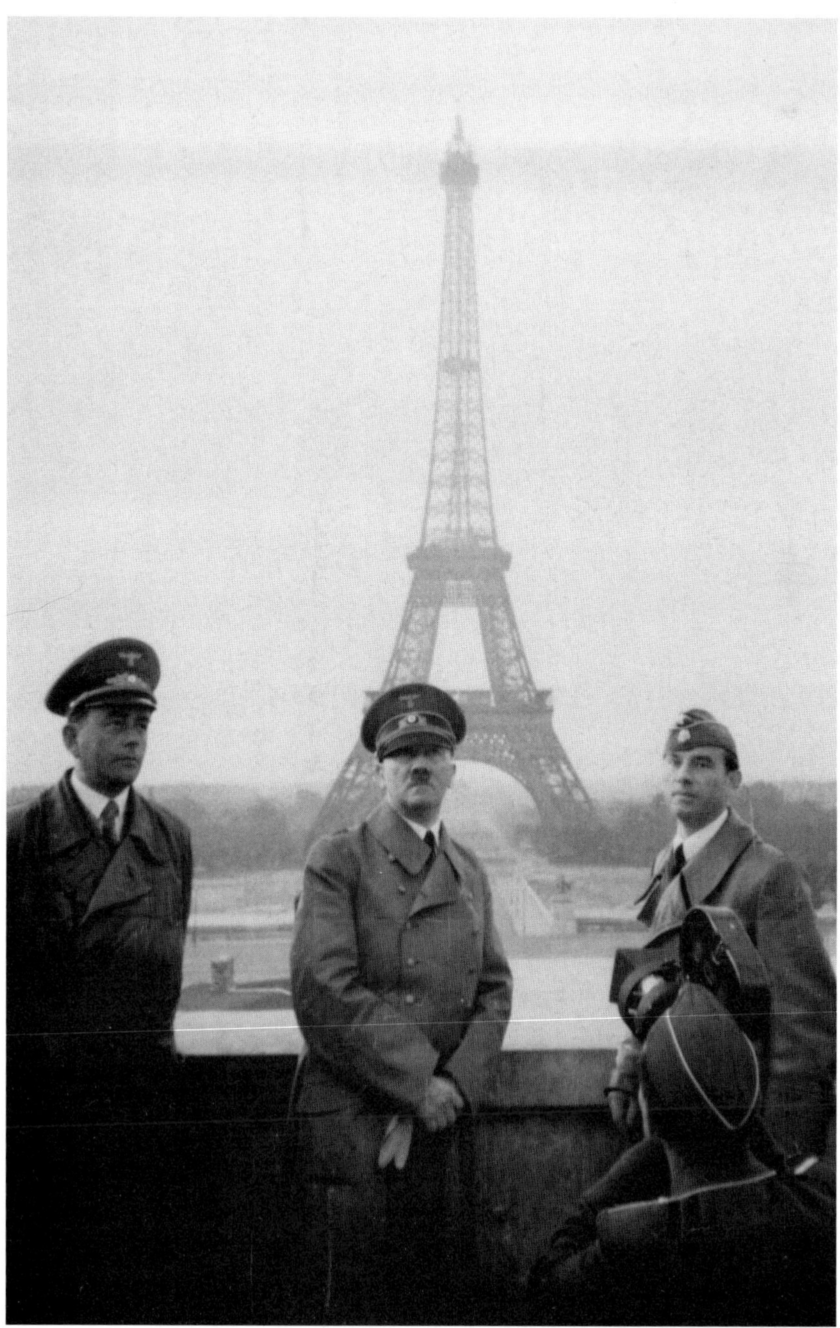

On June 28, 1940, Hitler celebrated his army's victory over France by visiting Paris. The Third Reich was at its apogee, and its forces looked unstoppable. Hitler admired the beauty of the city, but he told his favorite architect, Albert Speer (*left*), that "Berlin must be made more beautiful," befitting its role as the capital of a new Nazi world order.

On April 22, 1941, Prime Minister Winston Churchill viewed the damage that German bombers inflicted on Bristol. U.S. Ambassador John Winant stands behind him. Unlike his predecessor, Joseph Kennedy, Winant was a staunch supporter of Britain.

During the war, London was home to several governments-in-exile representing the nations of occupied Europe, while their troops who had managed to escape regrouped on British soil. Here General Władysław Sikorski, the Polish prime minister, and Churchill inspect a Polish unit.

Churchill welcomed President Franklin D. Roosevelt's election to a third term (above, FDR with his wife, Eleanor, on inauguration day, January 20, 1941). But the British leader pointedly reminded him that his country did not know "what the United States is planning to do, and we are fighting for our lives."

On August 23, 1939, Soviet Foreign Minister Vyacheslav Molotov (*seated*) and his German counterpart Joachim von Ribbentrop (*behind him*) signed the infamous Nazi-Soviet nonaggression pact while Joseph Stalin looked on.

At a reception in Hanover in November 1940, Molotov greeted Georg Thomas, the German Army's chief economist, who had tried to warn Hitler about the dangers of a wider war. Once those efforts failed, Thomas helped design the "Hunger Plan" for the Soviet Union.

At the start of 1941, Hitler and his top generals (Wilhelm Keitel, Walther von Brauchitsch, and Franz Halder) were already engaged in planning the invasion of the Soviet Union, which was launched on June 22.

From Tokyo, Soviet master spy Richard Sorge repeatedly warned the Kremlin about the pending German invasion, only to be dismissed by Stalin as "a little shit." Later, Sorge confirmed that Japan was ignoring German pleas to join in the attack on the Soviet Union. This freed up Red Army troops in the Far East, allowing them to play a critical role in the defense of Moscow.

No one opposed Roosevelt's policy of providing aid to Britain more fiercely than famed aviator Charles Lindbergh. Here, on April 23, 1941, he addresses a rally of the America First isolationist movement in New York. Lindbergh argued that the United States should not even attempt to stop Hitler's forces from conquering Britain.

German U-boats attacked ships seeking to maintain the flow of supplies to Britain, sinking many of them. But when they struck American ships, this only increased Roosevelt's determination to resist Nazi aggression and weakened the isolationist cause.

CBS's Edward R. Murrow (*above*), whose "*This* is London" broadcasts had a huge following, played a major role in winning popular support for Britain when it came under attack from the German Air Force. So did the celebrity foreign correspondent Dorothy Thompson (*below*), who lobbied intensely for the passage of the Lend-Lease bill. She visited Britain in the summer of 1941 to demonstrate her support for all those resisting Hitler. Here, she is on a submarine chaser of the Free French Navy.

Despite all the warnings he had received, Stalin was stunned when German troops launched Operation Barbarossa, the invasion of the Soviet Union, on June 22, 1941. At first, the invaders met minimal resistance. In some Ukrainian villages, they were even welcomed as liberators from Stalin's reign of terror.

Stalin entrusted the defense of Moscow and other key assignments to General Georgy Zhukov, who never flinched at sacrificing his men on the battlefield or executing anyone who tried to retreat.

General Heinz Guderian's panzer units pushed east all the way to Smolensk in less than a month. But Hitler's insistence on taking Kiev next proved to be a critical mistake, Guderian believed, since it delayed the assault on Moscow until the weather changed. German troops then found themselves caught in the autumn rains and mud, followed by the early winter cold.

Caught by surprise and often without weapons, hundreds of thousands of Soviet troops surrendered to the Germans in the early days of the German invasion. Kept in horrific conditions, most of these Soviet POWs quickly perished.

The Germans unleashed their own reign of terror wherever they advanced, hanging alleged Soviet partisans and deliberately starving the local population. The atrocities helped Stalin rally his people, including those who had suffered the most under his rule.

During the invasion of the Soviet Union, the first stage of the Holocaust was set in motion, the "Shoah by bullets." Einsatzgruppen, special killing squads, carried out mass executions in the newly conquered territories, methodically shooting their Jewish inhabitants along with Gypsies and other "enemies."

Soviet POWs were assigned the task of expanding the Auschwitz concentration camp, building the barracks for the Birkenau section (above) that soon became one of the major sites of the "Shoah by gas." The gas chambers at this and other camps made industrialized-style mass murder possible.

In August 1941, Churchill and Roosevelt held their meeting off the coast of Newfoundland to finalize the set of common principles known as the Atlantic Charter. Here, they meet aboard the British battleship *Prince of Wales* for a Sunday morning religious service with British and American sailors. "It was a great hour to live," Churchill recalled. "Nearly half those who sang were soon to die."

Churchill and Ambassador Ivan Maisky clink glasses at a lunch in the Soviet Embassy in London in August 1941. The veteran Soviet envoy frequently exasperated Churchill with his insistent demands on behalf of Stalin.

Roosevelt aide Harry Hopkins with Stalin during his visit to Moscow in August 1941. Maisky was convinced that Hopkins was "much more sympathetic" to Soviet needs than Churchill was.

Exhausted German soldiers near Moscow surrender to Red Army troops in full winter gear. Hitler's expectation of a swift victory before the extreme cold set in proved to be a major miscalculation.

The sinking of the battleship *Arizona* at Pearl Harbor on December 7, 1941. In a trans-Atlantic telephone call, Roosevelt told the British leader: "We are all in the same boat now." The surprise Japanese attack "certainly simplifies things," Churchill replied. "God be with you."

The day after Pearl Harbor, Roosevelt asked Congress to approve a declaration of war against Japan, which he signed while wearing a black armband. But, officially at least, the United States was still not at war with Germany.

Convinced that yet another expansion of the war would work to his country's benefit, Hitler put an end to any remaining uncertainty by declaring war on the United States in his speech to the Reichstag on December 11. He proclaimed his "unalterable determination to carry a fight once begun to its successful conclusion."

On December 26, 1941, Churchill addressed a joint session of Congress. Churchill warned that Britain and the United States still faced "a long and a hard war." But he was convinced that they would emerge victorious in the end. The events of 1941 were propelling Hitler's Third Reich, along with Japan, down the path to disaster.

"The task of defeating Hitler may be long and arduous," he declared. "There are a few appeasers and Nazi sympathizers who say it cannot be done. They even ask me to negotiate with Hitler—to pray for crumbs from his victorious table. They do, in fact, ask me to become the modern Benedict Arnold and betray all that I hold dear—my devotion to our freedom, to our churches, to our country. This course I have rejected—I reject it again." Then the president offered his most ringing proclamation yet: "Instead, I know that I speak the conscience and determination of the American people when I say that we shall do everything in our power to crush Hitler and his Nazi forces."

If Roosevelt had really wanted a casus belli, he could have seized upon a skirmish in the North Atlantic on September 4. A German U-boat fired torpedoes at the USS *Greer,* an American destroyer, but they missed. A British plane had spotted the U-boat earlier and dropped depth charges while the *Greer* was tracking it, which may have prompted the German crew to believe the American ship was responsible. After evading the torpedoes, the *Greer* dropped depth charges as well, but both vessels escaped unscathed.

A few days earlier, on August 31, the *Times* of London had vented its frustration with what it saw as American half measures. "The flood is raging, and we are breasting it in an effort to save drowning civilization," it opined. "America throws a line to us, and will give us dry clothes if we reach the shore. . . . We say this because we are frankly disappointed with the American contribution to the rescue."

Roosevelt's representatives in London shared some of those feelings. On the same day that the *Greer* was attacked, Ambassador Winant and General Lee compared notes over dinner. According to Lee, Winant declared that Britain had "no chance of winning" without full US support. On September 8 Lee's dinner partner was Eugene Meyer, the publisher of the *Washington Post*, who had just arrived in London. "He says that FDR is turning timid in his leadership of the country and feels very much bound by the sweeping campaign promises to keep the country out of war," Lee noted in his diary.

But at a lunch with British newspaper editors, Meyer defended the president, pointing out that he was taking action despite Lindbergh's most recent denunciations of "the British, the Jewish, and the Roosevelt administration" as warmongers. "I pointed out that Mr. Roosevelt is carrying out undeclared war and doing most of the things we would be doing if war were declared, and doing them more quickly than could be done through action by Congress," he recalled.

Lee was not convinced. On September 9 he wrote in his diary: "War is edging nearer to the United States, a nation which prefers to be unconscious of events. I cannot help wondering whether wisdom really does reside in the masses, because in so many cases lately, the masses have displayed less than no wisdom."

Roosevelt's response to the *Greer* incident was delayed because of the death of his mother on September 7. But in his fireside chat on September 11, he sounded eager to silence anyone who doubted his resolve. Ignoring the ambiguous background to the skirmish, he claimed that the German U-boat had launched its torpedoes in an unprovoked attack. "This was no mere episode in a struggle between two nations," he declared. "This was one determined step toward creating a permanent world system based on force, on terror, and on murder."

To block Hitler's bid to control the seas, he continued, the United States would pursue a policy of "active defense." His government "sought no shooting war with Hitler," he added, "but when you see a rattlesnake poised to strike, you do not wait until he has struck before you crush him. . . . From now on, if German or Italian vessels of war enter the waters, the protection of which is necessary for American defense, they do so at their own peril." In other words, American ships, especially those in convoys to Britain, were free to fire at will whenever they felt threatened.

Churchill was elated by those fighting words. "Roosevelt, this morning excellent," he wrote to the Earl of Athlone, the governor general of Canada, on the same day. "As we used to sing at Sandhurst [the Royal Military Academy], 'Now we *shan't* be long!' "

The prime minister was grateful for what he termed "the instant relief to our hard-pressed flotillas" as a result of the new American policy. In a letter on September 14 to Field Marshal Jan Smuts, Churchill explained the broader implications of Roosevelt's message. "Hitler will have to choose between losing the Battle of the Atlantic or coming into frequent collision with United States ships and warships," he wrote with evident satisfaction. As indicated by his citing the Sandhurst song in his previous letter to the Earl of Athlone, he felt increasingly confident that Roosevelt had positioned his country to move closer to direct involvement in the fighting. "American public have accepted the 'shoot at sight' declaration without knowing the vast area to which it is to be applied," he wrote, "and in my opinion, they will support the President in fuller and further application of this principle, out of which at any moment war may come."

Churchill knew he could not afford to air such thoughts in public. "All the above is for your own most secret information," he cautioned Smuts.

But friction was also a part of the rapidly evolving Anglo-American relationship, even when it came to their common goal of aiding Russia. As Churchill and Roosevelt had discussed in their meeting at sea, the two countries were planning to send a joint supply mission to Moscow. The idea was to assess Soviet needs and reassure Stalin that the Anglo-American powers would do everything possible to help. Roosevelt designated Averell Harriman, who was already in Britain coordinating the Lend-Lease program, to lead the US delegation, since Harry Hopkins was in no shape physically to make another grueling trip to Moscow. Lord Beaverbrook, the Canadian-British newspaper tycoon who had recently taken up the post of minister of supply in Churchill's War Cabinet after serving as minister of aircraft production, headed the British delegation.

When the two sides convened in London to map out their strategy, they immediately disagreed on a key point. Beaverbrook started the session on September 15 by proposing that the United States channel all aid for Russia through his ministry, allowing him to control its distribution. "The United States delegation was thunderstruck," Lee noted. "The proposal was a bald-faced bit of politics." Beaverbrook insisted this was the best way to handle the situation, but Harriman was having none of it. "If that is your attitude, we might as well go home," he told him. After that, according to Lee, Beaverbrook backed down—but the Americans in the room were still furious.

When the two sides got down to discussing what they could offer the Russians, they clashed again. Beaverbrook's team realized immediately that American generosity toward Russia would trigger cutbacks in supplies to Britain. This applied both to tanks and planes, which were badly needed by both combatants. It took Roosevelt's direct intervention to resolve those issues. The president ordered the doubling of US tank production, thus avoiding the feared reductions in shipments to Britain. And he acceded to British pleas not to send heavy bombers to Russia but compensated for this by increasing the number of other planes that could be sent there.

On September 19 Churchill invited most of the members of the British and American delegations heading for Russia to a lunch at 10 Downing Street. Lee was to remain in Britain, but he was in on the planning and also a guest at that luncheon. According to his account, Churchill rose after the meal and delivered a "very moving speech"—in effect, a pep talk for those who were to make the voyage. "The gist of it was that at this moving and solemn moment when the future of civilization is in the balance, the Anglo-American mission is starting out like a lifeboat to bring succor to the Russians, who are resisting such subhuman atrocities as the world has never seen before."

Lee was seated next to General Hastings Ismay, Churchill's

military adviser, who offered a more coolly pragmatic view. "He said there was no use in being too romantic about Russia," Lee noted, "that this was just a straightforward deal with Stalin, who is a crafty Oriental but who happens to be fighting Hitler."

The members of the mission to Moscow would quickly discover that negotiating with Stalin was hardly a straightforward exercise. Yet despite the occasional differences between them, the Brits and Americans on the team were increasingly committed to the common goal of bolstering Soviet resistance to the German invaders. In that sense, Hitler's latest act of aggression had already rebounded against him, since it was strengthening the partnership between London and Washington.

Beaverbrook, Harriman, and their senior aides traveled to Russia on a British cruiser, the HMS *London*, transferring to a Soviet destroyer when they reached the mouth of the Dvina River for the remaining twenty miles to Archangel. From there, four Soviet planes, accompanied by fighter aircraft, transported them to Moscow on September 28. The junior members of the US delegation had been dispatched in two American B-24 bombers that had flown directly to Moscow a few days earlier, helping provide a diversion while the leaders of the delegation made their secret journey by sea.

One of those making the direct flight was Quentin Reynolds, the *Collier's Weekly* reporter who had tried and failed to get a visa to Russia as a war correspondent. Instead, he had arranged with Harriman to go in as the mission's press officer, with his employer lending him out for that purpose. On the flight over, he sat in the frigid cabin next to Colonel Philip Faymonville, the former military attaché in Moscow who had been assigned to the Russian aid program. "He was one of the few Americans I had met who doubted the Germans could conquer Russia," Reynolds recalled. Members of both delegations kept debating that question even as they pursued their mission.

There were also decided splits on how to strike the right balance between meeting Stalin's demands for aid and protecting Western interests. Churchill cautioned Beaverbrook not to get carried away with his enthusiasm for his current assignment. "Your function will be not only to aid in the forming of plans to help Russia, but to make sure we are not bled white in the process," he instructed him. "And even if you find yourself affected by the Russian atmosphere, I shall be quite stiff about it here." Like the prime minister, Harriman believed that Beaverbrook was prone to be overly generous to the Russians "to the point of disregard of other considerations."

The visitors were anxious to gauge the mood of wartime Moscow. Having arrived early, Reynolds had the chance to walk about the "shabby" city and notice the long lines of people waiting in front of every food store. He noted that there were no able-bodied men in those lines or elsewhere, indicating they had all been called up for "the last ditch stand" to stop the Germans from taking the city. "At this point, the Nazis had overrun sixty thousand square miles of Russian soil and were only a little over two hundred miles away," he wrote. "That much the foreign correspondents knew, but little more, since none of them were being allowed anywhere near the fighting."

Nonetheless, Reynolds was impressed by the fact that new recruits were training daily in Red Square, and that the poorly dressed people he saw on the streets "looked anything but frightened." While there was "no rational reason" to believe that the Russians could stop the Germans from taking the city, he concluded, "I felt at least as confident as I thought the Muscovites felt."

When the planes carrying Harriman, Beaverbrook, and the rest of the delegation approached Moscow for landing, they had to dive for a low approach while antiaircraft guns opened fire to ward off any possible German pursuers. Harriman was hosted at Spaso House, the residence of US ambassador Laurence Steinhardt, which had several blown-out windows from earlier bombing raids. But to anyone like Harriman, who had spent time in London during the Blitz, Moscow appeared to have survived with relatively little damage to date. Still, he knew there was a chance they would all have to evacuate the city hastily if the Soviet defenses proved inadequate. "You had the feeling of going into a war area," he recalled later. "We could see the flash of Russian antiaircraft guns at night."

Beaverbrook and Harriman met for three consecutive evenings with Stalin, each time for about three hours. On those same days, other members of the delegation met with their Soviet counterparts in subcommittees to deal with the military supply issues. "The discussions were frustrating and achieved nothing," General Ismay complained. The Soviet officials largely stalled until they could take their lead from Stalin.

In theory, Stalin was the supplicant, but neither he nor his guests acted that way. Beaverbrook and Harriman signaled their desire to placate him. They decided to exclude Steinhardt and British Ambassador Stafford Cripps from their meetings, much to the envoys' chagrin. "We knew that Stalin had no very high regard for either of them, so there was nothing to be gained by taking them," Harriman explained. Disregarding normal practice, they also did not bring their own embassy interpreters with them; instead, they relied on a Soviet interpreter, former Foreign Minister Maxim Litvinov.

All of which only contributed to nervousness among embassy staffers, as Charles Thayer of the US embassy put it, that "too much be promised with not enough strings attached." Regardless of the outcome of the talks, those early preemptive efforts to please Stalin were based on the miscalculation that he would respond to such behavior with gratitude—rather than with even more insistent demands.

Beaverbrook and Harriman reported that their first session with Stalin was "extremely friendly." That may have been overstating things, but the Soviet leader reviewed the military situation and provided his wish list of supplies—tanks, antitank guns, planes, antiaircraft guns, even barbed wire—without taking any jabs at his guests. Although Foreign Minister Molotov was also present, Stalin did almost all the talking. Harriman was struck by how brusquely he cut off Molotov on the rare occasions when he tried to inject himself into the proceedings.

According to Harriman, the Soviet leader was blunt in presenting his country's critical situation. He talked about the three-to-one or even four-to-one ratio of German to Soviet tanks and emphasized "the vital importance of holding Moscow at all cost." If that effort failed, he vowed that his troops would continue to fight a defensive war from behind the Urals, but this would represent a loss of "the nerve center of all Soviet operations," and they would be severely limited in their ability to push back the Germans.

It was no accident that his analysis did not differ that much from the arguments that Heinz Guderian and other German generals had made to Hitler when they urged him to concentrate their forces on Moscow. According to Harriman's account, Stalin explained that Hitler had "blundered" in mounting an offensive on three fronts. "If he had concentrated his attack on Moscow, the city certainly would have fallen," he admitted.

There were a few awkward moments. Stalin again raised the possibility of British troops joining Soviet forces in the Ukraine. Like Churchill, Beaverbrook offered no encouragement. Taking his cue from Roosevelt, Harriman tried to raise the issue of religious freedom, noting that it was of concern to American public opinion, but Stalin hardly bothered to respond. Yet Beaverbrook and Harriman felt "more than pleased" by this first round, which bolstered their confidence that the Soviet leader intended to do everything possible to prevent the Germans from taking Moscow. At the same time, his no-nonsense demeanor suggested that he did not want to needlessly antagonize his new allies.

Stalin also impressed his visitors with his grasp of technical details. When Beaverbrook mentioned that the motor of the British Hurricane fighter plane had 1,350 horsepower, Stalin smiled as he corrected him: "No, it has only twelve hundred fifty." Recounting this exchange to Reynolds, Beaverbrook added: "And he was right." Like Hitler, Stalin loved to show off his superior knowledge on almost any subject.

During his Moscow visit, Beaverbrook instructed a junior diplomat in the British embassy to buy twenty-five pounds of caviar. He planned to share the bounty with Harriman and other members of the delegation during the return trip on the British cruiser, and then with friends back in London. Churchill was among the intended recipients, although there was no indication that the prime minister knew anything about this. But the junior diplomat made the mistake of mentioning his assignment to Philip Jordan, the Moscow correspondent of the London *News Chronicle*, who pounced on the tip.

According to Jordan's story, which received wide coverage elsewhere as well, all of the caviar was earmarked as a gift for Churchill. The furious prime minster immediately dispatched a telegram castigating Beaverbrook for embarrassing him by making it look like he was concerned with such luxuries in wartime. Beaverbrook then castigated the junior diplomat who was the source of the leak. But everyone had far more serious issues to worry about, which meant this was only a momentary flap.

The real drama played itself out when Beaverbrook and Harriman returned for their second evening of talks with the Soviet leader. "Stalin was very restless, walking around and smoking continuously, and appeared to both of us to be under an intense strain," Beaverbrook recounted. In his report, Harriman called the evening "very hard sledding." He wrote: "Stalin seemed discourteous and at times not interested, and rode us pretty hard." Both men were taken aback by his change of mood and his contemptuous disregard for them. He picked up the phone and made three calls in their presence, dialing himself. When Beaverbrook handed him a letter from Churchill, Stalin barely glanced at it and left it on the table, ostentatiously ignoring it.

On the issue of supplies, the Soviet leader was openly combative rather than grateful. "Why is it that the United States can only give me a thousand tons of armor plate steel for tanks—a country with a production of over fifty million tons?" he asked Harriman. When the American tried to explain that it took time to increase capacity for this type of steel, Stalin shot back, "One only has to add alloys." At another point, he appeared to write off the entire British-American effort to help his country. "The paucity of your offers clearly shows that you want to see the Soviet Union defeated," he said. The only time he appeared appreciative was when Harriman offered him five thousand American jeeps, and he immediately asked if more would be available.

Later, Beaverbrook and Harriman concluded that Stalin must have been preoccupied by a stream of new warnings that the Germans were about to seize Moscow. But, at the time, they knew very little about those increasingly alarming reports, and they returned to their respective embassies in a grim mood. Harriman recalled how "rattled" his British counterpart was—and what a failed mission might mean for him personally. "Beaverbrook was constantly thinking of his own reputation with his colleagues in the British government," the American pointed out. For that reason, Beaverbrook suggested that Harriman take the lead in the next and final meeting, presenting the list of supplies that both their governments could offer to Stalin. "Then, if things did not go well, the fire would be directed at me," Harriman concluded.

The next day, the Germans were proclaiming the talks a failure. Goebbels, the Nazi regime's chief propagandist, gloated that no agreement was possible between the visitors and the "Bolshevists." But when the downcast duo of Beaverbrook and Harriman arrived at the Kremlin for their final meeting, Stalin promptly signaled a change in tone. "It is up to the three of us to prove Goebbels a liar," he declared.

Despite his earlier recommendation that Harriman take the lead,

Beaverbrook responded by going down the list of supplies requested by the Soviet side, pointing out which ones Britain and the United States could provide quickly and adding some suggestions of their own. He also indicated which supplies would be harder to get, but Stalin was visibly pleased. Litvinov, the interpreter, jumped up and exulted: "Now we shall win the war!"

According to Harriman, "The meeting broke up in the most friendly fashion possible. Stalin made no effort to conceal his enthusiasm. It was my impression that he was completely satisfied that Great Britain and America meant business."

Before the delegations left Moscow, they were treated to a farewell banquet at the Kremlin. Like any good journalist, Reynolds was careful to note the details of this "twenty-three course orgy," which featured caviar in huge bowls, mushrooms sautéed in sour cream, sturgeon in champagne sauce, and pilaf of quail. All this was accompanied by endless vodka toasts, with glasses refilled from carafes of different varieties of the drink.

"Feasting thus, I found it a little difficult to remember that the Germans were now less than a hundred miles from Moscow—or to recall the lines of the hungry of this classless society doubtless even now waiting at the doors of the food stores," Reynolds wrote.

As pleased as Harriman was by the outcome of their talks, he was also struck by the surreal scene at the Kremlin dinner, and he made a similar point. "Churchill was always careful to conform to British rations, whereas the tables of the Russian officials were groaning with all kinds of delectable foods, and the people were hungry," he observed. "I thought it was disgusting."

Even on this occasion, Stalin could not resist reverting to form. He once again asked Beaverbrook why the British were not willing to open a second front on the Continent. "What is the good of having an army if it doesn't fight?" he said. "An army which does not fight will lose its spirit." General Ismay pointed out that the British army was fighting in the Middle East—and he could have added that it had fought earlier in France when Stalin was still adhering to his pact with Hitler. But nothing could stop Stalin from returning to the second-front theme again, again, and again.

The mission to Moscow allowed the Americans and British participants to try to take the measure of the Soviet leader. Their first impressions were often naïve, almost comically so—except for the fact that Stalin's already long record of mass murder and duplicity should have served as more than adequate warning not to fall into the traps set for them.

Reynolds saw Stalin for the first time at the Kremlin dinner, and he was, by his own admission, amazed by the figure coming to greet Beaverbrook and Harriman. From the pictures and omnipresent posters of Stalin, he had expected someone "huge, forbidding, surly." Instead, "the rather bowlegged little man who walked toward us, his face a broad grin when he caught sight of Beaverbrook and Harriman, was a shattering contradiction of the public image," Reynolds recalled. "I gathered that he wore elevator shoes." He quoted a British correspondent as saying, "He looks like the kindly Italian gardener you have in twice a week." Reynolds added: "It couldn't have been put better."

While those observations were all about Stalin's physical appearance and did not necessarily reflect political judgments, Beaverbrook and Harriman, who had spent a total of nine hours with him during their three talks, did not hesitate to blend the two. Beaverbrook observed the Soviet leader carefully, even noting that his doodling habits included "drawing numberless pictures of wolves on paper and filling in the background with red pencil" while Litvinov translated his remarks. Rather than seeing anything ominous in those sketches, Beaverbrook explained that he and Harriman had come to see him in a positive light. "We have got to like him; a kindly man, with a habit, when agitated, of walking about the floor with his hands behind his back," he declared. "He smoked a great deal and practically never shows any impatience at all."

Harriman summarized his impressions in a similar vein. "I left feeling that he had been frank with us and if we came through as had been promised and if personal relations were retained with Stalin, the suspicion that has existed between the Soviet government and our two governments might well be eradicated," he wrote. It was as if he and Beaverbrook were so relieved to find a more cordial Stalin at their final meeting and dinner that they had banished any memory of the boorish Stalin they had encountered earlier.

At least some of the other members of the delegation were less prone to see only what they wanted to see. Ismay observed that, at the dinner, Stalin was "the best-dressed man of the party," wearing civilian clothes that consisted of "long boots of fine leather, baggy trousers, and a well-cut blouse of a dove gray color and obviously expensive material." He was also surprised by Stalin's "diminutive" stature, but he was not fooled about his fundamental nature.

"He moved stealthily like a wild animal in search of prey, and his eyes were shrewd and full of cunning," Ismay noted. "He never looked one in the face. But he had great dignity, and his personality was dominating. As he entered the room, every Russian froze into silence, and the hunted look in the eyes of the generals showed all too plainly the constant fear in which they lived. It was nauseating to see brave men reduced to such abject servility."

Ismay also reflected on Stalin's "unmannerly" treatment of Beaverbrook and Harriman, particularly during their second evening together. "I wondered then, and I have often wondered since, whether we were right when confronted with that kind of behavior to turn the other cheek, as we persistently did throughout the war," he wrote in his memoirs. While he agreed with the policy of helping the Soviet Union in its struggle against the Germans, the general believed that it was "surely unnecessary, and even unwise, to allow them to bully us in the way they did." After all, Stalin desperately needed the help of the

Western powers. Those who argued that a tougher stance by London and Washington might drive Stalin back into the arms of Hitler were wrong, he maintained. "Stalin was a realist, and knew perfectly well that the only alternatives open to the Russians were either to keep on fighting for their lives or to become slaves of Hitler," he concluded.

Ismay's inclination to take a refreshingly unblinking view of his country's new ally was only strengthened by an incident that occurred shortly before the British and American teams left Moscow. James Allan, an emaciated British soldier, had showed up at the British embassy. Freed that morning from the Lubyanka, the notorious NKVD prison, "he had a shocking story to tell," Ismay recalled. While serving in France in 1940, Allan was captured by the Germans and sent to a POW camp in Germany. He then managed to escape to Poland, where "friendly Poles" kept him hidden. But he was determined to get back to Britain, so he crossed into Russia before that country was invaded. The Russians promptly labeled him a spy, locked him up, beat him daily, and nearly starved him to death. With the British delegation in town, they decided to let him go.

The visiting delegation took Allan back to England with them, and he was later awarded the Distinguished Combat Medal. But there was no public mention of what he had done to deserve this award. As Ismay pointed out bitterly, "The courageous endurance of devilries perpetrated on a British soldier by an ally of his country could not have been divulged at that time."

Right after they returned from Moscow, Beaverbrook and Harriman went for dinner with Churchill and Eden at Chequers to report further on their mission. Since both men had sent extensive reports earlier, they did not need to go into much detail. Instead, Beaverbrook, who was still smarting from Churchill's scolding over the caviar incident, immediately berated the prime minister for accusing him of "importing illicit caviar" from Russia. Churchill tried to deflect his anger by claiming he had not made such an accusation, and they moved on to other subjects. As Harriman put it, the British leader "seemed greatly reassured by our reports of Stalin's determination to fight on," and the dinner ended with everyone in good spirits.

As the four of them were leaving the dining room, Churchill turned to Beaverbrook and asked: "Now, after all this talk, where is that caviar?"

NINE

"WE WILL BREAK THEM SOON"

In *mid-September 1941, as Hitler* was finally ordering his generals to prepare for Operation Typhoon, the delayed push to reach Moscow, SS officer Otto Günsche visited his Wolf's Lair headquarters in East Prussia. Günsche had served on the Eastern Front and was on his way back to Bavaria for further training in the SS officer school there. Before the invasion of the Soviet Union, he had served as one of Hitler's SS bodyguards, and he would later become the personal adjutant to the German leader. Therefore, it was hardly surprising that he was friends with many of the men still on duty in Hitler's headquarters, and they greeted him warmly when he showed up.

Günsche was surprised by the impressive size of Wolf's Lair, contrasting it with the much more modest headquarters such as the Felsennest (Rock Nest), which had been set up south of Bonn for the conquest of Western Europe earlier. When he asked some of the officers stationed there whether this was where Hitler planned to spend the winter, they laughed as if this were an absurd idea. "Spend the winter? What are you thinking of?" one of them replied. "We are fighting a blitzkrieg against Russia. Christmas we will certainly be celebrating on the Obersalzberg as usual"—a reference to Hitler's Alpine retreat.

Once Hitler learned that Günsche was visiting, he summoned him to the conference room in his bunker, eager to hear his impressions from the Eastern Front. Judging by the way the Führer greeted him—he was whistling softly to himself—he was expecting good news. While conceding that the Russians were fighting hard, Günsche did not disappoint him. He reported that morale among the SS troops was high and that they were happy to be fighting.

Hitler offered a prediction that reflected his ebullient mood. "We will break them soon; it is only a question of time," he said. "I have ordered Panzer armies with over two thousand tanks to group before Moscow. Moscow will be attacked and will fall. Then we will have won the war."

After the Soviet forces defending the capital were defeated, he added, German troops would continue their drive all the way to the Urals, finally stopping there. The Luftwaffe would then be charged with bombing any Soviet troops that might regroup farther east, while the Russians in any unoccupied areas would be left to starve. Right before dismissing Günsche with a Fascist salute, he vowed, "As the reformer of Europe, I shall make sure that a new order is imposed on this land according to my laws!"

Over meals in Wolf's Lair during the next couple of weeks, Hitler expanded on his pet themes about Germany and Russia. "It's inconceivable that a higher people should painfully exist on a soil too narrow for it, whilst amorphous masses, which contribute nothing to civilization, occupy infinite tracts of a soil that is one of the richest in the world," he declared. "We must create conditions for our people that favor its multiplication, and we must at the same time build a dike against the Russian flood." His ambitions for conquest were only a reflection of natural law, he continued. "If today you do harm to the Russians, it is so as to avoid giving them the opportunity of doing harm to us. God does not act differently."

No aspect of the new order was too grandiose or too minute for him to consider. Once Russia was conquered, he pointed out, all Germans who traveled on trains would do so in "first or second class, so as to distinguish themselves from the natives." The difference between first and second class, he added, would be that in first class there would be places for three people to sit on each side of a compartment, while there would be four in second class. He did not bother to explain what conditions might be like in the sections where "the natives" would be crammed.

Hitler was clearly obsessed with the notion that Russia was home to hordes of *Untermenschen* whom he viewed as barbarian Asiatics, whether they lived in the European or Asian part of the country. "Asia, what a disquieting reservoir of men!" he mused. "The safety of Europe will not be assured until we have driven Asia back behind the Urals. No organized Russian state must be allowed to exist west of that line." He envisaged a wave of people "foaming down from Asia" that could overwhelm a complacent Europe, and it was up to the German occupiers to "meet it with a living wall," since it would be impossible to create a physical barrier to stop it. But he claimed to welcome this challenge. "A permanent state of war on the Eastern Front will help to form a sound race of men and will prevent us from relapsing into the softness of a Europe thrown back upon itself," he argued.

At the same time, the conquest of Russia would ensure prosperity for the German people, he insisted, allowing it to create "an empire of worldwide importance." Under German stewardship, the Ukraine's rich soil would produce harvests "several times" larger than in the Soviet era, he predicted, and the Black Sea would be "for us a sea whose wealth our fishermen will never exhaust." As a result, "In twenty years' time, European emigration will no longer be directed toward America, but eastward," to the new land of opportunity. None of this purported bounty would be shared by the current inhabitants of Russia, however, since they "will be supplied with no means of production whatsoever, except of absolute necessities."

He conceded that others might ask how he could condemn so many people to misery—or "how can the Führer destroy a city like Saint Petersburg?" His response: he had learned early that life is "a cruel struggle." Besides, "I plainly belong by nature to quite another species." He claimed that he would prefer not to see anyone suffer. "But when I realize that the species is in danger, then, in my case, sentiment gives way to the coldest reason."

Taking a speculative turn, he pondered his own life's course, especially his early days, which had taught him the logic of this kind of reason. "Who knows? If my parents had been sufficiently well-to-do to send me to a school of art, I should not have made the acquaintance of poverty, as I did," he told his mealtime companions. "Whoever lives outside of poverty cannot really become aware of it."

Hitler conveniently overlooked the fact that his failure to gain admission to the Academy of Fine Arts in Vienna had nothing to do with his financial situation. In 1907, he qualified to take the entrance exam and was completely convinced he would pass easily. Instead, he was rejected with the terse comment: "Test drawing unsatisfactory. Few heads." As Hitler admitted, this was "a bolt from the blue" for him.

Hitler never allowed facts to get in the way of his reasoning—or in the way of rewriting the story of his life, with its explicit message that fate was propelling him on a messianic mission. But his belief about certain victory in Russia would soon prove to be just as illusory as his conviction that he was destined to study art in Vienna.

Operation Typhoon was launched on September 30, just as Beaverbrook and Harriman were holding their talks with Stalin in the Kremlin. General Guderian, the tank commander who had tried in vain to convince Hitler to attack Moscow earlier, received his orders to lead the offensive from the south, where his troops had succeeded in capturing Kiev, inflicting massive casualties and taking 665,000 prisoners in the process.

But by then, the Wehrmacht had lost several precious weeks, and Guderian was no longer nearly as confident as he had once been that the attack on Moscow would succeed. "The Battle of Kiev was undoubtedly a great tactical victory," he noted. "But whether great strategic advantages were to be garnered from this tactical success remained questionable. It all depended on this: would the German army, before the onset of winter and, indeed, before the autumnal mud set in, still be capable of achieving decisive results?" During the battle of Kiev, heavy rains had already turned the area's unpaved roads into rivers of mud at times, signaling the kind of growing difficulties the general's panzer troops would face as the weather inevitably worsened.

Nonetheless, Guderian was quick to follow his orders to advance north toward Moscow, targeting Orel first. On October 2 Franz Halder, the Wehrmacht's chief of staff, received Guderian's report that his troops had broken through enemy lines and were already approaching that city. "TYPHOON has started with smashing force and is making excellent progress," Halder wrote in his diary. When Guderian's tanks rolled into Orel a day later, the local authorities were caught totally by surprise—so much so that the trams were running as if this were a normal day. Crates full of dismantled machinery and tools from local factories lined the streets, indicating that they had also failed to carry out their orders to evacuate such equipment for use farther east.

Vasily Grossman, the famous war correspondent for the Red Army newspaper *Krasnaya Zvezda,* recalled the pointed exchange he had with his editor after he returned to Moscow from covering the German push from the south. "Why didn't you write something about the heroic defense of Orel?" the editor asked. Grossman's reply: "Because there was no defense."

But three days after they seized Orel, Guderian's troops received a nasty surprise of their own. Attacked by Russian T-34 tanks, they sustained major losses. "This was the first occasion on which the vast superiority of the Russian T-34 to our tanks became plainly apparent," Guderian admitted. It also confirmed his earlier suspicions that the Soviets had been developing a better tank than his own troops' Panzer IVs. In order to be effective against the new Russian tank, the driver of a Panzer IV had to maneuver behind the T-34 and fire an extremely accurate shot at the grating above the engine to put it out of commission. From other angles, the Germans could only damage the tank but not disable it.

German pilots who were sent on missions to bomb Moscow were also discovering how effectively the capital had prepared for their attacks—and how the Soviet Air Force was beginning to recover from its huge initial losses. Lieutenant Richard Wernicke, who flew one of the notorious Junkers Ju-87 Stuka dive bombers, recalled how startled he was by the hail of antiaircraft fire that he and his fellow pilots faced as they dove down over their targets. "It was terrible: the air was full of lead, and they were firing very accurately," he said. "We hadn't seen anything like this before." Newly built Soviet fighters, such as the Yakovlev Yak-7, appeared in the sky, he added. "They were very dangerous. They even dived right behind us."

For Guderian, the other unpleasant discovery was the extent to which the continual combat, first in the Ukraine and now in the Russian heartland, was exacting a toll not only in higher than expected casualties and exhausted troops, but also in overextended supply lines. While the panzer units began to experience occasional food shortages, the general was especially worried about the looming change in the weather and the lack of warm clothing for his men. He asked repeatedly for winter clothing, only to be told that his soldiers would get what they needed "in due course," and he should stop making such "unnecessary requests." The same thing happened with his appeals for antifreeze for the engines of the vehicles. "We saw as little of this as we did of winter clothing for the troops," he noted bitterly. "This lack of warm clothes was, in the difficult months ahead, to provide the greatest problem and cause the greatest suffering to our soldiers—and it would have been the easiest to avoid of all our difficulties."

With Guderian's troops and other units already experiencing the heavy fall rains and first freezes of a winter that started early even by Russian standards, the elements appeared to be conspiring against them. "General Mud and General Cold are helping the Russian side," wrote Grossman, the Soviet war correspondent. The problem was that Hitler and many of his generals had talked themselves into believing that they would knock out the Soviet Union before the onset of extreme weather, which meant that they had failed to prepare for a winter war. Like Stalin in the early days of the invasion, Hitler was responsible for a growing number of self-inflicted wounds, and his troops were beginning to pay the price for them.

The German forces advancing on Moscow were still formidable and mostly victorious, but they were already not the juggernaut that they had been during the first stages of the offensive. They were feeling the strains of moving so far so fast—and, as in Guderian's case, of abruptly shifting course and targets. They were about to face their most difficult test to date, with a growing sense of unease about whether they were up to it.

For the German troops advancing from the west instead of the south, the first major target was Vyazma, which lay directly on the path to Moscow, 140 miles away. In early October they turned that town and its immediate surroundings into the next "cauldron": an inferno of death and destruction for the Red Army units that found themselves trapped there with almost no possibility of escape. The Soviet brass had failed to recognize how quickly the Germans were moving to encircle their troops. During less than two weeks, Army Group Center claimed it killed four hundred thousand and captured another six hundred thousand Red Army troops—a staggering one million tally. The Germans almost certainly inflated their figures, but not by an exponential amount. Soviet losses totaled in the hundreds of thousands.

Most Soviet histories of the war barely mentioned Vyazma. "In our literature, one can find hardly any information about this battle," Boris Oreshkin, one of its few survivors, pointed out. "It's quite normal: who wants to talk about defeats?" His account, published only in 1991, as the Soviet era was ending, offers graphic testimony about how the Red Army troops on the ground were the victims of a complete breakdown in command and communications.

Manning an observation post atop a high hill with three other soldiers, Oreshkin watched wave after wave of German planes flying overhead, followed by explosions and smoke on the horizon. They tried to report what they were seeing, but they could reach only a soldier standing guard at a nearby airfield, who showed no interest in their warnings. "I think that we—four ordinary soldiers—were the only people who could see clearly what was going on," he claimed.

Soon the bombs were falling closer, and Oreshkin found himself in a sea of soldiers desperately trying to break through the German positions. "People threw away gas masks, helmets, and bags," he recalled. "Everyone had just one thought: to have enough time to escape the encirclement." Thinking that he would be safe if he could make it only a short distance to the other side of the German lines, he even threw away his food bag, normally the last item that a panicked soldier abandons.

Oreshkin and the others spent the night running blindly back and forth in the woods, trying to avoid bursts of German machine-gun fire and cascades of artillery shells. At one point, he saw a blinding light as an explosion threw him to the ground. When he opened his eyes, he saw a friend who had fallen next to him with a gaping wound between his shoulder blades. "Dress my wound," the friend pleaded. Oreshkin tried to help him, but it was hopeless, and another round of shells quickly sent him sprawling again.

By the next morning, Oreshkin felt completely exhausted and

dispirited. "Even death felt like deliverance," he recalled. But then he saw a line of German troops approaching and Soviet soldiers struggling to their feet, barely able to raise their hands in surrender. Following the example of a junior officer, he threw his gun and documents into a pond and joined a group of about twenty surrendering soldiers. He was immediately struck by the disdainful confidence his captors displayed. "We were conveyed to a village by a single soldier," he noted. "He was walking ahead of us and didn't even think that it was necessary to hold the gun in his hands. He was sure that we would do nothing to him, and this fact finally broke me down, humiliated me, and showed me the whole helplessness of our situation."

Oreshkin would miraculously survive to fight again and, in 1944, to capture German troops who would feel as humiliated and defeated as he did then. But the overwhelming majority of those trapped in Vyazma didn't have a chance of making it. When the battle was over, Maria Denisova, a fifteen-year-old girl from one of the villages destroyed in the fighting, emerged from hiding in the basement of her house to a scene of pure horror. "There were so many dead bodies all over the place," she recalled. "We walked on them as if it was a floor covered with bodies. They were next to each other and on top of each other. Some didn't have legs, heads, or other parts. We had to walk on them, since there was no other place to step. . . . It's awful to remember! The river was red with blood, as if there was only blood flowing there."

In 2005 I accompanied a small team of "searchers"—mostly young Russian veterans who regularly return to World War II battlefields—on a camping trip to the dense woods near Vyazma. They were combing the area for—and still finding—the remains of soldiers, their gear and weaponry. They saw it as their mission to rescue the dead from anonymity. Since 1990, this group had found the remains of about a thousand soldiers and brought them to a small cemetery for burial; other groups had been active, too, and the cemetery held a total of thirty thousand remains at that point, all gathered in the same fifteen-year period since it was started. As Yegor Chegrinets, a member of the group I was with, pointed out, "You can't escape the war here. It just grows out of the ground."

On October 7, 1941, even before the fighting in Vyazma was completely over, General Halder described the operation in his diary as "a brilliant success." Two days later, Otto Dietrich, Hitler's press chief, announced that the victory at Vyazma meant that only "empty space" stood between Germany's forces and Moscow, indicating that the Soviet capital was doomed. According to the *Völkischer Beobachter*, the Nazi newspaper, "The military end of the Bolsheviks" was at hand.

But some of the German troops who participated in the battle for Vyazma recognized that it was far too early to celebrate. Joachim Pusch was a forward observer whose job was to spot and then relay the positions of Red Army troops firing mortars, so that German artillery units could direct their fire against them. "What I didn't like is that when I gave coordinates, all of a sudden you got only three shells per gun," he recalled. "That really disappointed me." Unlike in the early days of Operation Barbarossa, supply problems led to the rationing of ammunition, he pointed out, and this meant "things started to slow down."

After the war, General Gerhard Grassmann reported that his artillery regiment's experiences during the push to Moscow confirmed that these were not isolated shortages. "There was hardly enough ammunition for satisfying the requests from the infantry for direct fire support and for neutralizing definitely identified assemblies of enemy forces," he declared. During critical battles, he added, his men were able to fire only about one-third of the howitzer rounds that they had originally planned on firing.

The Wehrmacht had calculated it needed about thirty trainloads of supplies on a daily basis, especially ammunition and fuel, for the troops mounting the drive on Moscow. By then, however, only about twenty trainloads a day were reaching them.

This did not stop the German press from proclaiming victory in increasingly categorical terms. "Campaign in East Decided! The Great Hour Has Struck!" the headlines screamed.

Despite his assurances to Beaverbrook and Harriman that his forces would prevail in the end, Stalin was far from certain that they were capable of saving Moscow. The British and American delegations were barely gone when Stalin began scrambling to save the situation. On October 6 he called General Zhukov—whom he had dispatched earlier to handle the defense of Leningrad—and ordered him to fly back to Moscow at once. Arriving in the capital the next day, Zhukov went straight to Stalin's Kremlin apartment, where the Soviet leader was recovering from a bout of the flu.

Stalin pointed to a map. "Look, we're in really serious trouble on the Western Front, yet I cannot get a detailed report about what's going on," he complained. Zhukov's assignment, he told him, was to head there immediately and report what was happening. But Zhukov understood that Stalin had a far more ambitious task in mind: he was to find a way to stop the Germans from marching into Moscow and declaring victory.

While both Stalin and Hitler overruled their generals at will, and Stalin had ordered the purges of the top officers of the armed services in 1937, a key difference in the behavior of the two tyrants was rapidly emerging as their forces battled each other. Hitler continued to believe that he was far more qualified than any of his generals when it came to both strategy and tactics; he would never trust their judgment. Stalin, on the other hand, still did not hesitate to terrorize both his generals and troops, but he had developed a grudging respect for Zhukov's judgment and abilities. The general, in turn, appeared to be more self-confident than any of his peers, less fearful of speaking up honestly in Stalin's presence. Marshal Semyon Timoshenko claimed later that Zhukov was "the only person who feared no one. He was not afraid of Stalin."

This was an overstatement. Zhukov knew he was lucky to have survived the purges that swept away so many of his fellow officers. As he admitted, one reason was that he had not been promoted more quickly, which meant he was a less obvious target at the time. But he had felt anything but secure, knowing how easy it was to be labeled "an enemy of the people." According to his daughter Ella, he always kept a small brown suitcase packed with two changes of underwear and a toilet kit in case the next knock on the door was for him. She remembered how it stood near his bed and how her mother would put in fresh clothes from time to time. Even as a child, she could feel the pervasive atmosphere of fear. "We never spoke openly about it at home," she said.

After the major purges of the military had ended, Zhukov caught Stalin's eye because of his leadership of the Soviet army group in Mongolia in 1939. Japanese forces had attacked Soviet forces there, and Zhukov had responded by driving them back. Although his troops sustained heavy casualties, he scored a decisive victory that produced an agreement among Japan, the Soviet Union, and Mongolia to end hostilities. It also taught Japanese military leaders not to underestimate Soviet capabilities, something they would remember when Germany began pushing for them to join in the attack on Moscow in 1941.

Stalin particularly liked the fact that Zhukov never flinched when it came to sacrificing men on the field of battle. As soon as the Soviet leader had sent him to Leningrad in September 1941 to deal with the "almost hopeless" situation there, Zhukov began dismissing those generals he felt were not up to the job; he also insisted that the troops stop retreating and launch new attacks, no matter what the odds—or face the firing squad if they disobeyed. Like Stalin, Zhukov could be brutally tough on those who reported to him. He was famous for his tirades laced with obscenities. "You are not a general but a bag of shit!" he would tell subordinates.

By the end of the month, the German advance had been arrested, and it settled into what would become the nine-hundred-day German blockade of Leningrad to starve its inhabitants. According to official Soviet figures, 632,253 civilians would die during the siege, but the Germans never took the city.

Right after his talk with Stalin on October 6, Zhukov had gone to the headquarters of the Western Front to determine how the German drive toward Moscow could be stopped. He called Stalin from there at two thirty in the morning. "The principal danger is that the road to Moscow is almost entirely unprotected," he reported. The fighting at Vyazma and elsewhere had destroyed any continuous front, and there were few reserves left to fill in the gaps. He recommended concentrating any remaining forces on the Mozhaisk defensive line, which ran for 135 miles from north to south, at a distance of about sixty miles west from the capital.

Zhukov spared no one in trying to win time to build up those defenses. About four thousand cadets from the Podolsk military academies were ordered to fill one of the most glaring gaps in the line where German troops were advancing. The inexperienced cadets were completely outgunned and, according to official accounts, suffered about 80 percent casualties in just a few days of fighting.

Boris Vidensky, one of the survivors who went on to become a military historian, recalled that the cadets faced the additional threat from their own lines. "This was the first time I saw NKVD blocking units," he said, referring to the troops assigned to shoot any soldiers trying to retreat. "They were behind us." But whatever he thought of those terror tactics at the time, he expressed approval of them when looking back more than sixty years later. "The idea was to resist the Germans at any price," he said. "Such toughness brought us victory."

This illustrated another difference between Stalin and Hitler. The Führer directed his terror campaigns in the territories his army conquered primarily at perceived foreign enemies, whether military or civilian—only reinforcing their hatred of Nazi rule, in most cases. Stalin was prone to direct much of his terror against his own troops. An estimated 158,000 Soviet soldiers were sentenced to death during the war. By contrast, German military tribunals sentenced a total of 22,000 soldiers to death for desertion, not just on the Eastern Front but everywhere they served. When it came to condemning the soldiers and officers in his armed forces, Stalin far outdid Hitler.

Zhukov calculated that he had only about ninety thousand men left to stop the Germans from taking Moscow. He sent them out to defend key positions, while Muscovites hastily dug trenches and erected antitank barricades at the approaches to the city. But still the German forces kept coming, and it was no longer possible to hide the extent of the danger they represented. On October 13 Stalin ordered the evacuation of top Party, government, and military officials to Kuibyshev, the Volga River city about six hundred miles to the east that had been picked to serve as the temporary capital if Moscow fell.

On the morning of October 16, an official communique provided more bad news. "During the night of October 14–15, the position on the Western Front became worse," it declared. "The German-Fascist troops hurled against our troops large quantities of tanks and motorized infantry, and in one sector broke through our defenses."

Despite appeals from the Moscow Communist Party organization for "iron discipline, a merciless struggle against even the slightest manifestations of panic, against cowards, deserters, and rumor-mongers," the sense of panic was growing, while rumors flew that the Germans were about to enter the city. Faith was dwindling that either Stalin or Zhukov could prevent the looming catastrophe.

The American and British diplomats in Moscow were increasingly pessimistic as well. After sending his wife to safety in Sweden, US Ambassador Steinhardt gathered his staff at Spaso House on October

15 to discuss evacuation procedures for everyone else. Major Yeaton, his military attaché, had spent the previous night at the embassy dacha, eleven miles from the city on the Smolensk highway, waking that morning to artillery fire. When he looked out the window, he saw Red Army soldiers setting up machine guns in the front yard. He was convinced this was the end. "I knew I would never see the place again," he recalled. At the Spaso House meeting, he told his colleagues that Moscow could hold out only for another thirty-six hours.

Colonel Faymonville, Yeaton's nemesis and predecessor who had returned to the Soviet capital as part of the Harriman mission, was also at the meeting. Harry Hopkins had arranged for him to stay behind when the rest of the delegation departed so that he could coordinate aid for Russia there. But even Faymonville, who had earlier echoed Soviet propaganda claims that the invaders would be driven back, "now had completely lost his nerve and gave them only five hours more before the Germans would arrive," according to embassy staffer Charles Thayer.

During the discussion, Molotov summoned Steinhardt to the Kremlin, along with British Ambassador Cripps. He instructed the two envoys to evacuate all their personnel to Kuibyshev immediately. "The fight for Moscow will continue and the fight to defeat Hitler will become more serious," Molotov told them. When the two ambassadors asked to stay in the capital as long as he and Stalin were there, Molotov refused, telling them that he and Stalin would join them in Kuibyshev in a day or two. The message seemed clear: the fight for Moscow would have to continue from outside the capital.

Steinhardt returned to Spaso House and told his staffers that they all had to assemble at the Kazan Station for a train that same evening. He delivered the same message to the American correspondents, who now included Quentin Reynolds. Like Faymonville, Reynolds had stayed behind when the rest of the Harriman-Beaverbrook team left, resuming his regular job as a reporter for *Collier's Weekly*. Steinhardt told the newsmen: "You have no discretion in the matter."

While Reynolds also took this as a sign that Moscow was about to fall, Tina Sofiano, his Russian secretary and translator, refused to give in to the dark mood. "You Westerners do not understand our country," she told him. "In *War and Peace*, Tolstoy said of Napoléon's campaign, 'The maggot may gnaw at the cabbage, but the maggot dies before it has killed the cabbage.' That is what will happen."

At the Kazan Station, as the first snow of the year came down in large flakes that promptly turned into slush, the assembled foreign diplomats and journalists from all the countries represented in Moscow milled around for hours before finally getting the signal to board. They brought along whatever personal belongings they could carry themselves, along with food and drink for the journey. "Thanks to Sofiano, I had a roast chicken, some radishes, and two bottles of vodka," Reynolds reported with evident satisfaction.

Their train consisted of thirty-three coaches and one locomotive "that seemed to tire frequently," as he put it. The diplomats traveled in the "soft" cars, and the journalists traveled in the "hard" cars, but the five-day, snail-paced ride wasn't comfortable for anybody. Heat and drinking water were in short supply, and the train was frequently diverted to sidings as troop trains headed in the other direction, toward Moscow. On one occasion, they sat on a siding for seven hours "not at all cheered by the spectacle of a bomb- and machine-gun-scarred train on the next track," Reynolds noted.

When the exhausted passengers got their first glimpse of their new home—a dreary Volga city that nonetheless startled them with its twinkling evening lights, since it was far enough east not to require the blackouts that had been the norm in Moscow—they saw little reason to expect good news. After all, Molotov had all but conceded that it would be impossible to stop the Germans from taking the capital, and now they could monitor developments only at a distance, underscoring the desperation of the situation.

Back in London on October 15, the same day that the foreign diplomats and correspondents were evacuated from Moscow, Harriman met with Churchill one more time before flying back to Washington the next day. He asked the prime minister for his assessment of the war. "Well," Churchill replied, "Hitler's revised plan undoubtedly is now—Poland, '39; France, '40; Russia, '41; England, '42; and, '43, maybe America."

A threat hangs over Moscow and our country," the newspaper *Izvestia* wrote on October 16. Trying to inject a note of reassurance, it added: "As always, the Soviet people look danger right in the eye." But, like the earlier myth that Red Army troops had all resisted valiantly instead of surrendering in huge numbers when Hitler's armies crossed into the Soviet Union in late June, this was hardly the case. The scenes of chaotic evacuation and near anarchy, which included looting, strikes, and other previously unimaginable acts of defiance of the regime, belied the notion that Muscovites were always steadfast in their resolve and confident of victory. Instead, October 16 was a day of panic in the capital that most Soviet historians were eager to forget when they wrote their heroic accounts of the Great Patriotic War later.

With reports that the Germans were within striking distance of the capital and rumors that they were already filtering into its outskirts, the rush for the exits was transformed into a near stampede. The official registration statistics leave no doubt on that score. In September Moscow's population was 4,236,000. In October it had dropped to 3,148,000, and, by January 1942, to 2,028,000. While there was the official evacuation of top government and Party officials, key factories, and other installations deemed essential to the continuation of the regime, many of the city's inhabitants fled on their own.

The personal accounts of those who were in Moscow on October 16, along with the secret reports of alarmed NKVD agents, offer graphic examples of the startling scenes they witnessed. Dmitry Safonov, who was working at an artillery factory near Moscow that was to be evacuated to the Urals, had just returned to the city to collect some belongings. "All of Moscow seemed to be streaming out somewhere," he recalled. "I hardly recognized the city." The roads were clogged with cars and trucks loaded down with personal belongings, while many of the people rushing about on the street "didn't seem to know what to do." At the railroad station where he was hoping to catch a train, he saw suitcases, bags, clothes, lamps, even a piano—all abandoned either by those who had already managed to board a train or by those jamming the platforms in the hopes of doing so.

Some of the privileged Muscovites who tried to flee in their own cars discovered that the police had largely melted away, and they were at the mercy of the mob. G. V. Reshetin, an art editor, recalled how people blocked the cars and attacked them. "They pulled the drivers and passengers out of the cars, beat them, and threw their belongings on the ground," he wrote. Sometimes they hijacked the cars for themselves; at other times, they appeared to join in out of sheer vindictiveness.

Mikhail Zhuravlev, the head of the NKVD's directorate for Moscow and the Moscow region, filed a report two days later about the "anarchistic behavior" of factory workers. Some examples:

"Some workers of factory No. 219. . . . attacked cars with evacuees from Moscow who were traveling on the Highway of the Enthusiasts. . . . They began seizing the evacuees' belongings. Six cars were thrown into a ravine by this group."

A group of workers from a synthetic leather factory "stopped a car with the evacuated members of the same factory's workers' families. Some passengers were beaten unmercifully, and their belongings were seized."

At Factory Number Eight, there was "counterrevolutionary agitation," which consisted of an arson attack on a warehouse and the ransacking of the belongings of a group of workers and their families singled out for evacuation. "The damage from the fire is about 500,000 rubles."

At the same time, looters attacked stores, especially those with any remaining food items that had been rationed up to that point. They also broke into the apartments of those Muscovites who had already left, and they even attacked the now empty British embassy.

Black smoke rose from the chimney of the NKVD headquarters at Lubyanka Square, which local residents realized meant that the feared secret police were in a rush to burn their incriminating files. Some Muscovites also took the initiative to purge their dwellings of the symbols of the regime. Valeria Prokhorova, at the time a twenty-two-year-old graduate of the Institute of Foreign Languages, recalled: "People were dumping Communist literature and portraits of the Party leaders"—the turgid volumes of Marx and others, along with the obligatory portraits of Lenin and Stalin. Garbage bins were overflowing with the detritus of the Stalin era, which no one would have dared to throw away at any other time. At night, "criminals and drunks" roamed the streets, and the police were nowhere in sight, Prokhorova said. "It felt like doomsday."

Tamara Bylinina, the young widow of a military officer who had been executed during the purges a few years earlier, was one of the thousands of women assigned to digging trenches on the outskirts of Moscow. When word spread that the Germans were about to break through, she rushed back to her communal apartment in the city, which she shared with about a dozen other people. She saw immediately that the portraits of Stalin and Lenin were gone from the walls and that someone had incinerated a twelve-volume collection of Lenin's speeches and writings. "People were scared that the Germans could execute them for worshipping those idols," she explained.

Their fear was well founded, but not the only motivation for some of those who were engaged in such destruction. Prokhorova heard people cursing Stalin. "We suffered from hunger, and they kept telling us that we are living in the richest country," she quoted them as saying. "What about now? Where is Stalin? He has abandoned us."

Bylinina reported that some of her neighbors were eager to greet anyone who would rid the Kremlin of its current rulers. "Good, they've sucked enough of our blood," one said.

While all this was happening, Stalin and most of the rest of the Kremlin team remained largely invisible—except for Anastas Mikoyan. The Politburo member decided to intervene when he received an urgent plea for help from the director of the Stalin Motor Vehicle Plant, where the workers had gone on strike. When he drove up to the locked factory gates, he found five thousand to six thousand workers demonstrating there who immediately bombarded him with questions: Why hadn't they been paid in two weeks? Why were they locked out of their own factory? Why had the government fled Moscow, along with Party and Komsomol (Communist Youth League) officials from the factory? Why was no one explaining anything to them?

Mikoyan tried to calm them. "Comrades, why are you so outraged?" he said. "There is a war on, and anything can happen." He branded the "rumors" that the government had fled as "provocations." While he admitted that some government departments had been evacuated, he added, "Those who have to be in Moscow are in Moscow. Stalin is in Moscow, Molotov as well—all the people who have to be here." The workers should maintain their trust in the government, which was proceeding according to "well-prepared plans," he assured them. Those plans included provisions for their livelihood. What was needed, he concluded, was "composure and discipline to deal with the enemy."

Mikoyan's rare personal intervention appeared to produce the desired result, and the workers gradually dispersed. But he had been far from candid with them. He failed to tell them that the reason they were locked out of their factory was that explosives had already been planted on its grounds. A day earlier, Stalin had issued a directive "to blow up factories, storage facilities, and institutions that cannot be evacuated"—and their factory was one of the designated facilities. He also failed to mention that Stalin had already ordered many of his top officials to leave Moscow, and most of them assumed that he planned to join them very soon.

Mikoyan was not merely covering up for the regime. He was also genuinely uncertain about Stalin's next move. In the universe that was controlled by the decisions and whims of one man, the leader had not yet decided what that next move should be.

During those critical days when Moscow looked most likely to fall, Stalin appeared to share the assumption that he would have to abandon the city. On October 14 he and Molotov met with Georgi Dimitrov, the head of the Comintern. Dimitrov was struck by the degree that the Kremlin leaders, along with everyone else, assumed that evacuation was inevitable. "Since Moscow itself is becoming the front, preparations must be made for the worst possible scenario," he wrote in his diary. Molotov issued him clear instructions: "Evacuation is necessary. I advise you to leave before the day is out." According to Dimitrov, Stalin's message to him was simple: "Moscow cannot be defended like Leningrad."

As Dimitrov and Molotov prepared to leave, Stalin added, "Have to evacuate before the day is out!" According to Dimitrov, he said this as casually as if he were saying "Time for lunch!" Stalin did not specify when he might follow them, but Dimitrov was convinced it would be very soon.

Dmitry Volkogonov, the former Red Army general and Stalin biographer, insisted that the Soviet leader was anything but sanguine about taking such a drastic step. "He was tormented by alarming presentiments," he wrote. "In those dark days, the enemy struck blow after blow, and Stalin felt that only a miracle would save him."

Everything was prepared for Stalin's evacuation: a special train, fully equipped and waiting at the station, and—just in case he needed to make an even hastier exit—his personal Douglas DC-3 and three other planes.

On the evening of October 15, Stalin decided to drive to his dacha, only to be told that it was already mined in preparation for the Germans, and he shouldn't go there. Irritated, he ordered his aides to "clear the mines" and announced that he would stick to his plan to spend the night there. This was most likely just another case of his asserting his absolute power and did not yet signal a decision on whether or not he would leave Moscow.

The next day, as Stalin was driving back to the Kremlin, he came upon looters: "people carrying bags with flour, bundles of sausages, hams, boxes of macaroni and noodles," according to one of his bodyguards. Stalin ordered his driver to stop and got out of the car, and a crowd immediately gathered around him. Some people applauded, and someone asked him, "Comrade Stalin, when will we stop the enemy?"

Instead of offering his normal ringing assurances of victory, he merely replied, "There is time for everything." The fact that he reportedly did not rebuke or threaten anyone for looting showed how much the disorders on the streets must have taken him by surprise.

Arriving at the Kremlin, he told his entourage to proceed with the evacuation of the government to Kuibyshev—although some ministries were to be scattered in other cities. Even Politburo members were ordered to go there, while a few officials, including NKVD chief Beria, were to stay in Moscow until they completed arrangements for the underground resistance activities once the Germans took over, including the blowing up of key installations.

As late as 2005, in the midst of a building boom in Moscow, new evidence was discovered about the extent of those plans. When construction workers began demolishing the Hotel Moskva, the Stalin-era behemoth close to Red Square, they found more than a ton of explosives in the building's foundations. Luckily, the TNT had deteriorated over time, and there were no detonators, which suggested that either the hotel had served as a storage site for the explosives or the authorities had never finished their preparations. But there was no doubt that the hotel had figured in the planning for a German-occupied Moscow.

As for Stalin's own plans, he announced, "I'll go tomorrow in the morning." Given the increasingly alarming reports streaming into the Kremlin, this looked like the only reasonable choice. Mikoyan reported that German troops on motorcycles had been sighted about fifteen to eighteen miles from his family dacha, which was about nine miles southwest of Moscow. That meant the German troops were only about twenty-five miles from the city's outskirts. Other reports put their scouts even closer.

Yet despite the growing sense of danger and Stalin's assertion that he was about to leave the city, the Soviet leader was still undecided. He was reading a new biography of Field Marshal Mikhail Kutuzov, who had led the Russian army to victory over Napoléon in 1812, and tellingly underlined the sentence "Until the last minute, no one knew what Kutuzov intended to do." Air Force Marshal Alexander Golovanov saw Stalin sitting in his office on that day, October 16, asking himself again and again, "What shall we do? What shall we do?"

On October 18 Stalin went to the station where his special train was waiting. Pavel Saprykin, a railway worker who had helped prepare it for what promised to be a historic trip, recalled that he saw the Soviet leader there. Stalin walked up to the train, he said, and paced the platform beside it. It was as if he were only then making his final decision. Then, instead of boarding the train, he left the station.

From that moment on, Stalin vowed not to leave Moscow. His period of wavering was over, and he signaled that he was definitely in charge again by employing the tactic he had always relied on: brute force. Declaring martial law on October 19, he sent out NKVD troops with instructions to shoot almost anyone who acted or looked suspicious. Emergency tribunals were empowered to deal with looters and other lawbreakers, which meant issuing prompt death sentences.

More than six decades later, Yevgeny Anufriyev, a surviving member of one of the NKVD patrols, was still reluctant to discuss the details of what happened then. But he was clear about the instructions his unit received. "We had an amazing order to shoot spies and deserters on the spot," he recalled. "We were ordered to do this, but we didn't know how to figure out who was a spy. So the order had no practical significance." Perhaps in his case, it didn't. But he hinted that there were many cases in which it did. "Well, a lot of stupid things were done then. What more can I say?"

There's no reliable tally of how many Muscovites perished in the subsequent crackdown, but Stalin's message that draconian rule was back in force registered loud and clear. The looting and most other acts of random violence ended abruptly, and those Muscovites who had remained in the city sensed the new determination to stop the Germans from taking it.

In his carefully vetted memoirs, Zhukov claimed that most Muscovites had behaved well during the mid-October crisis. "But, as the saying goes, there are black sheep in every family, and, in this case, too, cowards, panicmongers, and self-seekers started fleeing the capital in all directions, spreading panicky rumors about an inevitable surrender," he wrote. The proclamation of martial law was necessary for "mobilizing the troops and civilians to repel the enemy and. . . . preventing a repetition of the panic stirred up by provocative elements on October 16." While cautiously worded, his account leaves no doubt that there were more than a few "black sheep" involved—and that the stakes were extremely high.

The panic had threatened to undermine not only the morale of Moscow's inhabitants but also the faith of all Soviet citizens that Stalin could ultimately prevail in the struggle against Hitler. Even people like Valeria Prokhorova, who distrusted the regime that had swept up many of her relatives in the purges, welcomed the abrupt change in mood. "We started to feel that we were being defended; we felt that the regime was defending our land," she said. "Nobody cared for Stalin, but people were fighting for our country."

This may have been true for intellectuals such as Prokhorova, but Stalin was more successful in conflating support for the country and for him as its ruler among ordinary citizens. Olga Sapozhnikova, a Komsomol activist at the Trekhgorka Cotton Mill in Moscow, looked back at those "dreadful days" a year later in a talk with the Russian-born BBC correspondent Alexander Werth. As a loyal Communist, she was privy to the planting of explosives in her factory. "It was only a case of pressing the button, and the whole factory would have gone up in the air," she said. On the same day that the factory managers were told not to blow up anything, she heard that Stalin had decided to stay in Moscow. "This made an enormous difference to morale," she recalled. "It now seemed certain that Moscow would not be lost."

In fact, not even Stalin felt this was certain at that point. Although the German chances for success evaporated by the end of 1941, the battle for Moscow would continue until April 1942, with record casualties. The combined losses of both sides—those killed, taken prisoner, or severely wounded—were 2.5 million, of which nearly 2 million were on the Soviet side. But this still represented the first time that Hitler's ground forces failed to achieve victory. In his postwar memoirs, Zhukov wrote that whenever he was asked about what he remembered the most from the war, his answer was always "the battle for Moscow."

A key factor in this failure of the German forces was Stalin's decision not to board the special train that was supposed to ferry him to safety. As his biographer Volkogonov put it, "In some respects, Stalin showed himself to be quite the psychologist. He knew that he must not leave Moscow." While Stalin's possibly impulsive decision was not in itself a guarantee of victory, a decision to flee to Kuibyshev would almost certainly have ensured continued chaos in the capital—and its possible collapse, which would have constituted a major blow to the entire war effort.

In the contest of wills with Hitler, Stalin was emerging as the more resolute leader: he had an intuitive feel for how to act when faced with a dire situation, even if it was always with the logic of a despot.

TEN

"NO MORE TRICKS LEFT"

Like a suitor who did not want to pop the question for fear of rejection, Churchill continued to woo Roosevelt while studiously not asking about what was on everyone's mind in London: At what point would the United States finally enter the war directly? This was a prospect that seemed tantalizing close at times, but then had a way of receding again and again.

The isolationist movement no longer looked like the threat it had been early in the year, especially after Charles Lindbergh's disastrous performance at an America First rally in Iowa on September 11. Immediately after Roosevelt delivered his fireside chat on that same day announcing that he had authorized the US Navy to "shoot on sight" any German or Italian ships in the American defense zone, Lindbergh responded with a speech on an inflammatory theme: the alleged role of Jews in pushing the United States toward war.

"It is not difficult to understand why Jewish people desire the overthrow of Nazi Germany," he told his audience of eight thousand in the Des Moines Coliseum. "The persecution they suffered in Germany would be sufficient to make bitter enemies of any race." But he warned of the dangers of a prowar policy, arguing that Jews "will be among the first to feel its consequences." And he proceeded to offer a standard denunciation of American Jews: "Their greatest danger to the country lies in their large ownership and influence in our motion pictures, our press, our radio, and our government."

In an apparent attempt to convey understanding, he only provided more ammunition to his many critics who already viewed him as an anti-Semite. "I am not attacking either the Jewish or British people," Lindbergh declared. "Both races, I admire." But the leaders of both groups, he continued, "for reasons which are not American, wish to involve us in the war. We cannot blame them for looking out for what they believe to be their own interests, but we must also look out for ours."

Although anti-Semitism was widespread at the time, this juxtaposition of American versus Jewish—in other words, foreign—interests met with a prompt backlash. His wife, Anne, wrote in her diary: "He is attacked on all sides, Administration, pressure groups, and Jews as now openly a Nazi, following a Nazi doctrine." *Liberty* magazine dubbed Lindbergh "the most dangerous man in America." According to his biographer A. Scott Berg, "Few men in American history had ever been so reviled."

On October 17 a German U-boat scored a hit on the USS *Kearny*, a destroyer protecting a British convoy southwest of Iceland. The American ship made it back to Reykjavik, but eleven of its sailors died in the attack. A week earlier, Roosevelt had asked Congress to amend the Neutrality Act, allowing for the arming of all American merchant ships and lifting the ban on sending them into war zones. After the *Kearney* attack, 61 percent of Americans favored allowing those ships to carry Lend-Lease aid to Britain, but public opinion was still divided on how far the United States should go in terms of its involvement in the war.

In a "personal and secret" message to Churchill on October 20, Averell Harriman reported from Washington on the contradictory signs. "The interventionists have increased in number and are more confident and aggressive," and "violent isolationists like Lindbergh have been discredited in the public eye," he explained. "And yet, with all this trend, it is not at all clear what or when something will happen to kick us into it"—by which he meant into the war. The attack on the *Kearny*, he added, "did not cause even a ripple. It seemed that the public had expected—and were thoroughly prepared for—such occurrences." An avowed interventionist, Harriman left no doubt that he was perplexed and frustrated by this indecisive state of affairs.

But Roosevelt was not about to allow the torpedoing of the *Kearny* to be written off as an almost routine incident. In his Navy Day address on October 27, he ratcheted up his anti-Hitler rhetoric to the point where it could be seen as providing the rationale for abandoning the remaining constraints on the use of American military might. After mentioning both the *Greer* incident in September and the subsequent attack on the *Kearny*, he declared flatly: "America has been attacked. The USS *Kearny* is not just a Navy ship. She belongs to every man, woman, and child in this nation."

The Germans had targeted the destroyer "to frighten the American people off the high seas—to force us to make a trembling retreat," Roosevelt continued. While warning Hitler that he had misjudged the American spirit, the president used the occasion primarily to disabuse his own people of any remaining illusions they might have about the German leader's goals. "Hitler has often protested that his plans for conquest do not extend across the Atlantic Ocean," he said. "His submarines and raiders prove otherwise. So does the entire design of his new world order."

To buttress his case, the president claimed to have obtained "a secret map made in Germany by Hitler's government" illustrating its plans to take over all of South America, dividing it into "five vassal states"—one of which would include the Panama Canal. "This map, my friends, makes clear the Nazi design not only against South America but against the United States as well." He also claimed to have another document produced by Hitler's regime vowing "to abolish all existing religions," replacing them with "an International Nazi Church." In reality, Roosevelt was citing fabricated documents produced by a British intelligence unit in Toronto.

Whether or not Roosevelt knew that he was relying on British disinformation, he seized the occasion to urge Congress to complete the process of amending the Neutrality Act, and to spur factories to keep increasing their output for the war effort, which now meant helping both Great Britain and Russia. "The forward march of Hitler and of Hitlerism can be stopped—and it will be stopped," he vowed. As for America's role, he added: "Every day that passes, we are producing and providing more and more arms for the men who are fighting on actual battlefronts. That is our primary task."

But the question still lingered: Could that remain its only task for much longer?

Churchill was quick to cable Roosevelt his appreciation. "Deeply moved by your wonderful speech," he said. Harold Nicolson, the Tory MP whose diary reflected the swings in mood of many of the prime minister's supporters, could hardly contain his enthusiasm. On October 28, the day after Roosevelt's address, he wrote: "A tremendous advance. . . . A very great date. Probably the turning point of the war. I walk the streets in silent elation."

Nicolson also reflected on the Anglo-American leaders and the stark contrast with their Italian and German counterparts. "What a master he [Roosevelt] has been! I am cheered when I think of the aged and bewildered Mussolini. . . . and the neurotic genius of Berchtesgaden—and then of dear Winston and that consummate politician of Hyde Park [Roosevelt's New York hometown]." He was further cheered when John Gunther, the visiting American writer, told him at a party that evening "that isolationism is dropping slowly like a pierced blimp."

The German and Italian leaders were paying close attention to Roosevelt's words as well. "Roosevelt's speech made a great impression," Count Ciano, the Italian foreign minister who was on a visit to Germany at the time, noted in his diary. "The Germans have firmly decided to do nothing to accelerate or cause America's entry into the war." But during a lunch that day, Ribbentrop "attacked" Roosevelt, he wrote. And the German foreign minister told his Italian counterpart: "I have given orders to the press to always write 'Roosevelt, the Jew.'" He then added, "I wish to make one prophecy: that man will be stoned in his own Capitol by his own people."

This was in keeping with the optimistic pronouncements Ribbentrop made at a dinner after a hunting expedition the previous day: "Next year, my dear Ciano, our game will be better, not only because we shall kill double the number of animals, but also because England will have finally realized that she can no longer win the war." In other words, Britain would be compelled to accept a Nazi-dictated peace.

Ciano concluded from his visit that Germany was "in fine shape." He was struck by the appearance of normality even as the war was intensifying. "The people are calm, well-fed, well-dressed, well-shod," he noted. "When the Americans speak of an internal collapse, they are mistaken. . . . Germany can hold out for a long time yet, especially since there is the spirit of victory."

Returning to Rome, he conveyed those impressions to Mussolini, who told him he was increasingly convinced that the United States would not enter the war. "It is quite clear that Roosevelt is barking because he cannot bite," he said. Recording those words in his diary, Ciano sounded less certain on that score. "Could he be right?" he asked.

On October 31 the Germans appeared to reinforce Roosevelt's message that America was under attack. A German U-boat torpedoed the USS *Reuben James,* another destroyer escorting a convoy to Britain. This marked the first sinking of a US Navy ship during the still-undeclared war, and 115 members of the 160-man crew were killed. The folk singer Woody Guthrie immortalized their loss with his lyrics:

> *Tell me, what were their names, tell me what were their names,*
> *Did you have a friend on the good* Reuben James*?*

Count Ciano was troubled by this news. "I fear that the incident this time is of such a nature to provoke, or at least accelerate, the crisis," he wrote on the day of the attack.

In Washington, the sinking of the ship helped Roosevelt's congressional allies win approval for the changes in the Neutrality Act—but it was still a close battle that demonstrated the degree to which the country remained divided. On November 7 the margin of the vote in the Senate was 50 to 37; a week later, the margin in the House of Representatives, a narrow 212 to 194.

In contrast to the militant tone of his Navy Day speech, Roosevelt did not issue any ringing new declaration following the sinking of the *Reuben James;* his voice was oddly muted. Like Harriman, Interior Secretary Harold Ickes, another interventionist, did not hide his irritation with Roosevelt's failure to take advantage of such attacks to make the case for going to war. "Apparently the President is going to wait—God knows for how long or for what," he wrote in his diary.

But according to presidential speechwriter Robert Sherwood, Roosevelt still felt "relatively powerless" to combat isolationist sentiment. The number of dedicated isolationists may have decreased, he added, but those that remained were "ever more strident." At the same time, many Americans simply wanted to avoid thinking about the dangers they faced. After the sinking of the *Reuben James,* he wrote, "The bereaved families mourned, but among the general public, there seemed to be more interest in the Army–Notre Dame football game."

After the *Kearny* incident earlier in October, General Robert E. Wood, the leader of the America First Committee, had challenged

Roosevelt to ask Congress for a declaration of war. According to Sherwood, that only reinforced the president's conviction that such an initiative "would meet with certain and disastrous defeat." His silence after the sinking of the *Reuben James*, Sherwood felt, was a result of the recognition that he was running out of credible options. "He had said everything 'short of war' that could be said," he wrote. "He had no more tricks left. The hat from which he had pulled so many rabbits was empty."

Across the Atlantic, some top British officials had concluded that Roosevelt's apparent lack of new rabbits boded ill for the entire war effort. In a telegram to Churchill on November 4, Field Marshal Jan Smuts declared: "I am struck by the growth of the impression here and elsewhere that the war is going to end in stalemate and thus fatally for us." To avoid that outcome, the United States needed to enter the war, which would serve to "warn off Japan and do more than anything else in keeping Russia in the war," he added. He urged Churchill to use his influence with Roosevelt to accomplish that goal. "I trust you are on the lookout for the right moment and manner of appeal to him for action," he concluded.

Churchill replied that he had already tried to convince Roosevelt and his team about the need for a declaration of war when they had met off the coast of Newfoundland in August. His message, as he summarized it for Smuts, was "I would rather have an American declaration of war and no supplies for six months than double the supplies and no declaration." But, he insisted, it would not help to make another such appeal now, since Roosevelt had made him appreciate the constraints he was working under.

"We must not underrate his constitutional difficulties," the prime minister explained. "He may take action as chief executive, but only Congress can declare war." In a more encouraging vein, he reported that Roosevelt had also told him: "I shall never declare war; I shall make war. If I were to ask Congress to declare war, they might argue about it for three months."

Churchill concluded his note by saying: "We must have patience and trust to the tide which is flowing our way and to events." He made a similar point to the rest of his War Cabinet on November 12. Reminding them that the United States was providing a steady stream of Lend-Lease supplies, and its navy was escorting the convoys, he emphasized once again that he did not want to make the mistake of pressuring Roosevelt to act "in advance of American opinion."

Churchill learned of the final vote in the House of Representatives on the Neutrality Act two days later when he was dining with his friend Lord Camrose. As his dinner companion wrote to his son afterward: "Winston was highly delighted. He said he did not care a damn about the smallness of the majority. The thing was that the President now had power to act, and the size of the majority would soon be forgotten. He anticipated great things from this new decision, and I could see he feels that it cannot now be many days before America is finally in the war."

In a note to Churchill on the same day, Lord Beaverbrook hailed the vote in Congress as a vindication of the prime minister's policy of patience in dealing with their American partners. "It is a victory for you in the Battle of the Atlantic, where you fought so long & such a lonely struggle," he wrote.

Although Stalin had decided to remain in Moscow, there was still widespread doubt about the outcome of the battle for the Soviet capital—and, therefore, about the Red Army's ability to recover and regroup after its string of initial defeats. The implications for the other major powers could hardly be overstated.

On October 18, the day when Stalin had flirted with the idea of boarding the special train that would have taken him to Kuibyshev, Interior Secretary Ickes spelled out how he saw the big picture from Washington. "I have believed for a long time that if Russia should find itself in difficulties, Japan would lose no time in attacking Siberia," he wrote in his diary. Noting that "a terrific battle" was raging and that Hitler had announced his intention of capturing Moscow before the start of winter, he concluded: "If the Russians can hold, the effect on the morale not only of Russia but of England will be enormous. And if Russia does hold, Japan will probably begin to cool off again."

Stalin had been worried about Japan's intentions all along. He desperately wanted to know whether he could redeploy some of his troops stationed in the Soviet Far East to the ongoing battles around Moscow and elsewhere in the western part of the country. But if he did so while the Japanese were still deliberating whether to heed German appeals for them to attack the Soviet Union from the east, he could make Siberia a more exposed—and tempting—target. Although Stalin despised Richard Sorge, the Soviet spy in Tokyo who had so accurately predicted the German invasion, he found himself increasingly looking to him for guidance about Tokyo's plans.

German Ambassador Eugen Ott, whom Sorge had cultivated as an unwitting source, had been trying to perform the same role for his bosses in Berlin. But Ott received mixed signals from his Japanese hosts throughout the summer and early fall. At times they sounded ready to join in the attack on Russia, and at other times they looked very hesitant. The politicians tended to be more dubious about German claims that they could score a quick victory than some of the military leaders were. "Now the opportunity to destroy the USSR has arrived," proclaimed General Sadao Araki.

In July Japan started a new mobilization and sent more troops north to Manchuria. Ott wanted to believe that this was preparation for a Japanese attack on Siberia. As for Sorge, this was "cause for anxiety" that he might be right. One member of Sorge's network of local spies that he had recruited reported on the kinds of uniforms the army was issuing to soldiers who were about to be deployed elsewhere. Summer uniforms indicated that the soldiers would be sent to Southeast Asia, where the Japanese were seeking to expand their Greater East Asia Co-Prosperity Sphere, despite mounting tensions with the United States and Britain. But some soldiers were receiving winter uniforms, which signaled they would be moving in another direction. The novelist Nagai Kafu picked up gossip from soldiers in the Tokyo area awaiting orders. "They have winter dress, so they think they will be sent not to the south but to Mongolia or Siberia," he wrote in his diary.

In August, Sorge and his accomplice Hotsumi Ozaki, a left-wing Japanese journalist, picked up more conflicting signals about Tokyo's intentions. Ozaki had heard reports that the Japanese would attack the Soviet Union on August 15; Sorge told him that Ott had heard the same reports and believed them. Ozaki was skeptical, since the Japanese realized that the German offensive against Moscow was not proceeding as smoothly and swiftly as originally predicted, and Soviet forces were putting up more effective resistance than they had earlier. As a result, Sorge's messages to Moscow did not provide a clear answer to the question of what the Japanese would do.

But a couple of weeks later, Sorge and Ozaki obtained more definitive information. Paul Wenneker, the German naval attaché, told Sorge that the Japanese navy wanted to rule out an attack on the Soviet Union, at least for the current year, so that they could push south. "The Japanese have weighed the risks and don't think they'll gain anything by getting involved," he said. "There's no guarantee of success before the winter." Sorge had also learned what was happening with Japanese troops sent to Manchuria. "Many soldiers have been issued with shorts . . . and from this, it can be assumed that large numbers will be shipped to the south," he reported to Moscow.

In another message, Sorge relayed the news that Ozaki had learned from top government officials about their attitude toward an attack on the Soviet Union. "They decided not to launch the war within this year, repeat, not to launch the war this year," he wrote with evident relief.

Now that he was sure of his information, Sorge still faced the challenge of convincing his bosses in Moscow. Stalin was always suspicious of the true loyalties of many of his own spies, and Sorge—who blended so fully into the German community in Tokyo and was well known for what the Soviet leader viewed as his dissolute lifestyle—easily inflamed those instincts. During the purges, some officers who were convicted of trumped-up charges of spying for Germany or Japan had mentioned Sorge, which was enough to establish guilt by association. Sorge's bosses in military intelligence had already considered the possibility that he might be an agent for the other side.

But unlike in the preinvasion days, when Sorge was delivering messages that Stalin did not want to hear, this time the master spy was reporting something that the Kremlin desperately hoped was true: it needed the reassurance that Japan would not attack from the east. The mounting evidence that Japan's leaders were more interested in pursuing their ambitions in Southeast Asia was welcome news. And in Moscow, General Aleksei Panfilov, a tank commander who was serving as a temporary chief of military intelligence, offered a rare endorsement of Sorge. "Considering his great possibilities as a source and the reliability of a significant amount of his previous reporting, this report inspires confidence," he wrote.

By September, according to Sorge, the Kremlin finally began to have "complete trust in my reports" that Japan had decided against an invasion of the Soviet Union. As a result, Stalin was able to make the decision to send a large part of his forces stationed in the Soviet Far East to defend Moscow. Starting in October, the Siberians, as those troops were called, were dispatched to the Soviet heartland. In this period of late 1941 and early 1942, about 400,000 troops made the one-to-two-week journey in hastily organized special trains. Approximately 250,000 were assigned to the defense of Moscow, and the rest were sent to Leningrad and other embattled regions. The arrival of these fresh troops, most of whom were outfitted with proper winter clothing, would dramatically bolster Moscow's chances for survival and shock the Germans, who were within striking distance of the city.

In mid-October Sorge once again demonstrated the reliability of his Japanese sources by predicting that "war with the United States will begin in the very near future." But before he had time to send this last report, his luck ran out. At six thirty in the morning on October 18, a Japanese police squad arrived at his door and arrested him while he was still in his pajamas; Ozaki and other members of his espionage ring were also rounded up.

Sorge had operated so effectively undercover for so long that he was caught completely by surprise. "It was never part of my calculation that I would be arrested," he told his captors later. During relentless interrogation sessions, he admitted his role, and he was sentenced to death.

The Japanese authorities were in no hurry to carry out that sentence. They kept him in prison until late 1944. By that time, the war was going badly for Japan, and it wanted to avoid further antagonizing the Soviet Union, which it feared would join the war in the Pacific. Japanese officials suggested several times that they would be willing to exchange Sorge for a Japanese prisoner held by the Soviet side. Each time, they were rebuffed. In one case, the response came directly from Stalin. "Richard Sorge?" he said. "I do not know a person by that name."

The Soviet leader was not about to do anything to help the spy who knew all about the warnings he had received and ignored when Hitler was preparing to invade his country—even if his intelligence later proved critical in saving Moscow. Spurned by the Kremlin masters he had served so well, Sorge was hanged in his Tokyo prison on November 7, 1944. That day happened to be the twenty-seventh anniversary of the Bolshevik Revolution.

As soon as Stalin had quelled the panic in Moscow in mid-October 1941 by imposing martial law, he turned his attention to that year's upcoming November 7 anniversary. Normally, this was an occasion for Red Army troops to flaunt their military might in a lavish parade on Red Square. To Molotov's and Beria's complete surprise, Stalin suddenly asked them: "How are we going to have the military parade? Maybe two of three hours earlier?"

Equally taken aback, General Pavel Artemyev, the Moscow military commander, argued that it would be impossible to hold the parade this time. After all, German forces were perilously close to the city, and their planes were still conducting frequent bombing runs. But as his question implied, Stalin had already made up his mind. "The antiaircraft defenses around Moscow must be reinforced," he declared. "The main military leaders are at the front. [Marshal Semyon] Budenny will take the parade, and General Artemyev will be in command. If there's an air raid during the parade, and there are dead and wounded, they must be quickly removed, and the parade will be allowed to go on." Clearly thinking of the propaganda value of such an event, he ordered the shooting of a newsreel of the parade and fulsome coverage by all newspapers.

Stalin added that he would use the occasion to give a major speech. "What do you think?" he asked.

Molotov raised the obvious objection. "But what about the risk?" he asked. Sensing his boss's determination, he backtracked immediately. "There would be a risk, though I admit the political response here and abroad would be enormous."

"So it's decided," Stalin concluded. "Make the appropriate arrangements."

For Stalin, the evident risks only increased the chances for a big payoff. If the parade could be pulled off successfully, it would boost the confidence not only of the shaken Muscovites but also of the whole country. That is, unless something went wrong and produced the opposite result.

On November 6, the eve of the anniversary, the ceremonies began somewhat inauspiciously in the Mayakovsky metro station. Stalin and other Kremlin leaders arrived on a subway train they had taken from a nearby station. Broadcast by radio and loudspeakers, the proceedings began with a burst of patriotic music. Then Stalin addressed the assembled delegates of the Moscow City Soviet and other civilian and military officials, who were seated on chairs brought from the Bolshoi Theatre for the occasion.

British correspondent Alexander Werth pointed out that most people attending the event understood all too well why this venue was chosen: it offered protection from possible German air raids. But that only underscored the tenuousness of their situation. "As many of the people who attended the meeting later told me, the underground setting of the speech was uncanny, depressing, and humiliating," he wrote. Stalin's speech was meant to lift their spirits, but, Werth added, it was "a strange mixture of black gloom and complete self-confidence."

After four months of fighting on Soviet soil, Stalin declared, the German invaders still represented a major danger. "I must emphasize that this danger—far from diminishing—has on the contrary increased. The enemy has captured the greater part of the Ukraine, Belorussia, Moldavia, and Estonia, and a number of other regions, has penetrated the Donbass, is looming like a black cloud over Leningrad and is menacing our glorious capital, Moscow." He also warned that the enemy "is straining all his strength to capture Leningrad and Moscow before the winter sets in, for he knows that the winter holds nothing good in store for him."

Then, trying to counteract the message of gloom with one of hope, he made the extravagant claim that the German losses—those who were killed, wounded, or taken prisoner—already amounted to four and a half million men, while Soviet losses were about one-third that number. This was pure fiction. As Western historians have pointed out, the Red Army routinely lost more men than the Wehrmacht even later in the war, when they were driving out the Germans. On average during the entire war, the Russians lost three times more men than the Germans did.

Stalin's main point, however, was that despite "temporary military setbacks," his forces were regaining the initiative against the invaders who "have already sunk to the level of wild beasts." He reminded his listeners of the struggle against Napoléon in the previous century, tying the modern conflict to the high points in Russia's national—as opposed to—ideological history. "Napoléon's fate must not be forgotten," he declared.

The Soviet leader not only promised victory but also revenge. "The German invaders want a war of extermination against the peoples of the USSR," he said. "Well, if the Germans want a war of extermination, they shall have it."

The military parade on Red Square was scheduled for eight o'clock the following morning. Due to the strict secrecy surrounding those plans, most of the commanders of the units involved learned about their assignments only at 2 a.m. But as the troops, tanks, and artillery began to assemble in the early-morning cold, fears of German air raids receded. Dark clouds had gathered, and a heavy snowfall started just as the parade did; Soviet planes still patrolled the skies, but there were no signs of enemy aircraft.

Although the winter weather provided welcome cover, it also contributed to some tense moments during the parade. With Stalin and the rest of the Kremlin leaders looking on from atop Lenin's empty mausoleum, artillery and tank brigades struggled to deal with slippery surfaces and snowdrifts, in some cases pushing recalcitrant artillery pieces. Two tanks abruptly stopped in the square and turned in the wrong direction, triggering momentary alarm, followed by visible relief when it became evident this was merely the result of a miscommunication. But most of the troops marched without incident—and immediately marched out of the city to rejoin the fighting at the nearby front.

In his speech to the assembled troops, Stalin returned to the themes that he had touched on the day before: how a lot of Soviet territory had been "temporarily lost" and "the enemy is before the gates of Leningrad and Moscow." But he insisted that the Germans "are straining their last forces." Taking a swipe at both the Germans and one of his favorite domestic targets, he added: "The enemy is not as strong as some terror-stricken would-be intellectuals picture him." More convincingly, he stressed the key advantage of the Soviet side in the contest between these two totalitarian systems. "Our reserves in manpower are inexhaustible," he declared.

Given the windy, snowy conditions, most of the troops who found themselves in Red Square that morning did not catch much of his speech. In fact, the cameramen and sound technicians were unable to get good footage and a clear recording. As a result, Stalin agreed to a reshoot in the Kremlin afterward. It was this version that Soviet citizens heard broadcast the next day and saw in the subsequent newsreel, with no knowledge that they were not hearing or seeing the original event.

But for the troops taking part, it was Stalin's presence that mattered far more than his words. "We marched past the mausoleum, and we saw him," Aleksandr Zevelev, a member of the NKVD special forces known as OMSBON, recalled decades later. "He was waving his arm." Leonid Shevelev, another OMSBON marcher, had heard the earlier rumors that Stalin may have left the capital. "It was very important for us to see that our leader chose to stay with us in Moscow," he said. "This made us march with the kind of determination as if we were nailing down the coffins of the advancing Nazis."

Stalin's show of bravado on November 7 had succeeded, but the Soviet leader was still far from convinced that he could make good on his promises to stop the German forces from taking the capital. On or around November 19, he called Zhukov. "Are you sure we are going to be able to hold Moscow?" he asked. "I ask with an aching heart. Tell me honestly, as a member of the Party."

Zhukov provided the answer Stalin wanted to hear: "There is no question that we will be able to hold Moscow." But he was also less than certain. Elena Rzhevskaya, who wrote extensively about her own wartime experiences as a German interpreter in the Red Army, met Zhukov in 1964 when he was working on his memoirs. As she recalled, "Marshal Zhukov considered November 1941 the most critical and most ominous month for Moscow, when its fate was decided in battle." In other words, at the time, he felt that the battle could go either way.

German commanders were also assailed by doubts. First their troops struggled with the mud during the autumn rains and then with plummeting temperatures. Their horses suffered, too. The Germans used about 750,000 horses during the early stages of Operation Barbarossa and a total of about 2.5 million of those animals during the entire war against the Soviet Union. They were used primarily to haul artillery and supplies. That was particularly difficult in the autumn, when the unpaved roads turned into rivers of mud. "All wheeled vehicles sink up to their axles in the slime," General Günther Blumentritt, the chief of staff of Army Group Center's Fourth Army reported. "Even tractors can only move with great difficulty."

While bullets and shrapnel killed the most horses, others died from overexertion, disease, and, as the weather changed, freezing temperatures. On average, about one thousand horses died during every day of the fighting. The Russians had horses that could withstand lower temperatures than the horses rounded up by the Germans in their occupied territories. Just as in the case of soldiers, those who were raised in the harsh Russian climate fared better than the new arrivals.

For the German troops, nothing was more disheartening than the lack of basic clothing and other gear. On November 14 General Guderian visited the 167th Infantry Division. "The supply situation was bad," he recalled. "Snow shirts, boot grease, underclothes, and, above all, woolen trousers were not available. A high proportion of the men were still wearing denim trousers, and the temperature was eight below zero!"

Guderian found a similar situation when he visited the 112th Infantry Division a few hours later. Some of those German troops had managed to survive by seizing winter coats and fur caps from the enemy. As for the clothing provided by the Wehrmacht, it was "a mere drop in the ocean," Guderian complained. When Siberian troops fresh off trains from the Far East launched a ferocious attack on those weary troops, he admitted, there was almost no contest. His "insufficiently clothed, half-starved men" were up against "the well-fed, warmly clad, and fresh Siberians, fully equipped for winter fighting." The resulting panic, he concluded, constituted "a warning that the combat ability of our infantry was at an end and they should no longer be expected to perform difficult tasks."

Not all the troops coming from the Far East were really Siberians. Vladimir Edelman, for example, was a Ukrainian Jew who had fought in the losing battle for Kiev. Many of his relatives died in the massacre of Jews at Babi Yar, but he managed to escape and ended up in an infantry unit in the Omsk region composed mostly of Siberian cadets. As a lieutenant with combat experience, Edelman was put in charge of a twenty-five-man unit. He quickly came to appreciate the shooting skills of his men. "They were excellent shots because they were hunters," he recalled.

While Edelman admitted that the Germans had better radios, machine guns, and mortars at that point in the war, he recognized the huge advantage his men had in other respects. They had been issued long underwear, sweaters, fur vests, cotton-wool pants, and gloves or mittens, along with winter coats and fur hats. With the temperature dropping to as low as minus 40 degrees Fahrenheit at times during November and December, German soldiers froze, as did some of the lubricants in their tanks and other vehicles.

Edelman recalled one particularly vivid scene he witnessed: a group of captured Germans standing at a crossroads where he was directing traffic. They were wearing summer uniforms with light coats and no hats. As they moaned and sighed, the only words he heard from them were, "*O Mein Gott! O Mein Gott!*" Every so often, one of them would drop to the ground, dead.

The other factor that undermined German morale was the stiffening—and, at times, near fanatical—resistance of the enemy they had been taught to disdain. "The Russians are so primitive that they won't give up even when they are surrounded by a dozen machine guns," General Ewald von Kleist, who commanded the First Panzer Army, recalled when he was held after the war in Nuremberg. "I would say it is a difference between German bravery and Russian bravery in the sense that the former is logical and the latter brutal."

A German soldier described his shock when he realized that some Red Army troops were employing the same kind of human wave tactics that were used during World War I. The attacks were "carried out by masses of men who made no real attempt at concealment but trusted in sheer weight of numbers to overwhelm us." He added that "the Ivans" kept attacking that way for days, marching straight into his unit's machine-gun fire. "It was uncanny, unbelievable, inhuman," he wrote.

General Halder's diary entries during this period indicate that he and others at headquarters were increasingly aware of the cumulative effect all of this was having on their troops in the field. He mentioned the "curtailment" of supplies, the "stiffening on the enemy front west of Moscow," and how, in some areas, "the troops here are finished." He was not predicting outright defeat, but on November 23 he concluded: "Despite our extraordinary performance, we shall not be able to totally destroy the enemy this year."

True to form, Hitler was largely in denial about the setbacks—and completely in denial about his own responsibility for them. Hearing that the Führer refused to believe the reports flowing into Wolf's Lair about the increasingly desperate situation of his troops, General von Bock remarked caustically: "Naturally, Hitler will not be convinced that it was his own strategic error last August that has gotten us into this mess." This was a reference to the German leader's orders to divert his troops south then, insisting that they take Kiev before starting the drive on Moscow.

By late November, some of the top German generals were not only convinced they would not be able to complete the drive on Moscow that year; several of them were visibly embittered, no longer in awe of Hitler's military and political genius. They would soon pay the price for such heresy.

In his November 6 speech in the Mayakovsky metro station, Stalin extolled "the coalition of the USSR, Great Britain, and the United States of America against the German-Fascist imperialists." He mentioned specifically the Beaverbrook-Harriman visit to Moscow and how this was leading to a new flow of vital supplies—tanks, planes, and other military equipment—from the Western powers. "The present war is a war of engines," he declared. "The war will be won by the side that has an overwhelming preponderance in engine production." Taken together, the three Allied powers could produce "at least three times as much as Germany," he maintained. "That is one of the grounds for the inevitable doom of Hitler's robber imperialism."

This would prove to be a rare acknowledgment of the Western role in supporting his country's military machine, since Soviet propaganda usually skirted that subject both during and after the war. But in those early days, when, in reality, nothing felt inevitable about the outcome of the conflict, Stalin was more willing to make some rhetorical gestures toward Britain and the United States. He contrasted Hitler's war "for the purpose of seizing foreign territory and subjugating foreign peoples" with the Allies' ambitions, which he claimed were limited to "a war of liberation."

Specifically, Stalin insisted that the Soviet Union had no other political or territorial ambitions in mind:

"We have not, and cannot have, any such war aims as that of imposing our will and our regime upon the Slavonic or other enslaved nations of Europe, who are expecting our help. Our aim is to help these nations in their struggle for liberation against Hitler's tyranny and then to leave it to them quite freely to organize their life on their lands as they think fit. No interference in the internal affairs of other nations!"

There was only one problem with such declarations: they were patently false. This had already become glaringly apparent during the negotiation of the Polish-Soviet treaty in London in July. Soviet Ambassador Maisky had steadfastly refused to promise a return to Poland's prewar borders, effectively signaling the Kremlin's goal of preserving the territorial gains it had made under the terms of the Molotov-Ribbentrop Pact.

When Harriman returned from Washington to London on November 18, he found Churchill and Eden preoccupied with Stalin's pressure tactics. According to Harriman's account, "Stalin was seeking the recognition of his new allies for Soviet claims to all the territories he had added to his domain during the brief term of his nonaggression pact with Hitler: the Baltic states, eastern Poland, a strip of Finnish territory, and (from Romania) the regions of Bessarabia and Bukovina."

During Beaverbrook's and Harriman's visit to Moscow, Stalin also insisted "that he wanted Russia's enemies to be treated as Britain's enemies," Harriman recalled. That would mean declaring war on Finland, Romania, and Hungary, which had all participated in the German attack on the Soviet Union. Churchill was hesitant, questioning whether it might make more sense to leave open the possibility of separating those countries from Germany at some point.

When the press reported on this disagreement, Stalin wrote to Churchill on November 8 complaining about "an intolerable situation" produced by the leaks of the Soviet position and Britain's negative attitude on this issue. "Why is all this being done?" Stalin asked. "To demonstrate the lack of unity between the USSR and Great Britain?" He ended with another complaint that left no doubt how irritated he felt: "May I call your attention to the fact (although this is a minor matter) that tanks, planes, and artillery are arriving inefficiently packed, that sometimes parts of the same vehicles are loaded in different ships, [and] that planes, because of imperfect packing, reach us broken?"

Now it was Churchill's turn to be irritated with what he dubbed "the almost hysterical note" from Stalin. But as the British leader observed, Stalin must have realized "that he had gone too far in the tone of this communication." On November 20 Maisky went to Anthony Eden to smooth things over. As Eden reported later, the Soviet envoy assured him that Stalin had not meant "to cause any offense to any members of the government, and least of all to the prime minister." But Stalin felt that Britain's refusal to declare war on Finland put him and his country "in a humiliated position," Maisky continued, implying that this accounted for his testy wording.

Churchill may not have been completely mollified, but he wanted to be sure that this disagreement did not impede continuing military cooperation. In a letter to Stalin a day later, the prime minister responded in a conciliatory vein. "My only desire is to work on equal terms of comradeship and confidence with you," he wrote. Specifically, he proposed that he send Eden and a team of military experts to Moscow "to discuss every question relating to the war."

At the same time, the British leader attempted to dampen Stalin's expectations that their two countries would immediately decide on "the postwar organization of peace." While they would be in constant communications about the war itself "however long it lasts," he asserted, it would only be once "the war is won" that the Soviet Union, Britain, and the United States "will meet at the council table of the victors" to map out the terms for the new era, "making a good plan for our mutual safety and rightful interests."

Reluctantly, Churchill followed up by delivering an ultimatum to Finland, Hungary, and Romania to cease fighting. When they refused, Britain issued the declaration of war against them that Stalin had wanted all along. But the larger question of the Soviet Union's postwar ambitions could not be solved so easily. As Eden prepared to travel to Moscow in December, both Churchill and Roosevelt knew that they would need to figure out how to handle Stalin's persistent pressure to dictate terms for a peace that was still a long way off.

Throughout this period of the rapidly developing relationship between Stalin and his Anglo-American counterparts, Churchill and Roosevelt had two overriding goals. The first was to make sure that they did everything possible to bolster the Soviet Union in its fight for survival against the German invaders. "There can be no question of our going back on our promises to Russia," Churchill instructed senior officials on November 3. The second goal was to make sure that Stalin did not renege on his commitment to the struggle against Germany and cut another deal with Hitler.

The notion that the two tyrants could once again make common cause sounded far-fetched at that point, but neither Churchill nor Roosevelt felt they could dismiss such a possibility completely. Ironically, Stalin's role as Hitler's enabler from the moment he agreed to the Nazi-Soviet pact on the eve of the German invasion of Poland until the German invasion of his own country provided him with extra leverage in his dealings with his new allies. Although never explicitly mentioned as such, it was a potential blackmail weapon: if the Soviet leader felt he was not getting what he wanted from London and Washington, or if he felt the German war machine could not be stopped, he might reconsider which side he was on.

According to his daughter Svetlana Alliluyeva's autobiography, Stalin never fully let go of the idea that he and Hitler could have stuck to their previous alliance. "Ekh! Together with the Germans we would have been invincible!" she quoted him as saying after the war.

Those British and American officials who argued for a tougher approach in the face of Stalin's demands were compelled to make the case that a separate peace between the totalitarian powers was no longer possible—and, therefore, should not be viewed as a credible blackmail threat. Among those strenuously making this point was William Bullitt, Roosevelt's first envoy to Moscow, who had subsequently served as the US ambassador to France. Bullitt had continued to offer advice to Roosevelt about Russia, arguing that Stalin would never make another pact with Hitler, since the German invasion had shattered any remaining trust between them.

Like George Kennan and some of the other Russia hands, Bullitt urged Roosevelt to view the United States as the party with the real leverage. As a condition for Lend-Lease aid, he wanted the president to pressure Stalin to guarantee a return to the prewar boundaries between his country, Poland, and the other neighboring states. By looking to Europe's future even as it was helping arm Britain and the Soviet Union, the United States could secure a place for itself as the "dominant political power," Bullitt explained.

Responding to Bullitt's letters, Roosevelt declared that he was in agreement with many of his points—but then offered a startlingly different view on how to deal with Stalin. "If I give him everything I possibly can and ask nothing from him in return, noblesse oblige, he won't try to annex anything," the president wrote. Bullitt fired back by pointing out that "he was not speaking of the Duke of Norfolk but of a Caucasian bandit whose only thought when he got something for nothing was that the other fellow was the ass."

But when faced with such rejoinders, Roosevelt's instinct was to rely even more on those members of his team who rationalized the policy of acceding to Soviet demands as much as possible. Joseph Davies, Bullitt's successor in Moscow, who had a well-deserved reputation as a fervent apologist for Stalin, was once again providing the president with regular advice. The tone of this advice could easily be deduced from his book *Mission to Moscow*, published shortly after the German invasion, in which he had expounded on the devotion of Soviet leaders to "the brotherhood of man" and world peace.

When Roosevelt received his copy of Davies's ode to the Soviet Union, he wrote in it: "This book will last." It was hardly surprising, therefore, that the president also remained unmoved by the warnings of Bullitt and others about Soviet territorial ambitions. "I do not think that we can worry about the possibility of Russian domination [of Europe]," he wrote to Admiral William Leahy, his envoy to the Vichy government.

Steinhardt, Davies's successor as ambassador to Russia, fell victim to the increasing pressures for a Russia policy based on such assumptions. The envoy was not a doctrinaire hard-liner: he supported the military aid program for Russia, but he opposed unconditional aid. His Moscow posting had turned him into a clear-eyed realist, with few illusions left about Stalin's motives and methods. During his visit to Moscow with Beaverbrook, Harriman reported that Stalin had openly expressed his displeasure with the envoy, denouncing him as "a defeatist, a rumormonger."

Claiming that he needed an ambassador who was better versed in production and supply issues, Roosevelt dismissed Steinhardt on November 5. But the Soviet side was in no mood to reward such gestures with a more open approach to the Westerners who were providing the country with vital aid. The Lend-Lease team, headed by Hopkins and Harriman, had requested visas for the American technicians who would help maintain the equipment dispatched to Russia. They were turned down flat, and the Kremlin announced that it had no need for such technicians.

Colonel Philip Faymonville, the former military attaché who now represented the Lend-Lease program in Russia, as usual made light of this latest evidence that the policy of trying to please Stalin at all costs was only making him a more difficult ally. Hopkins agreed with him, writing that there was no reason to keep pressing the issue of the technicians, since "that will only irritate the Russians over something that is not really important to us."

Within the administration, there were still disagreements on how far to go in accommodating Stalin. Harriman felt that nothing would be lost by entering into negotiations with the Soviet leader about the future boundaries in Europe. But Secretary of State Hull insisted that Britain and the United States stick to the position that any such negotiations should not take place before the war was won. As Anthony Eden was preparing for his trip to Moscow, Hull instructed John Winant, the US envoy in London, to read him a blunt message aimed at heading off any talks on that subject during his visit. It warned against "any willingness to enter into new commitments regarding specific terms of the postwar settlements" by Britain and the Soviet Union. "Above all, there must be no secret accords," he added.

But so long as doubts remained about Russia's ability to stand up to German might, and so long as the overall trajectory of the war remained uncertain, the emphasis in London and Washington was on keeping Stalin on their side at all costs. While the German drive on Moscow appeared to be faltering, Hitler's forces were still making gains elsewhere. On October 24, for instance, they had captured Kharkov, the second largest Ukrainian city. And farther afield, Axis troops were also demonstrating their capabilities. In late November German and Italian troops commanded by General Erwin Rommel, aptly known as "the Desert Fox," were engaged in fierce battles with British forces in Libya.

Back in London, Tory MP Harold Nicolson reflected the general mood of anxiety in his diary entry on November 26: "We may be faced with a very black week. Moscow may fall. Japan may come in against us. France may join the Axis. We may be beaten in Libya. I fear that all this will react very badly on Winston's prestige."

Far more than the British leader's prestige was at stake. The confluence of events as 1941 was drawing to a close suggested that the war was about to take a decisive turn.

ELEVEN

"THE FIFTH ACT"

O*n the evening of December* 7, US Ambassador Winant and Averell Harriman were among Churchill's guests for dinner at Chequers. Harriman recalled that their host looked "tired and depressed." Winant concurred that the prime minister looked "very grim" and was uncharacteristically silent, probably because he was worried that if Japan attacked British colonies in Asia, he could be facing a two-front war.

When Winant had arrived that day, Churchill told him that Britain would declare war on Japan if it attacked the United States. Then he asked pointedly: "If they declare war on us, will you declare war on them?" Winant ducked the question by pointing out that only Congress could declare war. The envoy knew exactly what Churchill was thinking: "He must have realized that if Japan attacked Siam or British territory, it would force Great Britain into an Asiatic war and leave us out of the war."

Harry Hopkins had sent Churchill a small $15 radio set, and, as he normally did on such evenings, the prime minister asked Frank Sawyers, his valet, to bring it into the dining room right before the nine o'clock news. Churchill was a "a bit slow" turning it on, according to Harriman, and missed the top headline about the Japanese attack on Pearl Harbor that morning. When the announcer repeated that news, there was momentary confusion about the target of the attack. Sawyers, who had stepped out briefly, returned and banished any doubts about what had happened. "We heard it ourselves outside," he said. "The Japanese attacked the Americans." The Admiralty also confirmed the news, leaving everyone momentarily stunned.

Churchill was suddenly a changed man, jumping up and proclaiming "We shall declare war on Japan!" as he headed for the door. Winant followed him. "Good God," the envoy told him, "you can't declare war on a radio announcement." Churchill paused and asked: "What shall I do?" Winant knew he would do whatever he had already decided, but he had posed the question "as a courtesy to the representative of the country attacked."

Winant offered to call Roosevelt. When the envoy was put through to the president, he told him that he had a friend who wanted to speak to him. "You will know who it is as soon as you hear his voice," he said.

Churchill took the phone from Winant. "Mr. President, what's this about Japan?" he asked.

"It's quite true," Roosevelt replied. "They have attacked us at Pearl Harbor. We are all in the same boat now."

"This certainly simplifies things," Churchill said. "God be with you." He promised that once the United States had declared war on Japan, Britain would immediately follow suit. As he learned a short time later, Japanese forces had also attacked Malaya, which meant that they had taken on the United States and Britain at the same time.

The British leader observed the reaction of Winant and Harriman to the "shock" of learning that their country had been attacked. "They wasted no words in reproach or sorrow," Churchill recalled. "In fact, one might almost have thought they had been delivered from a long path."

The prime minister's supporters at home could hardly believe this sudden turn of events. "I am dumbfounded by this news," Harold Nicolson wrote in his diary that day. Noting that the Japanese had been engaged in negotiations with the Americans right up until the last moment, he added: "The whole action seems as insane as Hitler's attack on Russia. I remain amazed."

The next day, in a special joint session of Congress, Roosevelt asked for the declaration of war against Japan. As the president promptly reported in a telegram to Churchill, the Senate approved the measure by a vote of 82 to 0, and the House passed it by a margin of 388 to 1. He repeated the message of their earlier phone call: "Today all of us are in the same boat with you and the people of the empire, and it is a ship which will not and cannot be sunk."

Even Charles Lindbergh recognized that he and his fellow isolationists were now in that same boat, conceding that his battle to keep the United States out of the war was over. In a statement he prepared for the America First Committee on December 8, he urged his countrymen to face the conflict "as united Americans regardless of our attitude in the past toward the policy our government has followed. Whether or not that policy has been wise, our country has been attacked by force of arms, and by force of arms we must retaliate."

The aviator's journal entry for that day put that sentiment in more personal terms. "If I had been in Congress, I certainly would have voted for a declaration of war," he wrote.

Across the Atlantic, Churchill addressed Parliament on the same day, making good on his promise to win support for a British declaration of war against Japan. Nicolson noted that Churchill entered the House of Commons "with bowed shoulders and an expression of grim determination on his face"—not with any sense of triumph. "The House had expected jubilation at the entry of America into the war and are a trifle disconcerted," he added.

The British leader cautioned the assembled MPs against underestimating "the gravity of the new dangers we have to meet, either here or in the United States." The Western powers and their Russian ally were engaged in a long, hard struggle, he continued, although assuring them that "our strength and willpower will be sufficient to sustain it."

He then pointed out how radically the balance of demographic and economic power had shifted after Pearl Harbor. "We have at least four-fifths of the population of the globe upon our side," he said. "In the past, we have had a light which flickered; in the present, we have a light which flames; and in the future, there will be a light which shines over all the land and sea." Both houses of Parliament offered unanimous support for the declaration of war.

Churchill deliberately failed to mention one inconvenient fact, which might have explained his reluctance to indulge in triumphalism: the United States was officially at war only with Japan at that point, not with Germany. But he was convinced that events were moving so fast that this second step was sure to follow. In his memoirs, he recalled the intensity of his emotional reaction to the fact that America had joined the fight. "No American will think it wrong of me if I proclaim that to have the United States at our side was to me the greatest joy," he wrote. "I do not pretend to have measured accurately the martial might of Japan, but now at this very moment, I knew the United States was in the war, up to the neck and in to the death."

As far as Churchill was concerned, this meant one thing: "So we have won after all!" While the war might go on for a very long time, he added, "England would live; Britain would live; the Commonwealth of Nations and the empire would live. . . .We should not be wiped out. . . . Hitler's fate was sealed. Mussolini's fate was sealed. As for the Japanese, they would be ground to powder."

Only "silly people," he added, would underestimate the United States. He recalled Sir Edward Grey's remark to him about that country thirty years earlier. Grey, who was Britain's foreign secretary in the early part of the century, told him that America was like "a gigantic boiler. Once the fire is lighted under it, there is no limit to the power it can generate."

To take advantage of that fire, Churchill proposed to Roosevelt that they meet again, this time in the United States. On December 9 he wrote the president that he could leave on the journey across the Atlantic almost immediately. His visit would allow them to "review the whole war plan in light of reality and new facts, as well as the problems of production and distribution," he wrote. "It would also be a very great pleasure to me to meet you again, and the sooner the better."

Late on December 7, George Kennan, the Russia specialist who had gone on to serve in the US embassy in Berlin after the war began, picked up a weak but audible shortwave news broadcast from the United States about the attack on Pearl Harbor. Since Washington had deliberately left the ambassador's post vacant for the previous couple of years, he called Leland Morris, the chargé d'affaires, who was already asleep, and several other embassy officers to arrange a hasty late-night meeting at the embassy. As Kennan recalled, the purpose was "to consider our course now that the end seemed near." Like Churchill, he assumed that Pearl Harbor signaled not just the beginning of the war with Japan but would also soon lead to war with Germany.

There were four days of "excruciating uncertainty" first, Kennan noted, while he and his colleagues waited for Hitler to decide whether Germany would demonstrate its support for Japan by declaring war on the United States. Since Roosevelt gave no indication he was eager to preempt him, it was up to the German leader to act. The signals in this period all indicated that Hitler had made up his mind. "One by one, during those four days, our channels of communication with the outside world ceased to function." Kennan reported. The telegraph office refused to take the embassy's telegrams, and by Tuesday, its phones stopped functioning. As a result, the American diplomats had no way of communicating with Washington. "We were now on our own," he pointed out.

Kennan and his colleagues decided by Tuesday night to start burning their codes and classified correspondence on the assumption that the German declaration of war was coming. They realized that "we would look like fools" if it didn't, Kennan wrote, but "we would appear as worse than fools if it did come, and we had failed to take this step." As the Americans burned their documents, ashes from the fires floated over nearby buildings, prompting a building inspector to warn the embassy that they were endangering the neighborhood.

On Thursday, Hitler addressed the Reichstag, offering a rambling denunciation of Roosevelt and "the full diabolical meanness of Jewry rallied round this man," claiming that he had rejected all of Germany's putative peace offers. Hitler then declared war on the United States, pledging "my unalterable determination to carry a fight once begun to its successful conclusion." As the Nazi leader was speaking, the phone at the embassy "suddenly and mysteriously came to life," Kennan reported, summoning Morris to see Ribbentrop. Almost simultaneously, a car with a protocol officer arrived to whisk him to the Foreign Ministry. There, Ribbentrop kept him standing as he read him the declaration of war and screamed: "Your president has wanted this war! Now he has it!"

But it was Hitler who, as in the case of the invasion of the Soviet Union, had convinced himself once more that yet another expansion of the war would work to his benefit, bringing a German victory closer. The day after Pearl Harbor, he had declared: "We can't lose the war at all. We now have an ally which has never been conquered in three thousand years." Based on such logic, Hitler's declaration of war made perfect sense—and it was a point of pride that he had insisted on it. "A great power doesn't let itself have war declared on it, it declares war itself," Ribbentrop explained.

In a call to Ciano on the same day, the German foreign minister sounded "joyful" at the widening of the war, his Italian counterpart reported. Hitler believed that Japan would now tie down the United States in the Pacific. As Goebbels put it, "Through the outbreak of war between Japan and the USA, a complete shift in the general world picture has taken place. The United States will scarcely now be in a position to transport worthwhile material to England let alone the Soviet Union."

Some of Hitler's generals were highly dubious about such claims. Field Marshal von Bock, whose Army Group Center was facing increasingly desperate conditions on the outskirts of Moscow, noted a day after Pearl Harbor that the anticipated outbreak of full hostilities with the United States only spelled more trouble. "The Americans now have a legal basis for assisting the English and the Russians, which they have been doing all along," he wrote in his diary. He then added wistfully: "How different would things be if the Japanese had attacked the Russians."

Italy was also swept up in the rush to declare war on the United States. Mussolini welcomed this "clarifying" of the showdown between the Allies and the Axis powers, as Ciano noted in his diary on December 8. But the Italian foreign minister added: "I am not so sure about the advantage." America's entry into what promised to be a long conflict, he wrote, would "permit her to put into action all her potential strength."

That was a message that Hitler had no interest in hearing. After failing to conquer Britain, he had argued that the defeat of the Soviet Union would convince the British to make a separate peace on his terms, with the added benefit of keeping the United States out of the war. Now that his troops had failed to achieve the anticipated swift knockout blow against the Kremlin, he viewed Japan's equally rash action as his salvation. Every escalation of the conflict was supposed to help him achieve the victory that always looked almost within his reach. He was once again proving himself to be a master of self-delusion.

On Saturday, it was Kennan's turn to be summoned to the Foreign Ministry in Berlin. He was told that the American diplomats were to vacate their apartments, taking only two pieces of luggage each, and then to report to the embassy the next morning. When the diplomats showed up as ordered, they found the embassy "already guarded by members of the Gestapo, and ourselves their prisoners," Kennan recalled. The remaining American journalists in the city had been detained earlier.

The American diplomats and journalists were bussed to the Potsdamer train station, where they boarded a special train. Their destination was Bad Nauheim, a spa town near Frankfurt. There they were housed in Jeschke's Grand Hotel, which had been closed at the start of the war. They were kept in this barely heated facility for five and a half months until an exchange could be arranged for the German diplomats and journalists in the United States. The latter group was held in much more luxurious conditions at the Greenbrier, the plush spa hotel in White Sulphur Springs, West Virginia. The Americans were hugely relieved when they finally returned home; some of their German counterparts probably later wished that they could have spent all of the war at the Greenbrier.

With the German offensive against Moscow rapidly losing steam, Stalin asked General Zhukov on November 29, "Are you sure that the enemy has reached a state of crisis and is incapable of introducing new groups into his forces?"

"The enemy is exhausted," Zhukov replied. But he hastily added that his forces could still be in jeopardy if the Germans managed to bring up fresh reserves. Neither side was sure of the remaining capabilities of its enemy, although it was increasingly clear that the balance of power had begun to shift on the outskirts of the Soviet capital.

While the German officers and men fighting those battles recognized as much, Hitler was the last to do so. On November 30 Army

Commander von Brauchitsch called Bock with a stunning declaration: "The Führer is convinced that the Russians are on the verge of complete collapse. He desires a definite commitment from you, Field Marshal von Bock, as to when this collapse will become a reality." Brauchitsch also insisted that the outcome of this struggle would be Bock's responsibility, signaling that Hitler had no intention of sharing any blame for failure.

"Unless we obtain ample reserve forces immediately, I cannot be responsible for the outcome," Bock protested. He also pointed out that he and his fellow officers had been "begging for winter clothing and supplies" for a long time, and while temperatures had plummeted, their troops "dressed only in field coats are fighting against an amply supplied enemy."

"But the winter supplies have been delivered," Brauchitsch replied, claiming that those deliveries had started in early October.

Bock pointed out that this was not the case. Perhaps, he added archly, "the necessary winter supplies are safely ensconced in storage areas and warehouses far behind the front. That is, if they exist at all." His Army Group Center, he continued, was "no longer in the position to achieve its objective."

Unwilling to hold back anything, Bock sent a telegram the next day with an equally blunt message to the Army High Command. "Any concept at higher headquarters that the enemy is collapsing is, as the events of the last few days will show, only a wild dream," he wrote. "The enemy now has numerical superiority before the gates of Moscow."

The evidence that he was right was not long in coming. On December 6, as temperatures plummeted to 50 degrees below zero, Zhukov acted on Stalin's order to launch the first Soviet counteroffensive of the war. The object was to drive the Germans back from their positions near Moscow, reversing the momentum. This only highlighted how exhausted and overextended the German troops were, and even Hitler finally had to give in to the appeals of his generals to acknowledge some of those realities.

On December 8 Hitler issued Directive Number 39 that abandoned the pretense that the drive to Moscow was on track. "The severe winter weather which has come surprisingly early in the East, and the consequent difficulties in bringing up supplies, compel us to abandon immediately all major offensive operations and to go over to the defensive," it read. Of course, the cold winter should not have been a surprise, and the failure to provide adequate supplies long predated those conditions. But this was all part of Hitler's habitual reordering of the facts to fit his narrative that always blamed others or external factors for any setbacks.

In the field, those setbacks were multiplying. On the same day that Hitler issued his directive, General Guderian wrote: "The Russians are pursuing us closely, and we must expect misfortunes to occur." Reviewing the losses of his troops in battle and to frostbite, along with the loss of many of his vehicles that could no longer function in the severe cold, he bemoaned the breakdown of the whole German offensive—and what this meant for the future of the war. "I am not thinking about myself but rather about our Germany, and that is why I am frightened," he wrote. In a letter to his wife two days later, he added: "The enemy, the size of the country, and the foulness of the weather were all grossly underestimated, and we are suffering for that now."

Fabian von Schlabrendorff, one of the German officers who later joined the conspiracy against Hitler, argued that the failure to seize Moscow was much more than just a military setback. "With it went the myth of the invincibility of the German soldier," he wrote in his memoirs. "It was the beginning of the end. The German army never completely recovered from that defeat."

But Hitler was a long way from abandoning such myths, which would have meant acknowledging his own mistakes. Instead, he signaled his intention to keep on deflecting blame while limiting his army's ability to fall back. "Scapegoats are being sought for grinding to a halt in the thrust on Moscow," Major Gerhard Engel noted in his diary on December 8. Despite the fact that Zhukov's forces had already launched their counteroffensive, Hitler's army adjutant revealed in the same entry that his boss was obstinately clinging to his illusions. "He did not believe in fresh Russian forces, considered it all a bluff, assumed it likely that these were the last reserves from Moscow."

By December 13, German forces had been driven back more than fifty miles, providing Moscow with welcome breathing room. *Pravda*'s headline on its lead story that day trumpeted this accomplishment: "Collapse of German Commanders' Plans to Surround and Seize Moscow—German Troops Defeated Near Moscow." This was not just propaganda. Vasily Grossman, the war correspondent for *Krasnaya Zvezda*, wrote in his diary: "Everything is very different than it was in the summer. There are lots of broken German vehicles on the roads and in the steppe, lots of abandoned guns, hundreds of German corpses, helmets and weapons are lying everywhere. We are advancing!"

Although Hitler had approved the shift from offensive to defensive positions, he was infuriated when he began hearing that German troops were retreating in the face of the Soviet counteroffensive. Guderian was convinced that the only way he could preserve the strength of his troops was to withdraw to positions farther back from the front lines—whenever possible, to areas where the troops had dug in and erected fortifications before the ground had frozen. "But this was exactly what Hitler refused to allow," Guderian complained.

Brauchitsch was more sympathetic, authorizing some limited withdrawals of Guderian's units. Learning of this, Hitler reached Guderian by phone on December 16. The connection was patchy, but the German leader made clear that no further withdrawals would be tolerated. General Halder, the army chief of staff, noted in his diary that Hitler reiterated those instructions to the whole command team at midnight. "General withdrawal is out of the question," Halder wrote, reflecting Hitler's instructions. "Enemy has made substantial penetration only in a few places. The idea to prepare rear positions is just driveling nonsense."

In his postwar memoirs, Field Marshal Erich von Manstein maintained that Hitler was repeating the mistakes Stalin made at the beginning of Operation Barbarossa when his troops faced overwhelming odds. "Hitler's reaction when the first crisis occurred in front of Moscow was to adopt Stalin's precept of hanging on doggedly to every position," he wrote. "It was a policy that had brought the Soviet leaders so close to the abyss in 1941." Manstein pointed out that this was a mistake that Hitler would repeat again and again as the war progressed, sticking obstinately to the belief that success required "clinging at all costs to what he already possessed."

Percy Ernst Schramm, the historian who later served as Hitler's war diarist, concurred that the German leader's behavior when Zhukov's forces struck back established a predictable pattern of his reactions to future setbacks. "He did not draw the obvious military conclusions from the grave crisis of the winter of 1941–1942, when the German armies were stopped at the gates of Moscow," he wrote, "nor from the catastrophe of Stalingrad in February 1943, nor from the collapse of Axis resistance in North Africa in May 1943, nor from subsequent blows." Instead, in each case, Hitler became "more obstinate, more unteachable."

Hitler was convinced that any failure to carry out his orders proved that his generals were not up to the task—not that the tasks he set them were impossible to begin with. As the failure to take Moscow became glaringly apparent, he dismissed Brauchitsch and took direct command of the army itself. "This little matter of operational command is something anyone can do," he told Halder, displaying his open contempt for his generals. "The task of the commander in chief of the army is to train the army in National Socialist ways. I know of no general who could do that as I want it done, so I have decided to take over the command of the army myself."

While Stalin also was convinced he was his country's best military strategist, he had begun to provide Zhukov with more leeway on handling day-to-day decisions. Not so, Hitler with his generals. Aside from ridding himself of Brauchitsch, he kept pressing Bock to follow his orders to "Stand and fight!" When Bock warned him that the result could be a disaster for his troops, he was placed on extended medical leave. On December 19 he left his headquarters at Army Group Center, telling his senior officers, "Better times will come, my trusted colleagues."

The next day, Guderian was summoned to Wolf's Lair, Hitler's headquarters. "Schneller Heinz" had once been a favorite of the German leader, impressing him with his bold leadership of his panzer troops as they scored their string of early victories in the war. But now he had fallen completely out of favor. As Hitler's adjutant Major Engel put it in his diary, "Clear to F. [Führer] that Guderian not able to lead." The general noticed the change in attitude immediately as he stepped into the dimly lit room where Hitler was meeting with his military leaders. "As Hitler came forward to greet me, I saw to my surprise, for the first time, a hard, unfriendly expression in his eyes," he recalled.

Describing the situation of his embattled, exhausted troops, Guderian reported that they were continuing the withdrawal that Brauchitsch had authorized earlier. "No! I forbid that!" Hitler shouted.

Guderian explained that the only way to prevent needless losses of his men was to continue with the redeployment to safer positions. But Hitler was having none of it. The troops "must dig into the ground where they are and hold every square yard of land!" he insisted.

Guderian refused to be cowed by commands that he viewed as absurdly unrealistic. "Digging into the ground is no longer feasible in most places, since it is frozen to a depth of five feet, and our wretched entrenching tools won't go through it," he said.

Hitler had a solution for that problem, too. "In that case, they must blast craters with the heavy howitzers," he said. "We had to do that in the First World War in Flanders."

"In Flanders, there was never such cold as we are now experiencing," Guderian retorted. "And apart from that, I need my ammunition to fire at the Russians."

When he also reminded Hitler that his troops still did not have winter uniforms, the German leader, just like Brauchitsch earlier, refused to believe him. He chastised Guderian for feeling "too much pity" for his men—something that, in Hitler's eyes, was a grievous failing.

Guderian concluded that his meeting with Hitler was "a complete failure." As with Brauchitsch and Bock, the price of that failure was to be borne by him, certainly not by Hitler. On December 26 Guderian, too, was stripped of his command.

In his farewell message to his troops, Guderian, like Bock, tried to remain upbeat. "I know that you will continue to fight as bravely as ever and that despite the hardships of winter and the numerical superiority of the enemy, you will conquer," he declared. But it was unlikely he believed his own words at that point.

In Rome, German ambassador Otto Christian Archibald von Bismarck, the grandson of the famous chancellor, did not even attempt to hide his belief that the dismissals of so many top military leaders constituted proof not of their incompetence but of Hitler's. "We have come to the fifth act of a great tragedy," he told Filippo Anfuso, Ciano's chief of staff at the Foreign Ministry. "This goes to show that Hitler is a blundering ass." Hearing of this remark, Ciano noted in his diary: "The young man is exaggerating, but he isn't the only one in Germany who plays at opposition."

The fifth act was still a long way off, but the young Bismarck was absolutely correct in recognizing that Hitler was already embarked on a path that was leading to Germany's ultimate defeat and destruction.

A week before he lost command of his troops, Bock offered an example of why he was so frustrated by his superiors. His diary entry dated December 11 contained this revealing passage:

"I was informed verbally that the army group is to be guaranteed the minimum number of trains required for its attack preparations. But at almost the same time, I received a report that several trains carrying Jews from Germany are being sent into the army group's rear area! I advised Halder that I would do everything I could to oppose this, because the arrival of these trains must result in the loss of an equal number of trains vital to supplying the attack."

Bock's objections to the deportations of Jews to the east, where many were immediately murdered, were purely practical; he never indicated any awareness that there could be moral objections as well. This raises an issue that has recently triggered renewed debate among Holocaust scholars: Did Hitler's determination to exterminate the Jews hamper Germany's war against the Allies?

In his 2014 book *Holocaust Versus Wehrmacht: How Hitler's "Final Solution" Undermined the German War Effort*, Yaron Pasher, a fellow at Yad Vashem in Jerusalem, argued that this was very much the case. The Holocaust "was assisted by logistics that were no less ambitious than those used by entire armies. . . . such logistics did not help Germany's war effort but rather were a burden on it," he wrote. During the critical stage of Operation Barbarossa, from mid-October to mid-December 1941, he pointed out, forty-three transports of Jews along with five transports of Gypsies were dispatched from the Reich to the east. This total of forty-eight trains could have been used to deliver more troops or vital supplies instead. "The situation was so delicate that every train counted," he wrote.

Over the course of the Holocaust, Pasher wrote, "somewhere between 3.5 and 4 million were transported by the Reichsbahn to their deaths. . . . which meant the Reichsbahn had to allocate 40,000 train wagons and between 2,500 and 3,000 locomotives." Coupled with the requirements for transporting and maintaining the guards and administrators who ran the concentration camps, this represented a major diversion of resources from the war effort, he concluded.

Other historians vigorously dispute the notion that the deportations had a significant impact on the German war effort. "Nothing could be further from the truth," wrote Peter Hayes in his 2017 book *Why? Explaining the Holocaust.* The Jewish transports constituted a tiny fraction of overall German daily rail traffic, he pointed out: no more than 1 percent to 2 percent even at the height of the mass deportations from Hungary later in the war. Similarly, while conceding that "tens of thousands of people" participated directly in the mass killings, Hayes claimed that this still did not amount to a significant drain on manpower, since the Nazis had "perfected a low-cost, low-overhead, low-tech, and self-financing process of killing with great speed."

Proponents of this view also point out that the Nazis benefitted from the wholesale looting of Jewish property and exploitation of slave labor—of both Jews and non-Jews. In other words, draconian measures, however immoral, could work to their short-term economic advantage, helping rather than hindering the war effort.

But the attempts to draw up a balance sheet of costs and benefits partly obscures the overriding fact that Hitler's racial policies were not based on any rational calculations. In his mind, the fulfillment of his vision required acting on his premise that Slavs were *Untermenschen* and Jews were vermin. Thus, there was no attempt to win over the conquered peoples of the Soviet Union—quite the contrary. And there was no incentive to keep Soviet POWs alive, even if many initially might have been willing to switch sides or, at the very least, could have provided a large pool of additional slave labor. As for the Jews, his idée fixe remained extermination, whatever the cost of doing so. While serving his prison sentence after the Nuremberg trial, Albert Speer wrote on August 24, 1960: "Hitler was even prepared to risk his plans of conquest for the sake of that mania for extermination."

It was a mania that came into full bloom during the second half of

1941—and ultimately did backfire against Hitler. Benjamin Ferencz, the chief prosecutor in the trial of the Einsatzgruppen commanders at Nuremberg, told me in 2016: “Their own policy helped doom them in the end. You can’t go around killing that many Jews and others, depriving yourself of part of your labor force.” He added that there was a reason why Hitler and other Nazis believed they did not have to worry about paying a price for their policies. “The fact is that Germany was so cocksure that it would win the war quickly that they didn’t think they might need more manpower,” he said. Based on the same assumption, the Germans had no need to try to win over the local inhabitants in the territories they conquered, since terror alone would keep them in line.

As with almost all of Hitler’s predictions in 1941, this critical assumption would prove to be flat-out wrong.

On January 20, 1942, top Nazi security officials met on the outskirts of Berlin for what became known as the Wannsee Conference. Contrary to popular belief, this gathering was not the key moment of decision about launching the full-scale Holocaust. The decision to substitute the Shoah by bullets with the Shoah by gas, thereby moving to industrialized-style mass murder, had already been taken in late 1941—not in a single moment but as a product of the evolution of Hitler’s and Himmler’s thinking on the subject. The Wannsee Conference’s purpose was to coordinate the complex logistics of the Holocaust, which could happen only once the fundamental decision about the fate of the Jews had been made.

The meeting at the Wannsee Villa was originally scheduled for December 9, 1941, which constitutes proof that there was no more room for debate on that question before the year was over. The Soviet counteroffensive and the Japanese attack on Pearl Harbor led to its postponement. But already in the fall, preparations were well under way for the construction of death camps on occupied Polish territory—in

Chelmno, Belzec, and Sobibor—while Auschwitz-Birkenau also conducted its first gassing experiments.

At Chelmno on December 8, one day before the originally scheduled conference, buses and trucks deposited Jews at the *Schloss* (manor house) at the heart of the camp, where they went through what would become an all-too-familiar procedure. Told that they were to be sent to work in Germany, they were instructed to undress and register their valuables so that they could be disinfected. They then were ordered into the cellar and, from there, up a ramp into a waiting airtight van. The doors were immediately closed and the victims gassed. Soon permanent gas chambers replaced vans in most camps.

Hitler's rhetoric had foretold the destruction of the Jewish people on more than one occasion, if not the means that would be used to accomplish this task. On January 30, 1939, he delivered his "prophecy" speech. "Today I will once more be a prophet," he declared. "If the international Jewish financiers in and outside Europe should succeed in plunging the nations once more into a world war, then the result will not be the Bolshevization of the earth, and thus the victory of Jewry, but the annihilation of the Jewish race in Europe!"

On November 16, 1941, Goebbels jubilantly proclaimed in his weekly newspaper *Das Reich* that "we are just experiencing the fulfillment of this prophecy." He added that Jewry "is now suffering the gradual process of annihilation which it intended for us. . . . It now perishes according to its own precept of 'An eye for an eye and a tooth for a tooth.' " He made this statement at a time when many top Nazis still believed that Hitler was leading them to victory. But even after the Soviet counteroffensive and Pearl Harbor, when it became obvious that, at the very least, Germany faced a long struggle, Hitler left no doubt that he would pursue his genocidal goals no matter what happened in the wider war.

On December 12, the day after he declared war on the United States, Hitler addressed about fifty top Nazi leaders in the Reich Chancellery. According to Goebbels's summary of his remarks, "With regard to the Jewish question, the Führer is determined to make a clean sweep of it." Hitler reminded his audience of his "prophecy" and declared: "That is no empty talk. The world war is here. The annihilation of Jewry must be the necessary consequence."

If 1941 was the year that Germany embarked on a path that could lead only to defeat, it was also the year that millions of Jews were condemned to die before the war was over.

There was one more reason why 1941 proved to be such a pivotal year: it was the year when Stalin already demonstrated his determination to exert pressure on his Western allies not only to provide maximum aid but also to accept a postwar world based on Soviet-dictated peace terms.

The irony was that the Western leaders should not have been cowed by the leader of a country that was fighting for its survival for that entire year. When Churchill instructed Eden in mid-November to travel to Moscow to try to bridge the differences between the Allies, the foreign secretary noted: "Winston is impressed with the strength of our hand in dealing with Stalin. His need of us greater than our need of him, I must not go to Moscow except the red carpet is out, etc. There is much force in all this."

But Stalin was not about to act like he was the weaker party. Nor was he willing to apologize for—or even to acknowledge—his most brutal actions during the period of his pact with Hitler. Less than two weeks before Eden arrived in Moscow, Polish Prime Minister Władysław Sikorski had preceded him, flying from London, via Cairo, Tehran, and Kuibyshev on his way to the Soviet capital. Meeting with Stalin on December 3 and 4, he pressed for the implementation of the terms of the Soviet-Polish treaty that had been concluded in the summer. This included freeing all Polish military personnel who had been taken prisoner by the Soviet invaders in 1939 so that they could form new units.

General Władysław Anders was to command those forces in future battles against the Germans, and he accompanied Sikorski in the meetings with Stalin. Anders was among those Poles who been freed from Soviet captivity, and Stalin asked him how he was treated. "Exceptionally badly in Lvov. In Moscow, slightly better," Anders replied, adding that "you understand yourself. . . . what is meant by 'better' in a prison when one is held for twenty months."

"Oh, well, such were the conditions," Stalin remarked, as if he had had nothing to do with those conditions.

Sikorski and Anders pressed him about the fate of approximately four thousand Polish officers who were captured and still unaccounted for. "Not one of these officers—and the number is probably at least twice as large as the four thousand shown on my list—has turned up as yet," Sikorski declared.

"That is impossible. They must have escaped somewhere," Stalin replied.

When an incredulous Anders asked where they could have escaped, Stalin persisted in feigning ignorance. "Well, to Manchuria maybe," he said. Of course, the Soviet leader knew that the officers in question had been executed in 1940 in the Katyn Forest near Smolensk, since he had ordered those killings.

Sikorski did manage to win Stalin's agreement to permit the former Polish prisoners who had survived to cross into Iran, where the British had promised to provide the supplies they needed to outfit themselves as a proper fighting force again. Known as Anders' Army, those troops would later fight in North Africa and, most famously, capture the monastery at Monte Cassino during the Italian campaign in 1944.

In return, Stalin tried to maneuver Sikorski into a discussion of the postwar boundary between Poland and the Soviet Union, claiming that the changes he was suggesting were "very slight." The Polish leader insisted that he had no right to discuss even the tiniest alterations in his country's "inviolable" borders, and Stalin dropped the subject.

But he was not about to do so with Eden, who was eager to avoid the topic of postwar borders altogether when he met for the first time with Stalin in Moscow on December 16. Roosevelt had been trying to convince the Poles that he and Churchill were sticking by their commitment in the Atlantic Charter that there would be no territorial changes "that do not accord with the freely expressed wishes of the people concerned."

At their first meeting, Stalin handed Eden drafts of two treaties: one for the wartime alliance between their countries; the other for dealing with postwar arrangements. While this was not totally unexpected, Eden was alarmed to see that the Soviet leader had also proposed a secret protocol to the second treaty, spelling out the future of European borders. "Russian ideas were already starkly definite," Eden noted later. "They changed little during the next three years, for their purpose was to secure the most tangible physical guarantees for Russia's future security." Stalin was seeking to annex eastern Poland and the Baltic states—repeating what the Soviet Union had done under the terms of the Molotov-Ribbentrop Pact—while Poland's borders would be moved westward, taking over previously German territory. He also wanted to discuss how the Allies would divide up military control of Germany after its defeat, foreshadowing the postwar occupation zones.

In their second meeting, Eden recalled, "Stalin began to show his claws," growing more insistent on the boundary issues. The British visitor tried to fend him off by telling him about Roosevelt's admonition against concluding any secret protocols about postwar boundaries. The broader form of a peace settlement, he said, would have to be worked out at a later date by the victorious powers. The atmosphere, Eden noted, had become "frigid."

At their final session on December 20, Stalin switched abruptly to a more conciliatory tone. He stuck by his call for recognition of the boundaries he wanted but declared that he understood the British and American sides needed to consult further before any treaty terms could be finalized. In the meantime, he expected relations between their two countries to improve, he added. Eden felt relieved that his talks were ending on a more upbeat note, but he wasn't fooled into thinking that those relations would ever prove to be easy.

That evening, Stalin invited the British delegation to the Kremlin for what Eden described as an "almost embarrassingly sumptuous" dinner. It featured borscht, sturgeon, a variety of meats, and "the unhappy little white suckling pig," along with the usual profusion of wine, champagne, and vodka.

But if this lavish display was meant to smooth things over, Stalin could not resist an opportunity to make the guest of honor squirm for a moment. Eden asked him about a bottle of a yellowish liquid that was on the table. "This is our Russian whisky," Stalin told him with a smile and poured him a large glass. In fact, it was pepper brandy. Ambassador Maisky, who had accompanied the British officials on the visit, recalled what happened when Eden took a big sip: "He grew terribly red, choked with his eyes nearly bursting from their orbits." Stalin then announced, "Only a strong people can take such a drink. Hitler is beginning to feel this."

All of those experiences convinced Eden that the Soviet leader would not be easily diverted from his goals. "Stalin, I believe, sincerely wants military agreements, but he will not sign until we recognize his frontiers, and we must expect continued badgering on this issue," he wrote to Churchill.

This was an understatement. The Stalin that Eden encountered in Moscow in December 1941 was very much the same Stalin who, at the Yalta Conference in February 1945, where he met with Churchill and Roosevelt, would nail down the terms that he had demanded all along. Those were the terms that set the stage for the Cold War.

On December 10, a day after Churchill had excitedly written to Roosevelt that he was ready to travel to the United States to meet with him, the British leader had to deliver grim news to the

House of Commons. "A report has been received from Singapore that HMS *Prince of Wales* and HMS *Repulse* have been sunk while carrying out operations against the Japanese in their attack on Malaya," he declared. The details only became known later: 840 officers and men of the two battleships had drowned, while 1,285 were rescued from the sea. This development immediately underscored the dangers for Britain of the expansion of the war after Pearl Harbor.

Churchill was still far more buoyed by what he saw as the huge new factor in the equation: the entry of the United States into the war. On December 12 he left for America, traveling on the battleship *Duke of York* for his rendezvous with Roosevelt. "Mr. Churchill has been panting to meet the President ever since he heard of Pearl Harbor," noted Lord Moran, his personal physician, who accompanied him on the journey. "He is a different man since America came into the war."

"The Winston I knew in London frightened me," Moran continued. "I could see that he was carrying the weight of the world, and wondered how long he could go on like that. . . . And now—in a night, it seems—a younger man has taken his place." Churchill spent most of his days on board in his cabin dictating a memo for Roosevelt on the war. "But the tired, dull look has gone from his eye; his face lights up as you enter the cabin. . . . And at night, he is gay and voluble, sometimes even playful."

Moran offered a strictly nonmedical explanation of his patient's mood: "The PM, I suppose, must have known that if America stayed out, there could only be one ending to this business. And now suddenly the war is as good as won, and England is safe; to be Prime Minister of England in a great war. . . . He loves every minute of it."

Churchill flew from Hampton Roads, Virginia, to Washington on December 22. Roosevelt was waiting to greet him at the airport and then drove with him to the White House, which would be his home for the duration of his stay. The two men conferred for several hours a day, including at lunch, when they were often joined by Hopkins. At their first dinner that evening, Roosevelt pointedly mixed the cocktails, and Churchill then took him in his wheelchair to the elevator "as a mark of respect," as the visitor recalled.

The quickly developing rapport between the two men was readily apparent. "As we both, by need or habit, were forced to do much of our work in bed," Churchill recalled, "he visited me in my room whenever he felt inclined, and encouraged me to do the same to him." Aside from taking over a bedroom, Churchill also installed what he called his "travelling map room" nearby. Roosevelt often came into the room to study the maps of the various theaters of the war, which included detailed representations of the military deployments on land and sea. As Churchill wrote with visible pride: "It was not long before he established a map room of his own of the highest efficiency."

As he did back home, Churchill frequently dictated his speeches, reports, and letters while sitting in the bathtub. At times, he continued to dictate after emerging from his bath, draped only in a large towel. Patrick Kinna, his shorthand writer during his White House visit, recalled one occasion when he was doing so in his bedroom and the towel fell to the floor. Seemingly oblivious, he kept pacing the room and dictating. At that moment, Roosevelt walked in. "Never being lost for words," as Kinna put it, Churchill declared: "You see, Mr. President, I have nothing to conceal from you."

It was hard for any of those who met the British leader to resist his charm. Addressing a joint session of Congress on December 26, he told the delighted lawmakers: "I cannot help reflecting that if my father had been American and my mother British, instead of the other way around, I might have got here on my own." But he also delivered sober reminders of how both their countries had failed to stop the conflagration that was now engulfing the world. "Five or six years ago, it would have been easy, without shedding a drop of blood, for the United States and Great Britain to have insisted on the fulfillment of the disarmament clauses of the treaties which Germany signed after the Great War," he said.

While he was enthusiastically cheered at the end of his speech, Churchill noticed how silent the Representatives and Senators were when he had effectively chastised both countries for not acting together earlier. He pointed out that reaction to Moran afterward, but added: "I don't think they would have taken that at all, even a few months ago."

The next morning, Churchill urgently summoned Moran back to the White House. He complained of "a dull pain over my heart" after he had strained to open a stubborn window the previous hot night. "It went down my left arm," he added. "It didn't last very long, but it has never happened before. What is it? Is my heart all right?"

The pain was gone when Moran made a cursory check on his heart, which meant that it was hard to tell what had happened. He concluded that at the very least "his symptoms were that of coronary insufficiency." But he was reluctant to examine him more closely, since he worried that he might discover something worse. "I felt that the effect of announcing that the PM had had a heart attack could only be disastrous," Moran recalled. The standard treatment in such cases was at least six weeks of bed rest. Once again engaging in political rather than medical analysis, he added: "And this at a moment when America has just come into the war, and there is no one but Winston to take her by the hand."

Fully cognizant that he would be vilified if Churchill died of a subsequent heart attack, he decided he had to take his chances and do nothing. "This is nothing serious," he reassured his patient. He told the prime minister only that his circulation was "a bit sluggish" and urged him to avoid overexerting himself.

One probable reason why Moran's gamble paid off was that Churchill was not about to allow any bad news to overwhelm his conviction that the Allies were now positioned to turn the tide of the war, no matter how long it would take and how high the price of victory. The events of 1941 made that outcome all but inevitable. As Ambassador Winant pointed out in his memoir, "The invasion of Russia and the attack on the United States were the great strategic blunders of the Axis powers. These decisions ignored the progress of science and the inexorable logic of the multiplication table."

Germany should have been able to do the calculations ahead of time. This was something some Nazi economic planners had tried to warn Hitler about before he launched Operation Barbarossa, but he was unwilling to listen. As Adam Tooze, the British historian who provided a detailed economic analysis of the war, explained, "Hitler was powerless to alter the underlying balance of economic and military force. The German economy was simply not strong enough to overwhelm all its European neighbors, including both Britain and the Soviet Union, let alone the United States."

Hitler's "attack on the whole world" in 1941, as the German author Joachim Käppner put it, amounted to a suicidal sequence of actions. In a recent US Army War College study, Jeffrey Record calculated the odds that were stacked against the Axis powers—Germany, Japan, and Italy—by the time both the Soviet Union and the United States were in the conflict. "The numbers are stark," he wrote. "The Allies (excluding China) enjoyed a 2.7:1 advantage in population and a 7.5:1 advantage in territory." They also controlled almost all of the world's oil reserves, and, during those war years, their collective gross domestic product was always at least twice the size of the collective GDP of the Axis countries.

Little wonder that Churchill was in high spirits during his stay in Washington and had no intention of slowing down. After his anxious talk with Moran about his heart, he acted as if there was nothing to worry about. He held discussions in the White House with General George Marshall, the US Army chief of staff, on how to allot command assignments to joint British-American military operations. They decided to establish the principle of appointing a shared supreme commander when both countries' troops were fighting in the same war theater.

On December 28, after Churchill and Roosevelt spent five hours talking with representatives of both Allied and neutral countries, the British leader boarded a night train to Ottawa, Canada. After meeting with Prime Minister Mackenzie King's War Cabinet and then with opposition leaders who Churchill concluded were "unsurpassed in loyalty and resolution," he was to address the Canadian Parliament on December 30.

Having delivered his major address to the US Congress only four days earlier, Churchill made a rare admission that he was facing a heavy workload. "The preparation of my two transatlantic speeches, transmitted all over the world, amid all the flow of executive work, which never stopped, was an extremely hard exertion," he wrote in his memoirs. He added: "I did my best."

He certainly did. The British leader mapped out how he envisaged the war from that point on. The first period of consolidation and preparation, he warned, would include "much heavy fighting," with the Allies "resisting the assaults of the enemy" as they marshaled their forces. The second phase would be one of liberation of the conquered territories. "The invaders and tyrants must be made to feel that their fleeting triumphs will have a terrible reckoning," he declared. He added that "quislings and traitors" would face particularly harsh punishment. The third and final stage, he continued, would be "the assault upon the citadels and the homelands of the guilty powers both in Europe and in Asia."

Churchill's audience had no way of knowing at that point how broadly accurate this forecast of the war's trajectory would prove to be. But they could not help but be impressed by the boldness of his vision—and by what he could already assert with full authority as 1941 was drawing to a close.

With a typically dramatic touch, he reminded the parliamentarians that, when France was collapsing in 1940, General Maxime

Weygand had offered a stark prediction: "In three weeks, England will have her neck wrung like a chicken." In other words, England would do no better than France in resisting the German onslaught.

Churchill then added: "Some chicken! Some neck!"

The British leader basked in the ensuing outburst of laughter and applause. But above all, he basked in the knowledge that, while the end of the war would be agonizingly long in coming and full of even more horrors on a previously unimaginable scale, the nature of that ending was no longer in doubt.

ACKNOWLEDGMENTS

The first stage of writing a book is a bit like trying to put together a complex jigsaw puzzle—looking at the scattered pieces and trying to see where they fit. But even more challenging is the task of figuring out what pieces are missing altogether and which of them can be tracked down. It helps if you have been gathering pieces for a long time, often without realizing it, even if they still represent only a small part of the future whole.

Thanks to my parents, grandparents, and their friends, I was always surrounded by people who could provide pieces of the story of World War II when I was growing up. My father was in the Polish army when Germany attacked in 1939, and, early during the Nazi occupation, escaped, ending up in a Polish paratrooper unit based in Scotland. My grandfather served in the Polish government-in-exile in London. When they moved to the United States, the stories of resistance movements and the political struggles that shaped the postwar world were staples of their writings and daily conversations.

During my tours in Germany, Poland, and Russia for *Newsweek*, I often found myself hunting for more pieces, whether for articles or, as my interest in these subjects deepened, for my earlier books. Many of the interviews I conducted then proved to be valuable input for this book as well, especially given the fact that so many members of the World War II generation have already died.

This is all the more reason to thank those who assisted me in finding survivors who I had not interviewed earlier. Don Patton, the retired US Army colonel who runs the World War II History Round Table in Minneapolis, and Peter Zharkov of the Russian Veterans Association in that city set up interviews for me with Russian and German veterans who took part in the fighting in 1941. Ina Navazelskis, a former journalistic colleague who now works at the United States Holocaust Memorial Museum, put me in touch with Walentyna Janta-Połczyńska, the wartime secretary of Polish Prime Minister Władysław Sikorski; she was still able to share her vivid memories at age 103.

Above all, I owe a debt to all the survivors in many locations at different times who were willing to tell their stories, quite a few of whom are included in these pages. Among them, I'd like to single out Benjamin Ferencz, the last surviving member of the US prosecution team at Nuremberg. I profiled him in my previous book, *The Nazi Hunters*, and he helped me see the emerging pattern of a key section of the puzzle that I was putting together for this project.

As in the past, the Hoover Institution was kind enough to host me so that I could dig in its impressive archives. I'd like to thank archivists Irena Czernichowska, Maciej Siekierski, and Carol Leadenham, along with Eryn Tillman, Argyle Roble, and Mandy MacCalla for their assistance there. Many others in a variety of locations offered suggestions and leads, including Rebecca Erbelding of the United States Holocaust Memorial Museum, Andrzej Bryk of the Jagiellonian University in Krakow, and Owen Johnson of Indiana University.

This is my fifth book where I have been fortunate enough to work with Alice Mayhew, as fine an editor as any writer could wish for. I always marvel at how skillfully she guides me through each project, spotting any danger signals early so I can adjust accordingly. It is a pleasure working with her and her able colleague Stuart Roberts, along with all the other members of the Simon & Schuster team: Amar Deol, Elizabeth Gay, Stephen Bedford, Alison Forner, Phil Metcalf, Brigid Black, and Lewelin Polanco. My thanks as well to Phil Bashe for his diligent copy editing.

I am also grateful to my agent Robert Gottlieb and his colleagues Dorothy Vincent and Erica Silverman at the Trident Media Group for their enthusiastic backing for this book. Robert keeps generating new ideas and offering new perspectives, and I always benefit from his insights.

Many friends—old friends from New York and other places where we have lived, and new friends we have made since we moved to St. Augustine in 2015—have also bolstered my spirits on a regular basis. At the risk of offering a very incomplete list, I want to express my appreciation to David Satter, Ardith and Steve Hodes, Eva and Bart Kaminski, Francine Shane and Robert Morea, Arlene Getz, Fred Guterl, Jeff Bartholet, Sarah Stern, Ryszard Horowitz and Ania Bogusz, Jerzy Kozminski, Grazyna and Bogdan Prokopczyk, Barbara and Antoni Moskwa, Monica and Frank Ward, Kim Miller and Vi Sudhipong.

My mother, Marie, died as I was nearing completion of this book, and until the end asked about its progress, offering her memories of life with Zygmunt, my father, in wartime Britain. I owe both of them a great debt. I also want to thank my sisters, Maria and Terry, their spouses, Roberto and Diane, and my sister-in-law Eva Kowalski, along with Andrzej Kowalski and Kinga Socha.

My four children—Eva, Sonia, Adam, and Alex—are a source of pride and joy, as are their spouses Eran and Shaun. There's also that very special place in my heart that is reserved for my seven grandchildren: Stella, Caye, Sydney, Charles, Maia, Kaia, and Christina.

That leaves the hardest person to thank. Krysia and I have been together since we first met in Krakow when I was an exchange student there. She has always been the anchor of our family, the one everyone turns to for just about everything. I certainly do, and I can't imagine writing this or any other book without her constant advice and support. There's so much more that I can't imagine without her, but I think she understands what I am trying to say.

BIBLIOGRAPHY

Archival Sources

Franklin D. Roosevelt Library, Hyde Park, NY
Hoover Institution Archives, Stanford, CA
Library of Congress, Washington, DC
United States Holocaust Museum Archives, Washington, DC

Unpublished Manuscripts

Jacob Beam, unpublished manuscript (with no title page), courtesy of Alex Beam.

David Marwell. "Unwonted Exile: A Biography of Ernst 'Putzi' Hanfstaengl," PhD diss., State University of New York at Binghamton, 1988.

Yeaton, Ivan D., "Memoirs of Ivan D. Yeaton, USA (Ret.)." Palo Alto, CA: unpublished manuscript donated to Hoover Institution on War, Revolution and Peace, 1976.

Publications

Alliluyeva, Svetlana. *Only One Year.* New York: Harper & Row, 1969.

Applebaum, Anne. *Gulag: A History.* New York: Doubleday, 2003.

Aron, Raymond. *Memoirs: Fifty Years of Political Reflection.* New York: Holmes & Meier, 1990.

Axell, Albert. *Marshal Zhukov: The Man Who Beat Hitler.* London: Pearson Longman, 2003.

Banac, Ivo, ed. *The Diary of Georgi Dimitrov 1933–1949.* New Haven: Yale University Press, 2003.

Beevor, Antony. *The Second World War.* New York: Back Bay Books/Little, Brown, 2013.

Beevor, Antony and Luba Vinogradova, eds. *A Writer at War: Vasily Grossman with the Red Army, 1941–1945.* New York: Pantheon Books, 2006.

Berezhkov, Valentin M. *At Stalin's Side: His Interpreter's Memoirs from the October Revolution to the Fall of the Dictator's Empire.* New York: Carol Publishing Group, 1994.

Berg, A. Scott. *Lindbergh.* New York: G.P. Putnam's Sons, 1998.

Beria, Sergo. *Beria, My Father: Inside Stalin's Kremlin.* London: Gerald Duckworth, 2001.

Beschloss, Michael R. *Kennedy and Roosevelt: The Uneasy Alliance.* New York: W. W. Norton, 1980.

Bock, Generalfeldmarschall Fedor von. Klaus Gerbet, ed. *The War Diary: 1939–1945.* Atglen, PA: Schiffer Military History, 1996.

Bohlen, Charles E. *Witness to History: 1929–1969.* New York: W. W. Norton, 1973.

Bormann, Martin, ed. *Hitler's Table Talk.* Chester, England: Ostara Publications, 2016.

Böhler, Jochen, Klaus-Michael Mallman, and Jürgen Matthäus, *Einsatzgruppen w Polsce.* Warsaw: Bellona, 2009.

Bor-Komorowski, Tadeusz. *The Secret Army.* London: Victor Gollancz, 1950.

Browning, Christopher R. *Ordinary Men: Reserve Police Battalion 101 and the Final Solution in Poland.* New York: HarperPerennial, 1992.

______. *The Origins of the Final Solution: The Evolution of Nazi Jewish Policy, September 1939–March 1942.* Lincoln and Jerusalem: University of Nebraska Press and Yad Vashem, 2004.

Bullock, Alan. *Hitler and Stalin: Parallel Lives.* London: Fontana Press, 1998.

Burdick, Charles B. *An American Island in Hitler's Germany: The Bad Nauheim Internment.* Menlo Park, CA: Markgraf Publications Group, 1987.

Burdick, Charles, and Hans-Adolf Jacobsen, eds. *The Halder War Diary: 1939–1942.* London: Greenhill Books, 1988.

Butler, Susan, ed. *My Dear Mr. Stalin: The Complete Correspondence Between Franklin D. Roosevelt and Joseph V. Stalin,* New Haven, CT: Yale University Press, 2005.

Churchill, Allen, ed. *Eyewitness: Hitler.* New York: Walker, 1979.

Churchill, Winston S. *The Second World War: The Gathering Storm.* Boston: Houghton Mifflin, 1948.

______. *The Second World War: The Grand Alliance.* Boston: Houghton Mifflin, 1950.

______. *The Second World War: Their Finest Hour.* Boston: Houghton Mifflin, 1949.

Ciechanowski, Jan. *Defeat in Victory.* New York: Doubleday, 1947.

Colville, John. *The Fringes of Power: Downing Street Diaries 1939–1955.* London: Hodder and Stoughton, 1985.

Conquest, Robert. *The Dragons of Expectation: Reality and Delusion in the Course of History.* New York: W. W. Norton, 2005.

______. *The Great Terror: A Reassessment.* New York: Oxford University Press, 1990.

Cooper, Duff. *Old Men Forget.* New York: Carroll & Graf, 1988.

Cuthbertson, Ken. *A Complex Fate: William L. Shirer and the American Century.* Montreal & Kingston: McGill-Queen's University Press, 2015.

Czech, Danuta. *Kalendarz Wydarzeń w KL Auschwitz.* Oświęcim: Wydawnictwo Państwowego Muzeum w Oświęcimiu-Brzezince, 1992.

Dallek, Robert. *Franklin D. Roosevelt: A Political Life.* New York: Viking, 2017.

Dallin, Alexander. *German Rule in Russia 1941–1945: A Study of Occupation Policies.* London: Macmillan, 1957.

Davies, Joseph E. *Mission to Moscow.* New York: Simon & Schuster, 1941.

Davies, Norman. *Heart of Europe: A Short History of Poland.* Oxford: Clarendon Press, 1984.

Deutscher, Isaac. *Stalin: A Political Biography.* New York: Oxford University Press, 1972.

De Gaulle, Charles. *The Army of the Future.* London: Hutchinson, 1940.

______. *The Complete War Memoirs of Charles de Gaulle.* Translated by Jonathan Griffin and Richard Howard. New York: Carroll & Graf, 1998.

Drawbell, J. W. *Dorothy Thompson's English Journey.* London: Collins, 1942.

Dunn, Dennis J. *Caught Between Roosevelt & Stalin: America's Ambassadors to Moscow.* Lexington: University Press of Kentucky, 1998.

Earl, Hillary. *The Nuremberg SS-Einsatzgruppen Trial, 1945–1958: Atrocity, Law, and History*. Cambridge: Cambridge University Press, 2010.

Eberle, Henrik and Matthias Uhl, eds., *The Hitler Book: The Secret Dossier Prepared for Stalin from the Interrogations of Hitler's Personal Aides*. New York: Public Affairs, 2005.

Eden, Anthony. *The Reckoning*. Boston: Houghton Mifflin, 1965.

Engel, Major Gerhard. *At the Heart of the Third Reich: The Secret Diary of Hitler's Army Adjutant*. London: Greenhill Books, 2005.

Erbelding, Rebecca. *Rescue Board: The Untold Story of America's Efforts to save the Jews of Europe*. New York: Doubleday, 2018.

Etkind, Alexander. *Roads Not Taken: An Intellectual Biography of William C. Bullitt*. Pittsburgh: University of Pittsburgh Press, 2017.

Ferencz, Benjamin B. *Less Than Slaves: Jewish Forced Labor and the Quest for Compensation*. Bloomington: Indiana University Press, 2002.

Fest, Joachim C. *Hitler*. San Diego: Harcourt Brace Jovanovich, 1992.

Filatov, V. P., and others. *Moskovskaia bitva v khronike faktov i sobytii*. Moscow: Voennoe Izdatelstvo, 2004.

Flannery, Henry W. *Assignment to Berlin*. New York: Alfred A. Knopf, 1942.

Friedlander, Saul. *The Years of Extermination: Nazi Germany and the Jews, 1939–1945*. New York: Harper Perennial, 2008.

Gibson, Hugh, ed. *The Ciano Diaries: 1939–1943*. Garden City, NY: Doubleday, 1946.

Gilbert, G. M. *Nuremberg Diary*. Boston: Da Capo Press, 1995.

Gilbert, Martin. *Churchill and America*. Toronto: McClelland & Stewart, 2005.

———. *Finest Hour: Winston S. Churchill 1939–1941*. London: Minerva, 1989.

———. *Road to Victory: Winston S. Churchill 1941–1945*. London: Minerva, 1989.

———. *The Second World War: A Complete History*. New York: Owl Books, 1991.

Glantz, David M. *Colossus Reborn: The Red Army at War, 1941–1943*. Lawrence: University Press of Kansas, 2005.

Glantz, David M., and Jonathan M. House. *When Titans Clashed: How the Red Army Stopped Hitler*. Edinburgh: Birlinn Limited, 2000.

Goldensohn, Leon, and Robert Gellately, eds. *The Nuremberg Interviews: An American Psychiatrist's Conversations with the Defendants and Witnesses*. New York: Alfred A. Knopf, 2004.

Gorinov, M. M., and others, eds. *Moskva Voennaia, 1941–1945: Memuary i arkhivnye dokumenty.* Moscow: Mosgorarkhiv, 1995.

Gorodetsky, Gabriel, ed. *The Maisky Diaries: Red Ambassador to the Court of St. James's, 1932–1943.* New Haven, CT: Yale University Press, 2015.

Grigorenko, Petro G. *Memoirs.* New York: W. W. Norton, 1982.

Gromyko, Andrei. *Memoirs.* New York: Doubleday, 1989.

Grossman, Vasily. *Life and Fate.* London: Collins Harvill, 1985.

———. *The Road: Stories, Journalism, and Essays.* New York: New York Review Books, 2010.

Guderian, General Heinz. *Panzer Leader.* London: Macdonald, 1982.

Gutman, Yisrael, and Michael Berenbaum, eds. *Anatomy of the Auschwitz Death Camp.* Bloomington: Indiana University Press, 1994.

Hanfstaengl, Ernst. *Hitler: The Missing Years.* New York: Arcade, 1994.

Harsch, Joseph C. *At the Hinge of History: A Reporter's Story.* Athens and London, University of Georgia Press, 1993.

———. *Pattern of Conquest.* New York: Doubleday, Doran, 1941.

Harriman, W. Averell, and Elie Abel. *Special Envoy to Churchill and Stalin 1941–1946.* New York: Random House, 1975.

Hastings, Max. *Inferno: The World at War, 1939–1945.* New York: Vintage Books, 2012.

Hart, B. H. Liddell. *The German Generals Talk.* New York: Quill, 1979.

Hartmann, Christian. *Operation Barbarossa: Nazi Germany's War in the East, 1941–1945.* Oxford: Oxford University Press, 2013.

Hasegawa, Tsuyoshi. *Racing the Enemy: Stalin, Truman and the Surrender of Japan.* Cambridge, MA: Belknap Press of Harvard University Press, 2005.

Hayes, Peter. *Why? Explaining the Holocaust.* New York: W. W. Norton, 2017.

Heffer, Simon. *Great British Speeches.* London: Quercus, 2007.

Herwarth, Hans von, with S. Frederick Starr. *Against Two Evils.* New York: Rawson, Wade, 1981.

Hessen, Robert, ed. *Berlin Alert: The Memoirs and Reports of Truman Smith.* Stanford, CA: Hoover Institution Press, 1984.

Hitler, Adolf. *Mein Kampf.* Boston: Houghton Mifflin, 1971.

Hoess, Rudolf. *Commandant of Auschwitz: The Autobiography of Rudolf Hoess.* London: Phoenix, 2000.

Höhne, Heinz. *Canaris: Hitler's Master Spy.* Garden City, New York: Doubleday, 1979.

Höss, Rudolf, Perry Broad, and Johann Paul Kremer. *KL Auschwitz Seen by the SS.* Warsaw: Interpress, 1991.

Hull, Cordell. *The Memoirs of Cordell Hull,* vol. 2. New York: Macmillan, 1948.

Huss, Pierre J. *The Foe We Face.* New York: Doubleday, Doran, 1942.

Ickes, Harold L. *The Secret Diary of Harold L. Ickes,* vol. 3, *The Lowering Clouds 1939–1941.* New York: Simon & Schuster, 1955.

Irving, David. *Hitler's War.* New York: Avon Books, 1990.

Ivanov, V. K. *Moskovskaia zona oborony. Eë rol' v zashchite stolitsy. 1941–1942 gg.* Moscow: Gosudarstvennyi Muzei Oborony Moskvy, 2001.

Jackson, Robert H., and John Q. Barrett, ed. *That Man: An Insider's Portrait of Franklin D. Roosevelt.* Oxford: Oxford University Press, 2003.

James, Robert Rhodes. *Victor Cazalet: A Portrait.* London: Hamish Hamilton, 1976.

Jones, Robert Huhn. *The Roads to Russia: United States Lend-Lease to the Soviet Union.* Norman: University of Oklahoma Press, 1969.

Judd, Denis. *George VI.* London, I. B. Tauris, 2012.

Jukes, Geoffrey. *The Defense of Moscow.* New York: Ballantine Books, 1970.

Kamieński, Łukasz. *Shooting Up: A Short History of Drugs and War.* Oxford: Oxford University Press, 2016.

Käppner, Joachim. *1941: Der Angriff auf die Ganze Welt.* Berlin: Rowohlt, 2016.

Karski, Jan. *The Great Powers & Poland 1919–1945: From Versailles to Yalta.* Lanham, MD: University Press of America, 1985.

Kennan, George F. *Memoirs: 1925–1950.* Boston: Little, Brown, 1967.

Kershaw, Ian. *Hitler, 1889–1936: Hubris.* London: Penguin Press, 1998.

———. *Hitler, 1936–45: Nemesis.* New York: W. W. Norton, 2000.

———. *Hitler, the Germans, and the Final Solution.* New Haven, CT: Yale University Press, 2008.

———. *The "Hitler Myth": Image and Reality in the Third Reich.* Oxford: Oxford University Press, 1987.

Kessler, Ronald. *The Sins of the Father: Joseph P. Kennedy and the Dynasty He Founded.* New York: Warner Books, 1996.

Khlevniuk, Oleg V. *Stalin: New Biography of a Dictator.* New Haven, CT: Yale University Press, 2015.

Kimball, Warren F. *Forged in War: Roosevelt, Churchill, and the Second World War.* New York: William Morrow, 1997.

______. *The Most Unsordid Act: Lend-Lease 1939–1941.* Baltimore: Johns Hopkins Press, 1969.

Knickerbocker, H. R. *Is Tomorrow Hitler's? 200 Questions on the Battle of Mankind.* New York: Reynal & Hitchcock, 1941.

Kochanski, Halik. *The Eagle Unbowed: Poland and the Poles in the Second World War.* Cambridge, MA: Harvard University Press, 2012.

Kumanev, Georgii. *Riadom so Stalinym: Otkrovennyye svidel'stva.* Moscow: Bylina, 1999.

Kurth, Peter. *American Cassandra: The Life of Dorothy Thompson.* Boston: Little, Brown, 1990.

Lehrman, Lewis E. *Churchill, Roosevelt & Company: Studies in Character and Statecraft.* Guilford, CT: Stackpole Books, 2017.

Leutze, James, ed. *The London Journal of General Raymond E. Lee 1940–1941.* Boston: Little Brown, 1971.

Lih, Lars T., Oleg V. Naumov, and Oleg V. Khlevniuk, eds. *Stalin's Letters to Molotov 1925–1936.* New Haven, CT: Yale University Press, 1995.

Lochner, Louis P. *Always the Unexpected: A Book of Reminiscences.* New York: Macmillan, 1956.

______, ed. *The Goebbels Diaries: 1942–1943.* New York: Doubleday, 1948.

______. *What About Germany?* New York: Dodd, Mead, 1943.

Lord Ismay. *The Memoirs of General Lord Ismay.* New York: Viking Press, 1960.

Lord Moran, *Churchill at War 1940–1945.* New York: Carroll & Graf, 2003.

Lucas, James. *War on the Eastern Front: The German Soldier in Russia 1941–1945.* London: Greenhill Books, Military Book Club edition, 1991.

Lukas, Richard C. *The Forgotten Holocaust: The Poles Under German Occupation 1939–1945.* New York: Hippocrene Books, 2012.

Lyttelton, Oliver, and Viscount Chandos. *The Memoirs of Lord Chandos.* London: Bodley Head, 1962.

Macmillan, Harold. *The Blast of War 1939–1945.* London: Macmillan, 1967.

Maisky, Ivan. *Memoirs of a Soviet Ambassador: The War 1939–1943.* London: Hutchinson, 1967.

Manstein, Field-Marshal Erich von. *Lost Victories.* Chicago: Henry Regnery, 1958.

Mazower, Mark. *Hitler's Empire: How the Nazis Ruled Europe.* New York: Penguin Press, 2008.

McLaughlin, John J. *General Albert C. Wedemeyer: America's Unsung Strategist in World War II.* Philadelphia: Casemate, 2012.

Meacham, Jon. *Franklin and Winston: An Intimate Portrait of an Epic Friendship.* New York: Random House, 2003.

Medvedev, Roy. *Let History Judge: The Origins and Consequences of Stalinism.* New York: Columbia University Press, 1989.

Megargee, Geoffrey P. *Inside Hitler's High Command.* Lawrence: University of Kansas, 2000.

Merridale, Catherine. *Ivan's War: Life and Death in the Red Army, 1939–1945.* New York: Metropolitan Books, 2006.

Mikoyan, Anastas. *Tak bylo.* Moscow: Vagrius, 1999.

Mikoyan, Stepan Anastasovich. *Memoirs of Military Test-Flying and Life with the Kremlin's Elite.* Shrewsbury: Airlife, 1999.

Miner, Steven Merritt. *Stalin's Holy War: Religion, Nationalism, and Alliance Politics, 1941–1945.* Chapel Hill: University of North Carolina Press, 2003.

Misiunas, Romuald J., and Rein Taagepera, *The Baltic States: Years of Dependence 1940–1980.* Berkeley: University of California Press, 1983.

Modelski, Tadeusz. *Byłem Szefem Wywiadu u Naczelnego Wodza.* Warsaw: Bellona, 2009.

Montefiore, Simon Sebag. *Stalin: The Court of the Red Tsar.* New York: Alfred A. Knopf, 2004.

Moorehouse, Roger. *Berlin at War.* New York: Basic Books, 2010.

Moskovskaia Bitva v Postanovleniiakh Gosudarstvennogo Komiteta oborony. Dokumenty i materialy 1941–1942. Moscow: Bol'shaiia Rossiiskaia Entsiklopediia i Gosudarstvennyj Muzei Oborony Moskvy, 2001.

Moskva Prifrontovaia 1941–1942. Arkhivnye dokumenty I materialy. Moscow: Mosgorarkhiv, AO Moskovskie uchebniki, 2001.

Mowrer, Edgar Ansel. *Germany Puts the Clock Back.* Paulton and London: Penguin Books, 1938.

———. *Triumph and Turmoil: A Personal History of Our Times.* New York: Weybright & Talley, 1968.

Murphy, David E. *What Stalin Knew: The Enigma of Barbarossa.* New Haven, CT: Yale University Press, 2005.

Murphy, Robert. *Diplomat Among Warriors.* London: Collins, 1964.

Murrow, Edward R. *This Is London.* New York: Schocken Books, 1941.

Muzeum Wojska Polskiego. *Generał Władysław Sikorski 1881–1943.* Warsaw: Bellona, 2013.

Musmanno, Michael A. *The Eichmann Kommandos.* MacFadden, 1962.

———. *Ten Days to Die.* New York: MacFadden, 1962.

Nagorski, Andrew. *The Greatest Battle: Stalin, Hitler, and the Desperate Struggle for Moscow That Changed the Course of World War II.* New York: Simon & Schuster, 2007.

______. *Hitlerland: American Eyewitnesses to the Nazi Rise to Power.* New York: Simon & Schuster, 2012.

______. *The Nazi Hunters.* New York: Simon & Schuster, 2016.

Nagorski, Zygmunt, Senior. *Wojna w Londynie: Wspomnienia 1939–1945.* Paris: Księgarnia Polska w Paryżu, 1966.

Nekrich, Aleksandr M. *Pariahs, Partners, Predators: German-Soviet Relations, 1922–1941.* New York: Columbia University Press, 1997.

Nel, Elizabeth. *Winston Churchill by His Personal Secretary.* New York: iUniverse, 2007.

Nicolson, Nigel, ed. *Harold Nicolson, The War Years 1939–1945: Vol. 2 of Diaries and Letters.* New York: Atheneum, 1967.

Ohler, Norman. *Blitzed: Drugs in the Third Reich.* Boston: Houghton Mifflin, 2017.

Olson, Lynne, *Citizens of London: The Americans Who Stood with Britain in Its Darkest, Finest Hour.* New York: Random House, 2010.

______. *Last Hope Island: Britain, Occupied Europe, and the Brotherhood That Helped Turn the Tide of War.* New York: Random House, 2017.

______. *Those Angry Days: Roosevelt, Lindbergh, and America's Fight over World War II, 1939–1941.* New York: Random House Paperbacks, 2014.

Oreshkin, Boris. *Viaz'ma,* in *Al'manakh "Podvig,"* issue 38. Moscow: *Molodaia Gvardiia*, 1991.

Overy, Richard. *The Dictators: Hitler's Germany, Stalin's Russia.* New York: W. W. Norton, 2004.

______. *Russia's War.* New York: Penguin Books, 1998.

______. *Why the Allies Won.* New York: W. W. Norton, 1995.

Pasher, Yaron. *Holocaust Versus Wehrmacht: How Hitler's "Final Solution" Undermined the German War Effort.* Lawrence: University Press of Kansas, 2014.

Peters, Charles. *Five Days in Philadelphia.* New York: Public Affairs, 2005.

Piper, Franciszek. *Ile Ludzi Zginęło w KL Auschwitz: Liczba Ofiar w Świetle Żròdeł i Badań 1945–1990.* Oświęcim: Wydawnictwo Państwowego Muzeum w Oświęcimu, 1992.

Piotrowski, Stanisław. *Hans Frank's Diary.* Warsaw: Państwowe Wydawnictwo Naukowe, 1961.

Pleshakov, Constantine. *Stalin's Folly: The Tragic First Ten Days of WWII on the Eastern Front*. Boston: Houghton Mifflin, 2005.

Prange, Gordon W. *Target Tokyo: The Story of the Sorge Spy Ring*. New York: McGraw-Hill, 1984.

Prażmowska, Anita J. *Britain and Poland, 1939–1945: The Betrayed Ally*. Cambridge: Cambridge University Press, 1995.

Pyle, Ernie. *Ernie Pyle in England*. New York: Robert M. McBride, 1945.

Raczynski, Count Edward. *In Allied London*. London: Weidenfeld and Nicolson, 1962.

Rayfield, Donald. *Stalin and his Hangmen: The Tyrant and Those Who Killed for Him*. New York: Random House, 2004.

Rayski, Adam. *The Choice of the Jews Under Vichy: Between Submission and Resistance*. Notre Dame, IN: University of Notre Dame Press, 2005.

Rees, Lawrence. *Auschwitz: A New History*. New York: PublicAffairs, 2005.

Resis, Albert, ed. *Molotov Remembers: Inside Kremlin Politics*. Chicago: Ivan R. Dee, 1993.

Reynolds, Quentin. *A London Diary*. New York: Popular Library, 1962.

______. *By Quentin Reynolds*. New York: McGraw-Hill, 1963.

Rhodes, Richard. *Masters of Death: The SS-Einsatzgruppen and the Invention of the Holocaust*. New York: Alfred A. Knopf, 2002.

Rich, Norman. *Hitler's War Aims: Ideology, the Nazi State, and the Course of Expansion*. New York: W. W. Norton, 1973.

Rogers, Clifford J., Ty Seidule, and Steve R. Waddle, eds. *The West Point History of World War II:* vol. 1. New York: Simon & Schuster, 2015.

Roseman, Mark. *The Villa, the Lake, the Meeting: Wannsee and the Final Solution*. London: Penguin Books, 2003.

Ross, Steven J. *Hitler in Los Angeles*. New York: Bloomsbury USA, 2017.

Rybin, A. T. *Riadom so Stalinym*. Moscow: Veteran, 1992.

Sanders, Marion K. *Dorothy Thompson: A Legend in Her Time*. Boston: Houghton Mifflin, 1973.

Seaton, Albert. *The Battle for Moscow*. New York: Jove, 1985.

Sevareid, Eric. *Not So Wild a Dream*. New York: Atheneum, 1976.

Schecter, Jerrold L., with Vyacheslav V. Luchkov, eds. *Khrushchev Remembers: The Glasnost Tapes*. Boston: Little, Brown, 1990.

Schlabrendorff, Fabian von. *The Secret War Against Hitler*. New York: Pitman, 1965.

Schramm, Percy Ernst. *Hitler: The Man and The Military Leader*. Chicago: Academy Chicago, 1999.

Seaton, Col. Albert. *The Battle for Moscow.* 1985: Jove edition, Jove.

Sehn, Dr. Jan. *Obòz Koncentracyjny Oświęcim-Brzezinka.* Warsaw: Wydawnictwo Prawnicze, 1960.

______. *Wspomnienia Rudolfa Hoessa, Komendanta Obozu Oswięcimskiego.* Warsaw: Wydawnictwo Prawnicze, 1961.

Service, Robert. *Stalin: A Biography.* Cambridge, MA: Belknap Press of Harvard University Press, 2005.

Seth, Ronald. *Operation Barbarossa: The Battle for Moscow.* London: World Distributors, 1965.

Shepherd, Ben. *War in the Wild East: The German Army and Soviet Partisans.* Cambridge, MA: Harvard University Press, 2004.

Sherwood, Robert E. *Roosevelt and Hopkins: An Intimate History.* New York: Harper & Brothers, 1948.

Shirer, William L. *Berlin Diary: The Journal of a Foreign Correspondent, 1934–1941.* New York: Galahad Books, 1995.

______. *The Rise and Fall of the Third Reich: A History of Nazi Germany.* Greenwich, CT: Fawcett Publications, 1965.

______. *"This Is Berlin": Radio Broadcasts from Nazi Germany.* Woodstock, NY: Overlook Press, 1999.

Shvetsova, L.I., and others, *Moskva i moskvichi – partizanskomu dvizheniiu Velikoi Otechestvennoi voiny.* Moscow: "Atlantida – XXI vek," 2000.

Siekierski, Maciej, and Feliks Tych, eds. *Widziałem Anioła Śmierci.* Warsaw: Rosner, 2006.

Smith, Howard K. *Last Train from Berlin.* New York: Alfred A. Knopf, 1942.

Snyder, Timothy. *Bloodlands: Europe Between Hitler and Stalin.* New York: Basic Books, 2010.

Spaak, Paul-Henri. *The Continuing Battle: Memoirs of a European 1936–1966.* Boston: Little, Brown, 1971.

Speer, Albert. *Inside the Third Reich: Memoirs.* New York: Simon & Schuster, 1970.

Stafford, David. *Roosevelt and Churchill: Men of Secrets.* Woodstock & New York: Overlook Press, 1999.

Stahel, David. *The Battle for Moscow.* Cambridge: Cambridge University Press, 2015.

Stalin, Joseph. *The War of National Liberation.* New York: International, 1942.

Stargardt, Nicholas. *The German War: A Nation Under Arms, 1939–1945.* New York: Basic Books, 2015.

Strasser, Otto. *Hitler and I.* Boston: Houghton Mifflin, 1940.

Stuart, Heikelina Verrijn, and Marlise Simons. *The Prosecutor and the Judge: Benjamin Ferencz and Antonio Cassese, Interviews and Writings.* Amsterdam: Amsterdam University Press, 2009.

Talbott, Strobe, ed. *Khrushchev Remembers.* Boston: Little, Brown, 1970.

Taubman, William. *Stalin's American Policy: From Entente to Détente to Cold War.* New York: W. W. Norton, 1982.

Taylor, Fred, ed. *The Goebbels Diaries: 1939–1941.* London: Sphere Books, 1983.

Thompson, Dorothy. *"I Saw Hitler!"* New York: Farrar & Rinehart, 1932.

Thompson, W. H. *Sixty Minutes with Winston Churchill.* London: Christopher Johnson, 1953.

Toland, John. *Adolf Hitler,* 2 vols. New York: Doubleday, 1976.

Tooze, Adam. *The Wages of Destruction: The Making and Breaking of the Nazi Economy.* New York: Penguin Books, 2006.

Trevor-Roper, H. R., ed. *Hitler's War Directives: 1939–1945.* London: Pan Books, 1966.

Turney, Alfred W. *Disaster at Moscow: Von Bock's Campaigns 1941–1942.* Albuquerque: University of New Mexico Press, 1970.

Ulam, Adam B. *Expansion and Coexistence: Soviet Foreign Policy, 1917–73,* 2nd ed., New York: Praeger, 1974.

Volkogonov, Dmitri. *Stalin: Triumph and Tragedy.* Rocklin, CA: Prima, 1991.

Weizmann, Chaim. *Trial and Error: The Autobiography of Chaim Weizmann,* vol. 2. Philadelphia: Jewish Publication Society of America, 1949.

Werth, Alexander. *Russia at War: 1941–1945.* New York: Avon Books, 1965.

Whymant, Robert. *Stalin's Spy: Richard Sorge and the Tokyo Espionage Ring.* New York: St. Martin's Press, 1998.

Williams, Charles. *The Last Great Frenchman: A Life of General De Gaulle.* New York: John Wiley, 1993.

Winant, John Gilbert. *Letter from Grosvenor Square: An Account of a Stewardship.* Boston: Houghton Mifflin, 1947.

Wortman, Marc. *1941: Fighting the Shadow War.* New York: Atlantic Monthly Press, 2016.

Zamoyski, Adam. *Moscow 1812: Napoleon's Fatal March.* New York: HarperCollins, 2004.

Zbarsky, Ilya and Samuel Hutchinson, *Lenin's Embalmers*, London: Harvill Press, 1999.

Zhukov, G. K. *Vospominaniia i razmyshleniia. V trekh tomah*. Moscow: Novosti, 1995.

Zhukov, Georgi K. *Marshal Zhukov's Greatest Battles*. New York: Pocket Books, 1970.

Selected Interviews

Yevgeny Anufriyev (2004)
Tamara Bylinina (2004)
Yegor Chegrinets (2005)
Katharine (Kätchen) Truman Smith Coley (2010)
Vyacheslav Dolgov (2004)
Yuri Druzhnikov (2004)
Benjamin Ferencz (2013, 2016)
Eric Hanfstaengl (2009)
Richard Hottelet (2009)
Walentyna Janta-Połczyńska (2016)
Yevgeniya Merlis (2017)
Sergo Mikoyan (2004)
Stepan Mikoyan (2004)
Franciszek Piper (1994)
Nikolai Pisarev (1994)
Valeria Prokhorova (2004)
Joachim Pusch (2017)
Pavel Saprykin (2004)
Leonid Shevelev (2004)
Angus Thuermer (2009)
Boris Vidensky (2004)
Ilya Vinitsky (2004)
Richard Wernicke (2004)
Mieczysław Zawadzki (1994)
Ilya Zbarsky (2004)
Aleksandr Zevelev (2004)
Ella Zhukova (2004)

NOTES

Introduction

1 *"We aren't"* and rest of Speer's account of Paris visit: Albert Speer, *Inside the Third Reich: Memoirs,* 171–73.

2 *"He folded"* and rest of Huss's account, Pierre J. Huss, *The Foe We Face,* 210–12.

3 *"Hitler is the nearest":* H. R. Knickerbocker, *Is Tomorrow Hitler's? 200 Questions on the Battle of Mankind*, 17–19.

3 *"the greatest":* Ian Kershaw, *The "Hitler Myth": Image and Reality in the Third Reich*, 153.

4 *"lead them":* Knickerbocker, *Is Tomorrow Hitler's?*, 48.

4 *A competing narrative* and Hitler's welcome in Berlin: Joachim C. Fest, *Hitler*, 636.

4 *"defend our island":* Simon Heffer, *Great British Speeches,* 171.

4 *"The Second World War":* Christian Hartmann, *Operation Barbarossa: Nazi Germany's War in the East, 1941–1945*, 4.

5 *"You know why":* W. H. Thompson, *Sixty Minutes with Winston Churchill,* 44–45.

5 *"You could not live":* John Gilbert Winant, *Letter from Grosvenor Square: An Account of a Stewardship,* 4.

6 *"Chinaman's chance":* Ronald Kessler, *The Sins of the Father: Joseph P. Kennedy and the Dynasty He Founded*, 201.

6 *"a defeatist":* Michael R. Beschloss, *Kennedy and Roosevelt: The Uneasy Alliance*, 196.

6 *"The Anglo-French":* Gabriel Gorodetsky, ed., *The Maisky Diaries: Red Ambassador to the Court of St. James's 1932–1943*, 279.

6 *"In three weeks":* Winston S. Churchill, *Their Finest Hour,* 213.

6 *"honourable death":* Nigel Nicolson, ed., *Harold Nicolson: The War Years 1939–1945,* vol. 2 *of Diaries and Letters,* 90.

7 *"attack on":* Joachim Käppner, *1941: Der Angriff Auf Die Ganze Welt.*

ONE: "Mad Logic"

11 *"This will be":* Gorodetsky, *Maisky Diaries*, 328.

12 *"A short blow":* Alexander Werth, *Russia at War: 1941–1945,* 84.

13 *"Undeserved and severe":* Alan Bullock, *Hitler and Stalin: Parallel Lives,* 4.

13 *Hitler's father:* Ian Kershaw, *Hitler, 1889–1936: Hubris*, 13, 19.

13 *"contempt for":* Dmitri Volkogonov, *Stalin: Triumph and Tragedy,* 155.

13 *"the oppressed nationalities":* Isaac Deutscher, *Stalin: A Political Biography,* 40.

14 *Stalin is:* Lars T. Lih, Oleg V. Naumov, and Oleg V. Khlevniuk, eds., *Stalin's Letters to Molotov 1925–1936,* app., 241–42.

14 *During 1937 and 1938:* Robert Service, *Stalin: A Biography,* 356.

15 *General Jonah Yakir:* Donald Rayfield, *Stalin and His Hangmen: The Tyrant and Those Who Killed for Him,* 324.

15 *Some of the "wives":* Robert Conquest, *The Dragon of Expectations: Reality and Delusion in the Course of History,* 115.

15 *"Hitler, what a":* Richard Overy, *The Dictators: Hitler's Germany, Stalin's Russia,* 53.

15 *"After the victory":* Valentin M. Berezhkov, *At Stalin's Side: His Interpreter's Memoirs from the October Revolution to the Fall of the Dictator's Empire*, 53.

15 *Valentin Berezhkov:* Ibid., 117.

16 *In her eyes:* author interview with Valeria Prokhorova.

16 *"Stalin struck me":* Hans von Herwarth with S. Frederick Starr, *Against Two Evils,* 54.

17 *Nobody had read* and rest of Otto Strasser's account: Andrew Nagorski,

Hitlerland: American Eyewitnesses to the Nazi Rise to Power, 4; Otto Strasser, *Hitler and I*, 58.

18 *"All who"* and subsequent quotes about Jews and race: Adolf Hitler, *Mein Kampf*, 169, 57, 296, 310, 637, 688.

18 *"Germany today":* Ibid., 644, 654.

18 *"excess population"* and *"then the law":* Ibid., 138–39.

18 *"by and large"* and other quotes in this paragraph: Ibid., 140, 138, 382, 654, 680.

19 *"without the slightest"* and *"The Allies":* Ibid., 196.

19 *"For such a policy"* and other quotes in this paragraph: Ibid., 140, 618, 681, 620.

20 *"There are two":* Speer, *Inside the Third Reich*, 101.

20 *"Knowing this"* and other Schramm quotes: Percy Ernst Schramm, *Hitler: The Man & the Military Leader,* 17, 21, 30.

20 *"an extraordinarily high":* Ibid., 34, 33.

20 *"astounding technical"* and *"Even in technological":* Ibid., 104, 106.

21 *"Economics is":* Hitler, *Mein Kampf*, 227.

21 *"The armed forces":* Adam Tooze, *The Wages of Destruction: The Making and Breaking of the Nazi Economy,* 254.

22 *"The plan was":* Jacob Beam, unpublished manuscript (courtesy of Alex Beam); Nagorski, *Hitlerland,* 238–39.

22 *"We had watched":* Erich von Manstein, *Lost Victories,* 23–24.

22 *"How different":* William L. Shirer, *Berlin Diary,* 145.

23 *In a memorandum* and Krosigk quotes and analysis: Tooze, *Wages of Destruction*, 272–73.

23 *The other key figure* and Thomas's quotes and actions: Ibid., 310.

24 *General Walter von Brauchitsch* and *"Germany's 'wartime'"* and *"that the Third Reich":* Ibid., 312, 315.

25 *"Was not well":* Ibid., 326.

25 *"mad logic":* Ibid., 317.

26 *"Never forget":* Hitler, *Mein Kampf*, 660–61.

26 *He had read* and *"His promises":* Volkogonov, *Stalin*, 352.

26 *As the two sides:* Andrew Nagorski, *The Greatest Battle: Stalin, Hitler, and the Desperate Struggle for Moscow That Changed the Course of World War II*, 17.

27 *"Hitler wants":* Jerrold L. Schecter with Vyacheslav V. Luchkov, eds., *Khrushchev Remembers: The Glasnost Tapes,* 46.

27 *"The general impression":* Charles Burdick and Hans-Adolf Jacobsen, eds., *The Halder War Diary: 1939–1942,* 42.

27 *"When I finished":* Fest, *Hitler*, 601.

27 *Interestingly, while:* Nicholas Stargardt, *The German War: A Nation Under Arms, 1939–1945*, 33.

28 *"He stuck unswervingly":* Speer, *Inside the Third Reich*, 165.

28 *On November 5* and *"sabotage":* Tooze, *Wages of Destruction*, 330.

28 *A month later* and *"The Führer himself":* Ibid., 337.

29 *"a significant shift":* Ibid., 317.

29 *"to beat our brains in":* Strobe Talbott, ed., *Khrushchev Remembers,* 166.

29 *"shamefully conducted":* Anastas Mikoyan, *Tak Bylo,* 385.

30 *"Most of our troops"* and subsequent Khrushchev quotes: Schecter with Luchkov, *Khrushchev Remembers*, 55.

30 *The casualty figures* and *"The Red Army":* Simon Sebag Montefiore, *Stalin: The Court of the Red Tsar,* 330.

30 *In 1938* and further purges and comments: Nagorski, *Greatest Battle,* 76–81.

30 *"This is worse":* Richard Overy, *Russia's War*, 30.

31 *"produced the most":* Stepan Anastasovich Mikoyan, *Memoirs of Military Test-Flying and Life with the Kremlin's Elite*, 106.

31 *"forged the defeats":* Volkogonov, *Stalin: Triumph and Tragedy,* 324.

31 *In April 1941:* Aleksandr M. Nekrich, *Pariahs, Partners, Predators: German-Soviet Relations, 1922–1941,* 220.

32 *"So while those sparrows":* Schecter with Luchkov, *Khrushchev Remembers*, 55.

32 *Dergachev* and *Ariets:* David E. Murphy, *What Stalin Knew: The Enigma of Barbarossa,* 63.

32 *"Nothing must be"* and *"The result of":* Heinz Höhne, *Canaris: Hitler's Master Spy*, 451–52.

33 *"Britain's hope"*: Burdick and Jacobsen, *The Halder War Diary*, 244–45.

34 *"We decided":* Herwarth with Starr, *Against Two Evils*, 115.

34 *"would only"* and *"My dear Canaris":* Höhne, *Canaris*, 450.

34 *"The gigantic spaces":* Fest, *Hitler*, 643.

35 *"the conclusion of"* and *In 1940* statistics: Tooze, *Wages of Destruction*, 321.

35 *"After some":* Alfred W. Turney, *Disaster at Moscow: Von Bock's Campaigns 1941–1942,* 25.

35 *"The German Armed Forces":* H. R. Trevor-Roper, ed., *Hitler's War Directives 1939–1945,* 93–98.

36 *BARBAROSSA was:* Nagorski, *Greatest Battle,* 22.

36 *"visibly at":* Overy, *The Dictators,* 490.

36 *"really intends war":* Major Gerhard Engel, *At the Heart of the Reich: The Secret Diary of Hitler's Army Adjutant,* 100–101.

36 *"Barbarossa: Purpose":* Burdick and Jacobsen, 314.

36 *"He regards":* Turney, *Disaster at Moscow,* 29.

37 *"If the rations":* Ibid., 31.

37 *"war against":* Tooze, *Wages of Destruction,* 424.

TWO: "Two Prima Donnas"

38 *"Looking back"* and *"No part":* Winston S. Churchill, *The Second World War: The Grand Alliance,* 3–4.

38 *The Battle of Britain* and forty-three thousand deaths: Clifford J. Rogers, Ty Seidule, and Steve R. Waddle, eds., *The West Point History of World War II,* vol. 1, 115.

39 *"The Führer is":* Hugh Gibson, ed., *The Ciano Diaries: 1939–1943,* 331.

39 *"We in Berlin":* Henry W. Flannery, *Assignment to Berlin,* 151.

39 *"There is no":* Nicolson, *Harold Nicolson,* 136–37.

40 *"Personally I feel":* Denis Judd, *George VI,* 179.

40 *"We were now":* Lord Ismay, *The Memoirs of General Lord Ismay,* 147.

40 *"France vanquished":* Robert Rhodes James, *Victor Cazalet: A Portrait,* 230.

40 *"For us":* Zygmunt Nagorski, Senior, *Wojna w Londynie: Wspomnienia 1939–1945,* 67.

40 *"Last Hope Island":* see Lynne Olson, *Last Hope Island: Britain, Occupied Europe, and the Brotherhood That Helped Turn the Tide of War.*

40 *"One hope":* Paul-Henri Spaak, *The Continuing Battle: Memoirs of a European 1936–1966,* 56.

40 *"the flame of": Charles de Gaulle, The Complete War Memoirs of Charles de Gaulle,* trans. Jonathan Griffin and Richard Howard, 83–84.

40 *Vers l'armée de métier* and *His book sold:* Charles Williams, *The Last Great Frenchman: A Life of General de Gaulle,* 76.

41 *"United Germany:* General Charles de Gaulle, *The Army of the Future,* 21.

41 *"I was starting":* De Gaulle, *Complete War Memoirs,* 82.

41 *"London is not":* Allen Churchill, ed., *Eyewitness: Hitler*, 210.

42 *"Remember, Mr. President,"* Martin Gilbert, *Churchill and America*, 211–12.

42 *"Britain has been":* Edward R. Murrow, *This Is London,* 229–30.

42 *"a has-been, which":* Robert Murphy, *Diplomat Among Warriors,* 51.

43 *"But there is":* John Colville, *The Fringes of Power: Downing Street Diaries 1939–1955,* 50.

43 *"it was a marvel":* Winston S. Churchill, *The Second World War: The Gathering Storm,* 650.

44 *"At last, we had":* Harold Macmillan, *The Blast of War 1939–1945,* 77.

44 *"similar positions"* and rest of FDR's letter: Jon Meacham, *Franklin and Winston: An Intimate Portrait of an Epic Friendship*, 45.

44 *"He [Kennedy] has":* James Leutze, ed., *The London Journal of General Raymond E. Lee 1940–1941,* 81.

45 *"I have always"* and rest of FDR's remarks to Kennedy: Beschloss, *Kennedy and Roosevelt,* 200; David Stafford, *Roosevelt and Churchill: Men of Secrets,* xvi.

45 *"follow public opinion":* Meacham, *Franklin and Winston*, 32.

45 *"peculiar difficulty"* and *"if he made":* Robert H. Jackson, *That Man: An Insider's Portrait of Franklin D. Roosevelt,* 81–82.

46 *"a victory by":* A. Scott Berg, *Lindbergh,* 382.

46 *"Democracy in Britain"* and *"In July of": Lewis E. Lehrman, Churchill, Roosevelt & Company: Studies in Character and Statecraft,* 14, 39.

46 *"The mighty Republic":* Ibid., 1.

47 *His son, Randolph,* and rest of exchange with his father: Meacham, *Franklin and Winston*, 51.

47 *On May 15* and *950 messages* and text of May 15 telegram: Winston S. Churchill, *The Second World War: Their Finest Hour,* 23–25.

47 *"live within":* www.let.rug.nl/usa/presidents/franklin-delano-roosevelt/state-of-the-union-1940.php.

48 *"a lone island":* Lehrman, 25.

48 *In his May 15 telegram:* Churchill, *Their Finest Hour,* 24–25.

49 *"Here's a telegram":* Gilbert, *Churchill and America*, 186.

49 *"Up till April":* Ibid., 197.

49 *On June 1:* Ibid., 188.

49 *"prayed for your":* Ibid., 206.

50 *"In a military":* www.presidency.ucsb.edu/ws/?pid=15917.

50 *"Neighbor, my garden":* Gilbert, *Churchill and America*, 209.

50 *"that there couldn't":* Robert E. Sherwood, *Roosevelt and Hopkins: An Intimate History*, 225.

50 *"the government of"* and *"give the president":* www.history.com/topics/world-war-ii/lend-lease-act.

51 *"I would have":* Hitler, *Mein Kampf*, 663.

51 *"His regret at":* Speer, *Inside the Third Reich*, 72.

51 *"Hitler knew nothing":* Ibid., 165.

52 *"Hopes Eng(lish)":* Engel, *At the Heart of the Reich*, 101.

52 *"merely as a":* Speer, *Inside the Third Reich*, 165.

52 "Germany's Will for": Stargardt, *German War*, 48.

52 *On March 4, 1940* and rest of Mooney account: Nagorski, *Hitlerland*, 283–84; Louis P. Lochner, *Always the Unexpected: A Book of Reminiscences*, 262–72.

52 *"The Führer is":* Burdick and Jacobsen, *The Halder War Diary*, 227.

52 *"When will"* and *"Their best weapons":* Taylor, 185.

52 *That same month:* Nagorski, *Greatest Battle*, 26.

53 *"If that's so":* Montefiore, *Stalin*, 340.

53 *"Churchill in the":* Speer, *Inside the Third Reich*, 165.

53 *"his big chance":* Ernst Hanfstaengl, taped interview by John Toland, Library of Congress.

53 *"If there is":* Ernst Hanfstaengl, *Hitler: The Missing Years*, 41.

53 *"It is Jews":* Hitler: *Mein Kampf*, 639.

54 *"because of her":* Ibid., 139.

54 *"America's rearmament":* Burdick and Jacobsen, 256.

54 *"The Americans had":* Speer, *Inside the Third Reich*, 121.

54 *"the biggest swindle":* Marc Wortman, *1941: Fighting the Shadow War*, 53.

54 *"I fear the":* Louis Lochner, "Round Robins from Berlin," *Wisconsin Magazine of History*, Summer 1967.

55 *On September 16* and *"We cannot":* "Franklin Roosevelt Approves Military Draft," History, www.history.com/this-day-in-history/franklin-roosevelt-approves-military-draft.

55 *"at no previous":* "Franklin D. Roosevelt, 1941 State of the Union Address "The Four Freedoms" (6 January 1941)," Voices of Democracy, voicesofdemocracy.umd.edu/fdr-the-four-freedoms-speech-text.

56 *"Never before"* and *"the most untruthful":* Lynne Olson, *Those Angry Days: Roosevelt, Lindbergh, and America's Fight over World War II, 1939–1941,* 276.

56 *On January 23* and description of Lindbergh's testimony, including his quotes and reactions, along with Hamilton Fish's role: Berg, *Lindbergh,* 413–16.

58 *"one of the ladies":* Colville, *Fringes of Power,* 326–27, 330; De Gaulle: *Complete War Memoirs,* vol. 1, 146–48.

58 *"Exile accentuates":* Raymond Aron, *Memoirs: Fifty Years of Political Reflection,* 135.

59 *"my personal representative"* and rest of Hopkins's arrival in Britain and first meetings, including quotes: Sherwood, *Roosevelt and Hopkins,* 232–36.

60 *"a bit down"* and account of lunch with Churchill: Ibid., 238–39.

60 *"God, what":* Meacham, *Franklin and Winston,* 87.

61 *"his sonorous elegance"* and rest of account of Ditchley dinner: Oliver Lyttelton, *The Memoirs of Lord Chandos,* 165–66.

61 *"very mellow":* Colville, *Fringes of Power,* 331.

61 *Shortly before* and story of Harriman's appointment, speeches and welcome to Britain, including quotes: W. Averell Harriman and Elie Abel, *Special Envoy to Churchill and Stalin 1941–1946,* 3–21.

62 *"If you elect":* Charles Peters, *Five Days in Philadelphia,* 177.

63 *Willkie's sister Charlotte:* Joseph C. Harsch, *At the Hinge of History: A Reporter's Story,* 55; Nagorski, *Hitlerland,* 305.

63 *"He is truly"* and Longfellow poem: Meacham, *Franklin and Winston,* 95.

63 *"deeply moved":* Gilbert, *Churchill and America,* 215.

63 *"He is astonished":* Nicolson, *Harold Nicolson,* 141–42.

64 *"There was no"* and *"There is great":* Murrow, *This Is London,* 235, 236–37.

64 *"It will require":* Nicolson, *Harold Nicolson,* 149.

THREE: "Wholly Misguided"

65 *"recognize and respect":* C. Peter Chen, "The Tripartite Pact," World War II Database, https://ww2db.com/battle_spec.php?battle_id=84.

65 *"We both":* Deutscher, *Stalin,* 452.

65 *"We must remain"* and description of Matsuoko's sendoff: Ibid., 453; Nagorski, *Greatest Battle,* 31–32

66 *When Schulenburg assured:* Adam B. Ulam, *Expansion and Coexistence: Soviet Foreign Policy, 1917–73*, 306.

66 *"I honestly believe":* Ronald Seth, *Operation Barbarossa: The Battle for Moscow*, 36.

66 *"the faintest idea":* Louis P. Lochner, ed., *The Goebbels Diaries: 1942–1943*, 87.

66 *"No hint":* Nekrich, *Pariahs, Partners, Predators*, 212.

66 *At a breakfast:* Turney, *Disaster at Moscow*, 35.

67 *"as more Nazi":* William L. Shirer, *The Rise and Fall of the Third Reich: A History of Nazi Germany*, 872.

67 *"Therefore, Germany":* Kershaw, *Hitler, 1936–45: Nemesis*, 364.

67 *On March 20* and other US and British warnings: David Murphy, 262; Churchill, *Grand Alliance*, 360–61.

67 *"There was near":* Herwarth with Starr, *Against Two Evils*, 162.

68 *The Soviet military intelligence* and reports from its agents, including Richard Sorge, along with Stalin's reaction: David Murphy, 64–66, 71–88, 101, 262–63; Rayfield, *Stalin and His Hangmen*, 394; Nagorski, *Greatest Battle*, 27–29; Gordon W. Prange, *Target Tokyo: The Story of the Sorge Spy Ring*, 3–16.

69 *"intimate with":* Robert Whymant, *Stalin's Spy: Richard Sorge and the Tokyo Espionage Ring*, 218.

70 *"extreme distrust":* Stepan Mikoyan, *Memoirs*, 102.

70 *"Now we have":* Speer, *Inside the Third Reich*, 173.

71 *"We only have":* Bullock, *Hitler and Stalin*, 759.

71 *"Russia will collapse":* Albert Axell, *Marshal Zhukov: The Man Who Beat Hitler*, 63.

71 *In January 1941* and Thomas's turnaround: Tooze, *Wages of Destruction*, 458–59.

71 *The Soviet Union's population* (as of 1941) and Germany's population (as of 1939): Ibid., 452.

72 *But while German* and lack of motorization of army: Ibid., 454–55.

72 *"The well-known"* and rest of Weizsäcker memo: Nekrich, 222.

72 *General Günther Blumentritt*, Hitler's time estimate: Overy, *The Dictators*, 490; Nagorski, *Greatest Battle*, 23.

73 *"Führer, we are"* and *"regrettable blunder":* Shirer, *Rise and Fall of The Third Reich*, 816–17; Nagorski, *Greatest Battle*, 24.

73 *"for new deployment":* Kershaw, *Hitler, 1936–45*, 361.

74 *The new government* and *"to smash":* Gilbert, *Churchill and America*, 166.
74 *"The beginning of"* and *"This postponement":* Shirer, *Rise and Fall of the Third Reich,* 824.
74 *"Our imminent":* Engel, *At the Heart of the Reich*, 106.
75 *"Russia will be"* and *"a dangerous game":* Gibson, 351–52.
75 *"a long, drawn-out":* Tooze, *Wages of Destruction,* 456–57.
75 *"Foreign Armies East," "Russian higher officers' corps,"* and *"Intelligence on":* Burdick and Jacobsen, *The Halder War Diary*, 350, 383, 329.
75 *As part of*, Guderian's conclusions, and *"had so befuddled":* General Heinz Guderian, *Panzer Leader,* 142–43.
75 *"Gentleman, do you":* Fabian von Schlabendorff, *The Secret War Against Hitler,*125; Nagorski, *Greatest Battle,* 100.
76 *"I believed in":* Leon Goldesohn and Robert Gellately, ed., *The Nuremberg Interviews: An American Psychiatrist's Conversations with the Defendants and Witnesses,* 160.
76 *"The war will"* and *"What does":* Turney, *Disaster at Moscow*, 36.
77 *"This war"* and *"Clash of two":* Burdick and Jacobsen, *The Halder War Diary*, 346.
78 *"surplus"* and estimate of 20 million to 30 million: Tooze, *Wages of Destruction,* 479.
78 *"to bring blessings":* Miner, *Stalin's Holy War: Religion, Nationalism, and Alliance Politics,* 54; Nagorski, *Greatest Battle*, 90.
78 *"If following":* Gerbet, 221.
79 *"The war can"* and starvation plans for cities: Tooze, *Wages of Destruction,* 479–80.
79 *On the eve*: Ibid., 478.
79 *"to occupy":* Prange, *Target Tokyo*, 338.
80 *In mid-1939* and statistics on German labor force and foreign labor: Tooze, *Wages of Destruction,* 358–59.
80 *"the old struggle":* Kershaw, *Hitler, 1936–1945,* 359.
80 *"the breaking of":* Turney, *Disaster at Moscow*, 41.
80 *Commissar Order* and *"We must":* Alexander Dallin, *German Rule in Russia 1941–1945: A Study of Occupation Policies*, 30–31; Nagorski, *Greatest Battle,* 90.
81 *"are the real":* Kershaw, *Hitler, 1936–45,* 358.
81 *"consider it"* and *"If international"* and *"pleaded with":* Engel, *At the Heart of the Reich*, 110, 113–14.

82 *"The German extermination"* and other quotations from the *Polish Fortnightly Review:* the private papers of Zygmunt Nagorski, Jr., my father who served in the Polish Army, first in Poland and then in Britain after his escape from Poland.

82 *"annihilation of Poland":* Burdick and Jacobsen, *The Halder War Diary*, 31.

82 *"It is essential":* Richard C. Lukas, *The Forgotten Holocaust: The Poles under German Occupation 1939–1944*, 4.

82 *"Housecleaning: Jews":* Burdick and Jacobsen, *The Halder War Diary*, 57.

82 *"we had to":* Stanisław Piotrowski, *Hans Frank's Diary*, 48.

83 *"If there is":* Stargardt, *German War*, 38.

84 *In fact, regular:* Ibid., 4.

84 *On February 6, 1940* and *"We bear":* Piotrowski, 49, 225.

84 *To achieve* and rest of information on Einsatzgruppen in Poland: http://ww2history.com/key_moments/Holocaust/Einsatzgruppen_operate_in_Poland; Jochen Böhler, Klaus-Michael Mallman, and Jürgen Matthäus, *Einsatzgruppen w Polsce*.

85 *"This extermination," Blaskowitz followed up,* and *Hitler's reaction:* Browning, *The Origins of the Final Solution: The Evolution of Nazi Jewish Policy, September 1939–March 1942*, 74–75; Richard Rhodes, *Masters of Death: The SS Einsatzgruppen and the Invention of the Holocaust*, 9–10; Stargardt, *German War*, 42–43.

85 *"those who": Polish Fortnightly Review*, December 15, 1940.

86 *Polish Jews quickly:* Maciej Siekierski and Feliks Tych, eds., *Widziałem Anioła Śmierci*, 8.

86 *On November 6, 1939:* Halik Kochanski, *The Eagle Unbowed: Poland and Poles During the Second World War*, 99, T. Bor-Komorowski, *The Secret Army*,18–19, and Lukas, 8–9.

86 *"The sole goal":* Kochanski, 99.

86 *"Polish intelligentsia":* Burdick and Jacobsen, *The Halder War Diary*, 73.

87 *Ironically, a year* and *In March 1940:* Kochanski, 101–2.

88 *"until the spring"* and *"Stalin, concerned":* Berezhkov, *At Stalin's Side*, 150, 181; Nagorski, *Greatest Battle*, 30.

88 *German planes* and NKVD and Beria orders: David Murphy, 165–66; Nagorski, *Greatest Battle*, 30–31.

88 *The Germans offered:* David Murphy, 167–70.

88 *"I'm not sure":* Montefiore, *Stalin*, 352.

89 *"so long as":* David Murphy, 167–70.

89 *"Stalin is about":* Ulam, 311.

89 *After all, as:* Deutscher, *Stalin,* 439.

89 *In March 1941* and *"Fulfillment of":* Volkogonov, *Stalin: Triumph and Tragedy,* 375–76.

89 *"Is the German army":* Ivo Banac, ed., *The Diary of Georgi Dimitrov,* 159–60.

90 *"I do not know":* Petro G. Grigorenko, *Memoirs,* 46–47.

90 *"between two groups"* and *"We see nothing":* David Murphy, 27.

90 *In an interview:* Note from the Polish Ministry of Information in London to the Polish embassy in Washington, June 11, 1941. Poland, Ambasada US, Box 10, Folder 2, Hoover Institution Archives.

91 *"Hitler is not":* Gorodetsky, *Maisky Diaries,* 362.

91 *"My people":* Montefiore, *Stalin,* 356.

FOUR: "Our Plymouth Brethren"

92 *"to keep Winston":* Winant, *Letter from Grosvenor Square,* 21–24.

92 *As the popular* and other Winant background and quotes, along with meeting with Roosevelt and love affair with Sarah Churchill: Winant, *Letter from Grosvenor Square,* 10–25, Lynne Olson, *Citizens of London: The Americans Who Stood with Britain in Its Darkest, Finest Hour,* 12–26, 111–13; "The Tragic Love Affair of Former NH Gov. John Winant and Sarah Churchill," New England Historical Society online, www.newenglandhistoricalsociety.com/tragic-love-affair-former-nh-gov-john-winant-sarah-churchill.

93 *"We are today":* Winant, *Letter from Grosvenor Square,* 21–24.

93 *When he landed* and *"It was the first":* Ibid., 26–40.

94 *"the British people":* Beschloss, *Kennedy and Roosevelt,* 241.

94 *"He was convinced"* and *"I hate":* Ibid., 235.

94 *"the President was":* Churchill, *Grand Alliance,* 139.

95 *"like hitting wads":* Warren F. Kimball, *The Most Unsordid Act: Lend-Lease 1939–1941,* 231.

95 *"this stocky figure":* Winant, *Letter from Grosvenor Square,* 37.

95 *"his unassertive shrewdness":* Colville, *Fringes of Power,* 372.

96 *"somewhat strange"* and *"to play":* Gordetsky, 339–40.

96 *At a lunch* and both Churchill's and Winant's remarks, along with press reaction: Olson, *Citizens of London,* 25–26.

97 *"not to antagonize":* Nicolson, *Harold Nicolson*, 153.

97 *"will depend on"* and rest of March 10 memo: Kimball, *The Most Unsordid Act*, 234.

98 *In the three months:* Churchill, *Grand Alliance*, 139.

98 *"Bombs came down"* and *"Certainly as":* Colville, *Fringes of Power*, 374, 376.

98 *"gravely depressed"* and rest of Colville's May 2 diary entry: Ibid., 381–82.

99 *"From the propaganda":* Nicolson, *Harold Nicolson*, 162.

99 *"was ever more"* and discussion about the word *"devastated":* "Raymond E. Lee, Retired General," *New York Times*, April 8, 1958.

100 *But given Washington's*, secrecy precautions, *"technical advisers"* and Sherwood quotes: Sherwood, *Roosevelt and Hopkins*, 272–74; John J. McLaughlin, *General Albert C. Wedemeyer, America's Unsung Strategist in World War II*, 35.

100 *But during his stopover* and nightmare and return to London: Leutze, *London Journal of General Lee*, 236–39.

101 *"What a contrast"*: Ibid., 241

102 *"I think I notice"* and rest of Lee's observations, *"Mr. Black,"* and Beaverbrook question to Arnold: Ibid., 243–51.

102 *"England's strength"* and *"The President is":* Harriman and Abel, *Special Envoy*, 31, 32.

103 *Dorothy Thompson* and quotes from her book: Nagorski, *Hitlerland*, 55–56, 83–86; Dorothy Thompson, *I Saw Hitler!*

104 The Battle of 1776 and quotes from Thompson's introduction: America First Committee, box 30, Hoover Institution Archives.

105 *Britain under Churchill* and Donovan-Mowrer mission: Edgar Ansel Mowrer, *Triumph and Turmoil: A Personal History of Our Times*, 314–17.

105 *"unless we are"* and *"The clash":* Shirer, *Rise and Fall of the Third Reich*, 592.

105 *In mid-1941* and bestseller lists: Ken Cuthbertson, *A Complex Fate: William L. Shirer and the American Century*, 280–82.

106 *"The question before":* Joseph C. Harsch, *Pattern of Conquest*, 303–4.

106 *"I was one":* Flannery, *Assignment Berlin*, 13.

106 *"on suspicion of"* and rest of Hottelet arrest: Richard C. Hottelet, "Guest of Gestapo," *San Francisco Chronicle*, August 3, 1941; author interview with Hottelet; Nagorski, *Hitlerland*, 305–6.

107 *"no longer hide":* Howard K. Smith, *Last Train from Berlin,* 226.
107 *"The United States had":* Duff Cooper, *Old Men Forget,* 287.
107 *"He spoke":* Murrow, *This Is London,* 125.
108 *"London yawned":* Quentin Reynolds, *A London Diary,* 153.
108 *"Murrow was not":* Eric Sevareid, *Not So Wild a Dream: A Personal Story of Youth and War and the American Faith,* 177–78.
108 *"In three months":* Ernie Pyle, *Ernie Pyle in England,* 226.
108 *"The British":* Sevareid, *Not So Wild a Dream,* 173.
109 *"I had been":* Pyle, *In England,* 134–35.
109 *"truly American":* Steven J. Ross, *Hitler in Los Angeles,* 307.
109 *"given up":* Taylor, 263.
109 *"frequent tirades"* and rest of Hitler's remarks: Engel, *At the Heart of the Reich,* 107–8.
110 *"If USA entered":* Burdick and Jacobsen, *The Halder War Diary,* 376.
110 *"have done everything":* Turney, *Disaster at Moscow,* 34.
110 *"We no longer"* and *"If he had":* Taylor, 309, 354.
111 *On May 10* and Hess mission, Duke of Hamilton and Hess conversation with Hitler earlier: Kershaw, *Hitler, 1936–45,* 369–81.
111 *A RAF wing commander:* www.undiscoveredscotland.co.uk/usbiography/d/douglasdouglashamilton.html.
112 *"I thought this":* Churchill, *Grand Alliance,* 48.
112 *"I suddenly":* Speer, *Inside the Third Reich,* 174.
112 *"Hess always":* Engel, *At the Heart of the Reich,* 112–13.
112 *"The Führer":* Taylor, 364.
112 *"discouraged and"* and *"a tremendous":* Gibson, 351.
113 *"appalling damage," "The main danger" and "We are dealing":* Taylor, 365, 367.
113 *"like other Nazi,"* Churchill letter to Roosevelt, and Churchill-Stalin encounter: Churchill, *Grand Alliance,* 51–55.
114 *This may have* and Hess's suicide: Andrew Nagorski, "The Ghost of Spandau," *Newsweek,* August 31, 1987.
114 *"Hess assured me":* Speer, *Inside the Third Reich,* 176.
115 *"I never attached":* Churchill, *Grand Alliance,* 49.
115 *"aggressor ships":* Gilbert, *Churchill and America,* 220.
115 *"Admiralty received"* and US extension of security zone: Churchill, *Grand Alliance,*141–42.
115 *On May 24* and *"Hell of a"* and *"For three days":* Harriman and Abel,

Special Envoy, 33–34; casualty figures for the *Hood:* "The Sinking of HMS *Hood:* A Summary," History in an Hour, last modified May 24, 2011, www.historyinanhour.com/2011/05/24/sinking-of-hms-hood-summary.

116 *about 2,300:* Kershaw, *Hitler, 1936–45,* 381.

116 *"From the point"* and Roosevelt's backpedaling the next day: Sherwood, *Roosevelt and Hopkins*, 298.

116 *"No matter how":* Berg, *Lindbergh*, 419.

117 *"Whatever the peril":* Sherwood, *Roosevelt and Hopkins*, 299.

117 *81 percent* and *"if it appeared":* Berg, *Lindbergh*, 421.

117 *"We are puzzled":* Nicholson, 172.

117 *"based on the":* Burdick and Jacobsen, *The Halder War Diary*, 400.

FIVE: "What Shall We Do?"

118 *Two days before* and German deserters: Anastas Mikoyan, *Tak Bylo,* 378; Nagorski, *Greatest Battle,* 46, 35–36; Montefiore, *Stalin*, 357–59. According to Montefiore, Liskov was interrogated but not shot, despite Stalin's order. The confusion of that day may have saved him.

119 *The German army* and numbers and organization of invading force: Nagorski, *Greatest Battle,* 47.

119 *"We are being"* and the rest of Corporal Busch's cable intercept: Seth, *Operation Barbarossa*, 54.

119 *At four o'clock* and Stalin's reaction and Molotov-Schulenburg meeting: Nagorski, *Greatest Battle,* 46–47.

120 *"continual infringements"* and rest of Goebbels's announcement on German radio: Stargardt, *German War*, 158–59.

121 *"Tactical surprise":* Burdick and Jacobsen, *The Halder War Diary*, 410.

121 *"Military developments"* and *"They are falling":* Taylor, 426–27.

121 *On the first* and *Major General I.I. Kopets:* Nagorski, *Greatest Battle,* 43; Constantine Pleshakov, *Stalin's Folly: The Tragic First Ten Days of World War II on the Eastern Front,* 126–27.

121 *"an awesome impression"* and rest of Herwarth account: Herwarth with Starr, *Against Two Evils*, 197–98.

122 *The letter that* and other letters from German soldiers: *Bulleten' Assotsiasii istorikov vtoroy mirovoy voyny*, issue 8, 2003, 21–25. Nagorski, *Greatest Battle,* 43–44.

123 *Vyacheslav Dolgov:* Nagorski, *Greatest Battle,* 42, and author interview with Dolgov.
124 *Ilya Druzhnikov:* Nagorski, *Greatest Battle,* 44–46, and author interview with his son Yuri Druzhnikov.
125 *"Comrade Boldin":* Werth, *Russia at War*, 159–60; Nagorski, *Greatest Battle,* 48–49.
125 *"to attack":* Werth, *Russia at War*, 165.
125 *It was no accident* and *"Let Molotov speak"* and *"That was certainly":* Nagorski, *Greatest Battle,* 49; Anastas Mikoyan, *Tak Bylo*, 388–89.
126 *"an unparalleled act":* Werth, *Russia at War*, 167–68; Montefiore, Stalin, 368.
126 *"minor successes":* Oleg V. Khlevniuk, *Stalin: New Biography of a Dictator,* 201.
127 *"Lenin left us"* and Stalin's behavior at the dacha: Volkogonov, 410–11.
127 *"Comrade Stalin":* Montefiore, *Stalin*, 374; Nagorski, *Greatest Battle,* 50.
127 *"Molotov said"* and officials' visit to dacha, along with Mikoyan's account: Volkogonov, *Stalin: Triumph and Tragedy,* 411; Montefiore, *Stalin*, 376–77; Nagorski, *Greatest Battle,* 50.
128 *"a different Stalin"* and *"Well, they talk":* Schecter with Luchkov, *Khrushchev Remembers*, 65.
128 *"Tell me"* and rest of Khrushchev-Malenkov exchange: Talbott, *Khrushchev Remembers,* 168, Nagorski, *Greatest Battle,* 50–51.
129 *"Comrades! Brothers":* Joseph Stalin, *The War of National Liberation,* 9–17. (I have corrected a few line of this translation), Nagorski, *Greatest Battle,* 51–54.
131 *On June 24* and evacuation plans and numbers: Overy, *The Dictators,* 500; Nagorski, *Greatest Battle,* 50.
131 *Ilya Zbarsky* and rest of account of Lenin's body: author interview with Ilya Zbarsky; Ilya Zbarsky and Samuel Hutchinson, *Lenin's Embalmers*; Nagorski, *Greatest Battle,* 53–58.
133 *"Since I struggled":* Dallin, 3. Nagorski, *Greatest Battle,* 59.
133 *"It is thus":* Burdick and Jacobsen, *The Halder War Diary*, 446–47.
133 *"It is the Führer's":* Ibid., 458.
133 *"Some of the":* Ibid., 472.
133 *Two days later* and subsequent events: Nagorski, *Greatest Battle,* 53.
134 *Over dinner* and rest of Hitler's July 27 remarks: Bullock, *Hitler and Stalin*, 764–65; Nagorski, *Greatest Battle,* 59–60.

134 *On July 28* and Engel diary entries: Engel, *At the Heart of the Reich*, 114–15.

135 *At the Brest Fortress* and *"Russians surrender":* Nagorski, *Greatest Battle,* 60; Pleshakov, 245.

135 *"Moscow has surrendered":* Werth, *Russia at War*, 164.

136 *"The Russians are defending":* Gerbet, 225.

136 *"The Russians are suffering":* Taylor, 431.

136 *"that the Russians":* Burdick and Jacobsen, *The Halder War Diary*, 433.

136 *"We were not":* B. H. Liddell Hart, *The German Generals Talk,* 179.

136 *"Lack of culture"* and *"This has made":* Gerbet, 225, 242.

137 *Of the 550,000:* Adam Zamoyski, *1812: Napoleon's Fatal March on Moscow,* 536.

137 *"The Führer has":* Bullock, *Hitler and Stalin*, 798.

138 *"I ban any":* Taylor, 446.

138 *"could be done":* Engel, *At the Heart of the Reich*, 114–15.

138 *"The enemy is":* Gerbet, 247.

138 *"The main thing":* Ibid., 265–66. Nagorski, *Greatest Battle,* 102–3.

138 *"Army Group Center":* Trevor-Roper, *Hitler's War Directives*, 146.

139 *"To Moscow"* and Guderian quotations, along with his confrontation with Hitler: Guderian, *Panzer Leader,* 193, 198–202.

139 *"to deprive"* and *"is not in"* and *"The most important":* Trevor-Roper, *Hitler's War Directives*, 150–51; Nagorski, *Greatest Battle,* 102–3.

141 *"destroying the"* and September 16 directive: Trevor-Roper, *Hitler's War Directives*, 153; Geoffrey Jukes, *The Defense of Moscow,* 77; Nagorski, *Greatest Battle,* 103–4.

141 *"utterly unscrupulous"* and other Manstein observations: Manstein, *Lost Victories,* 74–75, 177, 261–62, 275.

142 *"the injections began":* Norman Ohler, *Blitzed: Drugs in the Third Reich*, 116.

142 *The German military:* Łukasz Kamieński, *Shooting Up: A Short History of Drugs and War,* 111–13. This book also examines the use of drugs by other armies in other wars.

SIX: "Step on It!"

144 *"very tired":* Leutze, *London Journal of General Lee*, 315.

144 *"Winant Reports"* and *"British Position":* Winant, *Letter from Grosvenor Square*, 200.

144 *"a warning that":* "President Franklin Delano Roosevelt Message to the Congress on the Sinking of the Robin Moor, June 21, 1941," American Merchant Marine at War online, last modified April 6, 2002, www.usmm.org/fdr/robinmoor.html.

145 *"The Germans"* and *"contributed to":* Winant, *Letter from Grosvenor Square*, 194, 202.

145 *"want to find":* Leutze, *London Journal of General Lee*, 315.

145 *"Should this new"* and *"any announcement":* Churchill, *Grand Alliance*, 369.

146 *At dinner* and *After dinner*: Ibid., 370–370; Nagorski, *Greatest Battle,* 150–51.

146 *Woken at four* and Colville's account of the day, including Churchill's ribbing of Cripps: Colville, *Fringes of Power*, 405.

146 *Churchill's butler* and *"We savored":* Anthony Eden, *The Reckoning,* 312; Nagorski, *Greatest Battle,* 139.

147 *"We have reached"* and rest of Churchill's radio address: www.jewishvirtuallibrary.org/churchill-broadcast-on-the-soviet-german-war-june-1941

148 *On June 16*: Eden, *Reckoning*, 312, Nagorski, *Greatest Battle,* 138–39.

148 *"would go through":* Ismay, *Memoirs*, 226.

148 *"Germany will be":* Sherwood, *Roosevelt and Hopkins*, 303–4.

149 *"great skepticism"* and *"Psychologically, this":* Ivan Maisky, *Memoirs of a Soviet Ambassador: The War 1939–1943,* 368.

149 *"Apart from"* and *"The help given":* Ismay, *Memoirs*, 225–26.

149 *"Thus the ravings":* Churchill, *Grand Alliance,* 367–68.

150 *"A forceful speech!":* Maisky, *Memoirs*, 366.

150 *"The silence"* and *"We shall do"* and Churchill-Stalin correspondence: Churchill, *Grand Alliance,* 380–85; Nagorski, *Greatest Battle,* 151–52.

150 *"I received":* Churchill, *Grand Alliance,* 388.

151 *"He might as"* and *Let's have less*: Ismay, *Memoirs*, 227–28.

152 *"The murderers":* Berg, *Lindbergh*, 422.

152 *"The next day":* Sherwood, *Roosevelt and Hopkins*, 303.

152 *"No one has":* Berg, *Lindbergh*, 423.

153 *"all the aid"* and *"If we see":* Dennis J. Dunn, *Caught Between Roosevelt & Stalin: America's Ambassadors to Moscow,* 126–27; Nagorski, *Greatest Battle,* 152.

153 *"we should do":* George F. Kennan, *Memoirs: 1925–1950*, 133.

154 *"in order the better"* and other early diplomatic history, including Bullitt and Davies: Dunn, *Caught Between Roosevelt & Stalin*, 49; Nagorski *Greatest Battle,* 140–47. Dunn's book also offers a more detailed look at the records of the American ambassadors.

154 *"sly humor"* and *"It is my opinion"* and *"There were no":* Joseph E. Davies, *Mission to Moscow,* 357, 272, 280.

155 *"has been more":* Sherwood, *Roosevelt and Hopkins*, 306–8.

156 *"Had the president":* Kennan, 83.

156 *"all deliberation on":* Sherwood, *Roosevelt and Hopkins*, 317.

156 *"unbelievable reticence":* Colville, *Fringes of Power*, 408.

157 *"definite pro-Russian bias":* Charles E. Bohlen, *Witness to History: 1929–1969,* 47.

157 *"dependence on Soviet"* and other quotes from Yeaton: Ivan Yeaton: "Memoirs of Ivan D. Yeaton, USA (Ret.)," unpublished manuscript, Hoover Institution Archives; Nagorski, *Greatest Battle,*147–50, 156.

157 *"Hopkins assured":* Maisky, *Memoirs*, 375.

157 *"obvious sympathy for":* Ibid., 179, 183; Nagorski, *Greatest Battle,* 153.

158 *"I think the stakes":* Sherwood, *Roosevelt and Hopkins*, 318.

158 *"I'll explain"* and *"Such a visa":* Gorodetsky, *Maisky Diaries,* 376.

158 *"I still believe":* Winant, *Letter from Grosvenor Square*, 208.

158 *Ironically, though* and Archangel meal: Sherwood, *Roosevelt and Hopkins*, 321, 326.

159 *"I think we"* and *"a wealthy bourgeoisie":* Dunn, *Caught Between Roosevelt & Stalin*, 102–3, 107.

159 *In his first conversations*: Sherwood, *Roosevelt and Hopkins*, 327; Nagorski, *Greatest Battle,* 154.

160 *"Not once"* and *"Stalin said":* Sherwood, *Roosevelt and Hopkins*, 333–44.

161 *"Give us"* and Stalin's requests for supplies: Ibid., 328.

161 *"The might of"* and other quotes from Hopkins's report about his talks with Stalin: Susan Butler, ed., *My Dear Mr. Stalin: The Complete Correspondence of Franklin D. Roosevelt and Joseph V. Stalin,* 37–39.

162 *"all possible military"* and rest of Yeaton-Hopkins exchange: Yeaton, "Memoirs," 36–39; Nagorski, *Greatest Battle,* 156.

163 *Right before Hopkins* and Faymonville's actions: Robert Huhn Jones, *The Roads to Russia: United States Lend-Lease to the Soviet Union,*

41–42, Dunn, *Caught Between Roosevelt & Stalin*, 129; Nagorski, *Greatest Battle,* 154.

163 *On August 2*: FDR to Wayne Coy, memorandum, August 2, 1941, Franklin D. Roosevelt Library & Museum online, www.fdrlibrary.marist.edu/_resources/images/sign/fdr_32.pdf.; Nagorski, *Greatest Battle,* 158.

164 *"I wondered how"* and Reynolds's broadcast and visits with Churchill, including quotes: Reynolds, *By Quentin Reynolds*, 216–27.

166 *"I am sure":* Sherwood, *Roosevelt and Hopkins*, 320.

167 *By then, Thompson's*: Peter Kurth, *American Cassandra: The Life of Dorothy Thompson,* 331.

167 *The "indefatigable fighter":* Sherwood, *Roosevelt and Hopkins*, 319.

167 *"I was an":* Kurth, *American Casandra*, 336.

168 *"the great British," "The boats that," "I know Germany,"* and *"So much to do":* J. W. Drawbell, *Dorothy Thompson's English Journey,* 101, 222, 193–98, 113. Drawbell's book also includes other details of her visit.

169 *He wanted to publish*: Marion K. Sanders, *Dorothy Thompson: A Legend in Her Time,* 275.

169 *"Whatever it is"* and Hopkins's return journey: Sherwood, *Roosevelt and Hopkins*, 346–48.

170 *"Hopkins returned":* Robert Dallek, *Franklin D. Roosevelt: A Political Life,* 428.

170 *"He approaches"* and *"You'd have thought*: Sherwood, *Roosevelt and Hopkins*, 350–51.

170 *The cover story*, *"I feel a thrill," "At last," "The close-packed"* and FDR press conference: Dallek, *Franklin D. Roosevelt*, 428–32.

171 *"in ordinary times":* Churchill, *Grand Alliance,* 444.

171 *"no aggrandizement":* Ibid., 434; News release to press and radio from Franklin D. Roosevelt and Winston S. Churchill, August 14, 1941, Franklin D. Roosevelt Library & Museum online, www.fdrlibrary.marist.edu/_resources/images/sign/fdr_33.pdf.

172 *"We are at":* Susan Butler, ed., *My Dear Mr. Stalin: The Complete Correspondence of Franklin D. Roosevelt and Joseph V. Stalin,* 41–42; Nagorski, *Greatest Battle,* 158–59.

172 *"uplifted in":* Sherwood, *Roosevelt and Hopkins*, 364.

172 *"a wave of":* Dallek, *Franklin D. Roosevelt*, 434.

SEVEN: "Simultaneous Wars"

173 *"astonishingly cordial"* and rest of Herwarth's account of welcome: Herwarth with Starr, *Against Two Evils*, 201–3.

175 *In what had been* and account of events during Soviet occupation of the region, including Katyn massacre: Nagorski, *Greatest Battle,* 81–88.

175 *"At a time":* Norman Davies, *Heart of Europe,* 67.

176 *"Protest or not":* Anne Applebaum, *Gulag: A History,* 418.

177 *"warmly greeted":* Ben Shepherd, *War in the Wild East: The German Army and Soviet Partisans,* 73.

177 "hostile through": Ibid., 79–80.

177 *"It's hard to":* author interview with Yevgeniya Merlis.

178 *"resistance in the":* Shepherd, *War in the Wild East*, 74.

178 *In response to*: Overy, *The Dictators,* 520–21.

178 *"The order":* Manstein, *Lost Victories,* 180.

178 *"inconspicuously":* Overy, *The Dictators*, 513.

179 *"The main reason"* and *"We would insult":* Shepherd, *War in the Wild East*, 72, 74; Nagorski, *Greatest Battle,* 91.

179 *"One thing"* and *"Willingly or"* and *"The positive attitude":* David Stahel, *The Battle for Moscow,* 47, 46.

179 *the "senseless shootings," "still more,"* and *"should be taken":* Gilbert, *The Second World War: A Complete History* , 200–201.

180 *"no hangman's"* and Anset's actions: Stahel, *Battle for Moscow*, 27.

180 *"Asiatic, Mongol"* and *"At this stage":* Dallin, 69; Nagorski, *Greatest Battle,* 91–92.

181 *"Since then":* Stahel, 42.

181 *In 1941* and Hartmann quotes: Hartmann, *Operation Barbarossa*, 89–94.

181 *"The Russian must":* Overy, *The Dictators,* 537.

181 *"A ferocious"* and *"A whirling mass":* Stahel, *Battle for Moscow*, 42–43.

181 *"marching arm-in-arm":* Herwarth with Starr, *Against Two Evils*, 208.

182 *"the largest crime":* Hartmann, *Operation Barbarossa*, 89.

182 *During 1941*: Stahel, *Battle for Moscow*, 41.

182 *Nonetheless, by the end*: Hartmann, *Operation Barbarossa*, 89.

182 *A former army barracks* and early Auschwitz history: Nagorski, "A Tortured Legacy," *Newsweek*, January 16, 1995, and much longer original file that I sent to my editors. I donated that reporting, along with the

interviews I conducted with Auschwitz prisoners, to the Holocaust Memorial Museum Archives in Washington. They include the interviews with Mieczyslaw Zawadzki and Nikolai Pisarev that are quoted in this section.

184 *Pavel Stenkin*: Laurence Rees, *Auschwitz: A New History,* 65–66.

184 *But about six hundred*: Danuta Czech, *Kalendarz Wydarzen W KL Auschwitz,* 84. Czech notes that the Germans first gassed 250 Polish prisoners from the camp hospital before gassing the Soviet POWs on the same day (September 3, 1941).

184 *"A short, smothered"* and *"I must even":* Rudolf Hoess, *Commandant of Auschwitz,* 146–47.

184 *The original plan*: Rees, *Auschwitz*, 64.

185 *"Nazi Germany fought":* Rebecca Erbelding, *Rescue Board: The Untold Story of America's Efforts to Save the Jews of Europe,* 7.

185 *"The Jewish calamity":* Chaim Weizmann, *Trial and Error: The Autobiography of Chaim Weizmann,* vol. 2, 413.

185 *"ruthless, energetic"* and *"Where there's":* Shepherd, *War in the Wild East*, 88–89

185 *"The battle against":* Friedlander, 212.

186 *As soon as* and early massacres: Christopher Browning, *Ordinary Men,* 9–14, Nagorski, *Greatest Battle,* 93–94.

186 *"August 25"* and *"August 31":* Browning, *Ordinary Men,* 17.

186 *"the Shoah by":* Vasily Grossman, *The Road,* 67.

187 *"From the start"* and *six hundred thousand* Jews: Friedlander, 209; Browning, *Origins of the Final Solution,* 244. Here Browning puts the number of Jews killed by the end of 1941 as between five hundred thousand and eight hundred thousand.

187 *"the deliberate slaughter":* Andrew Nagorski, *The Nazi Hunters,* 53.

187 *One of the defendants* and Ohlendorf-Ferencz exchange: Nagorski, *Greatest Battle,* 94; Nagorski, *Nazi Hunters,* 55–57.

187 *"The Jews were":* Goldensohn and Gellately, *Nuremberg Interviews,* 389–90.

188 *"He died convinced":* author interview with Benjamin Ferencz.

188 *"The soldier must":* Friedlander, 210.

188 *"Drive the female"* and *"Driving women":* Browning, *Origins of the Final Solution,* 281.

189 *"Many gruesome scenes":* Hoess, 147–48.

189 *Those who did not*: See, for example, Browning, *Ordinary Men*, 67, the case of Georg Kageler, who was granted his wish to be released from the execution squad and reassigned to guard duty.

189 *"Ghetto plan":* Burdick and Jacobsen, *The Halder War Diary*, 59.

190 *"extremely sensitive"* and *"The rapid dying":* Browning, *Origins of the Final Solution*, 330–31, 120.

190 *"We cannot shoot":* Gilbert, *Second World War*, 35.

190 *When Germany invaded* and *Madagascar Plan*: Browning, *Origins of the Final Solution*, 88.

191 *SS Captain Theodor Dannecker*, his memorandum and *"an absence":* Adam Rayski, *The Choice of the Jews Under Vichy: Between Submission and Resistance*, 22–23.

191 *"In the first":* Engel, *At the Heart of the Reich*, 103.

191 *"the will of":* Browning, *Origins of the Final Solution*, 331.

191 *"the Jew would":* Martin Bormann, *Hitler's Table Talk*, 35.

192 *"first program of"* and *"a rehearsal":* "Euthanasia Program," United States Holocaust Memorial Museum online, www.ushmm.org/wlc/en/article.php?ModuleId=10005200.

192 *In Britain* and forced sterilizations in the United States: Teryn Bouche and Laura Rivard, "America's Hidden History: The Eugenics Movement," Scitable, last modified September 18, 2014, www.nature.com/scitable/forums/genetics-generation/america-s-hidden-history-the-eugenics-movement-123919444.

192 *"unworthy of life"* and euthanasia actions and other quotations: Browning, *Origins of the Final Solution*, 184–93; Kershaw, *Hitler, 1936–1945*, 252–61; "Euthanasia Program," US Holocaust Memorial Museum online.

194 *Some of the American* and other information about the origins and coverage of this story by American correspondents and diplomats: Thorsten Noack and Fred Flatow, "William L. Shirer and International Awareness of the Nazi 'Euthanasia' Program," *Holocaust and Genocide Studies* 30, no. 3 (Winter 2016).

194 *On October 26* and September 21 and November 25 Shirer diary entries: Shirer, *Berlin Diary*, 512, 569–75.

195 *"their murder of":* Flannery, *Assignment to Berlin*, 110.

195 *"On instructions"* and the rest of Galef's sermon: "Sermon of Cardinal von Galen—Part 1," Tradition in Action online, last modified August 27, 2012, www.traditioninaction.org/Cultural/E031_Euthania_1.html.

195 *While several priests*: www.britannica.com/biography/Blessed-Clemens-August-Graf-von-Galen
195 *"embarrassed by":* Stargardt, *German War*, 153.
196 *"The killing of":* Browning, *Origins of the Final Solution,* 193.
196 *"It was not":* Sergo Beria, *Beria, My Father: Inside Stalin's Kremlin,* 69.
196 *Stalin reacted by* and Stalin's orders: Nagorski, *Greatest Battle,* 70–73.
197 *Ilya Vinitsky*: author interview with Vinitsky. Fuller account of Vinitsky's experiences in Nagorski, *Greatest Battle*, 63–68.
198 *According to a NKVD Report*: Conquest, *Dragon of Expectations*, 128.
198 *"I am Stalin's son"* and rest of Yakov's story: Montefiore, *Stalin*, 379–80, 445–46; Nagorski, *Greatest Battle,* 71.
198 *"There are no":* Steven Merritt Miner, *Stalin's Holy War,*56.
199 *"I grew up":* Friedlander, 249.
199 *"Let us kill!":* Overy, *The Dictators,* 516.

EIGHT: **"The Kindly Italian Gardener"**

201 *"In present instance":* Leutze, *London Journal of General Lee*, 383.
201 *Two of the military attachés* and *A Japanese newspaper correspondent*: FSB archives courtesy of V. P. Yeroshin and V. Iampolskii, *Organy gosudarstvennoi bezopasnosti SSSR v Velikoi Otechestvennoi voine;* Nagorski, *Greatest Battle*, 156–57
202 *From inside*: Tsuyoshi Hasegawa, *Racing the Enemy,*17.
202 *Sorge, the Soviet spy*: Whymant, *Stalin's Spy*, 206–7.
203 *Colonel Alfred Kretschmer*: Ibid.
203 *"he felt that"* and rest of Hopkins-Molotov exchange: Sherwood, *Roosevelt and Hopkins*, 332.
203 *On July 26:* Max Hastings, *Inferno: The World at War, 1939–1945,* 186; "Secretary Hull's Statement on Japanese Aggression, January 15," US Department of State, publication 1983, *Peace and War: United States Foreign Policy, 1931–1941* (Washington, DC: US Government Printing Office, 1943), 118–49, available at "Discussions with Japan 1941 and Pearl Harbor," Mount Holyoke College online, www.mtholyoke.edu/acad/intrel/WorldWar2/pearl.htm.
204 *On August 29* and rest of Churchill letter and then September 4 exchange with Maisky: Churchill, *Grand Alliance,* 454–58; Maisky, *Memoirs,* 190–91; Nagorski, *Greatest Battle,* 159–61.

206 *Churchill promptly wrote* and *"Although nothing,"* Stalin telegram and Churchill's reaction: Churchill, *Grand Alliance,* 458–63.

207 *"They make a very":* James, *Victor Cazalet*, 235.

207 *"at the root":* Churchill, *Grand Alliance,* 390–91.

208 *The Poles wanted* and talks with Maisky: Nagorski, *Greatest Battle,* 275.

208 *"I explained that":* Maisky, *Memoirs,* 173.

208 *"Poles keep feeling*: James, *Victor Cazalet*, 262.

208 *"either be completely":* Count Edward Raczynski, *In Allied London,* 96.

209 *When Sikorski signed*: Tadeusz Modelski, *Byłem Szefem Wywiadu U Naczelnego Wodza,* 80.

209 *In an interview*: author interview with Walentyna Janta-Połczyńska.

209 *"The British government":* Jan Ciechanowski, *Defeat in Victory,* 36.

209 *"to abandon"* and *"We had the invidious":* Churchill, *Grand Alliance,* 391.

209 *"was in line with," "does not involve,"* and *"the first swallow":* Ciechanowski, *Defeat in Victory*, 40–41.

210 *A Gallup poll* and *"The American people":* Jones, *Roads to Russia,* 55.

210 *"might have":* Butler, *Dear Mr. Stalin*, 43; Nagorski, *Greatest Battle,* 159.

211 *"The task of defeating":* "Franklin D. Roosevelt, Labor Day Radio Address, September 1, 1941," American Presidency Project, www.presidency.ucsb.edu/ws/index.php?pid=16166.

211 *A German U-boat*: "USS *Greer*, Destroyer No. 145; DD 145," Destroyer History Foundation online, http://destroyerhistory.org/flushdeck/ussgreer.

211 *"The flood is raging"* and rest of Lee's account: Leutze, *London Journal of General Lee*, 383, 388, 391–92.

212 *"the British, the Jewish"* and *"I pointed out":* Meacham, *Franklin and Winston*, 127.

212 *"This was no mere"* and rest of fireside chat: "Fireside Chat 18: On the Greer Incident, September 11, 1941," Miller Center online, https://millercenter.org/the-presidency/presidential-speeches/september-11-1941-fireside-chat-18-greer-incident.

212 *"Roosevelt this morning":* Gilbert, *Finest Hour: Winston S. Churchill, 1939–1941,* 1188.

213 *"the instant relief"* and Churchill letter to Smuts: Churchill, *Grand Alliance,* 517.

214 *Beaverbrook started* and rest of dispute over Russian aid: Jones, *Roads to Russia*, 58–59; Leutze, *London Journal of General Lee*, 400.

214 *It took Roosevelt's* and trade-offs: Jones, *Roads to Russia*, 59.

214 *"very moving speech," "The gist of,"* and *"He said there":* Leutze, *London Journal of General Lee*, 402–3.

215 *Beaverbrook, Harriman*: Harriman and Abel, *Special Envoy*, 82–83.

215 *One of those* and *"He was one"* and Reynolds's observations about Moscow: Reynolds, *By Quentin Reynolds*, 229–35.

216 *"Your function" and "to the point of":* Harriman and Abel, *Special Envoy*, 82–83.

216 *When the planes* and Harriman's first impressions: Harriman and Abel, *Special Envoy*, 84–85.

217 *"The discussions were":* Ismay, *Memoirs*, 231.

217 *"We knew that," "too much,"* and decision about interpreter: Harriman and Abel, *Special Envoy*, 85–86.

217 *"extremely friendly"* and first meeting: Sherwood, *Roosevelt and Hopkins*, 387–88; Harriman and Abel, 87–88; Nagorski, *Greatest Battle*, 162.

218 *"No, it has":* Reynolds, *By Quentin Reynolds*, 235.

219 *During his Moscow visit* and caviar episode: Harriman and Abel, *Special Envoy*, 102–3.

219 *"Stalin was very"* and second and third rounds of talks with Stalin: Sherwood, *Roosevelt and Hopkins*, 388–89; Harriman and Abel, 88–90; Nagorski, *Greatest Battle*, 162.

220 *"Bolshevists"* and *"It is up to":* Jones, *Roads to Russia*, 61.

221 *"twenty-three course orgy"* and rest of Reynold's account of dinner, including physical description of Stalin: Reynolds, *By Quentin Reynolds,* 238–40.

221 *"Churchill was always"* and *"What is the good?":* Harriman and Abel, *Special Envoy*, 99, 101.

222 *"drawing numberless pictures":* Ibid., 92.

222 *"We have got to"* and *"I left feeling":* Sherwood, *Roosevelt and Hopkins*, 391.

223 *"the best-dressed man"* and other Ismay observations, including story of James Allan: Ismay, *Memoirs*, 231–35.

224 *Right after they* and account of dinner with Churchill and Eden: Harriman and Abel, *Special Envoy*, 105.

NINE: "We Will Break Them Soon"

226 *In mid-September* and account of Günsche visit to Wolf's Lair, including talk with Hitler: Henrik Eberle and Matthias Uhl, eds., *The Hitler Book,* 77.

226 *Felsennest (Rock Nest)*: "Führer Headquarters Felsennest," http://battlefieldsww2.com/fuhrer-headquarters-felsennest.html.

227 *"It's inconceivable"* and other Hitler quotes in this section: Martin Bormann, *Hitler's Table Talk,* 14–18. There have been questions about the reliability of the records of these talks, which have appeared in various translations. But Hitler's quoted remarks are largely consistent with statements he made on other occasions.

229 *"Test drawing"* and *"a bolt":* Kershaw, *Hitler: 1889–1936,* 24.

229 *General Guderian,* number of Soviet prisoners, and *"The Battle of Kiev":* Guderian, *Panzer Leader,* 225–26.

230 *Nonetheless, Guderian* and Orel scenes: Ibid., 231–32.

230 *"TYPHOON has":* Burdick and Jacobsen, *The Halder War Diary,* 544.

230 *Vasily Grossman* and *"Why didn't you":* Beevor, *A Writer at War,* 56.

230 *Attacked by Russian T-34* and other difficulties faced by Guderian's troops: Guderian, *Panzer Leader,* 233–37; Nagorski, *Greatest Battle,* 109–10.

231 *"It was terrible":* author interview with Richard Wernicke.

232 *"General Mud":* Beevor, *A Writer at War,* 223.

232 *For the German troops* and Vyazma battle account: Nagorski, *Greatest Battle,* 111–19.

233 *"In our literature"* and rest of Oreshkin's account: Boris Oreshkin, "Viaz'ma," anthology *Podvig,* issue 38, Moscow, *Molodaia Gvardiia,* 1991, 102–14.

234 *Maria Denisova*: Andrei Palatov interview with Maria Denisova. Palatov, who led the group of searchers I accompanied, recorded this interview with Denisova in 1996.

235 *Yegor Chegrinets*: author interview with Yegor Chegrinets.

235 *"a brilliant success":* Burdick and Jacobsen, *The Halder War Diary,* 549.

235 *"empty space"* and *"The military end":* Stargardt, *German War,* 187.

235 *Joachim Pusch*: author interview with Joachin Pusch.

235 *"There was hardly":* "Terrain Factors in the Russian Campaign," Office of the Chief of Military History, US Department of the Army, Craig H.W. Luther collection, Box 40, Hoover Institution Archives.

235 *The Wehrmacht had calculated*: Turney, *Disaster at Moscow,* 112.

236 *"Campaign in East":* Overy, *Russia's War,* 95.

236 *On October 6* and rest of Zhukov account, including conversations with Stalin and action till mid-October: Georgy K. Zhukov, *Marshal Zhukov's Greatest Battles* (including introduction by Harrison Salisbury), 21–46; G. K. Zhukov, *Vospominaniia i razmyshleniia,* vol. 1, 221–49; Nagorski, *Greatest Battle,* 119–35.

237 *"the only person":* Overy, *Russia's War,* 69.

237 *"We never spoke":* author interview with Ella Zhukova.

238 *"You are not":* Pleshakov, 165.

238 *According to official*: Overy, *Russia's War,* 112.

238 *Boris Vidensky*: author interview with Boris Vidensky.

239 *An estimated 158,000* and *By contrast*: Overy, *The Dictators,* 535, 517; Nagorski, *Greatest Battle,* 74.

239 *"During the night"* and *"iron discipline":* Werth, *Russia at War*, 232–33.

239 *After sending his wife* and rest of account of October 15 meeting at Spaso House and evacuation: Reynolds, *By Quentin Reynolds*, 242–45; Yeaton, "Memoirs," 40–44; Harriman and Abel, *Special Envoy* 106–7; Nagorski, *Greatest Battle*, 164–66.

242 *"Well," Churchill replied*: Harriman and Abel, *Special Envoy*, 107–8.

242 *"A threat hangs"* and other accounts of the mid-October 1941 events in rest of this chapter, including interviews with Dmitry Safonov, Valeria Prokhorova, Tamara Bylinina, Yevgeny Anufriyev: Nagorski, *Greatest Battle*, 167–85.

242 *In September Moscow's population*: Oleg Matveev, *"Bedstviia zatiazhnoi voiny," Nezavisimoe Voennoe Obozrenie,* 20.06.2003, no. 20 (335).

243 *G. V. Reshetin*: M. M. Gorinov, and others, eds., *Moskva Voennaia, 1941–1945: Memuary i arkhivnye dokumenty,* 111.

243 *Mikhail Zhuravlev* and his NKVD report: Ibid., 116–19.

245 *Anastas Mikoyan* and his intervention in the strike: Anastas Mikoyan, *Tak Bylo*, 420.

245 *"to blow up factories": Moskovstkaia Bitva v postanovleniiakh Gosudarstvennogo Komiteta oborony, 70.*

246 *"Since Moscow itself"* and Dimitrov's account: Ivo Banac, ed., *The Diary of Georgi Dimitrov: 1933–1949,* 196–200.

246 *"He was tormented"* and *a special train*: Volkogonov, *Stalin: Triumph and Tragedy*, 434–35.

247 *"clear the mines":* Montefiore, *Stalin*, 397.

247 *"people carrying bags":* A. T. Rybin, *Riadom so Stalinym,* 23.

247 *As late as 2005*: Kevin O'Flynn, "A Ton of Explosives Unearthed at Moskva," *Moscow Times,* July 11, 2005.

248 *Mikhail Kutuzov*: Montefiore, *Stalin*, 399.

248 *"What shall we do?":* Stepan Mikoyan, *Memoirs*, 108.

248 *Pavel Saprykin*: Saprykin recalled that episode in an interview in 2005, as he was approaching his hundredth birthday (Nagorski, *Greatest Battle*, 183).

249 *"But, as the saying":* Zhukov, *Marshal Zhukov's Greatest Battles,* 46.

250 *"It was only":* Werth, *Russia at War*, 236–38.

250 *The combined losses*: Nagorski, *Greatest Battle*, 2.

250 *"the battle for Moscow":* Zhukov, *Marshal Zhukov's Greatest Battles,* 93.

250 *"In some respects":* Volkogonov, *Stalin: Triumph and Tragedy,* 436.

TEN: "No More Tricks Left"

252 *"It is not difficult," "He is attacked,"* and *"the most dangerous":* Berg, *Lindbergh*, 426–28.

253 *61 percent*: Dallek, *Franklin D. Roosevelt*, 436.

253 *"personal and secret"* and *"The interventionists":* Harriman and Abel, *Special Envoy*, 109.

254 *"America has been"* and rest of FDR October 27 speech: www.presidency.ucsb.edu/ws/?pid=16030.

255 *In reality* and fabricated documents: Olson, *Those Angry Days,* 403; Warren F. Kimball, *Forged in War: Roosevelt, Churchill, and the Second World War,* 114.

255 *"Deeply moved":* Dallek, *Franklin D. Roosevelt*, 437.

255 *"A tremendous advance":* Nicolson, *Harold Nicolson*, 189.

256 *"Roosevelt's speech made"* and rest of Ciano diary entries in this section: Gibson, *Ciano Diaries*, 398–400.

256 *On October 31* and sinking of *Reuben James*: "A People at War—Prelude to War: The U.S.S. *Reuben James*," National Archives and Records Administration online, www.archives.gov/exhibits/a_people_at_war/prelude_to_war/uss_reuben_james.html.

257 *Tell me, what*: Woody Guthrie, "The Sinking of the *Reuben James*," Woody Guthrie online, http://woodyguthrie.org/Lyrics/Sinking_Of_The_Reuben_James.htm.

257 *On November 7* and congressional voting: Harriman and Abel, *Special Envoy*, 109.

257 *"Apparently the President"*: Harold L. Ickes, *The Secret Diary of Harold L. Ickes,* vol. 3, 650.

257 *"relatively powerless"* and other Sherwood quotes: Sherwood, *Roosevelt and Hopkins*, 382–83.

258 *"I am struck"* and *"that I would rather"*: Gilbert, *Finest Hour,* 1230.

259 *"in advance of," "Winston was highly,"* and *"It is a victory"*: Gilbert, *Churchill and America,* 239–40.

259 *"I have believed"*: Ickes, *Secret Diary*, 629–30.

260 *German ambassador Eugen Ott* and rest of Sorge's reporting from Japan and his fate: Whymant, *Stalin's Spy*, 194, 212–14, 232–34, 239, 258, 275; David Murphy, 88–90; Nagorski, *Greatest Battle*, 216–18.

264 *To Molotov's and Beria's* and rest of discussion about parade and November 6–7 events, including interviews with Aleksandr Zevelev and Leonid Shevelev: Volkogonov, 436; Montefiore, *Stalin*, 404–6; Werth, *Russia at War*, 240; Joseph Stalin, *The War of National Liberation, 18–38*; Gorinov, 147–52; Overy, *Russia's War,* 113–15; Nagorski, *Greatest Battle*, 193, 219–25. Details of reshoot of newsreel film provided by Boris Maklyarsky, son of senior NKVD official Mikhail Maklyarsky.

267 *"Are you sure"*: Zhukov, *Marshal Zhukov's Greatest Battles,* 62.

268 *"Marshal Zhukov considered"*: Elena Rzhevskaya, "Roads and Days: The Memoirs of a Red Army Translator," *Journal of Slavic Studies* 14 (March 2001): 59.

268 *Their horses suffered*: James Lucas, *War on the Eastern Front: The German Soldier in Russia 1941–1945,* 32–33; Nagorski, *Greatest Battle*, 228.

268 *"All wheeled vehicles"*: Seth, *Operation Barbarossa*, 151.

268 *"The supply situation"* and rest of Guderian's account: Guderian, *Panzer Leader*, 248–55; Nagorski, *Greatest Battle*, 231–32.

269 *Vladimir Edelman*: author interview with Vladimir Edelman.

270 *"The Russians are"*: Goldensohn, 344.

270 *"carried out by"*: Lucas, *War on the Eastern Front*, 32–33.

270 *General Halder's diary*: Burdick and Jacobsen, *The Halder War Diary*, 554–63.

270 *"Naturally, Hitler will"*: Turney, *Disaster at Moscow*, 132.

271 *"the coalition of"*: J. V. Stalin, "Speech at Celebration Meeting of the Moscow Soviet of Working People's Deputies and Moscow Party and

Public Organizations, November 6, 1941," Marxists Internet Archives, www.marxists.org/reference/archive/stalin/works/1941/11/06.htm.

272 *"Stalin was seeking":* Harriman and Abel, *Special Envoy*, 109–10.

272 *"an intolerable situation"* and rest of Stalin-Churchill exchange, along with visit by Maisky: Churchill, *Grand Alliance,* 529–31.

274 *"There can be no":* Gilbert, *Finest Hour,* 1229.

274 *"Ekh! Together":* Svetlana Alliluyeva, *Only One Year,* 392.

275 *Bullitt had continued* and rest of Bullitt-FDR correspondence: Alexander Etkin, *Roads Not Taken: An Intellectual Biography of William C. Bullitt,* 205–6.

275 *"the brotherhood of":* Davies, 511.

276 *"This book will last"* and *"I do not think":* Dunn, *Caught Between Roosevelt & Stalin*, 140–41.

276 *"a defeatist":* Harriman and Abel, *Special Envoy*, 93.

276 *But the Soviet side* and *"that will only irritate":* Dunn, *Caught Between Roosevelt & Stalin*, 143–44.

277 *Harriman felt that* and *"any willingness to":* Harriman and Abel, *Special Envoy*, 110.

277 *"We may be faced":* Nicolson, *Harold Nicolson*, 191.

ELEVEN: "The Fifth Act"

278 *"tired and depressed"* and rest of Harriman and Winant account of December 7 dinner: Harriman and Abel, *Special Envoy*, 110–12; Winant, *Letter from Grosvenor Square*, 275–79.

279 *"Mr. President, what's"* and rest of Churchill's account of reaction to Pearl Harbor: Churchill, *Grand Alliance,* 604–11.

280 *"I am dumbfounded":* Nicolson, *Harold Nicolson*, 194.

280 *The next day* and *"Today all of us":* Gilbert, *Churchill and America,* 244.

280 *"as united Americans"* and *"If I had been":* Berg, *Lindbergh*, 432.

280 *"with bowed shoulders":* Nicolson, *Harold Nicolson*, 194.

280 *"the gravity of":* Churchill, *Grand Alliance,* 611.

281 *"No American will"* and rest of Churchill's recollections along with the December 9 message to FDR: Ibid., 606–9.

282 *"to consider"* and rest of Kennan quotes about Pearl Harbor aftermath, including Ribbentrop's encounters with Morris: Kennan, 134–35.

283 *As the Americans*: Charles B., Burdick, *An American Island in Hitler's Reich: The Bad Nauheim Internment,* 9; Nagorski, *Hitlerland,* 313.

283 *"my unalterable":* www.jewishvirtuallibrary.org/hitler-s-speech-declaring-war-against-the-united-states.

283 *"We can't lose"* and *"Through the outbreak":* Kershaw, *Hitler, 1936–1945,* 442.

283 *"A great power":* Dallek, *Franklin D. Roosevelt*, 441.

283 *In a call* and *"I am not so sure":* Gibson, *The Ciano Diaries,* 416.

284 *"The Americans now":* Turney, *Disaster at Moscow*, 155.

285 *The American diplomats and journalists*: Nagorski, *Hitlerland,* 317.

285 *"Are you sure":* Zhukov, *Marshal Zhukov's Greatest Battles,* 72.

286 *"The Führer is"* and rest of Brauchitsch-Bock exchange, and *"Any concept at":* Turney, *Disaster at Moscow*, 146–49.

287 *"The severe winter":* Trevor-Roper, *Hitler's War Directives*, 166.

287 *"The Russians are"* and *"The enemy":* Guderian, *Panzer Leader*, 260–61.

287 *"With it went":* Fabian von Schlabrendorff, *The Secret War Against Hitler,* 131.

287 *"Scapegoats are being":* Engel, *At the Heart of the Reich*, 124.

288 *By December 13*: Turney, *Disaster at Moscow*, 156.

288 *"Collapse of":* Nagorski, *Greatest Battle,* 258.

288 *"Everything is":* Beevor, *A Writer at War,* 63.

288 *"But this was"* and *Brauchitsch was more*: Guderian, *Panzer Leader,* 259, 262–63.

288 *"General withdrawal":* Burdick and Jacobsen, *The Halder War Diary*, 590.

289 *"Hitler's reaction":* Manstein, *Lost Victories,* 279.

289 *"He did not":* Schramm, *Hitler*, 134–35.

289 *"This little matter":* Seth, *Operation Barbarossa,* 158.

290 *"Stand and fight!"* and *"Better times":* Turney, *Disaster at Moscow*, 158, 160.

290 *"Clear to F.":* Engel, *At the Heart of the Reich*, 125.

290 *"As Hitler came"* and rest of Guderian-Hitler meeting and dismissal: Guderian, *Panzer Leader*, 265–71; Nagorski, *Greatest Battle,* 256–57.

291 *"We have come"* and *"The young man":* Gibson, *Ciano Diaries,* 422–23.

292 *"I was informed":* Gerbet, 356.

292 *"was assisted by"* and other Pasher statistics quotes: Yaron Pasher, *Holocaust Versus Wehrmacht: How Hitler's "Final Solution" Undermined the German War Effort*: 1, 5, 11, 35.

293 *"Nothing could be":* Peter Hayes, *Why? Explaining the Holocaust,* 134–37.

293 *"Hitler was even":* Pasher, *Holocaust Versus Wehrmacht*, 290.

294 *"Their own policy":* author interview with Benjamin Ferencz.

294 *The meeting at the Wannsee Villa* (original planned date): Friedlander, 339.

294 *The Soviet counteroffensive*: Mark Roseman, *The Villa, The Lake, The Meeting,* 60.

294 *But already in the fall* and other early preparations for death camps, Chelmno details: Browning, *Origins of the Final Solution,* 365–66, 416–19.

295 *"Today I will once":* www.yadvashem.org/odot_pdf/Microsoft%20Word%20-%201988.pdf.

295 *"we are just":* Browning, *Origins of the Final Solution*, 391.

295 *"With regard to"* and *"That is no":* Kershaw, *Hitler, 1936–1945,* 490.

296 *"Winston is impressed":* Eden, *Reckoning,* 326.

296 *Less than two weeks* and Sikorski-Anders talks with Stalin: Ciechanowski, *Defeat in Victory*, 65–75; Nagorski, *Greatest Battle,* 276.

298 *At their first meeting,* rest of Eden's meetings with Stalin, including farewell dinner: Eden, *Reckoning*, 330–52; Nagorski, 277–82.

299 *"This is our"* and pepper brandy episode: Maisky, *Memoirs,* 236.

300 *"A report has been":* Churchill, *Grand Alliance,* 620.

300 *The details only* and numbers drowned and saved: Gilbert, *Second World War,* 276.

300 *"Mr. Churchill has been"* and *"He is a different":* Lord Moran, *Churchill at War 1940–1945*: 5, 8–9.

300 *The two men* and Churchill visit to US and Canada, including his quotations unless otherwise indicated: Churchill, *Grand Alliance,* 662–81.

301 *"Never being lost"* and *"I cannot help reflecting":* Gilbert, *Churchill and America*, 249.

302 *"I don't think"* and heart attack scare: Moran, 16–18.

302 *"a bit sluggish":* Gilbert, *Churchill and America*, 250.

303 *"The invasion of":* Winant, *Letter from Grosvenor Square*, 5.

303 *"Hitler was powerless":* Tooze, *Wages of Destruction,* xxv.

303 *"The numbers are stark":* Jeffrey Record, *Ends, Means, Ideology and Pride: Why the Axis Lost and What We Can Learn From Its Defeat,* the Letort Papers, Strategic Studies Institute, US Army War College, July 2017.

303 *He held discussions* and FDR-Churchill meetings with foreign representatives: Gilbert, *Churchill and America*, 250–51.

304 *"unsurpassed in loyalty"* and *"The preparation,"* Churchill speech: Churchill, *Grand Alliance,* 678–80.

INDEX

ABOUT THE AUTHOR

Andrew Nagorski, an award-winning journalist, was born in Scotland to Polish parents, moved to the United States as an infant, and has rarely stopped moving since. During a long career at *Newsweek*, he served as the magazine's bureau chief in Hong Kong, Moscow, Rome, Bonn, Warsaw, and Berlin. He is the author of six previous books and has written for countless publications. He lives in St. Augustine, Florida.